Sex, Hormones and Behaviour

The Ciba Foundation for the promotion of international cooperation in medical and chemical research is a scientific and educational charity established by CIBA Limited – now CIBA-GEIGY Limited – of Basle. The Foundation operates independently in London under English trust law.
Ciba Foundation Symposia are published in collaboration with Excerpta Medica in Amsterdam.

Excerpta Medica, P.O. Box 211, Amsterdam

Symposium on:

Sex, Hormones and Behaviour

Ciba Foundation Symposium 62 (new series)

1979

Excerpta Medica

Amsterdam · Oxford · New York

ISBN Excerpta Medica 90 219 4068 X
ISBN Elsevier/North-Holland 0 444 90045 4

Published in February 1979 by Excerpta Medica, P.O. Box 211, Amsterdam and Elsevier/North-Holland, Inc., 52 Vanderbilt Avenue, New York, N.Y. 10017.

Suggested series entry for library catalogues: Ciba Foundation Symposia.
Suggested publisher's entry for library catalogues: Excerpta Medica.

Ciba Foundation Symposium 62 (new series)
382 pages, 52 figures, 7 tables

Library of Congress Cataloging in Publication Data

Symposium on Sex, Hormones, and Behaviour, London, 1978.
Sex, hormones, and behaviour.

(Ciba Foundation symposium; 62 (new ser.))
"Held at the Ciba Foundation, London, 14th-16th March 1978."
Includes bibliographies and indexes.
1. Sex – Cause and determination – Congresses.
2. Hormones, Sex – Physiological effect – Congresses. 3. Human behavior – Congresses. 4. Sexual behavior in animals – Congresses. I. Porter, Ruth. II. Whelan, Julie. III. Title. IV. Series: Ciba Foundation. Symposium; new ser., 62. [DNLM: 1. Sex behavior – Physiology – Congresses. 2. Sex hormones – Physiology – Congresses. We C161F v. 62 1978 / WK900 S989s 1978]

Printed in The Netherlands by Casparie, Heerhugowaard

Contents

Participants

Symposium on Sex, Hormones and Behaviour, held at the Ciba Foundation, London, 14th-16th March 1978

E. J. SACHAR *(Chairman)* Department of Psychiatry, College of Physicians and Surgeons of Columbia University, 722 West 168th Street, New York, NY 10032, USA

D. H. ABBOTT MRC Reproductive Biology Unit, 2 Forrest Road, Edinburgh EH1 2QW, UK

J. BANCROFT MRC Reproductive Biology Unit, 2 Forrest Road, Edinburgh EH1 2QW, UK

F. A. BEACH Department of Psychology, University of California, Berkeley, California 94720, USA

G. W. BESSER Department of Endocrinology, St Bartholomew's Medical College, West Smithfield, London EC1A 7BE, UK

J. R. BRAWER Royal Victoria Hospital, Women's Pavilion, 687 Pine Avenue West, Montreal, PQ, Canada H3A 1A1

S. CROWN Department of Psychiatry, The London Hospital, London E1 1BB, UK

G. DÖRNER Institute of Experimental Endocrinology, Humboldt University, Schumannstrasse 20-21, 104 Berlin, German Democratic Republic

ANKE A. EHRHARDT Psychiatric Institute, Division of Child Psychiatry, Columbia University, 722 West 168th Street, New York, NY 10032, USA

B. J. EVERITT Department of Anatomy, University of Cambridge, Downing Street, Cambridge CB2 3DY, UK

R. W. GOY Regional Primate Research Center, University of Wisconsin, 1220 Capitol Court, Madison 53706, Wisconsin, USA

R. GREEN Department of Psychiatry and Behavioral Science, Health Services Center, State University of New York at Stony Brook, New York 11794, USA

J. HERBERT Department of Anatomy, University of Cambridge, Downing Street, Cambridge CB2 3DY, UK

P. HERTOFT Department of Psychiatry and Sexological Research Unit, Psychiatric Clinic, Rigshopitalet, Blegsdamveg 9, 2100 Copenhagen, Denmark

J. B. HUTCHISON MRC Unit on the Development and Integration of Behaviour, University Sub-Department of Animal Behaviour, Madingley, Cambridge CB3 8AA, UK

A. JOST Laboratoire de Physiologie du Développement du Collège de France, Place Marcelin Berthelot, 75231 Paris Cedex 05, France

E. B. KEVERNE Department of Anatomy, University of Cambridge, Downing Street, Cambridge CB2 3DY, UK

L. MARTEAU The Dympna Centre, 24 Blandford Street, London W1H 3HA, UK

E. NIESCHLAG Abtlg. Experimentelle Endokrinologie, Universitäts-Frauenklinik, Westring 11, 4400 Münster, Westphalia, German Federal Republic

K.-M. PIRKE Max-Planck-Institut für Psychiatrie, Kraepelinstrasse 10, 8000 München 40, German Federal Republic

R. V. SHORT MRC Reproductive Biology Unit, 2 Forrest Road, Edinburgh EH1 2QW, UK

Editors: RUTH PORTER *(Organizer)* and JULIE WHELAN

Chairman's introduction

E. J. SACHAR

Department of Psychiatry, College of Physicians and Surgeons of Columbia University, New York

I was asked to chair this symposium not because of any research I have done in this field, or any knowledge or sophistication that I have about it, but because of my naivety: I could be counted on to ask the most simple-minded questions about the relations of sex hormones to behaviour, which, it was hoped, would prompt the participants out of courtesy to take such questions seriously. So let me begin by posing the most naive and simple-minded questions: to what extent, by what mechanisms and under what conditions do hormones pre- and postnatally play a role as determinants of sexual behaviour in human beings—and if we don't know exactly, how can we find out? These simple-minded questions will, I hope, stay before us throughout the symposium, because the organizers hope very much that the time has come for the animal and human researchers to come together to discuss these issues, to explore the relevance of their findings to each other, to examine the appropriateness of their experimental models and hypotheses, and if possible to generate further interdisciplinary hypotheses and models.

It is especially appropriate that Dr Jost gives the first paper. As we all know, it was Dr Jost in his stunning experiments on rabbits a quarter of a century ago who clarified the role of testosterone in sexual differentiation. This illuminated a number of human endocrine syndromes—Turner's syndrome, gonadal agenesis, and testicular feminization. Not much later the work of Geoffrey Harris and others was beginning to suggest that this hormonal influence on sexual differentiation might extend to the hypothalamus itself and that there might be a male and a female hypothalamus. We shall hear from Dr Brawer how this differentiation may in fact affect the very structure of these organs. It was reasonable to ask, then, if prenatal hormone influences could have such an effect on somatic sexual differentiation and on certain aspects of the brain, whether it was possible for hormones prenatally to exert more subtle but nevertheless important enduring effects on dimorphic sexual behaviour postnatally. Dr Goy and Dr Phoenix were able to investigate this question in monkeys. It was a natural step for Dr Ehrhardt with Dr Money and then with Dr Meyer-Bahlburg to explore whether such effects could be noticed and were significant in boys and girls as well—work that is being pursued, as we shall hear from Dr Green, also on studies of the psychosexual development of boys and girls.

I have picked this particular sequence out because so many of the people involved are represented here and because it could provide an order for us to follow as we look for themes throughout the symposium, as the work moves from animal studies to experimental behavioural studies and to human work, adapting the model at each step along the way. We might ask during the course of the symposium whether similar interplays between animals and human models, experimental models, can clarify other questions for us: to what extent do hormones prenatally or postnatally play a role in other forms of 'sexual' behaviour, in homosexual or transsexual patterns? How do the hormonal changes at puberty contribute to the dramatic changes in sexual interest and aggressive behaviour at that time? What role do hormones play in maintaining sexual drives in the adult? What role do sex hormones play in social organization—in the traditional social role of the female and in determining dominance hierarchies in males and females?

All of us agree on the tremendous power of psychosocial influences in the human: of learning, of modelling, of the peer group. But nevertheless it is a legitimate question whether such influences are being exerted on a biological substrate which may be translated into significant inter-individual differences in innate vulnerability, susceptibility or predisposition. It is also legitimate to ask to what extent hormones play a role in providing the biological anlage on which psychosocial influences may be exerted.

We are particularly fortunate in having Dr Beach here. He took part in the Ciba Foundation meeting on Hormones, Psychology and Behaviour in 1950 (Beach 1952) and he is with us not only to provide a broad historical perspective but to caution us about the differences between responsible and irresponsible extrapolation from animal models to human situations, and to warn us also about being over-inclusive in the behaviour we define as sexual. He will emphasize the difference between those psychobiological systems we may define as sexual and those equally powerful psychobiological systems that subsume attachment behaviour, and how important it is to keep the two interrelated systems clearly in focus.

With this in mind and with a superb interdisciplinary group to participate, as chairman I am charged with the responsibility of trying to urge the discussion to become cross-disciplinary wherever I can and to turn us all into 'experimental cross-dressers' and role players, so that we shall ask the animal researchers to play the role of clinicians and the clinicians to play the role of animal researchers as the symposium develops. This is the way to increase our understanding of each other's work and of the subject we shall be discussing during the next three days.

Reference

BEACH, F. A. (1952) Sex and species differences in the behavioural effects of gonadal hormones. *Ciba Foundation Colloquia on Endocrinology,* Vol. III, pp. 3-14, Churchill, London

Basic sexual trends in the development of vertebrates

ALFRED JOST

Laboratoire de Physiologie du Développement, Collège de France, Paris

Abstract The chain of events occurring during sexual development involves successive steps: genetic sex, gonadal sex and body sex. The latter comprises the genital tract, secondary sex characters and neural structures mediating sexual interest and appetite. Body sex obeys a hormonal control. In the absence of any hormone it develops in conformity with the homozygous sex type—feminine in mammals, masculine in birds, newts and one lizard studied so far. Similar differences have been observed for sex behaviour in some mammals and birds. It has been suggested that the sex of the gonads is determined by the presence (or absence) of the histocompatibility antigen produced by the sex chromosome of the heterozygous sex (Y or W). However, in newt or *Xenopus* graft chimaeras as well as in bovine freemartins, testicular dominance over presumptive ovaries is obvious whatever the mode of chromosomal control of sex. A unifying concept for sex differentiation in all vertebrates, accounting for the long series of recognized data, is still difficult to delineate.

The reproductive function reaches its acme when sexual partners are attracted to each other and cooperate in sexual union, eventually permitting gametes to fuse into an egg cell and to initiate a new individual. The sexual developmental story of this descendant is marked for life from its very inception, when it is provided with pairs of paternal and maternal chromosomes.

In normal circumstances the 'genetic sex' (Fig. 1) established at fertilization determines sexual capacities and achievements for a lifetime. It first governs the differentiation of the gonads (gonadal sex). In turn the gonads control the sexual differentiation and functioning of the other parts of the body (body sex), including the nervous structures which mediate sexual interest or appetite. To what extent and in what way these developmental processes also dictate the type of sex behaviour or the choice of partner will be discussed during this symposium.

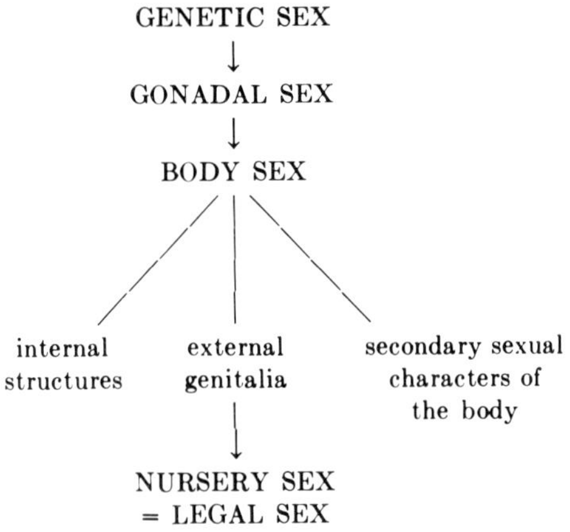

FIG. 1. Chain of events during sexual differentiation. (From Jost 1958).

SEXUAL TRENDS IN THE DIFFERENTIATION OF BODY SEX

The processes directing development of the genital tract or other body sex characters were studied experimentally thirty years ago. I surgically castrated rabbit fetuses *in utero* before sexual differentiation of the genital tract and observed that they acquired a feminine reproductive tract whatever their genetic and gonadal sex (Jost 1947, 1953). The genital structures obey an inherent trend (or programme) for femaleness, unless the fetal testes oppose the feminine programme and impose a masculine orientation (Fig. 2, right). This schematically summarized result was complemented with many consonant observations made on other mammals or in humans.

One point of importance for the following discussion was that the mammalian fetal testis imposes maleness by producing two kinds of morphogenetic secretion; on one hand androgens that stimulate the male structures, and on the other hand an inhibiting factor that induces the regression of the fetal Müllerian ducts (Jost 1953, 1965; Josso *et al.* 1977) and

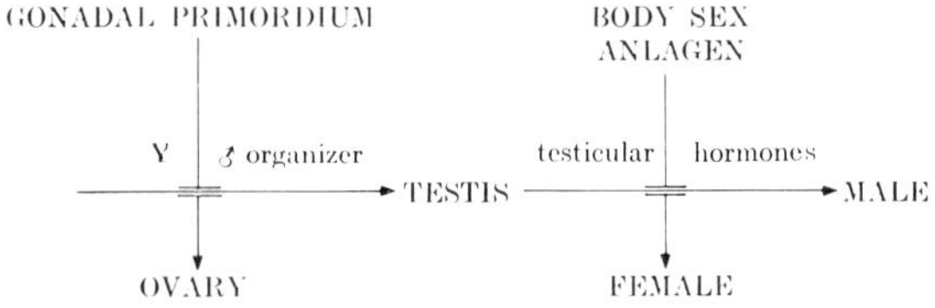

FIG. 2. Theoretical interpretation of sexual differentiation in mammals showing how feminine programmes for body sex and for gonadal sex are counteracted in males. (Slightly modified after Jost 1970).

perhaps has some effects on the gonads as well.

Wolff castrated duck embryos *in ovo* with a beam of X-rays (see Wolff & Wolff 1951). This species was chosen because it presents a pronounced sexual dimorphism at the level of the voice organ (syrinx) and the penis. In the absence of gonads these organs became masculine. These experiments, and others, established that in birds the basic sexual trend of body sex is masculine*—in contrast to mammals—and that during development maleness has to be repressed by the ovary to ensure female development in females.

Earlier experiments by de Beaumont (1933) on newts *(Triturus cristatus)* can be interpreted in the same way. He surgically castrated young animals (50-60 mm in length) and described a 'neutral' aspect of several sex structures in castrates of either sex. De Beaumont emphasized the stimulatory or inhibitory effects of gonadal hormones in the realization of the male or female genital tract respectively. Actually the 'neutral type' of some structures, for example the renal collecting tubules, is largely masculine (these tubules are confluent in males and open more or less independently into the Wolffian duct in females).

In the viviparous lizard *Lacerta vivipara,* young castrated with X-rays developed masculine copulatory organs (Dufaure 1966).

The opposite sexual trends in the differentiation of the genital tract in mammals on one hand (female trend) and in birds, lizards and newts on the other (male trend) parallel differences in the mechanism of chromosomal sex determination. In mammals the female is homozygous for the X chromosome, the male sex being heterozygous (XY) and heterogametic; the Y chromosome is the bearer of male-determining gene(s). The reverse applies to birds and newts (ZZ males and ZW females); female viviparous lizards may also be heterogametic (Chevalier 1969). It appears that the basic trend in body sex differentiation is that of the homozygous sex.

A very important milestone in studies on sex development was established by Phoenix *et al.* (1959) when they showed that in guinea-pigs the nervous structures mediating sexual behaviour in adulthood could be modified permanently by prenatally administered testosterone: prenatally androgenized guinea-pig females could be induced to display feminine behaviour when given female hormones as adults. On the other hand, castration of neonatal male rats (Grady *et al.* 1965) suppressed any possibility of later masculine behaviour in response to testosterone, whereas neonatal androgenization (or oestrogenization) of females permitted it. The critical period in rats for the

*This is not true for the Müllerian ducts, which depend on the testicular Müllerian-inhibiting hormone for their regression in males.

'masculinization' or 'defeminization' of the brain is within the first postnatal week. Similar permanent effects of hormones are known in only a few mammals.

Recent work in birds has demonstrated the counterpart of the observations made on mammals. In the adult quail (during short-photoperiod-induced gonadal atrophy), oestrogens induce receptivity to the male in either sex. By contrast, testosterone succeeds in inducing male behaviour (including mounting and cloacal contact movements) only in males, not in females (Adkins & Adler 1972). A similar difference was found in ring doves (Cheng & Lehrman 1975).

In adult female quails that had been treated on Day 9 of incubation with an antioestrogen (CI-628), testosterone could elicit male behaviour. It is likely that a so-called 'demasculinization' of the neural structures is produced by oestrogens secreted by the embryonic ovary and that the antioestrogen opposes this effect (Adkins 1976). Moreover, oestradiol or testosterone given to chick (Wilson & Glick 1970) or quail (Adkins 1975) embryos also demasculinizes them in such a way that in adulthood they cannot respond to testosterone with male behaviour.

Such data fit well the concept that the neutral body sex, including neural structures, is feminine in mammals and masculine in birds.

On that basis, one would expect the sexual behaviour of the frog *Xenopus laevis* (a species in which males are homozygous) to respond to hormones as does that of birds. Actually the clasping behaviour could easily be elicited, after castration, by testosterone in both sexes (Kelley & Pfaff 1976). No permanent 'demasculinization' is evident in females.

In conclusion, it would appear that in mammals and birds body sex shows a basic developmental trend corresponding to that of the homozygous sex. Characteristics of the heterozygous sex have to be actively imposed by the secretions of the corresponding gonads. Therefore the mechanisms controlling gonadal differentiation are of prime importance.

GONADAL DIFFERENTIATION

I tentatively suggested (Jost 1965, 1971; Jost *et al.* 1973) that the gonad as well as the body sex would develop in conformity with the homozygous sex, unless a triggering mechanism produced in the heterozygous sex initiates the differentiation of a testis in mammals (Fig. 2), or of an ovary in birds. Wachtel *et al.* (1975*b*) proposed that in mammals the H-Y histocompatibility antigen, a membrane protein controlled by a locus on the Y chromosome, is the factor responsible for the differentiation of testes; those individuals who do not produce the antigen form an ovary. The female cells of birds and of the frog *Xenopus laevis* produce an H-W antigen, held to be responsible for ovarian development. The mammalian H-Y and the avian or frog H-W antigens react with the same mouse anti-H-Y antisera, and therefore seem to be similar or identical (Wachtel *et al.* 1975*a*).

Ohno (1977) developed the theory that in the male mammal the H-Y antigen triggers the formation of a testis and therefore of testosterone, which masculinizes the body sex. The theory seems to overlook the significance of the inhibiting hormone produced by the fetal testis.

Along the same line of thought, Ohno *et al.* (1976) proposed a new interpretation of the freemartin condition in cattle. They suggested first that male cells colonize the female gonads and, second, that these cells disseminate the H-Y antigen in a hormone-like manner. H-Y antigen could be detected in the gonads of near-term freemartin fetuses; it was held to be responsible for the masculinization of the gonads. A similar interpretation was proposed for another old observation: a mouse (or calf) fetal testis cultivated *in vitro* in contact with a chick embryo testis 'feminizes' it by preservation of a cortical layer (Salzgeber 1963; Akram & Weniger 1968). This is assumed to result from the transfer of H-Y antigen from male mammalian tissue to avian tissue where it has feminizing effects (Wachtel 1977). The absence of masculinization of the mouse ovary by chicken ovary has not been discussed.

The unifying concept that in mammals (and in other species with heterozygous males) testicular organogenesis results from the local production or importation in the gonadal primordium of H-Y antigen, and that in birds (and in other species with heterozygous females) ovaries depend upon the H-W antigen, is of great interest. However, so far it does not really account for several old and recent observations.

It is of importance to compare the bovine freemartins and experiments with amphibians aimed at duplicating this condition. Let us first recall that, in cattle, female fetuses become abnormal (freemartins) when sharing the same uterus with a male twin: fusion of the chorions and of blood vessels permits exchange of blood. In amphibians the experiments of Humphrey (1929, 1931, 1945) are especially beautiful and significant. He made extensive use of a method of orthotopic exchange of lateral primordia, including the gonadal region, between early larvae of *Amblystoma tigrinum* or of axolotls. The chimaeras thus produced possessed their own gonad on one side of the body and the transplanted gonad on the other side. In other experiments amphibian larvae were united in parabiosis.

Without going into details here, suffice it to emphasize the great similarities in the developmental processes of the bovine freemartin fetuses (Jost *et al.*

1972, 1973, 1976) and experimental newts. In both, male gonads developed normally, while the female gonads (presumptive ovaries) became highly abnormal and finally were more or less sex-reversed. The sequence of events was very similar:

(1) The presumptive female gonads remained essentially like those of normal females for approximately ten days after the initial sex differentiation (40 days post-insemination in freemartins; 45 days after transplantation in newts).

(2) Growth of the gonads then stopped (after Days 50-55); the germ cells ceased to proliferate and meiotic cells became rare. The so-called germinal epithelium of the ovary was more or less completely suppressed. In both species the gonads remained stunted for several weeks.

(3) In the third phase, masculinization of the genetic females could occur. In the newts testicular-like nodules appeared in the hilar part of the inhibited gonads; they became conspicuous between 80 and 125 days and grew after the testis that induced the ovarian changes had been removed. After 9-12 months the testicular parts of the transformed gonads contained sperm. Humphrey (1945) obtained progeny from normal females and a female converted into a functional male. The reversed gonad produced male hormone and secured male behaviour. In freemartins, the stunted gonad was covered with an albuginea and contained a proportionally large rete (somewhat larger than in normal females). Structures similar to seminiferous tubules appeared around Day 90 in one animal, and much later in others, during a period of three months or more. In contrast to the newt, the germ cells disappeared from the freemartin gonad after the fifth month.

A probably very significant feature of the freemartins was that stunting of the ovary coincided with the disappearance of the tubal part of the Müllerian ducts in both the males and the freemartins during the second period mentioned above. Inhibition of Müllerian ducts and gonads occurred in the absence of any sign of masculinization and might well result from the activity of the testicular inhibiting hormone (Jost *et al.* 1972, 1976).

Another series of experiments, on *Xenopus laevis,* produced results similar to those described in cattle and newts, although the series of transformations involved was not followed in the same detail. Experimental parabiosis (Chang 1953) and testicular transplantation (Mikamo & Witschi 1963) caused extreme and prolonged reduction of the presumptive ovaries, and finally functional sex reversal, from female to male (fertilization of normal females by females converted to males) was obtained.

It is significant that in all three species reversal from female to male was observed, although only in cattle is the male heterozygous and produces H-Y antigen. In newts and in *Xenopus* the homozygous males were not feminized by the heterozygous female that produces the H-W antigen. In other experiments functional feminization of ZZ male *Xenopus* or newts *(Pleurodeles)* was obtained under the influence of oestrogen, in the absence of the W chromosome (see Gallien 1965). Therefore it would appear that H-W antigen is probably not a prerequisite for ovarian differentiation in these species.

As a whole, in mammals and in amphibians, when male and female embryos of the same developmental age and species are given a chance to influence each other, the trend is testicular dominance over the ovarian primordium and eventually sex reversal of the latter. This occurs whatever the mode of genetic determination of sex, and perhaps whatever the trend of body sex differentiation in gonadless young (if de Beaumont's observations on *Triturus* also apply to *Amblystoma* and to *Xenopus,* a possibility that still has to be explored).

Results in birds are at variance. For instance, in heterosexual pairs of chick embryos developed in eggs with two yolks, the ovaries of the female partner are neither reduced nor reversed, although the Müllerian ducts are partly inhibited; the testes of the males show minimal alterations (small and inconstant patches of superficial epithelium) (Lutz & Lutz-Ostertag 1959). Similarly, testes taken from older male embryos and grafted into the coelomic cavity of two-day-old female embryos did not modify the ovaries of the host, although they more or less inhibited the Müllerian ducts. Older ovaries grafted into younger males modified the embryonic testes in the same way as a low dose of oestradiol (Wolff 1947). Embryonic chicken testes are easily altered by steroids; ovaries are not.

In conclusion, it seems warranted to say that, at least in mammals and in birds, opposite basic trends in sex development correspond to opposite mechanisms of chromosomal sex determination. Not only is this true for the development and functioning of the entire reproductive system, but—at least in certain species—it clearly also applies to sexual behaviour. In other species, particularly in humans, behaviour depends on a more complex range of determinants; it is of importance to evaluate the exact contribution of its biological bases.

References

Adkins, E. K. (1975) Hormonal basis of sexual differentiation in the Japanese quail. *J. Comp. Physiol. Psychol. 89,* 61 – 71

Adkins, E. K. (1976) Embryonic exposure to an anti-estrogen masculinizes behaviour of female quail. *Physiol. Behav. 17,* 357 – 359

Adkins, E. K. & Adler, N. T. (1972) Hormonal control of behavior in the Japanese quail. *J. Comp. Physiol. Psychol. 81,* 27 – 36

Akram, H. & Weniger, J. P. (1968) Féminisation en culture in vitro du testicule embryonnaire du poulet par le testicule embryonnaire de veau. *Arch. Anat. Microsc. Morphol. Exp. 57,* 369

Chang, C. Y. (1953) Parabiosis and gonad transplantation in *Xenopus laevis* Daudin. *J. Exp. Zool. 123,* 1 – 28

Cheng, M. F. & Lehrman, D. (1975) Gonadal hormone specificity in the sexual behavior of ring doves. *Psychoneuroendocrinology 1,* 95 – 102

Chevalier, M. (1969) Données nouvelles sur le caryotype du Lézard vivipare (Reptile Lacertilien). Existe-t-il une hétérogamétie femelle de type $Z_1 Z_2 W$? *C.R. Hebd. Séances Acad. Sci.Sér. D Sci. Nat. 268,* 2098 – 2100

De Beaumont, J. (1933) La différenciation sexuelle dans l'appareil uro-génital du triton et son déterminisme. *Wilhelm Roux' Arch. Entwicklungsmech. Org. 129,* 120 – 178

Dufaure, J. P. (1966) Recherches descriptives et expérimentales sur les modalités et facteurs du développement de l'appareil génital chez le Lézard vivipare *(Lacerta vivipara* Jacquin). *Arch. Anat. Microsc. Morphol. Exp. 55,* 438 – 537

Gallien, L. (1965) Genetic control of sexual differentiation in Vertebrates, in *Organogenesis* (De Haan, R. L. & Ursprung, H., eds.), pp. 583 – 610, Holt, Rinehart & Winston, New York

Grady, K. L., Phoenix, C. H. & Young, W. C. (1965) Role of the developing rat testis in differentiation of the neural tissues mediating mating behavior. *J. Comp. Physiol. Psychol. 59,* 176 – 182

Humphrey, R. R. (1929) Studies on sex reversal in *Amblystoma.* II. Sex differentiation and modification following orthotopic implantation of a gonadic preprimordium. *J. Exp. Zool. 53,* 171 – 219

Humphrey, R. R. (1931) Studies on sex reversal in *Amblystoma.* III. Transformation of the ovary of *A. tigrinum* into a functional testis through the influence of a testis resident in the same animal. *J. Exp. Zool. 58,* 333 – 365.

Humphrey, R. R. (1945) Sex determination in ambystomid salamanders: a study of the progeny of females experimentally converted into males. *Am. J. Anat. 76,* 33 – 66

Josso, N., Picard, J. Y. & Tran, D. (1977) The antimüllerian hormone. *Recent Prog. Horm. Res. 33,* 117 – 167

Jost, A. (1947) Recherches sur la différenciation sexuelle de l'embryon de lapin. III. Rôle des gonades foetales dans la différenciation sexuelle somatique. *Arch. Anat. Microsc. Morphol. Exp. 36,* 271 – 315

Jost, A. (1953) Problems of fetal endocrinology: the gonadal and hypophyseal hormones. *Recent Prog. Horm. Res. 8,* 379 – 418

Jost, A. (1958) Chapter 2, in *Hermaphroditism, Genital Anomalies and Related Endocrine Disorders* (Jones, H. W. & Scott, W. W. eds.) (1st edn), Williams & Wilkins, Baltimore (2nd revised edn, 1971)

Jost, A. (1965) Gonadal hormones in the sex differentiation of the Mammalian fetus, in *Organogenesis* (De Haan, R. L. & Ursprung, H., eds.), pp. 611 – 628, Holt, Rinehart & Winston, New York

Jost, A. (1970) in *Mammalian Reproduction* (Gibian, H. & Plotz, J. E., eds.), pp. 4 – 32, Springer-Verlag, Berlin

Jost, A. (1971) A new look at the mechanisms controlling sex differentiation in Mammals. *Johns Hopk. Med. J. 130,* 38 – 53

Jost, A., Vigier, B. & Prépin, J. (1972) Freemartins in cattle: the first steps of sexual organogenesis. *J. Reprod. Fertil. 29,* 349 – 379

Jost, A. Vigier, B., Prépin, J. & Perchellet, J. P. (1973) Studies on sex differentiation in Mammals. *Recent Prog. Horm. Res. 29,* 1 – 41

Jost, A., Perchellet, J. P., Prépin, J. & Vigier, B. (1976) The prenatal development of bovine freemartins, in *Intersexuality in the Animal Kingdom* (Reinboth, R., ed.), pp. 392–406, Springer-Verlag, Berlin/Heidelberg/New York

KELLEY, D. B. & PFAFF, D. W. (1976) Hormone effects on male sex behavior in adult South African clawed frogs, *Xenopus laevis*. *Horm. Behav. 7,* 159–182

LUTZ, H. & LUTZ-OSTERTAG, Y. (1959) Free-Martinisme spontané chez les oiseaux. *Dev. Biol. 1,* 364–376

MIKAMO, K. & WITSCHI, E. (1963) Functional sex reversal in genetic females of *Xenopus laevis,* induced by implanted testes. *Genetics 48,* 1411–1421

OHNO, S. (1977) The Y-linked H-Y antigen locus and the X-linked *Tfm* locus as major regulatory genes of the mammalian sex determining mechanism. *J. Steroid Biochem. 8,* 585–592

OHNO, S., CHRISTIAN, L. C., WACHTEL, S. S. & KOO, G. C. (1976) Hormone-like role of H-Y antigen in bovine freemartin gonad. *Nature (Lond.) 261,* 597–599

PHOENIX, C. H., GOY, R. W., GERALL, A. A. & YOUNG, W. C. (1959) Organizing action of prenatally administered testosterone propionate on the tissues mediating mating behaviour in the female guinea pig. *Endocrinology 65,* 369–382

SALZGEBER , B. (1963) Modification expérimentale du développement de l'ovaire de Souris sous l'influence du testicule embryonnaire de Poulet. *J. Embryol. Exp. Morphol. 11,* 91–105

WACHTEL, S. S. (1977) H-Y antigen: genetics and serology. *Immunol. Rev. 33,* 35–57

WACHTEL, S. S., KOO, G. C. & BOYSE, E. A. (1975*a*) Evolutionary conservation of H-Y ('male') antigen. *Nature (Lond.) 254,* 270–272

WACHTEL, S. S., OHNO, S., KOO, G. C. & BOYSE, E. A. (1975*b*) Possible role for H-Y antigen in the primary determination of sex. *Nature (Lond.) 257,* 235–236

WILSON, J. A. & GLICK, B. (1970) Ontogeny of mating behavior in the chicken. *Am. J. Physiol. 218,* 951–955

WOLFF, E. (1947) Recherches sur l'intersexualité expérimentale produite par la méthode des greffes de gonades à l'embryon de Poulet. *Arch. Anat. Microsc. Morphol. Exp. 36,* 69–90

WOLFF, E. & WOLFF, E. (1951) The effects of castration on bird embryos. *J. Exp. Zool. 116,* 59–98

Discussion

Beach: What are the possibilities that the Müllerian-inhibiting substance acts as an embryonic inducer or organizer in relation to the central nervous system, instead of or in addition to testosterone?

Jost: I don't know of any evidence, but perhaps an answer could be provided by the human males who have a uterus. The most probable explanation of these individuals is that they lacked the Müllerian-inhibiting hormone during development. They have not been reported to lack male sexual behaviour. They may ignore their condition. This is one indication.

Ehrhardt: This is a rare condition, but over the years I have seen three boys who were discovered to have a uterus. In all other respects they were normal males.

Jost: They are not completely normal: usually they are sterile, which is some kind of abnormality!

Ehrhardt: Anatomically their external genitalia developed normally and their behaviour showed nothing which was not masculine.

Jost: A. Prader and M. Zachmann and their colleagues reported on familial cases of this condition (Brook *et al.* 1973).

Bancroft: What was the nature of their infertility? What happened to the testis?

Ehrhardt: I don't know.

Besser: It is not so rare a condition. One sees the occasional true hermaphrodite in any endocrine clinic.

Professor Jost was careful to exclude the human at the end of his paper, and wisely so, but nevertheless his concept of the Müllerian-inhibiting factor has allowed us to understand a number of clinical conditions like true gonadal agenesis, Turner's syndrome, Klinefelter's syndrome and testicular feminization. But the difficulties come in considering some cases of true hermaphroditism.

One group of true hermaphrodites have an ovary on one side with a tube and half a uterus, and a testis and male external genitalia on the other side. They conform fully with your concept. They are male in outlook and want to be male. Another group have ovotestes on both sides, or maybe on one side. I find this difficult to explain. They appear to be male, but they may present gonads in herniae; at operation there is a fallopian tube and uterus, usually, and the gonad is mixed. How is this explained?

Jost: The fetal gonadal hormones controlling the sex ducts are probably *not* distributed through the bloodstream during the early stages. They act locally. Moreover, the amount of these hormones produced in the normal or in the abnormal fetus could never be measured. The anatomical or histological structure of the gonad and its genetic constitution are not necessarily related to the release of hormones. I am not too disturbed by differences seen in different cases.

Besser: The secretion of testosterone and dihydrotestosterone from the testicular part of the ovotestis is often adequate to masculinize the external genitalia in these cases, so that is another dissociation between the Müllerian-inhibiting factor secretion, which acts early, and subsequent steroid secretion, and it confirms that they are two different hormones.

Jost: As to the role of testosterone and dihydrotestosterone in sexual differentiation, I wish to remind you of the excellent work by Jean Wilson (1973) at Dallas in rabbits and in rats showing that these hormones are unequally bound to different receptor organs; some structures probably respond to testosterone and others to dihydrotestosterone.

Herbert: The evidence in primates is rather *against* testosterone having the same kind of effects on the differentiation of sexual behaviour as it has in non-primates (see Herbert 1977).

What progress has there been in identifying the Müllerian-inhibiting factor? Do you think that some of the negative effects on behaviour and pituitary function when baby monkeys are treated with androgen are because one is not simultaneously treating them with Müllerian-inhibiting factor, and this may therefore play a positive role in the sexual differentiation of the brain as well as the gonads? This would go some way towards explaining the puzzling discrepancy between rodents and primates.

Jost: The effects of androgens on the behaviour of monkeys are certainly not the same as those in rats, but I cannot suggest an explanation. The isolation and chemical nature of the Müllerian-inhibiting hormone are being studied by Nathalie Josso (see Josso *et al.* 1977), who started this work in my laboratory. She has shown very convincingly that this hormone is produced by the Sertoli cells, not by the interstitial cells, and we have confirmed this. It is probably a large molecule, or it is linked to a large molecule. So far, the hormone has not been isolated yet.

Short: I was always intrigued by the descriptions of Van Niekerk (1974) in South Africa of 24 cases of true hermaphroditism in Bantu. He described how some of these patients, who were all chromosomally XX, grew up to have male external genitalia and to menstruate regularly through the penis. So they had an ovary or an ovotestis from which ovulations occurred, and a uterus that menstruated, but the external genitalia were masculinized. This poses a tremendous problem to our understanding of sex determination and differentiation.

Sachar: On the question of whether the Müllerian-inhibiting factor plays a role in the organization of the brain and of behaviour, and bearing in mind Dr Ehrhardt's point that in the three cases she has seen she could not find any difference from other boys, it is important to stress that if endocrinologists encounter further such patients they should refer them for psychological evaluation. Such children or young adults constitute one of the few available models for the investigation of the possible psychological role of this factor.

Jost: The point was raised of whether the gonads are normal in the absence of fetal Müllerian-inhibiting hormone. I know of two publications (Bergada *et al.* 1962; Jirasek 1970) showing that in human males with a uterus the testis is *not* completely normal and that there is a thick layer in place of the normally thin albuginea. I am myself convinced that the inhibiting hormone has something to do with the differentiation of the gonad itself.

Professor Besser mentioned testicular feminization. When I first visited Lawson Wilkins in 1949 and proposed explanations for Turner's syndrome and for several other abnormalities, he asked how I could explain his observations of 'hairless women with testes'. He suggested that this was loss of sensitivity of the receptor tissues to androgens. His interpretation has been amply confirmed. In these patients the Müllerian-inhibiting hormone is probably produced during fetal life, since the uterus is absent; the androgens remain ineffective.

Green: Professor Jost, has anyone suggested using antiserum to the H-Y antigen as a method of selectively destroying Y spermatozoa in humans?

Jost: Not in humans. It has been tried in mice by Bennett & Boyse (1973), who obtained approximately 45% males and 55% females in the progeny, which is not very significantly different from the normal sex ratio.

Green: Why wasn't the antiserum more successful in destroying the Y sperm?

Jost: There are many difficulties in such tests. Theoretically the Y antiserum should destroy 50% of the spermatozoa but actually it destroys more, sometimes 70% of cells. One possibility is that the sperm receiving the X chromosome also receives part of the membrane of the original XY cell with some Y antigen molecules on it. This could explain why some of the sperm carrying the X chromosome are killed in the test.

Short: I am glad that you raised a note of caution about acceptance of the H-Y antigen theory, Dr Jost. The idea is appealing because it is so simple, but there are problems (Short 1978). Firstly, there is the dogma, which I think is essentially correct, of the lack of haploid gene expression—the fact that the haploid spermatozoon does not express its genotype. We know, for example, that one cannot absorb out X chromosome-bearing spermatozoa with XgA antiserum, so why should we expect to absorb out Y-bearing sperm? And why should we expect the H-Y antigen even to be expressed in the spermatozoa?

Secondly, there is the question of the H-Y antigen and the germ cell. We know from Charles Ford's recent work (unpublished) that an XY germ cell can become a functional oocyte capable of being fertilized and giving rise to offspring. This is an example of a cell that has the H-Y antigen and, if put in a female environment, becomes a normal female cell. Contrariwise, we know that an XX germ cell when put into a testicular environment cannot survive. This suggests that the H-Y antigen does not determine the sex of the germ cell.

Finally, we have the XX male goat where an autosomal *recessive* gene controls the formation of the testis; this does not fit the H-Y antigen hypothesis.

Dörner: Dr Jost, what do you think about the idea that testosterone itself may participate as a local hormone in the organization of the testes?

Jost: I know of no evidence for that. My only experience is with the anti-androgen drug cyproterone acetate which I gave to pregnant rabbits, early in pregnancy, to see what effect it would have on the development of the testis. Giving it from Day 13 onwards does not prevent testicular differentiation

(Jost 1966). It prevents only the masculinizing effect of the testis on the genital tract, as previously reported by F. Neuman and W. Elger (see Elger 1966).

Nieschlag: In the offspring of rabbits immunized against testosterone we observed no effect on the testis itself, but in a few cases the testes did not descend, which is a rather unusual finding in rabbits (unpublished). In studies with cyproterone acetate this effect has to my knowledge not been noted.

Herbert: Is it reasonable to suggest that the H-Y antigen plays no part in hormonal response in adult life, because in a somatic cell it would be paired with the corresponding allele in the X chromosome, which is presumably dominant? Or would you expect the H-Y antigen to play a role in adult life as well as in differentiation?

Jost: The anti-Y antisera are produced by grafting skin from adult male mice to adult females; so it works as an antigen in adults.

Hutchison: The hypothesis that H-Y antigens are involved in the primary determination of sex (Wachtel *et al.* 1975) implies that once gonadal sex is determined it is irreversible, but there are many examples in lower vertebrates where gonadal sex can be reversed. A good example is the sex-reversing marine teleost *Anthias squamipinnis* in which a change in social structure, brought about by the removal of the male, leads to rapid sex reversal in the top-ranking female of the group (Shapiro 1977). How does sex reversal relate to the H-Y antigen theory?

Jost: As I mentioned (p. 11), complete sex reversal has been obtained in amphibians with sex hormones in the absence of the H-W antigen. The question has been raised of whether the antigen is produced as a *consequence* of sex hormones, or whether it is independent of sex hormones.

Short: A classical case was described by Professor Crew (1923) of a bird that underwent complete, spontaneous functional sex reversal. It started off as a hen laying eggs and ended up as a cockerel with spermatozoa in its ejaculate. That poses problems for the H-Y antigen theory too!

Beach: D. R. Robertson (1972) also described sex reversal in a coral-reef fish, *Labroides dimidiatus.* The social organization is such that one dominant male patrols a certain area in the sand and within that area are 3-6 adult females, each with her own nest and small territory. As long as the male is present he protects the total area and fertilizes eggs of all females. If he dies or is removed the most dominant female starts to display territory defence, eventually becomes completely male, and fertilizes the eggs of other females. There are spermatogenic crypts in the normal ovary which develop and become functional under the control of social stimulation.

References

BENNETT, D. & BOYSE, E. A. (1973) Sex ratio in progeny of mice inseminated with sperm treated with H-Y anti-serum. *Nature (Lond.) 246,* 308 – 309

BERGADA, C., CLEVELAND, W. W., JONES, H. W. & WILKINS, L. (1962) Gonadal histology in patients with male pseudohermaphroditism and atypical gonadal dysgenesis: relation to theories of sex differentiation. *Acta Endocrinol. 40,* 493 – 520

BROOK, C. G. D., WAGNER, H., ZACHMANN, M., PRADER, A., ARMENDARES, S., FRENK, S., ALEMAN, P., NAJJAR, S. S., SLIM, M.S., GENTON, N. & BOZIC, C. (1973) Familial occurrence of persistent müllerian structures in otherwise normal males. *Br. Med. J. 1,* 771 – 773

CREW, F. A. E. (1923) Complete sex-transformation in the domestic fowl. *J. Hered. 14,* 361 – 362

ELGER, W. (1966) Die Rolle der fetalen Androgene in der sexualen Differenzierung des Kaninchens und ihre Abgrenzung gegen andere hormonale und somatische Faktoren durch Anwendung eines starken Antiandrogens. *Arch. Anat. Microsc.Morphol. Exp. 55,* 657 – 743

HERBERT, J. (1977) Hormones and behaviour. *Proc. R. Soc. Lond. B Biol. Sci. 199,* 425 – 443

JIRASEK, J. E. (1970) The relationship between differentiation of the testicle, external genital ducts and genitalia in fetal and postnatal life, in *The Human Testis* (Rosemberg, E. & Paulsen, C.A., eds.), p. 19, Plenum Press, New York

JOSSO, N., PICARD, J. Y. & TRAN, D. (1977) The antimüllerian hormone. *Recent Prog. Horm. Res. 33,* 117 – 167

JOST, A. (1966) Steroids and sex differentiation of the mammalian foetus, in *Proc. 2nd Int. Congr. Hormonal Steroids (International Congress Series no. 132),* pp. 74 – 81, Excerpta Medica, Amsterdam

ROBERTSON, D. R. (1972) Social control of sex reversal in a coral reef fish. *Science (Wash. D.C.) 177,* 1007 – 1009

SHAPIRO, D. Y. (1977) *Social Organization and Sex Reversal of the Coral Reef Fish Anthias squamipinnis (Peters).* Ph.D. Thesis, University of Cambridge

SHORT, R. V. (1978) Sex determination and differentiation of the mammalian gonad. *Int. J. Androl.,* Suppl. 2, in press

VAN NIEKERK, W. A. (1974) *True Hermaphroditism: Clinical, Morphologic and Cytogenetic Aspects,* Harper & Row, New York

WACHTEL, S. S., OHNO, S., KOO, G. C. & BOYSE, E. A. (1975) Possible role for H-Y antigen in the primary determination of sex. *Nature (Lond.) 257,* 235 – 236

WILSON, J. D. (1973) Testosterone uptake by the urogenital tract of the rabbit embryo. *Endocrinology 92,* 1192 – 1199

The effects of oestrogen on hypothalamic tissue

J. R. BRAWER and F. NAFTOLIN

Departments of Obstetrics and Gynecology and Anatomy, McGill University School of Medicine and Woman's Pavilion, Royal Victoria Hospital, Montreal

Abstract Oestrogens exert potent influences on hypothalamic differentiation and on sexual function throughout life. During the period in which the hypothalamus differentiates, the availability of oestrogens (or aromatizable androgens) to the hypothalamus results in a male pattern of gonadotropin secretion and in male sexual behaviour in the adult. Lack of oestrogens during this period results in a cyclic schedule of gonadotropin secretion and in female sexual behaviour. Oestrogens or their metabolites determine future sex-specific activity by facilitating synapse formation in developing target circuits. The onset of puberty may also in part reflect oestrogen-stimulated synapse formation in the hypothalamus. In contrast, oestrogen given to an adult female rat causes specific multifocal lesions in the lateral arcuate nucleus. Such animals exhibit persistent oestrus and small multicystic ovaries. Since the same anovulatory syndrome can be produced by mechanical disruption of neuronal pathways from more anterior regions to the arcuate nucleus, it would appear that oestrogen could effect a 'disconnection' of the circuit responsible for cyclic drive of gonadotropin secretion. Furthermore, old female rats spontaneously exhibit the same type of reproductive derangement as well as the arcuate lesion. Thus direct effects of oestrogens on neuronal circuitry within the hypothalamus may be responsible for (1) sexual differentiation, (2) the onset of puberty and sexual activity, and (3) cessation of reproductive function in the female rat.

Specific actions of sex steroids on brain tissue have been examined from a variety of perspectives. The regional localization of steroid target areas in the brain has been explored by autoradiography (Stumpf 1970; Pfaff & Keiner 1973; Morrell *et al.* 1975; Stumpf & Sar 1976, 1977) and by examining the physiological effect of selective steroid implants (Lisk & Newlon 1963; Ramirez *et al.* 1964; Lisk 1967; Nadler 1973; Christensen & Clemens 1974; Kalra & McCann 1975; Hayashi 1976). Furthermore, oestrogen formation and metabolism as well as specific receptors have been demonstrated and extensively characterized in brain tissues (see McEwen 1976). The physiological and biochemical responses of populations of target neurons to sex steroids have contributed to a large literature on the role that these hormones play in regulating CNS neuroendocrine function.

It has become clear from these findings that although short-term interactions of sex steroids with the neuroendocrine brain may be rather grossly demonstrated pharmacologically, generally their long-term effects are the result of events which are subtle and complex. While it is obvious that gonadal steroids influence a range of functional parameters in target neurons and that all these effects must be taken into consideration if we are to understand the biological mechanisms and behavioural consequences of such interactions, consideration of all of these phenomena in a single paper is clearly impossible. This paper will focus, therefore, on the actions of sex steroids, principally oestrogen, in modifying developing neuronal circuits and on altering established 'wiring' in the adult.

From autoradiographic studies it is clear that there are oestrogen-receptive neurons throughout the limbic system, periventricular brain, brainstem, and spinal cord. Neuronal circuitry in all these areas may be subject to the direct modifying influences of oestrogen, which should be reflected in physiological activity and in behaviour.

Our attention has been focused on the effects of sex steroids on the neuronal organization in the hypophysiotropic hypothalamus. Specifically, we have examined a neuronal system that is responsible for regulating gonadotropin secretion. However, we believe the principles observed to be generally applicable to other hypothalamic functions, such as the determination of sexual behaviour. The circuitry has been reviewed at length previously (see Sawyer 1975; Brawer & Van Houten 1976). Briefly and simply, it consists of a two-neuron chain. The cyclic drive is initiated in the anterior hypothalamus (suprachiasmatic nucleus [SCH] and possibly medial preoptic area [MPOA]), and is transmitted by way of axonal connections to putative luteinizing hormone (LH) releasing factor (LRF) neurosecretory cells in the medial basal hypothalamus. This description, although essentially true, is a gross oversimplification since the MPOA itself contains LRF neurons and projects to the median eminence (Brawer & Van Houten 1976). In any event, a hypothalamic island consisting of medial preoptic area (MPOA), suprachiasmatic nucleus (SCH), medial basal hypothalamus (MBH), median eminence, and pituitary is sufficient to maintain cyclic surges of LH with subsequent ovulation in the female rat (Tejasen & Everett 1967; Halasz 1969; Taleisnik *et al.* 1970). This system has several advantages as a model for studying organizational effects of sex steroids on neuronal tissue. It is anatomically and physiologically simple and accessible. Clear sex differences in gonadotropin secretion are unequivocally diagnostic of sexual differentiation, and alteration in sexual cyclicity in the female can be directly related to anatomical changes in hypophysiotropic circuits, as will be explained shortly. There is, of course, also commensurate evidence of behavioural differentiation and activation in the same areas (see Beyer 1976). Sex steroids play a critical role in programming sexual behaviour in the adult. Since neuronal circuitry is generally considered the physical substrate of behaviour, it is probable that steroid modifications of hypothalamic regions associated with reproduction would be attended by altered reproductive behaviour. The behavioural consequences associated with oestrogen modifications of these hypothalamic circuits have not yet, however, been firmly established, nor has the applicability of these findings to other steroid-sensitive neuronal systems.

EFFECTS OF GONADAL STEROIDS ON DEVELOPING HYPOTHALAMIC TISSUE: SEXUAL DIFFERENTIATION

Sex-specific patterns of gonadotropin secretion and sexual behaviour are determined by exposure or lack of exposure of the hypophysiotropic hypothalamus to oestrogens or aromatizable androgens during a specific period of development (Gorski 1971; Gorski *et al.* 1977). The exposure of neonatal female rats to these sex steroids results in a tonic male pattern of gonadotropin secretion when the animals reach sexual maturity. Elimination of circulating gonadal steroid in neonatal male rats results in a cyclic 'female' schedule of gonadotropin release in adults. The perinatal interval in which sexual reversal can be effected, the so-called critical period, exhibits considerable species variability. However, within any one species, it appears to occupy a fixed constant interval in the developmental continuum. The question of how gonadal steroids effect the development of a defeminized hypophysiotropic hypothalamus has recently received considerable attention. There is good evidence that they actually 'fashion' sex-specific circuits. For example, Raisman & Field (1973) showed that the MPOA of the rat is sexually dimorphic. There are many more synapses of non-amygdalar origin on dendritic spines of MPOA neurons in the female than in the male. Furthermore, the development of a dimorphic non-amygdalar circuit appears to be under the direct influence of gonadal steroids. For example, gonadectomy of neonatal male rats resulted in cyclic (female) schedules of gonadotropin release when the animals reached sexual maturity. Moreover, the brains of these sexually reversed rats exhibited typical female synaptology in the MPOA. Injection of androgen into the neonate resulted in male gonadotropin secretion patterns and male synaptology in the MPOA of the adults. 'It has been subsequently shown that dendritic patterns within the MPOA of the hamster also exhibit sexual dimorphism (Greenough *et al.* 1977), but the response of these patterns to neonatal androgenization or gonadectomy has not yet been reported in detail.

The timing of hypothalamic development of the MPOA has been studied in the neonatal rat (Reier *et al.* 1977). At birth, the MPOA consists of immature cells and a few definitive adult-type synapses. During the first two postnatal weeks, there is a sharp increase in the number of adult-type synapses within the MPOA. The undeveloped state of this area at birth, and the development of synapses and morphologically mature neurons within the first fourteen days of life, Days 21-35 post-conception, indicate that the MPOA establishes much of its connections during the critical period of hypothalamic differentiation, which in the rat is about the first ten postnatal days. The authors report no differences in either morphology or rates of development of the MPOA between male and female animals. It must be emphasized, however, that the sexual dimorphism reported by Raisman & Field occurred among synapses that had been identified and distinguished from strial synapses by lesioning the stria and identifying and quantifying the synapses that did not undergo subsequent degeneration. Obviously, the appreciation of quantitative differences in synaptology would depend upon such identifications and would not have come to light in an ordinary fine-structural study. Exactly what role the MPOA's dimorphic circuitry plays in reproduction is unclear, since recent evidence (Brown-Grant & Raisman 1977; Brown-Grant *et al.* 1977; Raisman & Brown-Grant 1977) strongly suggests that the suprachiasmatic nucleus of the rat rather than the MPOA is responsible for driving the cycle of gonadotropin secretion. Interestingly, sexual dimorphism in the internal morphology of dendrites has also recently been reported in the suprachiasmatic nucleus of the rat (Guldner 1976). In any case, the steroid-sensitive dimorphic circuit in the MPOA could be associated with sex-specific behaviour (Lisk 1967).

Toran-Allerand (1976) has recently examined the efects of sex steroids on neonatal mouse hypothalamus in organ culture. She found that addition of oestradiol or testosterone to the culture medium caused an accelerated and intense proliferation of neuronal processes as compared to the same region of hypothalamus cultured in control media. Addition of non-aromatizable androgens such as 5α-dihydrotestosterone to the media resulted in growth patterns and rates identical to those of the untreated controls (personal communication), suggesting that the organizational action of androgens on these hypothalamic tissues depends on prior ring A aromatization. Addition of antibody to oestrogen to normal culture media resulted in severe retardation of neuritic growth. Thus it appears that oestrogen facilitates growth in neonatal hypothalamic tissue. The finding that tissue from the hypothalamus of 21-, 22- and 23-day post-conceptional rats (−1, 1, 5 and 10 days in relation to birth) is capable of aromatizing androgens (Reddy *et al.* 1974), and that these areas are capable of forming catechol oestrogens (Fishman & Norton 1975), implies that this metabolism may be important in the modelling of the nervous system as described.

It is not yet certain from Toran-Allerand's study whether oestrogen stimulates the formation of definitive synapses. So far she has reported only on the growth and complexity of neurites at the light microscopic level. However, *in vivo* investigations suggest that oestrogen is synaptogenic. Matsumoto & Arai (1976*a*) found that treatment of female rats with oestradiol benzoate during the first 30 days *post partum* resulted in twice as many axodendritic synapses in the arcuate nucleus as in oil-treated controls.

The arcuate nucleus of the MBH contains a population of LRF hypophysiotropic cells. The LRF release patterns of these cells are thought to be driven by afferent axonal connections from the more anterior cyclic drive regions (SCH and MPOA). Thus, the final adult pattern of LRF and subsequent LH secretion could reflect, in part, the modelling of this circuit. Availability of gonadal steroids to the hypothalamus during the time of development would obviously result in a configuration of synaptic connections not seen in the hypothalamus unexposed to steroid during the critical period of development.

Dr Walsh, of our laboratory, has examined the fine structure of the developing arcuate nucleus in male rats (Walsh & Brawer 1978). As in the case of the neonatal MPOA, the arcuate nucleus of the neonate contained very few mature synapses. Interestingly, many neuronal perikarya of the arcuate nucleus appear to be cytologically mature, which may account for the gonadotropin secretion known to occur in neonates. Matsumoto & Arai (1976*b*) also observed very few synapses in the arcuate nucleus of early neonatal female rats. There was a large increase in the numbers of synapses between the fifth and twentieth day *post partum*. The paucity of synapses in the neonatal arcuate nucleus indicates, as in the neonatal MPOA, that the major afferent connections have yet to be established and that the patterns of development of these connections could be subject to modifying influences of gonadal steroids during the critical period of differentiation.

It appears, therefore, that oestrogen (regardless of the source) is responsible for influencing the physical development and remodelling of circuits in the regions of the hypothalamus associated with sex-specific patterns of gonadotropin secretion and behaviour. A hypothetical mechanism of action of sex steroids in fashioning sexually dimorphic circuits has been suggested by

Toran-Allerand (1976). Briefly, sex steroid-facilitated circuits would grow faster than non-facilitated afferents and therefore compete more successfully for synaptic space on recipient neurons. In the steroid-exposed hypothalamus – for example, in the normal male rat – the subsequent behaviour of the recipient neurons would be dominated by the steroid-facilitated afferents whereas in unexposed hypothalamus, as in the normal female rat, the steroid-facilitated afferents would have no growth advantage and would compete more or less equally with all other afferent synapses for synaptic space.

IDENTIFICATION OF OESTROGENS AS THE KEY STEROIDS IN BRAIN DIFFERENTIATION

It has been known for many years that the presence of a functioning testis during the critical period is required for sexual differentiation. Recent evidence indicates that the testicular androgens serve mainly as prohormones and are converted to oestrogens in order to affect hypothalamic circuitry, as described in this paper. Several key pieces of evidence support this idea. The first is the failure of ring A-reduced metabolites of androgens to cause brain differentiation (Brown-Grant *et al.* 1971). On the other hand, aromatizable androgens including 19-hydroxy intermediates between C_{19} and C_{18} steroids are effective (McDonald & Doughty 1974). The most potent compounds in this area are the oestrogens (Gorski 1963; Sutherland & Gorski 1972; Gorski *et al.* 1977). Supporting the idea that oestrogens are the critical compounds in brain differentiation are the ability of non-steroidal antioestrogens to block the effects of aromatizable androgens such as testosterone (Doughty & McDonald 1974), the finding of areas sensitive to intra-hypothalamic oestrogen implants (Hayashi 1976), and the ability of the rat neuroendocrine hypothalamus to convert (aromatize) androgens to oestrogens (Reddy *et al.* 1974).

The presence of a binding protein in the rat during the critical period (Raynaud *et al.* 1971; Nunez *et al.* 1971) probably protects the developing rat brain from the effects of circulating oestrogens during pregnancy. The existence of such a protein provided a model with which to confirm the oestrogen hypothesis, since minute amounts of diethylstilboestrol, a relatively weak non-steroidal oestrogen which is not bound by the oestrogen-binding proteins of the perinatal rat, can be the cause of brain differentiation (Gorski 1966).

Correlative studies showing the effect of oestrogen in developing nervous tissues (described elsewhere in this paper, p. 22) also support the oestrogen hypothesis. Recently it has been shown that catechol oestrogens can also effect brain differentiation (Parvizi & Naftolin 1977); they have also been shown to be formed in the rat brain (Fishman & Norton 1975).

PUBERTY

It may be that the hypothalamic events initiating puberty also stem from sex steroid facilitation of target circuits within the hypothalamus. It has recently been demonstrated that pregnant mare serum gonadotropin injected into 28-day-old female rats advances puberty and also results in a sharp increase in the number of mature synapses in the arcuate nucleus as compared to the normal or ovariectomized controls (Matsumoto & Arai 1977).

Similarly, it has been demonstrated that a unilateral lesion of the MBH advances puberty in the female rat (YoungLai *et al.* 1976). Preliminary observations in our laboratory (R. Walsh, K. B. Ruf & J. R. Brawer) show many more adult-type synapses in the lateral arcuate nucleus on the non-lesioned side than in arcuate nuclei of non-lesioned controls. Lesions of this sort result in elevated circulating oestrogen levels (YoungLai *et al.* 1976). It should be noted that the lateral region of the arcuate nucleus has been shown to be particularly sensitive to oestrogen in both its short-term (Price *et al.* 1976) and long-term (Brawer *et al.* 1978) effects. Arrival at the final adult complement of synapses in the female arcuate nucleus is reported to require 45 days of postnatal life (Matsumoto & Arai 1976*b*), which suggests that synaptic development and hypothalamic circuitry are still subject to the modifying influences of gonadal steroids until this time.

ADULT

The action of sex steroids in modifying hypophysiotropic circuitry in the sexually mature adult appears to differ markedly from the effects of steroids in neonatal and prepubertal animals. Whereas, in the latter case, the effects of steroids appear to be largely trophic, affecting specific parameters of development, in the adult these hormones can be dystrophic – that is, they appear to effect the disconnection of specific circuits.

Attention was first drawn to this possibility in a study of the effects of repeated high doses of oestradiol valerate (OV) on hypothalamic cytology in the adult female rat (Brawer & Sonnenschein 1975). Monthly injections of 2 mg OV over four to eleven months produced large adenomas of the pituitary. The fine structure of the hypothalamic arcuate nucleus was examined in these animals in order to evaluate the effects of such treatment on a known hypophysiotropic nucleus. It was found that in treated animals a gradually progressive, multifocal lesion developed in the lateral arcuate nucleus extending from its most anterior to its most posterior limits.

After three monthly injections, multiple foci, characterized by degenerating axons, terminals, and dendrites, appear primarily along the lateral border of the arcuate nucleus. This degeneration is accompanied by reactive microglia containing phagosomes and also by an extremely unusual variety of reactive astrocytes. The astrocytes within degenerative foci contain numerous pleomorphic pools of dense lipid-like material in addition to large bundles of fine filaments. In more extensively treated animals (e.g. for 6-11 months) the microglia are very large and filled with masses of degenerating debris. These intensely reactive cells are invariably situated among clusters of degenerating axons and dendrites. Between degenerative foci, the neuropil appears cytologically normal, suggesting that the degenerative process is not simply the result of a generalized non-specific phenomenon.

Many of the degenerating axons are not much thicker than ordinary mitochondria and therefore they do not display the easily observable signs of anterograde degeneration characteristic of larger axon systems. Dr L. Renaud (personal communication) has calculated axon diameters of afferents from

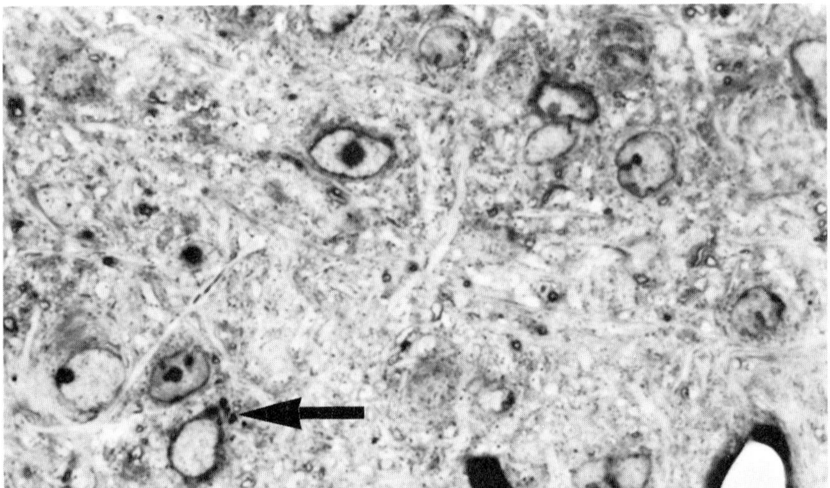

FIG. 1. Arcuate nucleus of normal cyclic female rats in dioestrus. The arrow indicates a normally appearing astrocyte with several dense bodies (gliosomes) (× 250).

the MPOA to the arcuate nucleus on the basis of conduction velocities in antidromically fired units. He concluded that many such axons must have diameters of about a single micrometre. Because of the fine diameters of these axons, the glial response to degeneration within the arcuate neuropil appears far more prominent than the axonal and terminal degeneration. However, the neural damage undoubtedly represents the primary pathological event. Because of their prominence in light or electron microscope preparations the glia serve as an excellent, albeit indirect, index for evaluating the arcuate lesion after exposure to steroids (Figs. 1 and 2).

If the progressive development of this lesion depends upon constantly elevated circulating oestrogens maintained by the monthly injections, discontinuation of the injections should result in remission of the lesion. However, sexually mature female rats given a single injection of OV and studied 1-6 months later showed arcuate pathology which progressed with time course, intensity, and distribution similar to that seen in animals receiving the monthly injections (Brawer *et al.* 1978). No evidence of remission was seen. Gross reproductive alterations follow this single exposure to OV. Daily

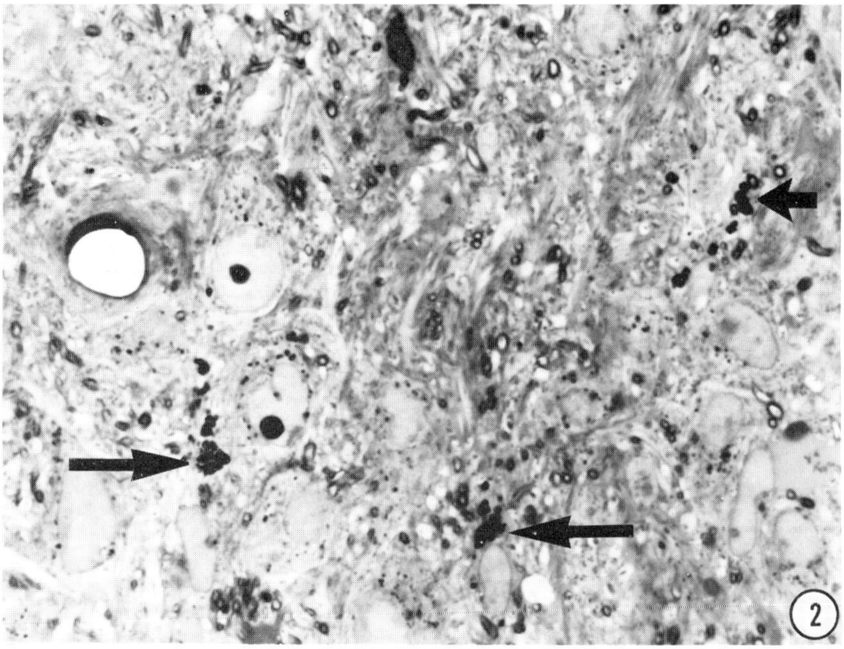

FIG. 2. Arcuate nucleus of a female rat injected three months previously with 2 mg oestradiol valerate. Arrows indicate astrocytic processes filled with large accumulations of gliosomes (× 250).

vaginal smears showed that the great majority of animals exhibited irregular changes in vaginal cytology for about six weeks after injection, followed by persistent oestrous smears that lasted for the duration of the experiment (six months). Serum prolactin levels rose sharply immediately after injection and then declined to control levels within one month. Serum LH was maintained at a steady level in the high-normal range and serum follicle-stimulating hormone (FSH) declined to a steady low-normal level. Circulating oestradiol (E_2) concentrations were very high after injection. The values dropped and reached a plateau by six weeks at a steady state level of about 30 pg/ml serum, which is rather high for the rat. The ovaries of these animals in persistent oestrus were small and contained many cystic follicles. The onset of the persistent oestrous condition was characterized by multicystic ovaries; high-normal LH and low-normal FSH levels closely paralleled the appearance of a histologically identifiable lesion in the arcuate nucleus, 4-6 weeks after injection.

A cause-and-effect relationship between the hypothalamic lesion and the development of the polycystic ovary-persistent oestrus syndrome was suggested by the fact that surgical disruption of the connections between the MPOA-suprachiasmatic area and the MBH results in the same endocrine and reproductive derangements as those seen in animals six weeks after an injection of oestradiol valerate (Halasz 1969; Blake *et al.* 1972, 1973; Willoughby *et al.* 1977). Since the oestradiol lesion involves deterioration of axons, terminals, and dendrites within the lateral arcuate nucleus, it may be that large doses of oestrogen in the sexually mature adult rat cause selective degeneration in target circuits within the hypothalamus, thus effecting a 'disconnection' of the MBH from the more anterior cyclic drive regions. This hypothesis is currently being tested in collaboration with Dr K. Ruf, by stimulating the MPOA in oestradiol-lesioned animals and comparing the subsequent elevation in plasma LH levels with that in stimulated normal cyclic controls. Our preliminary results indicate a significantly reduced LH surge after MPOA stimulation in animals injected three months previously with OV.

The physiological implications of the oestradiol lesion require clarification, since we have arbitrarily employed a single supra-pharmacological dose of OV to obtain the model. We are at present using a diminishing dose schedule to establish the minimum effective dose. It should be noted, however, that circulating E_2 concentrations rose and fell to a plateau level of about 30 pg/ml within the first month after injection (before the appearance of either the lesion or persistent oestrus). This suggests that the initial dose upset some parameter within the brain-pituitary-gonad axis, resulting in moderately elevated circulating oestradiol levels. We believe that the OV clears after its initial effect and that the lesions and polycystic ovary-persistent oestrus syndrome develop in response to only the gonadal activity characterized by mildly elevated E_2 levels. This is further suggested by the fact that the lesion does not develop in injected animals that were ovariectomized one day before injection. We have also observed that the lesion develops in animals in persistent oestrus as a result of constant light exposure. In such animals, circulating E_2 is only moderately elevated.

The selective destruction of target circuits for oestradiol may be significant in explaining a variety of hypothalamic anovulatory syndromes in humans (Katz & Carr 1976; Rebar *et al.* 1976). Furthermore, many adult female rats normally exhibit this type of anovulation with age (Aschheim 1976). That is, they spontaneously develop persistent oestrus at an age at which the ovaries are still competent and the pituitary is still responsive to LRF.

Interestingly, we have found that older female rats, particularly those in senile persistent oestrus, exhibit spontaneous degenerative foci in the lateral arcuate nucleus, characterized by populations of reactive astrocytes and microglial cells. This might be attributed to the normal ageing of the CNS in general except for the fact that the distribution and intensity of the reaction resembles that in young rats that have received OV several months previously. Furthermore, as in the case of injected animals, the anterior hypothalamic nucleus and dorsomedial nucleus were completely free of reactive glia, suggesting that general ageing is insufficient to account for degenerative foci in the arcuate nucleus. We are now testing the role of oestradiol in hypothalamic ageing by ovariectomizing young rats and letting them age. Arcuate histology of these animals will be compared to that of age-graded controls.

SUMMARY

We have reviewed data concerning the role of oestrogen (formed distally or locally) in hypothalamic structure and function. Oestrogens are apparently operative throughout life in modifying hypothalamic circuitry, to account for functional reproductive changes that characterize the different stages of the reproductive history of the animal. The role of oestrogens early in life is primarily trophic in that they model and fashion developing hypothalamic circuitry destined to support specific sexual activity (behavioural and endocrinological) in the young adult. In the adult hypothalamus, the long-term anatomical-functional role of oestrogens seems to be primarily destructive, resulting in deterioration of synaptic structures in the hypothalamus. The result of this process may be disconnection of hypothalamic circuits terminating in a functional hypothalamic anovulation, as is characteristic of the old female rat. The cause-and-effect relationship between oestrogen-induced MBH lesions and the polycystic ovary syndrome is, at present, unproven. Furthermore, the behavioural role of the affected circuit is unclear in general, so that behavioural correlates of this type of hormone-induced neuronal modification are a matter of pure speculation. It is also questionable whether the target circuit that is subject to trophic influences in the neonate (Naftolin & Brawer 1977) is the same as that which degenerates under the influence of oestrogen in the adult.

With these reservations in mind, the question may be asked why the effect of oestrogen on the hypothalamus reverses in the adult. It may be over-simplistic to regard the two actions of oestrogen described above as separate and distinct processes. They may actually represent different facets of a single phenomenon. For example, it has been shown that in the posterior ventro-lateral region of the hypothalamic ventromedial nucleus in the normal adult male rat, degeneration of neuronal processes, attended by reactive astrocytes and microglia, occurs spontaneously (Van Houten & Brawer 1978). Interestingly, growth cones also appear intermingled among the degenerating elements in the same region. This suggests that degeneration of established connections may be accompanied by formation of new ones; that is, degeneration and growth may operate in synchrony, resulting in synaptic remodelling. Whether or not the anatomy of this particular system (posterior ventromedial nucleus) is subject to hormonal influences is not yet known. Nevertheless, in neonatal rats, the growth effect of oestrogen may predominate, whereas later in life the growth potential of the tissue may be minimal and the degeneration effect could be accentuated. Whatever the explanation, it is clear that oestrogen effects are critical at all ages for determining hypothalamic circuitry and therefore the physiological activity and behaviour dependent upon circuits.

ACKNOWLEDGEMENTS

This work was supported by MRC Grant MA 5948 to J. R. Brawer and MRC Grant MT 5823 to F. Naftolin. J. R. Brawer is an MRC Scholar.

References

Aschheim, P. (1976) Aging in the hypothalamic-hypophyseal ovarian axis in the rat, in *Hypothalamus, Pituitary, and Aging* (Everitt, A. & Burgess, J., eds.), pp. 376-418, Thomas, Springfield, Ill.

Beyer, C. (1976) Neuroendocrine mechanisms in sexual behavior, in *Subcellular Mechanisms in Reproductive Neuroendocrinology* (Naftolin, F., Ryan, K. J. & Davies, J., eds.), pp. 471-484, Elsevier, Amsterdam

BLAKE, C., WEINER, R., GORSKI, R. & SAWYER, C. (1972) Secretion of pituitary luteinizing hormone and follicle stimulating hormone in female rats made persistently estrous or diestrous by hypothalamic deafferentation. *Endocrinology 90,* 855-861

BLAKE, C., SCARAMUZZI, R., HILLARD, J. & SAWYER, C. (1973) Circulating levels of pituitary gonadotrophins and ovarian steroids in rats after hypothalamic deafferentation. *Neuroendocrinology 12,* 86 – 97

BRAWER, J. R. & SONNENSCHEIN, C. (1975) Cytopathological effects of estradiol on the arcuate nucleus of the female rat. A possible mechanism for pituitary tumorigenesis. *Am. J. Anat. 144,* 57 – 89

BRAWER, J. R. & VAN HOUTEN, M. (1976) Organization of luteinizing hormone releasing factor delivery systems, in *Subcellular Mechanisms of Reproductive Neuroendocrinology* (Naftolin, F., Ryan, K. J., & Davies, J., eds.), pp. 1 – 21, Elsevier, Amsterdam

BRAWER, J. R., NAFTOLIN, F., MARTIN, J. & SONNENSCHEIN, C. (1978) Effects of a single injection of estradiol valerate on the hypothalamic arcuate nucleus and on reproductive function in the female rat. *Endocrinology, 103,* 501-512

BROWN-GRANT, K. & RAISMAN, G. (1977) Abnormalities in reproductive function associated with the destruction of the suprachiasmatic nuclei in female rats. *Proc. R. Soc. Lond. Ser. B Biol. Sci. 198,* 279 – 296

BROWN-GRANT, K., MUNCK, A., NAFTOLIN, F. & SHERWOOD, M. (1971) The effects of the administration of testosterone propionate alone or with phenobarbitone and testosterone metabolites to neonatal female rats. *Horm. Behav. 3,* 1 – 10

BROWN-GRANT, K., MURRAY, M., RAISMAN, G. & SOOD, M. (1977) Reproductive function in male and female rats following extra- and intra-hypothalamic lesions. *Proc. R. Soc. Lond. Ser. B Biol. Sci. 198,* 267 – 278

CHRISTENSEN, L. W. & CLEMENS, L. (1974) Intrahypothalamic implants of testosterone or estradiol and resumption of masculine sexual behaviour in long-term castrated male rats. *Endocrinology 95,* 984 – 990

DOUGHTY, C. & MCDONALD, P. (1974) Hormonal control of sexual differentiation of the hypothalamus in the neonatal female rat. *Differentiation 2,* 275 – 285

FISHMAN, J. & NORTON, B. (1975) Catechol estrogen formation in the central nervous system of the rat. *Endocrinology 96,* 1054 – 1059

GORSKI, R. A. (1963) Modification of ovulatory mechanisms by postnatal administration of estrogen to the rat. *Am. J. Physiol. 205,* 842 – 844

GORSKI, R. (1966) Localization and sexual differentiation of the nervous structures which regulate ovulation. *J. Reprod. Fertil.,* Suppl. 1, 67 – 88

GORSKI, (1971) Gonadal hormones and the perinatal development of neuroendocrine function, in *Frontiers in Neuroendocrinology* (Martini, L. & Ganong, W., eds.), pp. 237 – 290, Oxford University Press, New York

GORSKI, R., HARLAN, R. & CHRISTENSEN, L. (1977) Perinatal hormonal exposure and the development of neuroendocrine regulatory processes. *J. Toxicol. Environ. Health 3,* 97 – 121

GREENOUGH, W., CARTER, C., STEERMAN, C. & DEVOOGD, T. (1977) Sex differences in dendritic patterns in hamster preoptic area. *Brain Res. 126,* 63 – 72

GULDNER, F. (1976) Synaptology of the rat suprachiasmatic nucleus. *Cell Tissue Res. 165,* 509 – 549

HALASZ, B. (1969) The endocrine effects of isolation of the hypothalamus from the rest of the brain, in *Frontiers in Neuroendocrinology* (Ganong, W. F. & Martini, L., eds.), pp. 307 – 342, Oxford University Press, New York

HAYASHI, S. (1976) Sterilization of female rats by neonatal placement of estradiol micropellets in anterior hypothalamus. *Endocrinol. Jap. 23,* 55 – 60

KALRA, P. S. & MCCANN, S. M. (1975) The stimulatory effect on gonadotropin release of implants of estradiol or progesterone in certain sites in the central nervous system. *Neuroendocrinology 19,* 289 – 302

KATZ, M. & CARR, P. (1976) Abnormal luteinizing-hormone response patterns to synthetic gonadotrophin releasing hormone in patients with polycystic ovarian syndrome. *J. Endocrinol. 70,* 163 – 171

Lisk, R. (1967) Sexual behavior: hormonal control, in *Neuroendocrinology,* vol. 2 (Martini, L. & Ganong, W. F., eds.), pp. 197 – 239, Academic Press, New York

Lisk, R. & Newlon, M. (1963) Estradiol: evidence for its direct effect on hypothalamic neurons. *Science (Wash. D.C.) 139,* 223 – 224

Matsumoto, A. & Arai, Y. (1976*a*) Effect of estrogen on early postnatal development of synaptic formation in the hypothalamic arcuate nucleus of female rats. *Neurosci. Lett. 2,* 79 – 82

Matsumoto, A. & Arai, Y. (1976*b*) Developmental changes in synaptic formation in the hypothalamic arcuate nucleus of female rats. *Cell Tissue Res. 169,* 143 – 156

Matsumoto, A. & Arai, Y. (1977) Precocious puberty and synaptogenesis in the hypothalamic arcuate nucleus in pregnant mare serum gonadotropin (PMSG) treated immature female rats. *Brain Res. 129,* 375 – 378

McDonald, P. & Doughty, C. (1974) Effect of neonatal administration of different androgens in the female rat: correlation between aromatization and the induction of sterilization. *J. Endocrinol. 61,* 95 – 103

McEwen, B. (1976) Steroid receptors in neuroendocrine tissue: topography, subcellular distribution, and functional implications, in *Subcellular Mechanisms in Reproductive Neuroendocrinology* (Naftolin, F., Ryan, K. J., & Davies, J., eds.), pp. 277 – 304, Elsevier, Amsterdam

Morrell, J., Kelly, D. & Pfaff, D. (1975) Sex steroid binding in the brains of vertebrates, in *Brain-Endocrine Interaction, II* (Knigge, K. & Scott, D., eds.), pp. 230 – 256, Karger, Basel

Nadler, R. (1973) Further evidence of the intra-hypothalamic locus for androgenization of female rats. *Neuroendocrinology 12,* 110 – 119

Naftolin, F. & Brawer, J. R. (1977) Sex hormones as growth promoting factors for the endocrine hypothalamus. *J. Steroid Biochem. 8,* 339 – 343

Nunez, E., Savu, L., Engelmann, F., Benassayag, G., Crepy, O. & Jayle, M. (1971) Origine embryonnaire de la protéine sérique fixant l'oestradiol chez la ratte impubère. *C.R. Hebd. Séances Acad. Sci. Sér. D Sci. Nat. 273,* 242 – 245

Parvizi, N. & Naftolin, F. (1977) Effects of catechol estrogens on sexual differentiation in neonatal female rats. *Psychoneuroendocrinology 2,* 409 – 411

Pfaff, D. & Keiner, M. (1973) Atlas of estradiol-concentrating cells in the central nervous system of the female rat. *J. Comp. Neurol. 151,* 121 – 158

Price, M., Olney, J. & Cicero, T. (1976) Proliferation of lamellar whorls in arcuate neurons of the hypothalamus of castrated and morphine-treated male rats. *Cell Tissue Res. 171,* 277 – 283

Raisman, G. & Field, P. (1973) Sexual dimorphism in the neuropil of the preoptic area of the rat and its dependence on neonatal androgen. *Brain Res. 54,* 1 – 29

Raisman, G. & Brown-Grant, K. (1977) The suprachiasmatic syndrome: endocrine and behavioural abnormalities following lesions of the suprachiasmatic nuclei in the female rat. *Proc. R. Soc. Lond. Ser. B Biol. Sci. 198,* 297 – 314

Ramirez, V. D., Abrams, R. M. & McCann, S. M. (1964) Effect of estradiol implants in the hypothalamo-hypophysial region of the rat on the secretion of luteinizing hormone. *Endocrinology 75,* 243 – 248

Raynaud, J., Mercier-Bodard, C. & Baulieu, E. (1971) Rat estradiol binding protein (EBP). *Steroids 18,* 767 – 788

Rebar, R., Judd, H., Yen, S., Rakoff, J., Vandenberg, G. & Naftolin, F. (1976) Characterization of the inappropriate gonadotrophin secretion in polycystic ovary syndrome. *J. Clin. Invest. 57,* 1320 – 1325

Reddy, V., Naftolin, F. & Ryan, K. (1974) Conversion of androstenedione to estrone by neural tissues from fetal and neonatal rats. *Endocrinology 94,* 117 – 121

Reier, P., Cullen, M., Froelich, J. & Rothchild, I. (1977) The ultrastructure of the developing medial preoptic nucleus in the postnatal rat. *Brain Res. 122,* 415 – 436

Sawyer, C. (1975) Some recent developments in brain-pituitary-ovarian physiology. *Neuro-*

endocrinology 17, 97 – 124

Stumpf, W. (1970) Estrogen-neurons and estrogen-neuron system in the periventricular brain. *Am. J. Anat. 129,* 207 – 218

Stumpf, W. & Sar, M. (1976) Steroid hormone target sites in the brain: the differential distribution of estrogen, progestin, androgen and glucocorticosteroid. *J. Steroid Biochem. 7,* 1163 – 1170

Stumpf, W. & Sar, M. (1977) Steroid hormone target cells in the periventricular brain: relationship to peptide hormone producing cells. *Fed. Proc. 36,* 1973 – 1977

Sutherland, S. & Gorski, R. (1972) An evaluation of the inhibition of androgenization of the neonatal female rat brain by barbiturate. *Neuroendocrinology 10,* 94 – 108

Taleisnik, S., Velasco, M. & Astrada, J. (1970) Effect of hypothalamic deafferentation on the control of luteinizing-hormone secretion. *J. Endocrinol. 46,* 1 – 7

Tejasen, T. & Everett, J. (1967) Surgical analysis of the preoptico-tuberal pathway controlling ovulatory release of gonadotropins in the rat. *Endocrinology 81,* 1387 – 1396

Toran-Allerand, C. D. (1976) Sex steroids and the development of the newborn mouse hypothalamus and preoptic area *in vitro:* implications for sexual differentiation. *Brain Res. 106,* 407 – 412

Van Houten, M. & Brawer, J. R. (1978) Regional variations in glia and neuropil in the hypothalamic ventromedial nucleus. *J. Comp. Neurol., 179,* 719-738

Walsh, R. & Brawer, J. (1978) Cytology of the arcuate nucleus in newborn male and female rats. *J. Anat. (Lond.),* in press

Willoughby, J., Terry, L., Brazeau, P. & Martin, J. (1977) Pulsatile growth hormone, prolactin, and thyrotropin secretion in rats with hypothalamic deafferentation. *Brain Res. 127,* 137 – 152

YoungLai, E. V., Holmes, M. J. & Ruf, K. B. (1976) Changes in the concentration of LH, FSH and estrogen in the immature female rat during precocious sexual maturation induced by electrochemical stimulation of the brain. *Horm. Res. 7,* 34 – 42

Discussion

Sachar: Have you seen whether you can protect the hypothalami of your rats after the initial oestrogen injection by giving clomiphene two weeks later?

Brawer: We are doing that now, so we have no results yet.

Everitt: I am confused about your use of the terms ‘suprachiasmatic nucleus’ and ‘preoptic area’, particularly since there is little or no evidence to suggest that neurons of the suprachiasmatic nucleus are involved in the action of oestradiol on the release of gonadotropin.

Brawer: Recent work (Brown-Grant & Raisman 1977; Raisman & Brown-Grant 1977) suggests that the deafferented suprachiasmatic nucleus is capable of driving cyclicity, and that the medial preoptic area (MPOA) may not be necessary.

Everitt: But how is that related to what oestrogen does, since the suprachiasmatic nucleus neurons do not take up and bind this hormone?

Brawer: One could just as well ask how the MPOA is related, since Kawakami’s group has shown that the MPOA may not be the primary recipient of positive oestrogen feedback, despite the fact that it has been shown to be a target for exogenous E_2.

Herbert: I wonder if we can try to extrapolate what you have been describing to primates and humans? It seems to me that one ought to focus on areas of disagreement and of similarity between your and others' data in the rat, and the very different information people are getting in humans. There seem to be two major distinctions. First, in the primate there is no evidence for circadian organization of the LH surge, whereas there is in the rat (Knobil & Krey 1976). That is, ovulation doesn't occur in relation to the light-dark cycle in the human, or monkey, as it does in the rat. This is an important difference, because you have related ovulation to the suprachiasmatic nucleus. All the evidence suggests that this nucleus is intimately concerned with generating circadian rhythms, since lesions here abolish rhythms in, for example, adrenal corticoid secretion and locomotor activity (Stetson & Watson-Whitmyre 1976).

The second difference is the fact that there is little or no evidence that prenatal or postnatal androgens in the female primate can prevent the LH surge, whereas they can do so in the rat (Goy 1968). Now, how does the evidence that you produce allow us to correlate those two findings?

Brawer: Regarding the episodic release of LH, one must keep in mind that the rat has a four-day cycle as opposed to the monthly cycle in women. Several hours in the rat cycle could well correspond to one whole day in the human cycle. As far as sexual differentiation is concerned, I don't know that parallels can be drawn.

The primate brain is formidably complicated in its organization and synaptic connections. So far there are very few data on the synaptic organization of the medial basal hypothalamus and there is no evidence yet, except for the ependyma, of sexual dimorphism. I think we are going to wait a long time for this information.

Ehrhardt: Has it been documented in the primate that the LH surge can come at any time of the day and that it is not part of a diurnal variation?

Besser: The only time that there is a circadian rhythm in LH secretion in humans is in the pubertal development period. The adult ovulatory surge of LH can occur at any time.

Short: Dr Brawer, you used the phrase 'a centre which drives the cycle'. I think the evidence is becoming rather strong that there is no centre in the brain that drives the oestrous or menstrual cycles (Short 1974).

Brawer: I used the word 'centre' not because it reflects true normal physiological function but because the MPOA is capable of sustaining cyclicity. The MPOA is, in a sense, no different from any other neural system. You have in all mammals, including humans, a series of redundant circuits all capable of doing the same thing – for example, pyramidal and non-pyramidal routes from cortex to spinal cord. I don't think anyone would deny that the MPOA when disconnected will drive cyclicity and support conception and pregnancy. This is not to say that it by itself is ordinarily capable of doing this. Clearly, the amygdala, the midbrain and the hippocampus are all normally involved in the regulation of cyclicity. The medial preoptic area-medial basal hypothalamus is, however, a convenient circuit to look at as having the capability to drive the cycle independently. Furthermore, many of the extra-hypothalamic inputs that modify the cycle feed through that region.

Short: I would be a lot happier if you didn't use the phrase 'drive the cycle', because I really don't think that there is any evidence for a CNS centre that drives it. Why don't you just say 'permit the cycle'?

Brawer: The MPOA-suprachiasmatic nucleus could be described as normally regulating the cycle and having the capacity to drive the cycle independently.

Goy: It seems to me that you are in a paradoxical situation. On the one hand you claim that early oestrogenization is synaptogenic and that having too many synapses disrupts cyclicity. On the other hand, in the adult female, you claim that oestrogens are synaptolytic and that too few synapses disrupt the cyclicity.

Brawer: We don't know that the synapses that are steroid-facilitated are the same as those that are subject to the dystrophic influences of oestrogen in the adult. Furthermore, in the neonatal rat in the developing mediobasal hypothalamus there is also degeneration. What it means, we don't know. It could be that oestrogen simultaneously effects growth and degeneration in developing hypothalamic tissue whereas the degenerative effect predominates in the adult. There are other systems, for example in the ventromedial nucleus of the normal adult male rat, in which one finds growth cones and degeneration in the same area.

Goy: If in early differentiation oestrogen is both synaptogenic and synaptolytic, in the differentiation of the normal male the critical connections may be *removed* (those sustaining cyclicity); the other ones that can't function in that way are then replacing them.

Brawer: This is possible.

Hutchison: On this theme of the synaptogenic action of oestrogen, I am not clear what evidence there is that oestrogen, derived by aromatization from androgen, acts specifically in the ventrobasal hypothalamus. Are the aromatase enzymes found in that region of the hypothalamus only, or are there synaptogenic effects of oestrogen in other brain regions which might also be affecting the differentiation of the neuroendocrine systems? And are the truly androgenic effects excluded completely from this system?

Brawer: My prejudice is that they are. The bulk of evidence is that it really is oestradiol which is exerting the effect, since ring A-reduced androgens don't work at all.

Goy: I would have no question that in the rat, and maybe other species too, oestrogens are masculinizing, but that brings up another point about the divergence we face when we use the rat as a model and also want to think in terms of other mammals. In the data I have collected on rhesus monkeys it is clear that dihydrotestosterone, a non-aromatizable androgen, effects all the changes, and to the same degree, that testosterone can effect. Conversely, there is no evidence in the human being, although many unfortunate girls were exposed to diethylstilboestrol before birth for long periods, that those girls are anovulatory or display abnormal cycles or are behaviourally or psychologically masculine.

Brawer: Perhaps they are protected.

Green: You certainly have an interesting model for the Stein-Leventhal syndrome; how do you propose to collaborate with clinicians, using your model? Also, do we have clinical data on women exposed, either for long durations or to high doses of oral contraceptives with oestrogens, regarding the degree to which they are unable to ovulate when they stop taking the contraceptives?

Brawer: On your first question, our first step in evaluating the clinical importance of these findings is to examine human hypothalami (autopsy specimens) of people who were treated with massive doses of oestrogen or oestrogenic agents for a variety of cancers. Simple histological examination should tell us if these compounds have a pathological effect on the hypothalamus and whether it would be worthwhile pursuing this further. Also, we shall probably start to examine the effects of oestrogen on the non-human primate hypothalamus.

On the effect of the oral contraceptives, there is a considerable debate about this. Many clinicians say that there is no connection between the pill and development of the hypothalamic anovulatory syndrome. I have no idea myself, but my inclination is to wait to see what happens to human brains exposed to high levels of gonadal steroids before we try to extrapolate to that possibility. A nerve cell, however, is a nerve cell, in whatever species, and if oestrogen has pronounced growth or lytic properties in one species, it has the potential of having those properties in others.

Besser: While I understand the attractiveness of using your work as a model of the polycystic ovary syndrome, one must be careful. One can get this reaction in an ovary in a wide variety of situations which are totally at variance with this model. For example, about 20% of patients with polycystic ovaries are hyperprolactinaemic. You also see it with congenital adrenal hyperplasia, with adrenal carcinomas, or even with androgen-secreting ovarian tumours. What is the adrenal androgen production in your rats with the oestrogen-determined lesions?

Brawer: We haven't looked at that yet. We are doing the assays now.

Besser: The hyperprolactinaemic patients often have excessive amounts of adrenal androgens as well.

Brawer: Our rats may also!

Besser: I am worried about analogy with the ageing rat, because my understanding is that a number of such rats have hyperprolactinaemia, and if you give an ergot alkaloid, ergocryptine, Dr Meites showed that you can get them cycling again (Simpkins *et al.* 1977).

Brewer: A small percentage of female rats don't go into persistent oestrus, but into dioestrus, with high prolactin concentrations. Most, however, go into persistent oestrus and show more or less the hormone changes that we found, so there are certainly these two populations.

Besser: Finally, to revert to your involvement of the hypothalamus in the cycle, there is good evidence that you don't actually need 'electrical activity' to have a menstrual cycle in the human, and Knobil has repeated our work in monkeys, showing that you can give luteinizing hormone-releasing hormone (LH-RH) and nothing else to patients who have either gonadotropin deficiency or hypothalamic or pituitary tumours, and get normal puberty, normal ovulation patterns and pregnancy (Mortimer *et al.* 1974, 1976). So all you need is a signal to the pituitary to release gonadotropin and the modulation then comes from feedback from the ovaries. The ovaries are obviously conducting the orchestra!

Brawer: That depends on whom you read! In monkeys, according to Knobil (1974) the ovaries conduct the show, but according to Spies *et al.* (1974) this is not the case.

Pirke: Your data indicate that puberty in the female rat can be advanced by giving oestrogens. Can puberty in the male rat as judged by plasma testosterone levels also be advanced by oestrogen?

Brawer: Yes. The problem is measuring puberty in the male rat.

Herbert: It seems to me that there is an assumption in this discussion that the degeneration you are studying, Dr Brawer, has a parallel in normal development. You are giving very large doses of oestrogen. There are instances where large amounts of a normal constituent produce degeneration in cells which are sensitive to them, for example using glutamic acid or kainic acid or thiogluose, or even perhaps in the case of the neurotoxic agents such as the dihydroxytryptamines. Are you looking at that mechanism rather than at one normally involved?

Brawer: It is impossible to say, because we don't know much about the degenerating axons. We have to determine where they are coming from and what cells they belong to.

Herbert: My point is that if you exposed a sensitive neuron to very large amounts of a transmitter to which it responds, the substance might become neurotoxic.

Brawer: We do not have to expose them to very much oestrogen. If you consider the constant-light situation, for example, where oestrogen concentrations rise to only about 10 pg/ml, that is not a great deal of oestrogen and lesions form in those circumstances as well.

Bancroft: I would like clarification on one of the points that Dr Goy raised. Is he saying that the aromatization of androgens is not relevant in the primate?

Goy: To refer to 'the primate' here would be too broad. I am absolutely *sure* it's not relevant in the rhesus monkey. I don't think it is relevant in humans, because the clinical evidence from the use of diethylstilboestrol indicates that it has little or no masculinizing properties.

Bancroft: Is there agreement on that point, or is there still disagreement as far as other primates are concerned?

Jost: Some experts, namely Dr Naftolin, have introduced the idea that other oestrogens could be at work, catechol oestrogens and substances like that. This could be relevant here.

Brawer: Catechol oestrogens are made by hypothalamic tissue; it was also recently shown by Parvizi & Naftolin (1977) that catechol oestrogens are apparently effective in defeminizing neonatal female rats, so they may play a role in brain differentiation. Naftolin is interested in the possible role of catechol oestrogens in the formation of the hypothalamic lesion. What we want to look at, of course, are the catecholamines, to see what happens to the catecholamine content of the hypothalamus.

Jost: Could the catechol oestrogens have different effects from oestradiol?

Brawer: Yes; catechol oestrogens have the possibility of tying up catechol *O*-methyltransferase, and consequently they can lock into a system that other oestrogens would not have access to.

Sachar: It does look as if there is a competition between catechol oestrogens and catecholamines for catechol *O*-methyltransferase (Paul & Axelrod 1977).

Bancroft: Has anyone given oestrogens to castrated monkeys or humans, and do they replace the effect of androgens?

Goy: They do not. One cannot enhance male patterns of sexual behaviour in the castrated male monkey by giving either oestrogens or androgens that are rapidly aromatized to oestrogens.

Pirke: Oestrogens have been given to castrated men suffering from carcinoma of the prostate. In these patients castration causes a decrease in sexual interest and sexual activity. These symptoms are unchanged when patients are treated with oestrogens. This observation indicates that – in contrast to the rat – testosterone cannot be replaced by oestrogens in human males.

Dörner: With regard to the organizing effect of oestrogen on the brain and sexual behaviour, we have found a mimicking of the effect of androgens – that is, a masculinizing effect on the brain – in rats, but a demasculinizing effect on the brain in domestic pigs (Dörner *et al.* 1977).

Goy: The failure of oestrogens to mimic androgens in terms of masculinizing effects is *not* limited to rhesus monkeys, in my own experience. In adult male guinea-pigs one cannot augment mounting behaviour or intromission-like behaviour or anything else by injecting large amounts of oestradiol, but a non-aromatizable androgen, dihydrotestosterone, injected into castrated male guinea-pigs or castrated adult male monkeys, effectively and quickly augments male behaviour. The pictures for the rat and the monkey are totally different, and the guinea-pig is more like the monkey than the rat.

Brawer: We have to be careful when separating the effects. I have been talking about organizational and growth effects; you are talking about something entirely different, namely a hormone-target tissue effect.

Goy: We are talking about activation, but organizational effects on behaviour can also be brought about by non-aromatizable androgens in the rhesus monkey. Moreover, in monkeys, organizational effects of androgens given or present before birth seem to be more pervasive and more enduring than experiential influences.

References

BROWN-GRANT, K. & RAISMAN, G. (1977) Abnormalities in reproductive function associated with the destruction of the suprachiasmatic nuclei in female rats. *Proc. R. Soc. Lond. B Biol. Sci. 198,* 279 – 296

DÖRNER, G., HINZ, G. & SCHLENKER, G. (1977) Demasculinizing effect of prenatal oestrogen on sexual behaviour in domestic pigs. *Endokrinologie 69,* 347 – 350

GOY, R. W. (1968) Organizing effects of androgens on the behaviour of rhesus monkeys, in *Endocrinology and Human Behaviour* (Michael, R. P., ed.), pp. 12 – 28, Oxford University Press, London

KNOBIL, E. (1974) On the control of gonadotropin secretion in the rhesus monkey. *Recent Prog. Hormone Res. 30,* 1 – 46

KNOBIL, E. & KREY, L. C. (1976) Neuroendocrine control of gonadotropin secretion in the rhesus monkey, in *Neuroendocrine Regulation of Fertility* (Anand Kumar, T. C., ed.), pp. 278 – 285, Karger, Basle

Mortimer, C. H., McNeilly, A. S., Murray, M. A. F., Fisher, R. A. F. & Besser, G. M. (1974) Gonadotrophin releasing hormone therapy in hypogonadal males with hypothalamic pituitary dysfunction. *Br. Med. J. 4,* 617–621

Mortimer, C. H., McNeilly, A. S. & Besser, G. M. (1976) Gonadotropin releasing hormone therapy. *Ann. Biol. Anim. Biochim. Biophys. 16,* 235–243

Parvizi, N. & Naftolin, F. (1977) Effects of catechol estrogens on sexual differentiation in neonatal female rats. *Psychoneuroendocrinology 2,* 409–411

Paul, S. M. & Axelrod, J. (1977) Catechol estrogens: presence in brain and endocrine tissues. *Science (Wash. D.C.) 197,* 657–659

Raisman, G. & Brown-Grant, K. (1977) The suprachiasmatic syndrome: endocrine and behavioural abnormalities following lesions of the suprachiasmatic nuclei in the female rat. *Proc. R. Soc. Lond. B Biol. Sci. 198,* 297–314

Short, R. V. (1974) Rhythms of ovulation, in *Chronobiological Aspects of Endocrinology (Symposia Medica Hoechst 9),* pp. 221–228, Schattauer, Stuttgart

Simpkins, J. W., Mueller, G. P., Huang, H. H. & Meites, J. (1977) Evidence for depressed catecholamine and enhanced serotonin metabolism in aging male rats: possible relation to gonadotropin secretion. *Endocrinology 100,* 1672–1678

Spies, H., Resko, J. & Norman, R. (1974) Evidence of preoptic hypothalamic influence on ovulation in the rhesus monkey. *Fed. Proc. 33,* 222

Stetson, M. H. & Watson-Whitmyre, M. (1976) Nucleus suprachiasmaticus: the biological clock in the hamster? *Science (Wash. D.C.), 191,* 197–199

Psychosexual development: an examination of the role of prenatal hormones

ANKE A. EHRHARDT and HEINO F. L. MEYER-BAHLBURG

New York State Psychiatric Institute and Department of Psychiatry, Columbia University, New York

Abstract Naturally occurring endocrine syndromes and the offspring from steroid-treated pregnancies are the major sources of evidence for a role of prenatal hormones in psychosexual development in man. Effects of prenatal androgens have been established for the sex-dimorphic behaviour clusters of energy expenditure (increased), parenting rehearsal (decreased), peer associations (shifted to male), and grooming-related behaviour (decreased); most of the information was obtained on the syndrome of congenital adrenal hyperplasia and in progestin-induced female hermaphroditism. Studies of children and adults exposed prenatally to exogenous oestrogens and/or progestagens suggest slight demasculinizing effects but cannot yet be considered conclusive. Gender identity is largely dependent on the sex of rearing; a direct role of prenatal hormones in its formation has not been shown. The evidence for the role of prenatal hormones in the development of sexual orientation is inconclusive.

SEX-DIMORPHIC BEHAVIOUR

Animal experimental research has suggested intriguing relationships between hormones and the developing central nervous system. Direct evidence for effects of androgens on brain differentiation, for instance, comes from the implantation of testosterone into the neonatal rat. Hayashi & Gorski (1974) reported anovulatory sterility after the implantation of testosterone propionate bilaterally into both ventromedial-arcuate and anterior hypothalamic sites of three-day-old female rats. Raisman & Field (1973) observed structural differences in the rat brain between normal males and females and were able to produce the same difference between neonatally castrated males and females treated neonatally with testosterone – a clear proof of the importance of hormonal effects during a critical phase of brain differentiation.

When we consider the evidence from animal studies it is indeed tempting to speculate that sex hormones may also have an important function in the psychosexual development of human beings. Over the last 15 years or so, several research workers have examined children, adolescents and adults who have a documented unusual prenatal hormonal history. The goal of these studies on human behaviour has been to assess whether high or low levels of prenatal androgens, oestrogens or progestagens may have effects on subsequent behavioural development in human beings. In contrast to animal experimentalists, human researchers typically are unable to design ideal experimental studies, but rather depend on spontaneous endocrine abnormalities or unusual prenatal hormone histories due to drug treatment of the pregnant mother for health reasons. This, of course, often requires compromises in research design and subject selection.

The aspects of behaviour that have been studied in non-human primates and in people cluster in a few areas. The first one is related to energy expenditure. In human beings this has been measured as active outdoor play and athletic skills. In non-human primates the comparable behavioural aspect is rough-and-tumble play. Intense physical energy expenditure of this type seems to be an essential aspect of psychosocial development and appears to be influenced by sex steroid variations before birth.

The second behaviour cluster possibly related to levels of prenatal hormones has to do with parenting rehearsal in human beings, such as doll play, maternal role rehearsal, wanting to have children and paying attention to infant care. While we have no parallel data in this regard from non-human primate studies, observations on lower mammalian species also suggest that the intensity of parenting behaviour may be sexually dimorphic and related to the type and level of prenatal hormone exposure.

The third sex-dimorphic behaviour area in psychosocial development concerns peer contacts, friends, and patterns of group interaction. In non-human primates, dominance behaviour and sex segregation of play groups have received special attention. The fourth behaviour cluster only applies to human beings. It combines the gender-role labelling, for example, tomboyism, of a given child by his/her social environment on the basis of play behaviour patterns and the child's gender-role preference.

The fifth area which has come up repeatedly as a possible behavioural sequel to prenatal hormonal abnormalities in human beings is attention to appearance, in relation to clothes preference, jewelry, makeup, hairdo and other adornments. We do not have systematic studies of grooming behaviour in relation to prenatal hormonal abnormalities in other primates.

These five behaviour clusters of sex-dimorphic behaviour seem to have been the focal points of all presently reported studies examining the role of prenatal sex hormones in the emergence of behavioural sex differences. Any variations seem to be due to different terms and are mainly dependent on the specific tests or interview measures used, but they do not differ in substance from these five areas.

A brief review of studies on human beings follows. We have evidence from two groups of patients with a definite history of prenatal androgenization on the possible effects of high levels of androgens on sex-dimorphic behaviour in genetic females and genetic males. One group is of patients with congenital adrenal hyperplasia, a condition well known as a genetically transmitted enzyme defect of the adrenal cortex with a resulting production of high levels of androgen rather than of cortisol. Findings on studies with two different designs have been reported: (1) comparison of patients with matched normal control groups (Ehrhardt *et al.* 1968*a*); (2) comparison of patients with unaffected siblings (Ehrhardt & Baker 1974). Both studies included genetic females who were early treated and early surgically corrected. The results can be summarized as follows: Females with congenital adrenal hyperplasia tend to have a characteristic pattern of psychosexual behaviour with a cluster of high energy expenditure, on the one hand, and a cluster of decreased parenting behaviour, on the other. There is a question whether these two behaviour clusters are independent or whether decreased parenting behaviour is the result of a high level of physical energy expenditure as a basic temperamental trait.

We also have the evidence from one study of boys with congenital adrenal hyperplasia and their sex-dimorphic behaviour (Ehrhardt 1975). The only difference between them and a male sibling control group was a higher level of energy expenditure in play and sports.

The evidence on the role of prenatal androgen exposure in human behaviour thus suggests effects in the direction of higher energy levels for both males and females and decreased parenting behaviour for females.

Studies on children whose mothers took drugs with androgenizing side-effects showed the same pattern of psychosexual behaviour in relation to energy expenditure as the studies on children with congenital adrenal hyperplasia (Ehrhardt & Money 1967).

The role of oestrogens and progestagens in central nervous system development is much less clear. In animals, oestrogens sometimes have an androgenizing effect and, at other times, an antiandrogenizing effect. In human beings the evidence is also less consistent than are the results of prenatal androgenization. There is one study on the sons of diabetic mothers who were treated with varying combinations of oestrogens and progestagens (Yalom *et al.* 1973). Typically there was no effect on genital differentiation. However, some subtle temperamental differences between the experimental and control groups in the direction of demasculinization were observed. The main problem of this study was the lack of an adequate control group. The group used did not consist uniformly of diabetic mothers without prenatal drug treatment. Therefore, it remains undecided whether maternal health state may have been a crucial intervening variable. If future studies can rule out that diabetes of the mother affects sex-dimorphic behaviour in the offspring, one may be able to conclude that exogenous oestrogens and certain progestagens during pregnancy may have a slight antiandrogenizing effect in human males.

Progesterone has been suggested as an antagonist of normal androgens in human males and females. A study on children of toxaemic pregnancies whose mothers were treated with progesterone suggests a slight effect in the area of energy expenditure in both males and females and in the dressing behaviour of females (Zussman *et al.* 1975). Again, maternal health state was not controlled and therefore cannot be excluded as a major intervening variable. In a recent study, we attempted to correct some of the problems of previous research (Meyer-Bahlburg *et al.* 1977; Ehrhardt *et al.* 1977). The follow-up of children from a pregnancy research population made it easier for us to rely on systematic prenatal histories and on matching for pregnancy condition. Thirteen males who were exposed to Provera (medroxyprogesterone acetate) because of maternal intake for mild pregnancy complications were studied extensively in late childhood or early adolescence. No differences were found between experimental and control males.

In females, medroxyprogesterone acetate seemed to have slight effects on the frequency of tomboyism and aggression and on their clothes preference. Girls who were exposed to Provera tended to be less frequently long-term tomboys and were slightly less aggressive than their peers. They were also more often described as having a greater interest in feminine clothing.

From the studies described, it seems that treatment with oestrogens and/or progestagens before birth may result in slight antiandrogenizing effects which are too mild to be of clinical importance but which are of interest as a possible factor shaping specific behaviour patterns within the spectrum of normal psychosexual development. However, because of the methodological weaknesses mentioned, the empirical evidence cannot yet be considered conclusive.

GENDER IDENTITY

The study of hermaphrodites has taught us some important principles of gender-identity differentiation (Money & Ehrhardt 1972):

(1) Gender identity typically depends on a person's sex of rearing, as long as this is consistently in one or the other sex.
(2) Gender-identity formation usually occurs in the first 2-3 years of a child's life. Once a female or male gender identity is formed, it becomes irrevocably a part of a girl's or boy's personality.
(3) However, if confusion about a child's sex of rearing persists beyond infancy in the mind of parents and others, there is a risk of ambiguity in the child's gender identity formation.

Of course, cases of hermaphroditism are rare, which makes systematic investigation difficult. Considering the complexities of clinical observations, it is even more remarkable how consistent a picture has emerged for children who are born with sex organ abnormalities. No new evidence has come to the fore since the original studies by Money and Hampson (Money *et al.* 1955) in regard to gender-identity formation. For our culture the original theory of Money is still as valid as fifteen years ago.

The evidence for the powerful effects of early social environmental conditioning on gender identification is even stronger when you consider the finding that children with both ambiguity of their sex organs at birth and subsequent exposure to confusion by pubertal hormones and secondary sex characteristics discordant with their sex of rearing usually identify firmly with their assigned gender (Ehrhardt 1978).

HOMOSEXUALITY

Since the discovery of the sex steroids, the development of homosexuality – defined as a lasting sexual orientation towards the same sex, expressed in attraction, erotic imagery, and sociosexual experience—has been repeatedly ascribed to endocrine abnormalities. No wonder, then, that the psychoendocrine hypothesis was reformulated in terms of prenatal hormone effects when animal research documented the important function of pre- and perinatal androgens in the sexual differentiation of the brain and the subsequent development of sex-dimorphic behaviour. If early androgenization or deandrogenization can have such dramatic effects on male and female patterns of mating behaviour in lower mammals, it is tempting to extrapolate these findings to the human situation. Dörner is the foremost representative of this approach and describes his findings in his own chapter in this volume. His underlying assumptions are challenged by Beach in another chapter. Here, we shall limit ourselves to a brief discussion of the human evidence (for a more comprehensive discussion see Meyer-Bahlburg 1977, 1978).

Pertinent human data come from two sources: (1) the screening of homosexual subjects for prenatal endocrine abnormalities, and (2) the assessment of patients with known congenital prenatal sex-hormone disorders as to their sexual orientation. A potential third source are individuals who have been exposed to exogenous steroid hormones *in utero* (because of hormone treatment of the pregnant mother), but systematic data on their sexual orientation have not yet been published.

In the screening of homosexual individuals the most obvious indicator of prenatal abnormalities of sex-hormone production or utilization would be intersexed genitalia. However, investigations that included physical examinations did not provide any evidence that homosexuals have a higher prevalence rate of intersexed genitalia and/or of sex chromosome abnormalities than heterosexual subjects. Although we do not have any truly epidemiological large-sample data on this issue, the conclusion is warranted that genital and/or chromosomal intersexuality does not explain homosexual orientation in the vast majority of cases. Yet, recent developments in animal-based neuroendocrine research make it likely that the utilization of androgens by the brain involves biochemical processes other than those operating in the periphery. This allows for the hypothetical construct of an intersexed central nervous system in the absence of hermaphroditic genitalia. This speculation has drawn support from findings of abnormalities in the neuroendocrine regulation of luteinizing hormone (LH) in male homosexuals and transsexuals (Dörner *et al.* 1975, 1976) and in female transsexuals (Dörner *et al.* 1976; Seyler *et al.* 1978). The reported abnormalities concern the effects of oestrogen administration on LH secretion (i.e. the so-called positive feedback effect of oestrogen on LH) and include a somewhat feminized pattern of the LH response in male homosexuals, and a somewhat defeminized, masculinized pattern in female transsexuals. If replicable by other laboratories, these findings may have potentially great significance for a neuroendocrine theory of sexual orientation. Their interpretation, however, is not simple, since the neuroendocrine regulation of LH in primates seems to involve both a negative and a positive feedback effect of which only the negative one appears to be influenced by prenatal hormone levels (Steiner *et al.* 1976); moreover, postpubertal oestrogens may exert their effects in synergism with androgens, at least in males (Resko *et al.* 1977). Thus, quite sophisticated and elaborate experimental designs are required to elucidate the importance of the LH data for the hormonal theory of homosexuality.

Prenatal abnormalities of sex-hormone production and of hormone utilization by the central nervous system should be reflected in aberrations of sex-hormone production after puberty. Therefore, it is worth examining the available data on hormone levels in postpubertal individuals. The numerous studies on male homosexuals have been surveyed by one of us (Meyer-Bahlburg 1977), who concluded that the vast majority of homosexual men investigated have normal testosterone levels, while the reported findings on other relevant hormones are too contradictory to permit any general statement. By contrast, the small number of available studies on female homosexuals and transsexuals, including the recent reports by Gartrell *et al.* (1977) and Sípová & Stárka (1977), have consistently shown an elevation of plasma testosterone concentrations above the normal female range in about a third of the study subjects (Meyer-Bahlburg 1978). It is conceivable, but not a necessary implication, that these individuals were already exposed to elevated testosterone levels *in utero;* however, in explaining their potential effects on sexual orientation, one would have to assume that the prenatal androgen levels were only moderately elevated and that the prenatal central nervous system is much more sensitive to such testosterone elevation than are the genital tissues, because of the absence of intersexed genitalia. On the other hand, elevated testosterone levels in adulthood – irrespective of the timing of the onset of the elevation – may be responsible for the abnormalities in the neuroendocrine regulation of LH found in transsexual women. However, this factor had been excluded in the study by Seyler *et al.* (1978). The interpretation of minor-to-moderate sex-hormone abnormalities in adulthood becomes even more complicated when one takes into account that the production of a given hormone may not only contribute to certain behavioural developments but may in itself be strongly influenced by behavioural and environmental variables.

The other major sources of evidence for a potential role of prenatal sex-hormone abnormalities are studies of pertinent endocrine syndromes. The major syndromes of interest in XY individuals are those of complete or partial androgen insensitivity; affected patients have a male chromosome complement and functioning testes but their peripheral end-organs respond only little or not at all to the circulating androgens, so that the external genitalia are intersexed or totally female. The available studies (Masica *et al.* 1971; Money & Ogunro 1974) on a total of 20 patients show that sexual orientation in these patients follows the sex of rearing. For XX individuals, the major syndrome is congenital adrenal hyperplasia. Data are available on a total of 56 patients (Ehrhardt *et al.* 1968*b*; Ehrhardt & Baker 1976; Money & Daléry 1976; Money & Schwartz 1977), three of whom were raised as males. The majority of females were described as heterosexual; some were bisexual, and none exclusively homosexual; this was true even of the patients who did not have adequate medical treatment before late adolescence and adulthood and were not only partially masculinized before birth but quite markedly virilized in later years until they were finally treated. Whether the incidence of bisexuality in the female patients was any higher than in endocrinologically normal women is questionable but cannot be decided because control groups were not used. The three patients raised as males were heterosexual with respect to their sex of rearing.

In spite of the small size of the samples of patients investigated, we can conclude that the decisive variable for the sexual orientation of intersex patients is the sex of rearing rather than the prenatal hormonal status. In no way does the assumption seem justified that prenatal hormones by themselves determine the sexual orientation, and even a merely facilitatory neuroendocrine predisposition by prenatal hormones for a homosexual orientation has not yet been established, although the current evidence does not rule it out either.

CONCLUSION

The evidence accumulated so far strongly suggests that man is no exception with regard to the influence of sex steroids on the developing brain and subsequent behaviour, although the hormonal effects demonstrated are quite limited. Best established are the effects of prenatal androgens on physical energy expenditure and play rehearsal of parenting behaviour; effects on peer preferences and grooming behaviour may be related to the former. The development of gender identity seems to depend largely on sex of rearing; gender identity may become ambiguous if there are inconsistencies in parental sex-typing. The evidence for the role of prenatal hormones in sexual orientation is currently inconclusive.

ACKNOWLEDGEMENTS

The authors' research is supported in part by a grant from the Spencer Foundation.

References

DÖRNER, G., ROHDE, W., STAHL, F., KRELL, L. & MASIUS, W.-G. (1975) A neuroendocrine predisposition for homosexuality in men. *Arch. Sex. Behav. 4,* 1 – 8

DÖRNER, G., ROHDE, W., SEIDEL, K., HAAS, W. & SCHOTT, G. (1976) On the evocability of a positive estrogen feedback action on LH-secretion in transsexual men and women. *Endocrinology 67,* 20 – 25

EHRHARDT, A. A. (1975) Prenatal hormone exposure and psychosexual differentiation, in *Topics in Psychoendocrinology* (Sachar, E. J., ed.) *(Seminars in Psychiatry Series),* pp. 67 – 82, Grune & Stratton, New York

EHRHARDT, A. A. (1978) Psychosexual adjustment in adolescence in patients with congenital abnormalities of their sex organs, in *Proceedings of the Birth Defects Institute Symposium VII on Genetic Mechanisms of Sexual Development,* Academic Press, New York, in press

EHRHARDT, A. A. & BAKER, S. W. (1974) Fetal androgen, human CNS differentiation and behavior sex differences, in *Sex Differences in Behavior* (Friedman, R. C., Richart, R. M. & Vandewiele, R. L., eds.), pp. 53 – 76, Wiley, New York

EHRHARDT, A. A. & BAKER, S. W. (1976) Prenatal androgen exposure and adolescent behavior (unpublished paper, International Congress of Sexology, Montreal, Quebec)

EHRHARDT, A. A. & MONEY, J. (1967) Progestin-induced hermaphroditism: IQ and psychosexual identity in a study of ten girls. *J. Sex Res. 3,* 83 – 100

EHRHARDT, A. A., EPSTEIN, R. & MONEY, J. (1968*a*) Fetal androgens and female gender identity in the early-treated adrenogenital syndrome. *Johns Hopk. Med. J. 122,* 160 – 167

EHRHARDT, A. A., EVERS, K. & MONEY, J. (1968*b*) Influence of androgen and some aspects of sexually dimorphic behavior in women with the late-treated adrenogenital syndrome. *Johns Hopk. Med. J. 123,* 115 – 122

EHRHARDT, A. A., GRISANTI, G. C. & MEYER-BAHLBURG, H. F. L. (1977) Prenatal exposure to medroxyprogesterone acetate (MPA) in girls. *Psychoneuroendocrinology 2,* 391-398

GARTRELL, N. K., LORIAUX, D. L. & CHASE, T. N. (1977) Plasma testosterone in homosexual and heterosexual women. *Am. J. Psychiatr. 134,* 1117 – 1119

HAYASHI, S. & GORSKI, R. A. (1974) Critical exposure time for androgenization by intracranial crystals of testosterone propionate in neonatal female rats. *Endocrinology 94,* 1161 – 1167

MASICA, D. N., MONEY, J. & EHRHARDT, A. A. (1971) Fetal feminization and female gender identity in the testicular feminizing syndrome of androgen insensitivity. *Arch. Sex. Behav. 1,* 131 – 142

MEYER-BAHLBURG, H. F. L. (1977) Sex hormones and male homosexuality in comparative perspective. *Arch. Sex. Behav. 6,* 297 – 325

MEYER-BAHLBURG, H. F. L. (1978) Sex hormones and female homosexuality: a documentation. *Arch. Sex. Behav.,* in press

MEYER-BAHLBURG, H. F. L., GRISANTI, G. C. & EHRHARDT, A. A. (1977) Prenatal effects of sex hormones on human male behavior: medroxyprogesterone acetate (MPA). *Psychoneuroendocrinology 2,* 383 – 390

MONEY, J. & DALÉRY, J. (1976) Iatrogenic homosexuality: gender identity in seven 46,XX chromosomal females with hyperadrenocortical hermaphroditism born with a penis, three reared as boys, four reared as girls. *J. Homosex. 1,* 357 – 371

MONEY, J. & EHRHARDT, A. A. (1972) *Man and Woman, Boy and Girl: The Differentiation and Dimorphism of Gender Identity from Conception to Maturity,* The Johns Hopkins University Press, Baltimore

MONEY, J. & OGUNRO, C. (1974) Behavioral sexology: ten cases of genetic male intersexuality with impaired prenatal and pubertal androgenization. *Arch. Sex. Behav. 3,* 181 – 205

MONEY, J. & SCHWARTZ, M. (1977) Dating, romantic and non-romantic friendships, and sexuality in 17 early-treated adrenogenital females, aged 16 – 25, in *Congenital Adrenal Hyperplasia* (Lee, P. A., Plotnick, L. P., Kowarski, A. A. & Migeon, C. J., eds.), pp. 419 – 451, University Park Press, Baltimore

MONEY, J., HAMPSON, J. G. & HAMPSON, J. L. (1955) An examination of some basic sexual concepts: the evidence of human hermaphroditism. *Bull. Johns Hopk. Hosp. 97,* 301 – 319

RAISMAN, G. & FIELD, P. M. (1973) Sexual dimorphism in the neuropil of the preoptic area of the rat and its dependence on neonatal androgen. *Brain Res. 54,* 1 – 29

RESKO, J. A., QUADRI, S. K. & SPIES, H. G. (1977) Negative feedback control of gonadotropins in male rhesus monkeys: effects of time after castration and interactions of testosterone and estradiol-17beta. *Endocrinology 101,* 215 – 224

SEYLER, L. E., CANALIS, E., SPARE, S. & REICHLIN, S. (1978) Abnormal gonadotropin secretory responses to LRH in transsexual women after diethylstilbestrol priming. *J. Clin. Endocrinol. Metab. 47,* 176 – 183

ŠIPOVÁ, I. & STÁRKA, L. (1977) Plasma testosterone values in transsexual women. *Arch. Sex. Behav. 6,* 477–481

STEINER, R. A., CLIFTON, D. K., SPIES, H. G. & RESKO, J. A. (1976) Sexual differentiation and feedback control of luteinizing hormone secretion in the rhesus monkey. *Biol. Reprod. 15,* 206–212

YALOM, J. D., GREEN, R. & FISK, N. (1973) Prenatal exposure to female hormones: effect on psychosexual development in boys. *Arch. Gen. Psychiatr. 28,* 554–561

ZUSSMAN, J. U., ZUSSMAN, P. P. & DALTON, K. (1975) Post-pubertal effects of prenatal administration of progesterone. (Unpublished paper, meeting of the Society for Research in Child Development, Denver, Colorado)

Discussion

Crown: Professor Green, in your studies of the effects of exogenous hormones given prenatally, mentioned by Dr Ehrhardt, was attention paid to the possible influence of early parental expectations? It seems particularly important to know what the parents were told when they were given these hormones in pregnancy, because the child's environment starts before birth and by the age of one year it has gone on for some time.

Green: In the studies done at the Joslin Clinic on diabetic mothers (Yalom *et al.* 1973) no specific information was given to the parents on the behavioural effects the hormones might have. They were told that much of the morbidity of diabetic gestation was due to improper metabolism of female hormones and that they would be given supplementary hormones which would enable them to carry their fetuses to term. They weren't given clues that this might affect behaviour.

May I describe a case which is in partial contradiction to something Dr Ehrhardt said, and relates to the pseudohermaphrodite children in the Dominican Republic who showed a deficiency in steroid 5α-reductase with absence of conversion of testosterone to dihydrotestosterone (Imperato-McGinley *et al.* 1974)? It is alleged that these children, at least in the first generation, were raised as females, then began to become virilized at puberty, and during adolescence converted to a male identity. They develop a male body habitus and what looks like a culturally appropriate male identity. Dr Maria New at Cornell University has referred a child to me who was born with ambiguous genitalia. Unfortunately, there was procrastination and indecision about whether this was a male or female child. There was also parental ambivalence, one parent thinking the child was a boy and the other thinking it was a girl. Many things that can go wrong in the clinical management of intersex states went wrong here. Finally, but still in the first year, a decision was made to raise the child as female. At the age of three the testes were removed to prevent pubertal virilization. The child is now nine years old and has more of a male identity even though being raised as a girl. There are a number of questions. Is the female identity not 'taking' because of the early ambiguity with respect to what the parents were told and their ambivalence, or because the central nervous system was so considerably influenced by testosterone before birth that no matter what is done postnatally, there will be a primarily male identity? Very early in life, by the second birthday, the mother of this child reports buying her dolls with the child refusing them and playing only with trucks and her brother's toys. She would not play with her sister's toys. She formed a male peer group. She has been 'supertomboyish' from early on and has said repeatedly that she wants to be a boy. She is now approaching adolescence; the endocrinologists are considering giving her exogenous oestrogens in the hope of feminizing her body and, they hope, her behaviour. This may be problematic. So we have here a possible exception to the theory of postnatal socialization overriding prenatal hormones.

Bob Stoller has described a case of a child raised unambiguously as a girl who always felt like a boy, behaving like a pre-female-to-male transsexual throughout childhood (Baker & Stoller 1968). At 12 or 13 she developed what was thought to be a sore throat because of hoarseness, which did not clear. This led to hospitalization, and laparotomy revealed intraabdominal testes which were allowed to remain. The individual was told she was really a male, remarked that she had felt that way all along, and commenced living as a man. There was no difficulty in transition here at all. Stoller had suggested that there is a 'biological force' behind gender identity. There was no other way to account for that case, because there had been no parental ambivalence. The endocrine defect in this individual has been shown to be in the conversion of androstenedione to testosterone. The patient had low testosterone and relatively normal dihydrotestosterone concentrations, in contrast to the pseudohermaphrodite children in the Dominican Republic (Imperato-McGinley *et al.* 1974) and the child I described, who have normal testosterone and lower dihydrotestosterone concentrations. My patient may be the product of parental ambivalence and the doctors' delayed communication of a clear identity and sex designation to the parents. Dr Stoller's case could also be explained as the concurrence of transsexualism and an enzymic defect. Or they may both represent experiments of nature which will make us challenge some of the Money & Ehrhardt thesis (1972) of postnatal socialization influences overriding whatever biological forces are present.

Ehrhardt: You are right to stress the importance of ambiguity in the parents' minds. Money has reported several children who changed their sex at age 10 years where this ambiguity in their environment persisted. Clearly, if there is sufficient ambiguity in the parents' minds which is transmitted to the child, then ambiguity about gender identity can only go one way, to the other sex. If you consider Money's two cases of congenital adrenal hyperplasia where there was sufficient ambiguity in the first 1½ or 2 years, the children changed their sex to male and to female respectively (Money 1968). Gender identity formation is crucially dependent on reactions from the environment. On Dr Stoller's example, we recently saw someone with a very similar history. The child was raised as a girl but was very heavily virilized at 14; though she looked very masculine she had a clear female gender identity and wanted to get rid of her maleness and continue to live as a female. Unfortunately such cases are rare, which makes a systematic study difficult.

Marteau: I wonder which comes first in this question of gender identity. Is there first a biological difference which is picked up by the parents and then reflected back, causing a final gender identity problem, or does the parental dynamic affect the biological state? I had a patient who was brought up as a girl, but was always called 'boy' because the parents could not understand how to care for little girls, 'they were so different'. They have gone on treating her unconsciously as a boy all through life, backing up anything she did that was boyish and not accepting anything she did that was feminine. This girl has not shown any ambivalence biologically or physiologically about her gender identity. But she has been unable to accept any sort of response to her physical body. For eight years she was unable to take a bath, wash her bra, or accept her physical female form at all, and has to live in a world of fantasy where her body does not exist. This is a 'cut out' which does not require a gender change, even though there was total ambivalence on the part of both parents.

Ehrhardt: That is very much like the history of many female transsexuals in childhood — not all, but certainly of a subgroup.

Bancroft: On the question of ambiguity, in the study of Imperato-McGinley *et al.* (1974) referred to by Dr Green the information given about the upbringing of these children was limited, but I had the impression that they were brought up in the community not as females so much but as a special group who were recognized as being a bit different.

Green: They used the terms 'penis at 12' or 'eggs at 12'. These authors' contention is that in the first generations, when the intersex state was not recognized in childhood, no hermaphroditic label was applied. Only in later generations was the label given. In addition they are now finding isolated cases in rural communities where the intersex label is not being given.

Ehrhardt: This evidence is shaky, because the people of the *first* generation have in many instances refused to speak about the topic. It is hard enough for a researcher to contend with retrospective data. In addition, to go into another culture, where what is known about masculinity and femininity is different from in our culture, makes an interpretation of specific observations almost impossible. Imperato-McGinley recently stated that, in fact, these children knew that something was odd by 6-7 years of age, because they obviously had testes. Therefore one cannot say that they were raised as normal girls. We don't and can't know how much ambiguity was in their minds during childhood.

Goy: Nevertheless, none of them has refused to accept the male role at adolescence, with one exception.

Sachar: At what age is it believed that gender identity is fairly well fixed in our culture?

Ehrhardt: By the time of language development of the child, around 2-3 years of age.

Sachar: The work is *done* before that age, then, so the child is fairly clear about who he or she is even before two years?

Ehrhardt: Yes, but before the age of two, some ambiguity and flexibility still exist. Subsequently, it begins to go more and more in one direction. With the beginning of language acquisition a child shows distinct modelling behaviour and begins to draw the conclusions 'I have a penis like daddy', 'boys do this', and so on; but before some language development has occurred there seems to be no firm concept of gender identity.

Sachar: There is an implication here for psychoanalysts and psychotherapists who are trying to explore retrospectively with patients the possible origins of disturbances in gender identity. This is a period which is traditionally regarded as relatively inaccessible to psychoanalytic recovery; if a lot of work is done before the acquisition of language, it means that there are severe limitations on our efforts to reconstruct the psychological origins using the psychoanalytical method.

Dörner: To return to the study by Imperato-McGinley *et al.* (1974) of 24 male pseudohermaphrodites born with ambiguity of the external genitalia and virilization at puberty, biochemical evaluation revealed a marked decrease in plasma dihydrotestosterone, as Dr Green said, which is secondary to a decrease in steroid 5α-reductase. The decrease in dihydrotestosterone *in utero* resulted in incomplete masculinization of the external genitalia. Thus the affected males (46,XY) were born with this external ambiguity and were raised as girls before the disorder became obvious to the community. Eighteen of the affected males were reared as females. Their psychosexual orientation, however, was unequivocally male. They considered themselves as males and their libido was directed toward females. Despite being reared as girls, the affected subjects were able to change gender identity at the time of puberty.

By contrast, genetic males with gonadal dysgenesis or testicular feminization, who have a primary testosterone deficiency or testosterone insensitivity, show a female-like sex drive directed toward males as well as female orientation and female gender identity. Hence, exposure to testosterone *in utero* seems to be most important for the development of a male sex drive, male sexual orientation and even male gender identity.

Sachar: Dr Ehrhardt, there is an additional problem with the studies of children with congenital adrenal hyperplasia who are given prednisone replacement therapy and studied while receiving that treatment. In adults prednisone is a psychoactive drug and often produces a certain degree of activation, almost an amphetamine-like effect. Therefore prednisone itself may alter the activity level or the energy level of the children being studied.

Ehrhardt: One has to keep in mind that it is replacement therapy rather than the administration of additional prednisone or cortisone. Also, the study of girls whose mothers were treated with progestinic drugs makes it unlikely that cortisone plays a major role in the behaviour pattern of girls with this syndrome. Progestinic drugs also had an androgenizing effect, so that these babies were born with an enlarged clitoris. The abnormality was surgically corrected and they were raised as girls from birth onwards. They showed the same kind of tomboyish behaviour as girls with congenital adrenal hyperplasia, even without any kind of exposure to cortisone.

Besser: This is an important question and I don't think that it is so simple. Medroxyprogesterone has some glucocorticoid activity, although weak. Of the androgenic progestagens, no-one has really studied whether they have glucocorticoid activity, since it is only recently that some progestagens have been shown to have such activity. When we come to congenital adrenal hyperplasia, we have to be careful about interpreting the data, because it is now clear that patients who on conventional criteria appear to be controlled are not. Their levels of ACTH frequently stay high; their 17α-hydroxyprogesterone levels are frequently high. Clinically they do well. The simple, classical criteria such as the urinary androgenic metabolites are grossly inadequate ways of following the patient. We have to review all the old studies in the light of new techniques. It is not necessary to give supraphysiological doses of steroids to these patients to control them, but one must manipulate their physiology by giving a replacement dose in such a way that the circadian rhythm of steroid administration is reversed. Glucocorticoids are stimulants; we normally say that to give a replacement of hydrocortisone is no different from normal adrenal function, but this isn't necessarily true if you use a reversed circadian rhythm method of steroid therapy. You will not control congenital adrenal hyperplasia by giving a replacement dose of any steroid in such a way that the patient has a normal circadian rhythm of ACTH. One must abolish the rhythm to control them on a dose that won't give them Cushing's syndrome. Dr Sachar's point is well made, and we have to be careful in interpreting these results. If you really mean that the patients were controlled on cortisone, I have never seen a patient who is controllable on cortisone in a physiological replacement dose, because of the kinetics of the conversion of cortisone to cortisol in the body. If some were controlled on prednisolone, that is a different matter.

Sachar: This is why it was particularly valuable to study girls who were exposed to androgens prenatally and received nothing after that. Those results were in the same direction, which is reassuring. In the absence of that report we would be concerned.

Jost: I want to come back to the cases where progesterone was given to pregnant women. It was reported several years ago by Dr Katharina Dalton (1968) that progesterone increased intelligence and gave intellectual advantages to infants born to mothers who had received large amounts of progesterone during pregnancy. Was that confirmed? If so, I wonder whether that would be considered as a sign of masculinization or feminization!

Ehrhardt: We have looked at the effects of antenatal medroxyprogesterone on mental abilities and we could not confirm Katharina Dalton's findings (Meyer-Bahlburg & Ehrhardt 1977). The children we studied were not different in IQ and other mental abilities from their controls. Congenital adrenal hyperplasia has also been linked to high IQ. We did a complete family study in Buffalo examining that question. We also found higher IQ's in patients with congenital adrenal hyperplasia. However, they were not different from the IQ's of their unaffected siblings and parents (Baker & Ehrhardt 1974).

Herbert: There is a well-established sex difference in verbal and visuo-spatial abilities; were these affected by progesterone?

Ehrhardt: We have not completed the data analysis in the medroxyprogesterone study, so I am not sure yet. In the children with adrenal hyperplasia we did not find a pattern of cognitive strengths and weaknesses that is more typical for males than for females.

Bancroft: I am confused, because in the studies where progesterone was given for toxaemia you suggested that in the female children there was some reduction in activation and perhaps some degree of demasculinization, whereas where progesterone was given for spontaneous abortion, there was activation.

Ehrhardt: In the latter case a synthetic progestin was administered which is quite different from Provera (medroxyprogesterone acetate) or the progesterone which Dr Dalton used. The synthetic progestins were compounds that sometimes had a virilizing effect on the genitalia of the children.

Bancroft: Natural progestagens do not have an androgenic effect?

Ehrhardt: No.

Nieschlag: I should like to ask for some advice as a clinician. As Dr Besser has pointed out, we have much better parameters now for the surveillance of congenital adrenal hyperplasia patients. Just as in the diabetic patient blood glucose is used for adjusting the insulin dose, 17α-hydroxyprogesterone in serum is now used for adjusting the cortisol dose in the adrenal hyperplasia. Thus the patient can be monitored more effectively than was previously possible with urinary 17-ketosteroids. To improve the therapy even more, which psychological test would you suggest that we use so that we can see whether they are well or badly adjusted?

Ehrhardt: The observation of increased tomboyish behaviour is not relevant clinically, since tomboyishness is acceptable for girls in our culture. I would only become concerned if the patient during childhood begins to show gender identity confusion, which is very rare in congenital adrenal hyperplasia; or if you are dealing with a girl who begins to reject her femininity in puberty, which again is rare in this condition. If that occurs, as for instance in a girl who does not want to menstruate or have breast development, as one finds in female transsexuals, I would become concerned.

Nieschlag: So there is no psychological test which helps us to adjust the patient's dose of steroid on a short-term basis?

Ehrhardt: I would certainly not pay any attention to physical activity. If a mother comes to me complaining of tomboyishness in her daughter, I reassure her.

Sachar: Later Dr Green will tell us about some behaviour patterns that we ought to worry about!

References

BAKER, S.W. & EHRHARDT, A.A. (1974) Prenatal androgens, intelligence and cognitive sex differences, in *Sex Differences in Behaviour* (Friedman, R.C., Richart, R.M. & Vandewiele, R.L., eds.), pp. 33 – 51, Wiley, New York

BAKER, H. & STOLLER, R. (1968) Can a biological force contribute to gender identity? *Am. J. Psychiatr. 124,* 1653 – 58

DALTON, K. (1968) Ante-natal progesterone and intelligence. *Br.J. Psychiatr. 114,* 1377 – 1382

IMPERATO-MCGINLEY, J., GUERRERO, L., GAUTIER, T. & PETERSON, R.E. (1974) Steroid 5α-reductase deficiency in man: an inherited form of male pseudohermaphroditism. *Science (Wash. D.C.) 186,* 1213 – 1215

MEYER-BAHLBURG, H.F.L. & EHRHARDT, A.A. (1977) Effects of prenatal hormone treatment on mental abilities, in *Progress in Sexology* (Gemme, R. & Wheeler, C.C., eds.), pp. 85 – 92, Plenum Press, New York

MONEY, J. (1968) Psychologic approach to psychosexual misidentity with elective mutism: sex reassignment in two cases of hyperadrenocortical hermaphroditism. *Clin. Pediatr. 7,* 331 – 339.

MONEY, J. & EHRHARDT, A.A. (1972) *Man and Woman, Boy and Girl: The Differentiation and Dimorphism of Gender Identity from Conception to Maturity,* The Johns Hopkins University Press, Baltimore

YALOM, J.D., GREEN, R. & FISK, N. (1973) Prenatal exposure to female hormones: effect on psychosexual development in boys. *Arch. Gen. Psychiatr. 28,* 554 – 561

Sex-dimorphic behaviour development in the human: prenatal hormone administration and postnatal socialization

RICHARD GREEN

Departments of Psychiatry and Behavioral Science, and Psychology, State University of New York at Stony Brook

Abstract An interdisciplinary integrative approach must be utilized in the study of psychosexual differentiation. The approach must capitalize on data derived from non-human models, from experiments of nature, and from experiments of nurture.

Studies from non-human primates strongly suggest the influence of prenatal sex hormone levels on postnatal sexually dimorphic behaviours. Starting from this basis we have studied sixty young adult men whose mothers received, during pregnancy, diethylstilboestrol, diethylstilboestrol and natural progesterone, natural progesterone, or synthetic progesterone. They have been compared with matched controls not exposed *in utero* to exogenous hormones.

Studies of socialization patterns must document the differential developmental experiences, if any, of childeren with atypical and typical sex-typed behaviours. To this end, we are studying 60 boys whose behaviour before puberty was decidedly feminine, and their parents, and contrasting them with masculine boys and their parents. We are also studying 50 girls whose behaviour before puberty was 'masculine', and contrasting them with 'feminine' girls.

Additionally, we are studying the sexually dimorphic behaviour of children of sexually atypical parents. The parents have either undergone sex-change surgery (male-to-female or female-to-male) or arc homosexual.

Data from the three studies are presented. A call is made to researchers working with non-human primates to test and extend these findings.

I shall present three strategies for studying the development of sexually dimorphic behaviour. I shall borrow from the work of non-human primate research workers and extend its application to human study. And I shall report on human studies and challenge those studying the non-human primate to extend these findings.

STRATEGY ONE

This strategy locates children whose sexually dimorphic behaviours are culturally atypical and contrasts them with typical children. It includes males and females. Parents and children are studied, cross-sectionally and longitudinally.

During the past eight years we have evaluated 60 boys who at initial evaluation preferred the clothes, toys, activities and companionship of girls, typically role-played as females, and generally stated their wish to be girls. Their age when initially seen ranged from 4 to 11 years. Forty-six per cent were 8–11, 26% 6–8, 19% 5–6, and 10%, 4–5 years. Parents had observed 62% of these boys cross-dressing over 20 times. Three-quarters began cross-dressing by the fourth birthday and 94% by the sixth. The persons to whom the boys related best were same-age girls for 41%, older girls for 22%, and adult females for 12%. Female-type dolls were either the favourite toys of or frequently played with by 57%. The role taken when playing house was typically mother for 38%, sister for 7%, and another female for 13%. Eighty-three per cent had frequently or occasionally stated their wish to be girls. The boys had an aversion to rough-and-tumble play, were socially stigmatized, and were very low on the peer hierarchy.

These children have been given psychological tests, including the It-Scale for Children, the Draw-a-Person test, the Family Doll Preference Test, the Parent and Activity Preference Test, and additionally have been observed in an experimental playroom. They have been interviewed. Several have also had periodic determinations of plasma testosterone concentrations and electroencephalograms. Parents have completed questionnaires describing the child's behaviour, have completed a variety of attitude scales, and have been systematically interviewed.

Fifty of these families have been matched with families in which a boy of the same age manifests culturally typical sex-dimorphic behaviours. Matching has been on boys' age, sibling sequence, parental marital configuration, ethnic background, and parents' educational level. The same evaluation methods have been used in both sets of families. The psychological tests and behavioural descriptions clearly discriminate the samples of boys (Green *et al.* 1972*a, b;* Green 1974, 1976).

Evaluations of the data on the parents have yielded few differences between feminine- and masculine-boy families on the time spent by each parent with child, marital role division, attitudes toward women, and sex education for children, among other factors. A final analysis is under way in which we are comparing transcribed interview segments with parents from the feminine-

and masculine-boy families. The segments assess several parameters of the marital relationship, and the relationship between each parent and the index child and siblings. Most families are being followed longitudinally, the majority of the boys being now in early teenage. Later reports will describe their mid- and late-adolescent sex-dimorphic behaviours.

More recently we have generated a sample of 50 girls, age 4–11 years, who dislike dresses and dolls, prefer the companionship of boys, and, when role-playing, usually portray a male. These children are considered as 'tomboys' by their parent(s). So far, about half have been demographically matched with females who prefer dresses, enjoy doll play, have a female peer group, and typically role-play as a female.

Thirty nine per cent of the 'tomboys' have frequently expressed the desire to be boys and another 42% have expressed this desire occasionally. As for play with 'Barbie' doll or a similar female-type doll, this is a rare or non-existent behaviour for 75%. Forty-seven per cent frequently play with trucks. Interest in truck play began early, in 88% by age four years. As for gun play, this is a frequent activity for 22% and an occasional activity for another 50%. These girls are seen as more 'rough-and-tumble' types than most girls by 75% of the mothers. Two-thirds of the mothers see their daughters as participating in sports more than the average girl. As for peer group, 80% of the girls relate better to males. For those girls who play 'house', 47% frequently or always role-play a male. Only 20% typically role-play a female. Socially, half the girls are seen as good mixers, 29% as leaders and 22% as loners. None are seen as rejected by the female peer group.

The girls and their parents are being evaluated by the same methods as used for the two male samples (Williams *et al.* 1978). The female sample, too, will be followed into adolescence.

Thus this research strategy consists of the study of disparate groups of male and female children and their families, and their early socialization experiences. In this regard, what can we learn from non-human primate research? Can we study the influence of various peer group compositions on later sexuality? It is an aphorism of human developmental research that a homosocial childhood peer group is associated with a later heterosexual orientation, and vice versa. Research workers studying non-human primates are also looking at peer socialization. One report described modifications in the early socialization experiences of two male rhesus monkeys (Erwin & Maple 1976). These two monkeys later showed ambisexual behaviour, with male-male anal penetration and an affectional preference for each other over female partners. Can we look at social hierarchy, participation in rough-

and-tumble play, and affectional bonds between the young monkey and an adult male and female, and correlate these variables with later social dominance, sex-dimorphic behaviours, and genital sexuality? What is the effect of raising non-human primates with exclusively same- or other-sex peers, with or without same- or other-sex adults? The non-human primates which might offer the most promise for this study would be man's closest relatives, the chimpanzee, baboon and orang utan, especially if juvenile sex-dimorphic behaviours can be documented as clearly as with the rhesus monkey (Rosenblum 1971). The prenatal endocrine status of these animals should also be determined, a procedure not possible in the above research on human samples. However, a model in which some manipulation of the prenatal hormonal milieu occurred and later sex-dimorphic behaviours were studied will be presented later (p.64).

STRATEGY TWO

The next strategy looks at sexually atypical parents and the influence of their behaviour on the psychosexual development of their children. Two types of atypicality have been studied: parents who have undergone sex-change procedures (transsexuals) and parents who are currently homosexual (Green 1978). The transsexuals have undergone hormonal and surgical conversion from male to female or female to male. The homosexuals are females who are divorced from the fathers of their children, are currently living a homosexual life style with a female partner, and have custody of their children.

Pre-teenage children were evaluated on sex-dimorphic behaviours such as peer group composition, favourite toy, whether they are considered 'sissy' or 'tomboy', and vocational aspiration. Teenage children have been evaluated on whether they have been considered 'sissy' or 'tomboy', vocational aspiration, and content of erotic fantasies (sexual orientation).

Fourteen children being raised by transsexual parents and 21 by homosexual parents have been evaluated. Seven children are being raised by three female-to-male transsexuals. Their age range is 13 to 20 years. They have lived in the transsexual households for 8–16 years. Five have known of the transsexual nature of their male-appearing parent for 4–15 years. Two are unaware after 14 years. The mean age at which the others knew was eight years.

Seven children are being raised by three male-to-female transsexuals. Their age range is 3 to 13 years. They have lived in the transsexual households for 1–3 years. The age at which they knew of the transsexual nature of the female-appearing parent ranges from 2 to 10 years (mean, 5).

Among children being raised by female-to-male transsexuals, no males were called 'sissy', and one female had been called 'tomboy'. All had culturally typical sex-typed vocational aspirations (e.g. housewife, engineer). All were exclusively heterosexual. Of the children being raised by male-to-female transsexuals, no males were called 'sissy' and one female was called 'tomboy'. All had culturally typical sex-typed vocational aspirations (e.g. policeman, mommy). The two who were old enough to report erotic attractions were exclusively heterosexual.

The age range of the 21 children being raised by seven female homosexual parents is 5 to 14 years; the mean is eight years. They have lived in the households for 2–6 years (mean, 3.5 years). Their age when their mother commenced her homosexual life style ranges from 2 to 9 years (mean, 4.5). The peer group of 19 is consistent with the sex of anatomy, the favourite toy of 20 is consistent with conventional sex-dimorphic preferences, and the vocational choice of all is culturally typical. The three oldest report exclusively heterosexual fantasies.

Some notes of caution. The four currently heterosexual children raised by female homosexuals are still in early teenage. Some adult female homosexuals do not report their first awareness of lesbianism until mid- to late teenage. Also, the age at which these children were initially exposed to their parents' homosexual life style was 7–9 years, possibly beyond a 'critical period' for influence on the child's sexual orientation.

The two currently heterosexually oriented children of the male-to-female transsexuals are also younger than mid-teenage. The ages when they became aware of their parents' transsexualism were 7 and 10 years.

However, the children raised by the female-to-male transsexuals, all of whom are heterosexual, include mid-teenagers and young adults. Two knew of the transsexual nature of their parent at 4 and 5 years.

Granting the preliminary nature of this report, the absence of follow-up evaluations, and the somewhat advanced ages at which exposure to the parents' atypicality commenced, the most remarkable thing about these children is just how *un*remarkable they are.

What model can this provide for those studying non-human primates? To what degree can atypical parent figures be introduced? We have the classic studies of surrogate parents of Cross & Harlow (1965), but these were gender-*absent* figures. Could male and female non-human primates be 'raised by', or exposed to adult males only? Could males and females be raised only in the presence of adult females? Could the two groups of younger monkeys be compared?

STRATEGY THREE

The third strategy best utilizes the concept of adapting findings from research into non-human primates to the human. It capitalizes on the pioneering work of Young *et al*. (1964), who showed that levels of prenatal androgens influence postnatal sex-dimorphic behaviours in the rhesus monkey, and proceeds from the exciting analogous findings of Ehrhardt & Baker (1974) in the human female. As is well known, Young *et al.* (1964) injected androgen into pregnant rhesus monkeys and observed the play behaviours of their female offspring. The latter, in addition to being somewhat anatomically virilized, were also behaviourally masculinized in their juvenile play patterns. Ehrhardt & Baker (1974) studied females with the adrenogenital syndrome, persons whose adrenals, beginning prenatally, overproduce androgen. These females were compared to their hormonally normal sisters. The girls with the adrenogenital syndrome show masculine, or less feminine, juvenile behavioural patterns.

Another situation exists in which the human fetus may be exposed to unusual amounts of 'sex' hormones. This is where women who have been habitual aborters (unable to carry a conception to term) have been treated with exogenous hormones.

We have studied a sample of 140 males between 18 and 30 years of age (Green *et al.* 1978). They were selected by reviewing obstetrical charts of approximately 12 000 patients at one clinic. Sixty-six male subjects exposed *in utero* to one of four hormone regimens were located. Each was matched against a control not exposed to sex hormones, selected from the same patient files. Controls were matched by age, age of mother, and, in most cases, prior number of siblings. The drug regimens and numbers in each group were: 18 males exposed to diethylstilboestrol, 24 males exposed to diethylstilboestrol and natural progesterone, 10 males exposed to natural progesterone, and 14 males exposed to synthetic progesterone.

The data are still being analysed, but our preliminary impressions will be described. The value of these data here is not in the degree to which they will stand up to further analytic refinements, but rather in providing a model of the potential applicability of experimental findings in the non-human primate to data available on the human. Our preliminary findings which will be summarized here are derived from paired and unpaired *t*-tests, and paired and unpaired regression analyses.

The psychological test instruments used were the Bem Sex Role Inventory (BSRI), the Guilford-Zimmerman Temperament Survey (GZTS), the Strong Vocational Interest Blank (SVIB), and the Embedded Figures Test

(EFT). There was also an interview with the son, and a questionnaire for the mother.

On the BSRI, a test that yields *separate* masculine and feminine scores rather than a combined score, subjects exposed to diethylstilboestrol (DES), those exposed to DES plus natural progesterone, and those exposed to synthetic progesterone had elevated feminine scores compared to controls. Subjects exposed to natural progesterone had lower masculine and feminine scores (an undifferentiated response) and those exposed to synthetic progesterone had elevated masculine, in addition to elevated feminine, scores (an androgynous response). Those exposed to DES plus natural progesterone tended to score higher on the feminine score of the GZTS, and exposure to DES and natural progesterone in trimesters 1 and 2 was associated with higher feminine scores on the SVIB. Exposure in the third trimester was associated with higher masculine scores. Other drug regimens were not associated with score differences.

The GZTS also measures other factors. Effects on activity, submissiveness and hostility will be described here. Except for DES, where no association was found, hormone exposure tended to be associated with lower activity scores. For submissiveness, when a drug association was found, there was a modest trend for these scores to be higher. Natural progesterone alone, or in combination with DES, lowered hostility scores (countered by increasing DES dosage) and synthetic progesterone raised hostility.

The SVIB also has several factors. Mathematics, science, mechanical aptitude, military activities, and adventure will be reported. On the mathematics scale, exposure to DES plus natural progesterone with higher dosages of DES was associated with lower scores. On the science scale, subjects exposed to DES and natural progesterone in trimester 1 also scored lower, as did higher-dose progesterone subjects. Those exposed to natural progesterone also scored lower. On the mechanical score, exposure to DES plus natural progesterone in trimester 1 and to natural progesterone in trimester 2 led to lower scores. Subjects exposed to natural progesterone in trimester 1, and to synthetic progesterone in trimester 2, had higher adventure scores. Exposure to natural progesterone in trimester 3 was associated with lower military activities scores.

Several parameters of boyhood behaviours were noted. Subjects exposed to DES recalled doing ‘girl-type’ things less often than controls. Those exposed to DES and natural progesterone also recalled ‘girl-like’ things less often in association with higher dosages of DES.

As for being called ‘sissy’, boys exposed to DES in trimesters 2 and 3 were called this more often than controls and those exposed to DES in trimester 2 only were called 'sissy' less often. For DES plus natural progesterone, those exposed in trimester 1 only and trimesters 2 and 3 only were called 'sissy' more, while others were called this less.

For boyhood cross-dressing, subjects exposed to DES recalled this behaviour less and those exposed to DES plus progesterone recalled it more than controls. Subjects exposed to synthetic progesterone in trimester 3 cross-dressed more than all other subjects. On peer group composition, subjects exposed to DES plus natural progesterone in trimester 1 had more female best friends than controls. Those exposed to synthetic progesterone also had more female best friends and increasing doses were associated with a more female peer group.

Regarding interest in fighting and rough-and-tumble play, boys exposed to DES plus natural progesterone tended to fight more than controls. Exposure to natural progesterone in high dosage was associated with more interest in rough-and-tumble play, but less involvement in fighting.

As for favourite toys, exposure to DES plus natural progesterone, with increasing dosages of DES, was associated with more masculine toy preference. However, the two subjects exposed only in trimester 1 recalled more female-type doll play. Subjects exposed to synthetic progesterone at high dosages, and those with early trimester drug initiation, recalled more selection of feminine toys.

As for sports interest, DES-exposed subjects rated themselves higher than controls. Subjects exposed to DES plus natural progesterone participated less. Natural progesterone-exposed subjects were more interested, notably those exposed in the first two trimesters and to higher dosages.

For brevity, I shall not discuss adolescent or adult behaviours, except heterosexual-homosexual fantasies and overt behaviours during adulthood. The four subjects exposed to DES plus progesterone in trimester 1 had more homosexual fantasies than any other subjects. Those exposed in trimester 1 only had more homosexual activity. For natural progesterone, higher dosages were associated with a greater degree of homosexual fantasy and activity. However, for DES, there was only one subject who was more than incidentally homosexual (Kinsey 2+; Kinsey *et al.* 1948) (6%); for DES and natural progesterone there were two (10%), for natural progesterone there were three (fantasy only) (30%), and for synthetic progesterone there was one (8%). For all hormone-exposed subjects this totalled 11%. The results are the same as with the control group who had not been exposed to hormones.

A major methodological difficulty with this study and similar ones (Yalom *et al.* 1973; Reinisch & Karow 1977; Meyer-Bahlburg *et al.* 1978; Zussman *et al.*

1977) is that they were not designed as experiments. Dosages of hormone vary enormously, the time of drug initiation varies greatly, and many of the treatment groups contain few subjects. Here I turn back to those studying non-human primates and ask them for additional experiments. We need studies of androgen deprivation or excessive oestrogen exposure of the male fetus, coupled with postnatal observations of sexually dimorphic behaviours.

CONCLUSION

This paper is a plea for the construction of a bridge. It was the hope of Joe Herbert and myself when we considered the formulation of this symposium that an era would ensue in which research workers investigating the sexual and sex-typed behaviours of non-human and human primates would examine their data, exchange ideas and models, and then propose studies uniquely available to either discipline. Ethical and methodological considerations should be the only limiting factor. The limit must not be set by disciplinary provincialism.

ACKNOWLEDGEMENT

This work was supported by grants from the National Institute of Mental Health (Dept of Health, Education, and Welfare, US Public Health Service).

References

Cross, M. & Harlow, H. F. (1965) Prolonged and progressive effects of partial isolation on the behavior of macaque monkeys. *J. Exp. Res. Pers. 1*, 39–49

Ehrhardt, A. A. & Baker, S. W. (1974) Fetal androgen, human CNS differentiation and behavior sex differences, in *Sex Differences in Behavior* (Friedman, R. C., Richart, R. M. & Vandewiele, R. L., eds.), pp. 53–76, Wiley, New York

Erwin, J. & Maple, T. (1976) Ambisexual behavior with male–male anal penetration in male rhesus monkeys. *Arch. Sex. Behav. 5*, 9-14

Green, R. (1974) *Sexual Identity Conflict in Children and Adults*, Basic Books, New York/Duckworth, London/Penguin, New York

Green, R. (1976) One-hundred ten feminine and masculine boys: behavioral contrasts and demographic similarities. *Arch. Sex. Behav. 5*, 425–446

Green, R. (1978) Sexual identity of thirty-seven children raised by homosexual or transsexual parents. *Am. J. Psychiatr. 135*, 692-697

Green, R., Fuller, M. & Rutley, B. (1972*a*) It-Scale for children and draw a person test: 30 feminine vs. 25 masculine boys. *J. Pers. Assess. 36*, 349–352

Green, R., Fuller, M., Rutley, B. & Hendler, J. (1972*b*) Playroom toy preferences of fifteen masculine and fifteen feminine boys. *Behav. Ther. 3*, 425–429

Green, R., Kester, P., Finch, S. & Williams, K. (1978) Prenatal female hormone administration and later psychosexual development in human males, in preparation

KINSEY, A. C., POMEROY, W. B. & MARTIN, C. E. (1948) *Sexual Behavior in the Human Male,* Saunders, Philadelphia

MEYER-BAHLBURG, H. F. L., GRISANTI, G. C. & EHRHARDT, A. A. (1978) Prenatal effects of sex hormones on human male behaviour: medroxyprogesterone acetate (MPA). *Psychoneuroendocrinology, 2,* 383–390

REINISCH, J. & KAROW, W. (1977) Prenatal exposure to synthetic progestins and estrogens: effects on human development. *Arch. Sex. Behav. 6,* 257–288

ROSENBLUM, L. (1971) The ontogeny of mother-infant relations in macaques, in *Ontogeny of Vertebrate Behavior* (Moltz, H., ed.), Academic Press, New York

WILLIAMS, K., GREEN, R. & GOODMAN, M. (1978) Patterns of sexual identity development: a preliminary report on the 'tomboy', in *Research in Community and Mental Health* (Simmons, R., ed.), JAI Press, Greenwich, Connecticut

YALOM, J. D., GREEN, R. & FISK, N. (1973) Prenatal exposure to female hormones: effect on psychosexual development in boys. *Arch. Gen. Psychiatr. 28,* 554–561

YOUNG, W. C., GOY, R. W. & PHOENIX, C .H. (1964) Hormones and sexual behavior. *Science (Wash. D. C.) 143,* 212–218

ZUSSMAN, J. U., ZUSSMAN, P. P. & DALTON, K. (1977) Unpublished data, annual meeting of the International Academy of Sex Research, Bloomington, Indiana

Discussion

Goy: We have been trying to uncover the influences of peer group composition and environment on the development of sex-typed behaviour in rhesus monkeys. We have studied 37 different groups of monkeys—heterosexual peer groups (half males, half females; not sibs)—and the pattern of development of mounting behaviour in these heterosexual groups. We have studied the animals from the age of three months to 3½ years old, observing them daily and counting every mount that every animal shows, and whom it shows it to. The normal intact males in the first year mount at a certain constant rate. The mounting behaviour of normal females is very low; in fact the typical female does not mount in this heterosexual environment. Then we take the monkeys away from their mothers at one year of age. That releases the males from maternal inhibition, and their rates of mounting rise. But separation from mothers doesn't affect the mounting of females. In the following years these males continue to mount at a quite high rate. The females may show small increases in mounting, but there remains a big sex difference.

One might conclude from this study that being reared with males inhibits mounting in females. I am not sure that that is the mechanism—it is just the term for it. But females reared in all-female peer groups show a higher level of mounting. When we take them away from their mothers they show a facilitation, again much like the male—in other words, the rate of mounting increases. But the frequency never equals that of males reared in heterosexual groups. I should add that males mount male partners just as often as they mount female partners at these ages.

In the females raised in isosexual groups the mounting rate gradually subsides and they end up as adolescent females not mounting significantly more often than normal females. So there is no lasting effect of being reared in what, for the monkey, is a very abnormal social environment.

We have done another experiment to show the lability of the phenomenon in female rhesus monkeys. We had a large group of juvenile monkeys, 9 males and 11 females, aged about $1^1/_2$ years when we began working with them. (We didn't start with their early development.) They were living amicably together and the males, true to form, were doing most of the mounting in the group. Then we removed the alpha and beta animals from the group, both of which were males, to see whether that would influence mounting of the remaining animals, and it did. But it only affected the mounting behaviour of the remaining males. They were 'disinhibited' by the removal of their oppressors and mounted much more frequently than when the alpha and beta males were present. Then we removed all males from the group, leaving an isosexual female peer group. These females now became disinhibited and mounted much more frequently than before, but never as often as the males did when males were present or when they were alone in their isosexual group.

To see whether this manipulation had any enduring effects on the psychological make-up of these females we reunited the groups, putting the males back in, and immediately the mounting behaviour frequency of the females declined to their previous baseline. So peer manipulations in monkeys have consequences for the kind and frequency of behaviour shown, but, so far as we are able to tell, do not alter the fundamental psychosexuality of the individuals.

Green: Could you comment on the report by Erwin & Maple (1976) on the so-called 'male bisexuals' that preferred males to females?

Goy: I don't think that this is so very uncommom in *male* monkeys. Male rhesus monkeys are probably not a good model for human beings, although they may be a perfect model without our realizing it. That is, male rhesus monkeys are capable of enjoying homosexual relationships, so far as I know; they ejaculate intra-anally and it is not uncommon to see male monkeys that have been 'peripheralized' in social development, in social groups, engage in this homosexual activity, one male playing the female role until the first male ejaculates, and then immediately taking his turn at the male role. This kind of bisexuality is quite characteristic of adult male rhesus monkeys, providing that their social circumstances render the females inaccessible.

Ehrhardt: Have you ever seen any preference for homosexual partners in monkeys?

Goy: No. This paper by Erwin & Maple claims a preference but it is the only study to give a feasible demonstration of this.

Crown: Professor Green's data seem to be unique, but I was disturbed by an implication of part of his work. He seems to imply that there was previously a normal environment in the families of the transsexuals, and that the environment *became* abnormal to these children when the parent had the sex change or when the children, interviewed afterwards, said they first recognized an abnormality. I am not experienced with transsexuals but from those I have seen I would feel that the environment must have been abnormal from the beginning in these families.

Secondly, what methods did you use to assess these people? Was depth interview used, or how was it done?

Finally, these studies have important implications. There are many social experiments in coupling of various sorts at present, particularly in the US and the UK, and the problem of whether children should be allowed to be brought up by deviant couples, such as lesbian or homosexual couples, seems to be a very important one.

Green: With respect to the 'normal' environment of the children before the dramatic transition in the lesbian or transsexual households, by contrast to what went on later, the environment was *relatively* normal before. That is not to say they were not atypical households in some way, but the dramatic transition took place at the time when, for example, the father began to cross-dress repeatedly, or the mother left the father and took in a female lover. In most cases we were not able to evaluate the home before this dramatic transition, but it is a gross transition that takes place.

The degree of evaluation of the families varies. In some families I have followed the parents for many years during the metamorphosis of transsexualism and have seen the children concurrently. In other cases it has been more of a cross-sectional study, particularly for the lesbian families where the study has often been done in the context of court litigation which has involved the so-called 'best interests of the children', in child custody cases. We have in another study 50 lesbians and at least 80 children, plus the 21 children reported here, and we are not seeing anything remarkable in the children. We have seen only a few children being raised by homosexual fathers, or by homosexual fathers with male lovers, because in the US mothers generally get custody of the children. One could play devil's advocate and say that in most cases the children's awareness of the atypical nature of the parent may have come later than the critical life period when an effect might take place. On the other hand, when one looks to see how much of the variance in the child's psychosexual development comes from the parent rather than from various other influences, it may be quite small. The influence of the mass media and of peer groups, and peer group parents, may be far greater. So our results might not be so surprising.

Sachar: If we are concerned about homosexuality and the possible determinants of a homosexual choice in adolescence and adulthood, these date are baffling in terms of some of our hypotheses. If we take Dr Green's studies and Dr Ehrhardt's, and the studies she reviewed on the effect of prenatal hormone administration, the outcome of homosexuality is no different from that in a control group, as far as one can see. On a second hypothesis that homosexuality has something to do with modelling behaviour in terms of the influence of parents, we have a small group of children raised with very deviant models—and your point that there may have been trouble much earlier, or something sensed much earlier, would only emphasize this—yet these children are not growing up to be homosexual or sexually variant in any respect.

One other piece of information here is that when Dr Green made a psychological evaluation of the parents of the boys who were dressing up as girls, and compared them with a control group of parents of children growing up normally, there were no striking differences in the psychological picture. The children in the two groups were more different than the parents, in fact. So one is puzzled and unsatisfied by hypotheses of either parental influences or hormonal influences as aetiological.

Hertoft: There is another factor here, because it is rare that transsexuals or homosexuals attribute their behaviour to the fact that their fathers or mothers were homosexual or transsexual.

Keverne: In trying to determine to what extent transsexual behaviour is environmentally or socially determined, Dr Green, have you been able to look at parental attitudes towards the children, rather than at the parent's own psychosexual orientation? For example, with the growth of the women's movement in the US, especially in its most extreme form where parents refuse to provide their children with a gender identity or even gender role, is there any evidence for an increase in transsexualism or homosexuality among such children?

Green: The male sample was generated largely before the advent of the 'unigender' or feminist movement in the US, a decade ago, when the movement hadn't taken much hold. Also, we have a number of sub-samples of families here. Clearly the parents who photograph their children dressing in the clothes of the other sex are conveying some degree of positive feedback and reinforcement to the children's atypical behaviour. But most of the parents do not take pictures of their sons cross-dressed. We are currently analysing interviews of mothers and fathers of the feminine boys compared to the same interviews with parents of the masculine boys. We are looking at intra-family dynamics as well as inter-family dynamics. We look, for example, at favouritism in the family—mother/father, mother/son, or father/son alliances. In comparing families we don't see very much but looking within families, we may.

The most dramatic example is a pair of monozygotic male twins in which one twin was decidedly feminine and the other typically masculine. There was a clear schism in the family. When the boy who became feminine was ill from 3 $1/2$ to 7 years he spent almost all his time with his mother, while the pre-masculine twin spent most of his time with the father. They were dramatically different by eight years. This is an example where we begin with relatively constant genetics, then have a dramatically different socialization pattern, and then a different gender role differentiation. Interestingly, in adolescence, *both* boys have become heterosexual. This makes me wonder whether the heterosexuality could have been 'written in' beforehand and all that the atypical socialization did was to modify gender role behaviour toward femininity during grade school years. However, when genital sexuality became paramount it was identical for both twins.

Marteau: You showed us photographs (not reproduced) of cross-dressing boys taken by their parents. I am interested in what happens when the parents did *not* take photographs of their cross-dressing children, because it struck me that there was something peculiar about the families that did. Not every child who dresses up in his mother's clothes necessarily becomes homosexual, and a lot more children dress up than are taken notice of by the parents. What interests me is why these parents took notice of it and whether their reactions to this behaviour have some dynamic effect. Is there something pathological about the parents, reinforced in the children by photographing?

On the other hand, I also wonder how many heterosexual men might admit to having a picture of themselves in their family album attired in a similar fashion. Even in psychiatry there is a danger of pointing to various forms of deprivation as causes of later aberrations. However, my experience as a pastor for 15 years in a deprived area has modified my opinions in this direction. I have seen just as many good results arising from the same forms of deprivation. To draw all our experience from one group, the deviant, is to lack the scientific approach which always calls for a control group.

Short: Dr Green, have you any information on the time of onset of masturbation in normal boys, as opposed to those who are effeminate? How closely do you reckon that the onset of masturbation is related to the hormonal changes of puberty in normal boys?

Green: We know that boys masturbate from the neonatal period onwards. There is an increase in frequency at puberty, in what people remember and what they tell us. I am not convinced that there is much difference between our two groups so far, but it appears that the content of masturbation differs. We are finding more bisexual and homosexual fantasy in the previously feminine boys than in the previously masculine boys, but since so many are only just beginning to report masturbation it is too early to be sure of a significant difference. We are collecting information on the onset, frequency and content of masturbation in both groups of boys.

Goy: Dr Sachar said that homosexuality in Dr Ehrhardt's series of individuals is not a conspicuous feature. Isn't it strange, however, to think of virilized women (the congenital adrenal hyperplasia syndrome) who are reared as boys and then want to get married to women as *not* lesbians? They have a psychosexual orientation in adulthood where the female is the preferred partner; isn't it a bit wilful to say that that is *not* a lesbian relationship?

Ehrhardt: It is a question of terminology. If we talk about homosexual partner choice, we usually refer to a preference for same-sex partners by persons who present as and look and feel like women or men. The people you refer to are 'males' in all social contacts and in body habitat. They are totally male in their gender identity and prefer females as erotic partners just as most other men do. To call that a homosexual relationship is, in my opinion, a mysticism of genetics or a confusing terminology.

Bancroft: It is an arbitrary issue and depends on what one is trying to demonstrate or prove. This comes across with some transsexual patients, who say they want a relationship with someone of the same genetic sex, but wouldn't contemplate using their genitalia. That *would* be homosexual, for them. They imagine the relationship in fantasy without their genitalia.

Goy: By the same token, the male individuals Dr Green describes who cross-dress from the beginning and then want to consort with males are not having homosexual fantasies; they are having *heterosexual* fantasies. But they have been referred to by Dr Green as having *homosexual* fantasies.

Pirke: Dr Green, I would like to ask you about the boys born to mothers who were treated with oestrogens during pregnancy. Were there any endocrinological abnormalities in these subjects which might at least in part explain the behavioural abnormalities?

Green: We have looked at fertility, because one report (Bibbo 1976) suggests that males exposed to diethylstilboestrol have an increased rate of infertility in adulthood. Many of our males are too young to have tested their fertility and we were not able to do semen analyses. However, the group includes a number of fathers.

Ehrhardt: I don't think anyone has systematically studied endocrine functions in adulthood in men who were prenatally exposed to progesterone or oestrogen.

Everitt: Dr Green, much of your behavioural analysis was concerned with establishing patterns of gender identity and gender role in your children, and you made a plea for experimental workers to try to assess the same things. The kinds of behavioural analyses that Dr Goy has done with his young monkeys might tell us something about gender role, but I wonder how you, as a psychiatrist faced with an experimental situation, would address the question of establishing gender *identity* in monkeys? Furthermore, how would you attempt to measure the influence of maternal and paternal behaviour on infants in that context?

Green: For gender identity, for a start, I would look at sexually dimorphic behaviour such as rough-and-tumble and threatening, chasing behaviour. I would look at interest in newborns of the species, interest in picking them up and holding them ventro-ventrally.

Everitt: Isn't that much more appropriate to role play than to identity? Is it possible to ask questions of this kind, in fact, about identity in non-human species? I believe this to be an important point for us to decide upon.

Beach: It is important to emphasize that rhesus monkeys do not cross-dress or play with dolls, and that we don't talk about girls and boys mounting each other. To be a male monkey and to be a masculine human being are two quite different things. We must not lose track of these important species differences in the *meaning* of being a male monkey as against the meaning of being a male human being. Otherwise we can be misled by similarities in hormonal effects on behaviour which is only crudely analogous.

Green: In sub-human primates do you not find social placements and troop formations? Would that be an index of identity? I understand that some primate troop formations have clear places for males and females. If a monkey misplaced himself or herself in the periphery or at the centre, would that give some indication of an atypical identity?

Beach: We must beware of reference points that *may* be superficial! If we don't fully understand the development of sex differences in even one species of primate such as the rhesus monkey, surely we are ill-advised to start jumping from one species to another.

Herbert: There are two separate issues here. One is whether you can get a monkey to reveal its identity; I would have thought you could, because the first thing to ask is how a monkey recognizes the sex of other monkeys. I am sure it can be done. You have to apply the principles of cognitive psychology to reveal identity. We know, for example, that monkey mothers look at male infants differently from female infants (see Hinde 1970), so it is possible.

The second problem was raised by Dr Beach, and I disagree with him here. He is saying that being a male monkey is different from being a male human. I don't think so. The difference lies in what we (as observers) actually look at. If we look at male monkeys, because we are interested in sexual behaviour, we look at mounting behaviour, which is one aspect of 'maleness'. We also know that rough-and-tumble play, for example, is also sexually dimorphic. In humans we don't look at sexual behaviour because overtly there is very little of it; most is inside the child's head and we can't get at that, very obviously, so we are forced to study other behaviours. So I would go the opposite way to Frank Beach and say that the similarities are greater than the differences and that the monkey model may be a good one for the human, rather than being a poor one.

Goy: Dr Beach is quite right to suggest that I don't really understand sex differences in monkeys! I don't understand them in anything. But one thing I have begun thinking about – and I notice that it is never talked about in clinical work – is what the *function* of sex differences really is. What is the adaptive significance of sex differences in behaviour, or any other character? Clearly, sex differences serve the function, at least in adulthood, of sexual attractiveness. But we never look at the development of sex differences in that way. Rough-and-tumble play in monkeys is a sexually dimorphic trait; males show a lot more of it than females do. I am convinced that there is a very similar but not exact parallel in human beings, and in my study of it in monkeys it is *not* a sex dimorphism that serves as a sexual attractant. It serves as a sorting out, separating the sissies from the boys, and it does it very rigorously and ruthlessly. It may be very important in the decision (critical for the rhesus monkey) of which males are going to be allowed to remain as the central males in the troop and which will be peripheralized and tolerated as possible portable sperm banks in case the central males get killed off. That is a sexual dimorphism that in some ways is unique and is characteristic of all the higher primates. That is the function that I believe it serves, and I think it serves the same function in human beings.

Keverne: You are talking about a particular group structure, namely a polygamous monkey society. In the gibbons, for example, a totally different social organization is found and their behaviour is quite different too. They have developed a lot of territorial traits, such as early-morning song vocalizations, and being monogamous they are much more protective towards their females. So, looking at primate sexual dimorphism in evolutionary terms, and thinking about how adaptable this is, we have to think about the kind of social organization with which we are dealing.

Herbert: Another point is that different monkey societies show very different amounts of parental behaviour by males, so that although we assume that playing with dolls and so on is a sexually dimorphic feature, it would depend on the species. The male gibbon shows a lot of parental activity, the rhesus monkey rather little.

Goy: Unquestionably, some sexually dimorphic traits are adaptive only in the sense that the division of labour for rearing the young and producing the next generation is essential and therefore males serve as protectors, females as feeders; or the opposite can happen in another species with the male as the feeder and the female as the protector.

Green: Can one study deviants within a species? Would that be part of the answer?

Goy: I think it would, but you can't identify that by abstracting a particular kind of behaviour and saying that if you are not a protector of the young you are not a male. That is not true; it is only in a certain species that if you are not a protector of the young, you are not a male.

Bancroft: Dr Green divided cross-dressing behaviour into the fetishistic transvestite type on the one hand and the transsexual on the other, illustrating this with a child transsexual. Another point to consider is that many adult transsexuals, particularly adult males, have gone through a phase of what you call fetishistic transvestite behaviour when they did not have clearly transsexual identities but were cross-dressing and behaving in a way congruent with their identity, and over a period of time their identity changes, *as if* to make it consistent with their sexual behaviour. This seems to be serving a need to keep their identities as people in some sort of order. I don't know how one would translate that into animal terms, but I believe that the majority of adult transsexuals that we see have gone through that kind of development. They give histories that tend to distort the past to make it consistent with their present; if one can follow them through one sees this change happening. They are different, I think, from the child transsexuals where this identity is assumed at a very early age.

Marteau: One of the exercises done in awareness groups is to challenge the individuals in a group as to what animal they see themselves as, or what animal they see the other members of the group as. This produces a number of projections which often help to elucidate the real feelings in the group. It strikes me that if we are going to look at the animal kingdom and try to learn something about man from it, we have to admit that as individual personalities we may each share some facets with a particular species. There may be some who function socially more like rhesus monkeys and others more like gibbons or whatever. If this is so, we shall not derive a full understanding of human behaviour by studying one species in depth. We need to examine the whole animal kingdom in breadth. Particular species, with their own particular social behaviour, may give us an insight into one element of a particular human being's behaviour. On this basis, one wonders if there is any species in the animal kingdom which displays specific homosexual behaviour or change of sexuality besides the fish: the slippery characters who are indeterminate about their sexuality but change it according to the needs of the time. It may seem unscientific to suggest that we might profit from the artistic model in this matter. A comparison of two works of art in the scientific mode might well produce some interesting facts, but a proper critique will only arise from standing well back and seeing each as a whole. This would seem to be another way in which we might derive some concepts about man from the animal kingdom.

Short: It seems to me that we are at sea on sexual dimorphism and I think we need a bit of structure to our thinking. Maybe it would help if we went back to Darwin's classical ideas on sexual selection and thought of different types of sexual selection (Short 1977): inter-sexual selection, whereby one sex makes itself attractive to the opposite sex, and intra-sexual selection whereby members of one sex, usually the males, compete with one another for access to the opposite sex. It is interesting to look at a sex behavioural characteristic and ask what its evolutionary significance is in terms of inter- or intra-sexual selection. In a highly polygamous species, like the rhesus monkey, we can expect to find enhanced intra-sexual selection between males, which will show up as increased male aggression and increased body size in the male, whereas in a monogamous primate we would expect to find little evidence of intra-sexual selection amongst males. David Abbott's paper will emphasize this in the marmoset.

Goy: Even more important than that, if clinicians could sort through *their* thoughts in those terms it would help towards bridging the gap that now exists between animal and human work.

Sachar: There is an interesting interplay here, because it is quite possible that the sex hormones like testosterone influence both dimensions, dominance and inter-sexual attractiveness.

Green: Earlier in this discussion Dr Goy described a study of rhesus monkeys in which the composition of the peer group was controlled. Has the composition of the adult group been controlled? In other words, do infants raised only by adult males or only by adult females show differential types of later behaviour?

Goy: Nothing that I can think of has a bearing on that, apart from the fact that all the young groups of monkeys raised in heterosexual groups had their mothers with them for the first year but no adult males. This procedure was followed because I wanted to avoid the interpretation that the males developed male behaviour because they had a male model to follow. So in that sense that was an abnormal environment; however, one might obtain even better 'male' behaviour if adult males were present.

Green: I was thinking of the atypical human parent model I described, and what it might do to children.

Goy: To my knowledge, such studies have not been done.

Jost: I would like to ask the clinicians whether, taking the measures of sexual behaviour that can be studied in humans, they find differences between patients seen 20 years ago, before the advent of sexual liberation, and patients now, and what change it has made to these measures.

Sachar: There was a report several years ago (Ginzberg *et al.* 1972) that clinicians were increasingly seeing men with performance anxiety – impotence connected with the worry of being unable to satisfy their female partner. In other words, women were becoming more demanding and expecting that they too should have the right to orgasm and equality, and this was producing a certain amount of cold sweat in their male partners. Many clinicians feel that they are seeing more of that but I know of no systematic studies.

Bancroft: One of the most interesting changes is in the incidence of bisexuality, particularly in women, which does seem to have increased in recent years.

Ehrhardt: There is a definite increase in bisexual experimentation among contemporary American women. This may be due to the encouragement provided by the women's movement as well as an accepting climate in women's colleges and within smaller more intimate women's groups. It is fascinating to note that that kind of bisexuality can suddenly increase because of a marked societal change. We should keep this phenomenon in mind when we assess the role of biological determinants in homosexuality.

Hertoft: There also seems to be an increase in the number of women who masturbate, and a shift in the attitude to female masturbation – a change both in women and men. Also, the increase in bisexual behaviour may be an expression of greater acceptance of female sexuality and human sexuality as such.

Ehrhardt: I wanted to say something about how little the behaviour of children is affected by current societal changes. For instance, there appears to be no immediate effect on a child if her mother alters her role as a full-time homemaker to include pursuing a career. The women's movement seems to have had little or no effect in this area as yet (A. A. Ehrhardt, S. E. Ince & H. F. L. Meyer-Bahlburg, in preparation 1978). I have just finished interviewing 70 girls between ages 8 and 12, a middle-class group, where a number of mothers were doctors or lawyers. The children were very traditional in their role play, in their expectation of what they wanted to be as adults. This emphasizes several things: one is that children may have to dichotomize gender role behaviour more than adults in order to identify clearly with one or the other sex; the other, beautifully illustrated by Dr Goy and too often ignored, is the importance of peer groups. The assumption has been that parents are the major model figures for behaviour and this idea has been promoted by many theories, including psychoanalytic ones. But the influence of the peer group may turn out to be much more important than that of the parents. This may apply to the aetiology of homosexuality, too. The assumption that parents, just because they are homosexual, produce homosexual children, is a very naive one.

Hertoft: Dr Green has photographs of small boys learning to walk in their mother's shoes. Peer group intervention cannot explain such behaviour.

Bancroft: That is not necessarily true; the peer group could have a very important role in how that sort of gender confusion could develop.

Hertoft: Yes, if it happens when the children are 3–4 years old, but these children were $1^1/_2$ years old. Of course I accept the influence of the peer group, but as far as I can see peer group influence does not explain the special effeminate behaviour of $1^1/_2$-year-old children.

Marteau: But the peer group seems to reject the deviant?

Hertoft: Yes, but that happens a bit later on.

Ehrhardt: It is very often already as early as that.

Nieschlag: I would like to ask Dr Goy about the sexual orientation of rhesus monkeys in regard to the concentrations of circulating androgens. In humans there are varying reports of androgen and oestrogen concentrations in homosexuals; in the rhesus monkey, with marked seasonality and varying testicular production of testosterone throughout the year, do you see any changes in sexual orientation correlated with plasma testosterone levels? Is there a higher level of homosexual orientation at any season of the year?

Goy: Seasonal changes have not been studied from that point of view. The general impression one obtains from looking at a troop of monkeys under seasonal influences is that both sexes during the non-breeding season simply become sexually inactive and sexually indifferent. They don't change their preferred partners necessarily or switch roles at that time. One has always to bear in mind, however, that both homosexual and heterosexual mounting behaviour are displayed by both sexes throughout the year, and such behaviour is important to inter-individual bonding and thereby to the cohesiveness of the troop.

References

BIBBO, M. (1976) DES: Potential risks for men too. *Med. World News,* January 26th

ERWIN, J. & MAPLE, T. (1976) Ambisexual behaviour with male–male anal penetration in male rhesus monkeys. *Arch. Sex. Behav. 5,* 9–14

GINZBERG, G. L., FROSCH, W. A. & SHAPIRO, T. (1972) The new impotence. *Arch. Gen. Psychiatr. 26,* 218–220

HINDE, R. A. (1970) *Animal Behaviour: A Synthesis of Ethology and Comparative Psychology* (2nd edn.), McGraw-Hill, New York

SHORT, R. V. (1977) Sexual selection and the descent of man, in *Reproduction and Evolution* (Calaby, J. H. & Tyndale-Biscoe, C. H., eds.) *(4th Int. Symp. on Comparative Biology of Reproduction),* pp. 3–19, Australian Academy of Sciences, Canberra

Hormones and sexual differentiation of the brain

G. DÖRNER

Institute of Experimental Endocrinology, Humboldt-University, Berlin, GDR

Abstract Male rats castrated on the first day of life exhibited predominantly heterotypical (homosexual) behaviour after androgen substitution in adulthood. In addition, an increased evocability of a positive feedback effect of oestrogen was observed in such genetic males. In homosexual men, an increased evocability of a positive oestrogen feedback on luteinizing hormone (LH) secretion was also found as compared to heterosexual men. These findings suggest that male homosexuality may be based, at least in part, on androgen deficiency during a critical period of brain differentiation. In addition, we have found significantly increased plasma follicle-stimulating hormone (FSH) and LH levels associated with decreased plasma free testosterone levels in homosexual men, but only in effeminate homosexuals. In view of these data, sexual deviations in the human may be based, at least in part, on discrepancies between the genetic sex and a sex-specific sex-hormone level during brain differentiation in prenatal life. Methods were therefore developed for determining genetic sex and sex-specific sex-hormone levels in amniotic fluid, in order to detect and possibly correct such discrepancies.

Sex hormone-dependent brain differentiation may be mediated, at least in part, by neurotransmitters, which may be regarded as local hormones of the brain. Interestingly enough, we have found permanent abnormalities of mating and other non-mating behaviour associated with permanent structural and chemical alterations in discrete brain regions of rats after neonatal treatment with psychotropic drugs known to affect neurotransmitter metabolism in the brain. Therefore, changes in neurotransmitter concentrations and/or turnover rates induced by psychosocial influences as well as by systemic hormones (particularly by sex hormones), when occurring during differentiation and maturation of the brain, may permanently affect sexual behaviour, sexual orientation and gender role behaviour throughout life.

NEUROENDOCRINE CONTROL OF THE GONADS AND SEXUAL BEHAVIOUR

The gonadotropic function of the pituitary gland was first demonstrated by Aschner (1912), who observed gonadal atrophy in dogs after hypophysectomy. Subsequently the gonadotropins were discovered by Aschheim & Zondek (1927) in our laboratories and simultaneously by Smith & Engle (1927) in America.

In 1932 Hohlweg & Junkmann envisaged a so-called sex centre in the central nervous system as controller of hypophyseal gonadotropic functions. Later Barraclough & Gorski (1961) distinguished a so-called cyclic sex centre in rats, located in the preoptic hypothalamic region and regulating cyclic gonadotropin secretion in females, and a so-called tonic sex centre located in the hypothalamic ventromedial arcuate region responsible for tonic gonadotropin secretion in both sexes. Recent data suggest that structures of the limbic system, especially of the amygdala, are also involved in cyclic gonadotropin release (Kawakami & Terasawa 1974; Döcke *et al.* 1975).

Our present knowledge of the hypothalamo–hypophyseal–gonadal system may be summarized as follows. In the medial basal hypothalamus a gonadotropin-releasing hormone (Schally *et al.* 1971) is secreted under the influence of neurotransmitters (Kamberi 1974; Sawyer 1975). It is transported by the hypothalamo-hypophyseal portal vessels to the anterior pituitary, stimulating there the secretion of gonadotropins. The sex hormones exert either only an inhibitory (negative) or also a stimulatory (positive) feedback effect on gonadotropin secretion, depending on sex hormone concentrations during a critical period in the differentiation period of the brain and in the postpubertal functional period as well (Dörner 1976*a*).

Finally, sex hormones can sensitize hypothalamic mating centres to sensory stimulation which reaches the diencephalon by pathways from the cerebral cortex and/or subcortex mediated by neurotransmitters (Dörner 1972, 1976*a*). In 1941, Brookhart & Dey demonstrated by means of intrahypothalamic lesions in guinea-pigs a central nervous mating centre responsible for sexual behaviour. In 1968–1969, we distinguished a so-called male mating centre located in the preoptic anterior hypothalamic area and a female centre located in the hypothalamic ventromedial nuclear region (Dörner *et al.* 1968*a*, 1969). In rats of either sex, predominantly male or female sexual behaviour could be selectively stimulated or abolished either by intrahypothalamic implants of sex hormones or by electrolytic lesions in these hypothalamic regions. Similar findings were meanwhile described by other authors (Nadler 1972; Powers 1972; Carrer *et al.* 1973/74; Barfield & Chen 1977).

We also found that the decrease in female sexual behaviour after bilateral or even unilateral hypothalamic lesions of the ventromedial nuclear region – that is, of the so-called female centre – was associated with a simultaneous increase in male behaviour in rats (Dörner *et al.* 1968*b*, 1975*a*). Similar findings were obtained in homosexual men, namely decreased female and increased male sexual behaviour after unilateral lesion of the ventromedial nucleus (Roeder & Müller 1969; Müller *et al.* 1974; Dieckmann & Hassler 1975). On the other hand, lesions of the medial preoptic area – that is, of the so-called male centre – resulted in decreased male and increased female behaviour in rats (Powers & Valenstein 1972).

The following conclusions may therefore be drawn. Different neuronal reflex circuits are responsible for male and female sexual behaviour. In the medial preoptic anterior hypothalamic area a sex hormone-sensitive control centre is located belonging to a neuronal reflex circuit responsible for male behaviour, whereas in the ventromedial nuclear region a sex hormone-sensitive control centre is located belonging to a neuronal reflex circuit regulating female behaviour. Some antagonistic interrelationships appear to exist between these male and female mating centres (Dörner 1976*a*).

SEX HORMONE-DEPENDENT DIFFERENTIATION OF SEXUAL BEHAVIOUR

As early as 1936 Pfeiffer observed that in rats, independent of the genetic sex, the lack of testes during a critical neonatal differentiation phase resulted in cyclic release of gonadotropin from the pituitary, whereas the presence of testes during this critical phase gave rise to tonic gonadotropin secretion by the pituitary in later life. In 1938, Vera Dantchakoff reported a remarkable observation on sex hormone-dependent brain differentiation and sexual behaviour which was later confirmed by Phoenix and co-workers (Phoenix *et al.* 1959). Female guinea-pigs, exposed to androgens prenatally, showed increased male and decreased female behaviour in adulthood. On the basis of these results, Phoenix *et al.* distinguished an early organization period and a postpubertal activation period.

Adult females of other species, such as rats (Barraclough & Gorski 1961; Dörner 1972), golden hamsters (Carter *et al.* 1972; Swanson *et al.* 1974) and rhesus monkeys (Eaton *et al.* 1973), were then also found to exhibit predominantly masculine behavioural patterns in adulthood after androgen administration during critical organization periods. On the other hand, Grady & Phoenix (1963) and Harris (1964) reported that male rats orchiectomized shortly after birth showed especially strong female sexual behaviour when treated with oestrogen in adulthood. Similar findings were obtained in adult male rats which had been treated with antiandrogen drugs during perinatal life (Neumann *et al.* 1967). All these observations pointed to the significance of the sex hormone level during a critical differentiation phase for the development of sexual behaviour.

OUR OWN INVESTIGATIONS ON SEX HORMONE-DEPENDENT BRAIN DIFFERENTIATION

In the last decade the following findings have been obtained in our laboratories on sex hormone-dependent brain differentiation and sexual behaviour (Dörner 1976*a*):

1. Male rats castrated on the first day of life showed predominantly heterotypical behaviour after androgen substitution in adulthood (Dörner 1967, 1969, 1970, 1972). In other words, genetic males exposed to a temporary androgen deficiency during the hypothalamic organization period, but to normal or approximately normal androgen levels in adulthood, were sexually excited preferentially by partners of the same sex.
2. These neuroendocrine-conditioned, female-like behavioural patterns could be prevented by androgens administered during the critical hypothalamic differentiation period (Dörner *et al.* 1968*b*).
3. The higher the androgen level during the hypothalamic differentiation phase, the stronger was the male and the weaker the female sexual behaviour during the postpubertal functional phase, irrespective of the genetic sex. We even observed a complete inversion of sexual behaviour in male and female rats after androgen deficiency in males and androgen excess in females during the hypothalamic differentiation period. According to these findings a neuroendocrine predisposition for primary hypo-, bi- and homosexuality may be based on different degrees of androgen deficiency in males and androgen excess in females during sex-specific brain differentiation (Dörner 1969, 1970).
4. The higher the androgen level during the critical hypothalamic differentiation period, the smaller were the nuclear volumes of the neurons in specific hypothalamic regions regulating sexual behaviour and/or gonadotropin secretion as well as in the medial amygdala, throughout life (Dörner & Staudt 1968, 1969; Staudt & Dörner 1976).
5. In male rats castrated on the first day of life, a strong positive oestrogen feedback effect on luteinizing hormone (LH) secretion (Hohlweg effect) could be induced, similar to that obtainable in normal females, but it could not be induced in males castrated on the 14th day of life or in neonatally androgenized females (Dörner & Döcke 1964; Döcke & Dörner 1966). From these findings it appears that a strong positive oestrogen feedback effect can only be evoked in adulthood if there was a low androgen level during brain differentiation.
6. More recently we have noted the following correlations between sex hormone levels during the hypothalamic differentiation and/or functional periods, on the one hand, and the evocability of a positive oestrogen

feedback effect on LH secretion on the other (see Fig. 1). After a single injection of oestrogen in postpubertally castrated and oestrogen-primed female rats a distinct surge of LH secretion was evoked, while castrated and androgen-primed females displayed a diminished and delayed surge of LH secretion. On the other hand, postpubertally castrated and oestrogen-primed male rats exhibited only a slight, but significant surge of LH secretion, whereas castrated and androgen-primed males did not show any surge of LH secretion after oestrogen injection. These findings suggest that the evocability of a positive oestrogen feedback action on LH secretion

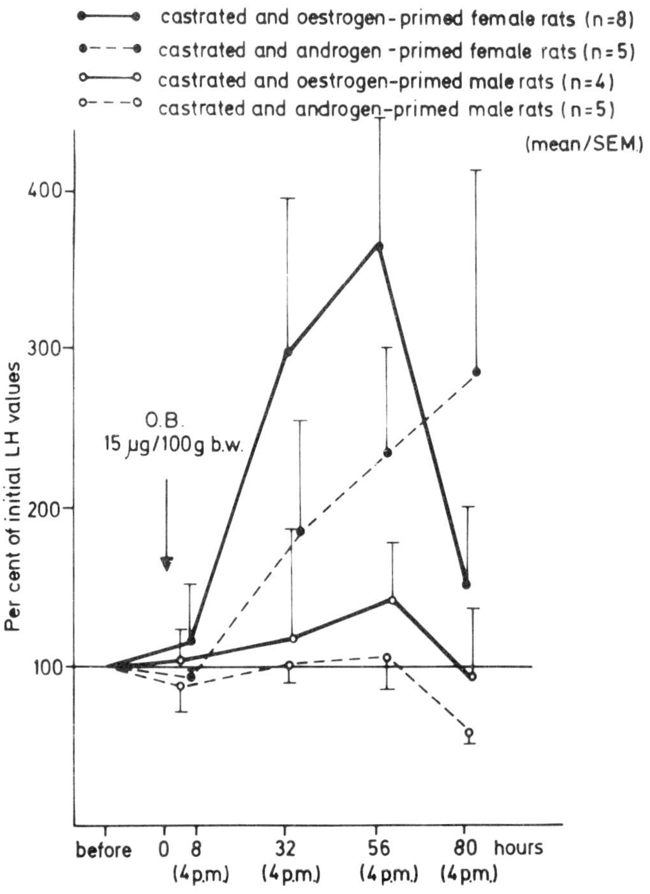

FIG. 1. Serum LH response to a subcutaneous injection of oestradiol benzoate (15 μg/100 g body wt.) expressed as a percentage of the mean initial LH values in postpubertally castrated and oestrogen- or androgen-primed female and male rats (means ± S.E.M.).

depends on the sex hormone level during the critical hypothalamic differentiation phase and the postpubertal priming phase as well.

As shown in Fig. 2, a positive oestrogen feedback effect could also be elicited in intact homosexual men, in contrast to intact heterosexual and bisexual men (Dörner *et al.* 1972, 1975*c*). This finding suggests that homosexual men may possess—at least in part—a predominantly female-differentiated brain. On the other hand, in postpubertally castrated and oestrogen-primed men, a slight positive oestrogen feedback effect could be elicited (Dörner *et al.* 1975*b*), as in postpubertally castrated and oestrogen-primed rhesus monkeys (Knobil 1974).

7. More recently, the basal plasma levels of free and total testosterone as well as of follicle-stimulating hormone (FSH) and LH have been measured in homosexual and heterosexual men (Rohde *et al.* 1977). As shown in Fig. 3, significantly lower levels of free plasma testosterone were found in effeminate homosexuals than in heterosexual men. In contrast to the free testosterone levels, no significant difference in total plasma testosterone levels was observed between homosexual and heterosexual males (Fig. 4).

As shown in Fig. 5, significantly higher plasma concentrations of FSH were found in homosexual males, but only in effeminate homosexual males and transsexual males, than in heterosexual males. Significantly higher

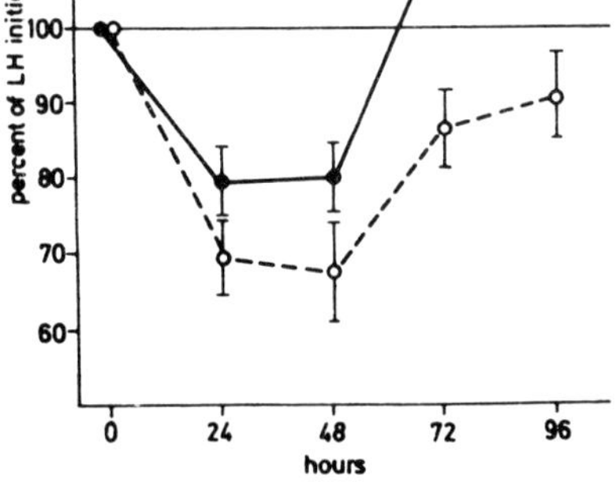

FIG. 2. Serum LH response to an intravenous oestrogen injection expressed as a percentage of the mean initial LH values in homosexual and hetero- or bisexual men.

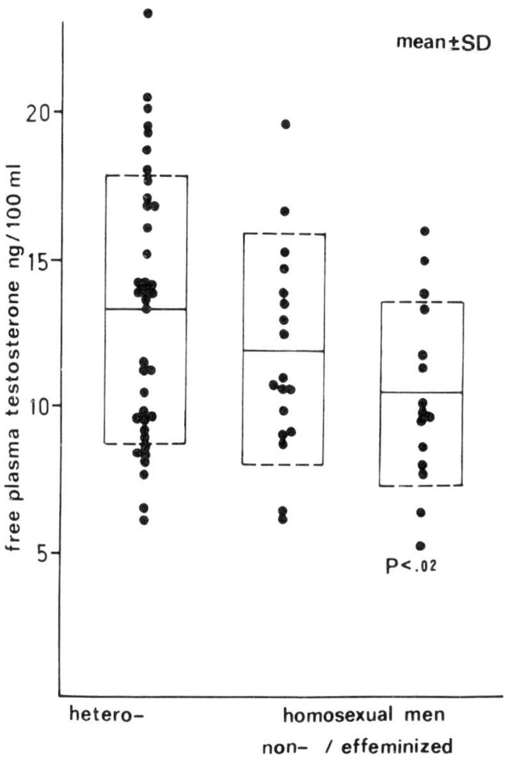

FIG. 3. Free plasma testosterone concentrations in heterosexual men and in non-effeminate and effeminate homosexuals.

plasma concentrations of LH were also observed in homosexual males, particularly in effeminate homosexuals, and in transsexual males, than in heterosexual males (Fig. 6).

In view of our experimental and clinical data, the following hypothesis may be deduced. An androgen deficiency in genetic males during a critical period of brain organization gives rise to predominantly female differentiation of the brain. This androgen deficiency in early life can be largely compensated by increased hypophyseal gonadotropin secretion in later life. Thus, the predominantly female-differentiated brain is postpubertally activated by an approximately normal androgen level, leading to homosexual behaviour.

8. In genetic females, the results of animal experiments in various species, supported by some clinical findings, suggest that androgen excess during a

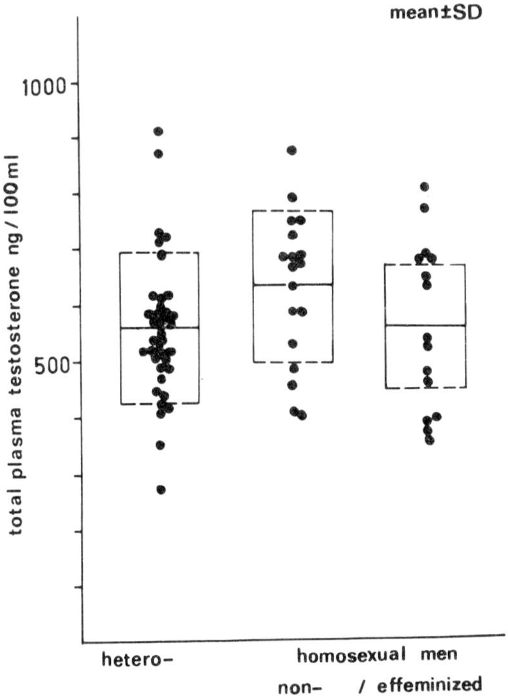

FIG. 4. Total plasma testosterone concentrations in heterosexual men and non-effeminate and effeminate homosexuals.

critical period of brain differentiation can lead to a predisposition to hypo-, bi- or even homosexual behaviour in postpuberal life. In female rats, unphysiologically high androgen and/or oestrogen levels during the hypothalamic differentiation period caused anovulatory sterility and/or a neuroendocrine predisposition to female hypo-, bi- or homosexuality (Dörner 1971*a*; Dörner & Hinz 1972). In this context it should be mentioned that androgens are converted to oestrogens, at least in part, by the neural tissue of fetal and neonatal rats (Reddy *et al.* 1974). A complete masculinization of sexual behaviour in female animals was observed after combined pre- and postnatal androgen treatment (Dörner 1968; Ward 1969; Sachs & Pollak 1973).

9. As demonstrated in Fig. 7, we have observed a slight increase in the plasma testosterone level in lesbian women. However, a significant increase was only found in those (nine out of 21) lesbian females showing some virilism (Dörner *et al.*, unpublished data). Similar findings were obtained by Griffith *et al.* (1974).

Recently, Money & Schwartz (1977) reported on 17 young women with the adrenogenital syndrome (congenital adrenal hyperplasia) who were diagnosed and hormonally corrected from early infancy. They were delayed in establishing dating, romantic and erotic interests. Most of all, those who were older showed an increased rate of awareness of bisexuality in fantasy, with or without actual experience. These findings were also attributed to a possible delayed effect of excess androgenization on the fetal central nervous system.

In view of the described data, sexual deviations in the human may be based, at least in part, on discrepancies between the genetic sex and a sex-specific sex-hormone level during brain differentiation. Therefore, a genuine prophylaxis may become possible, if it is desirable at all, in the future by the prevention of such discrepancies during the period of sexual differentiation of the brain.

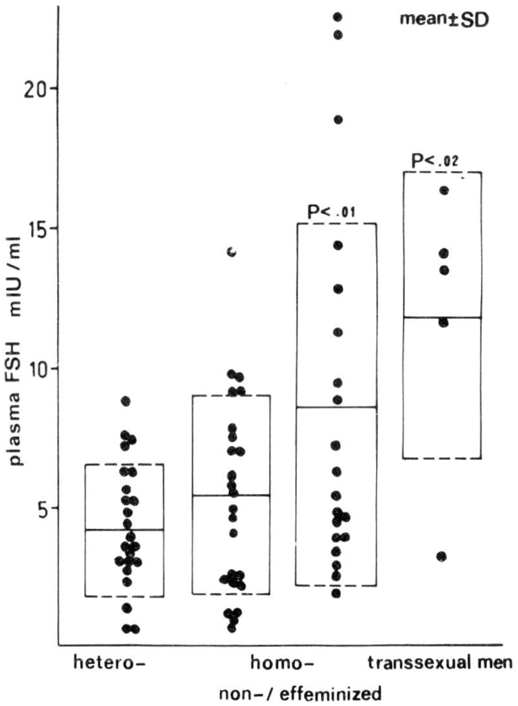

FIG. 5. Plasma FSH concentrations in heterosexual men, non-effeminate or effeminate homosexuals, and transsexual men.

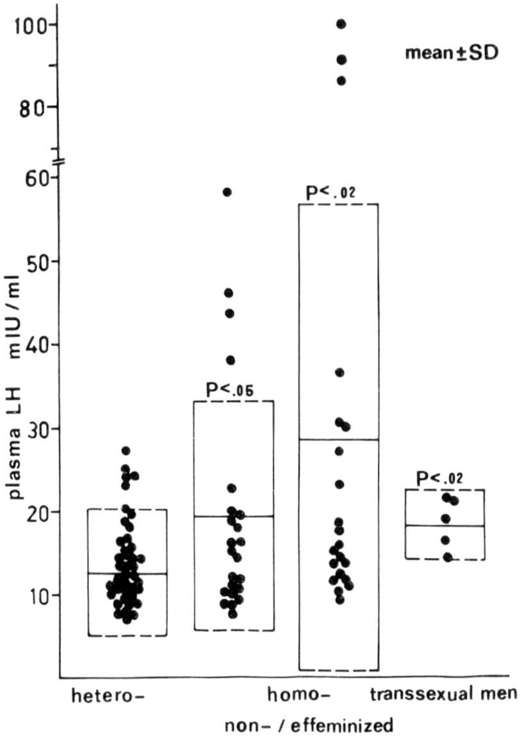

FIG. 6. Plasma LH concentrations in heterosexual men, non-effeminate and effeminate homosexuals, and transsexual men.

Three preconditions for this aim have already been achieved:

1. Our comparative studies of the morphogenesis of the hypothalamus in 84 human fetuses and hundreds of rats have led to the conclusion that the critical period of sex-specific brain differentiation occurs in the human between the fourth and seventh months of fetal life (Dörner & Staudt 1972).
2. A simple and reliable method for the prenatal diagnosis of genetic sex was developed using fluorescence microscopy of amniotic fluid cells (Dörner *et al.* 1971*b*).
3. As shown in Fig. 8, levels of testosterone glucuronide (TG) and also of unconjugated testosterone were found to be significantly increased and FSH levels significantly decreased in the amniotic fluid of male fetuses as compared to that of female fetuses between the 16th and 26th week of pregnancy (Dörner 1972, 1976*a*; Clements *et al.* 1976; Dörner *et al.* 1977*b*).

Therefore, the examination of amniotic fluids for genetic defects should be supplemented in the future by the determination of hormone levels in order to detect abnormalities that might lead to maldifferentiation, especially of the brain; this is all the more important as hormone-induced teratogenic effects may be accessible to preventive therapy.

In conclusion, unphysiological concentrations of hormones (e.g. of sex hormones) occurring during brain differentiation can act as 'teratogens'.

They can lead to permanent disorders of mating and non-mating behaviour associated with permanent structural alterations in discrete regions of the brain (Dörner & Staudt 1968, 1969; Raisman & Field 1971).

NEUROTRANSMITTERS AS ENVIRONMENT-DEPENDENT ACTIVATORS (OR INHIBITORS) AND ORGANIZERS OF THE BRAIN

In my opinion, hormones may be defined as chemical messengers that are produced in specific cells and exert biological effects on other cells of the same

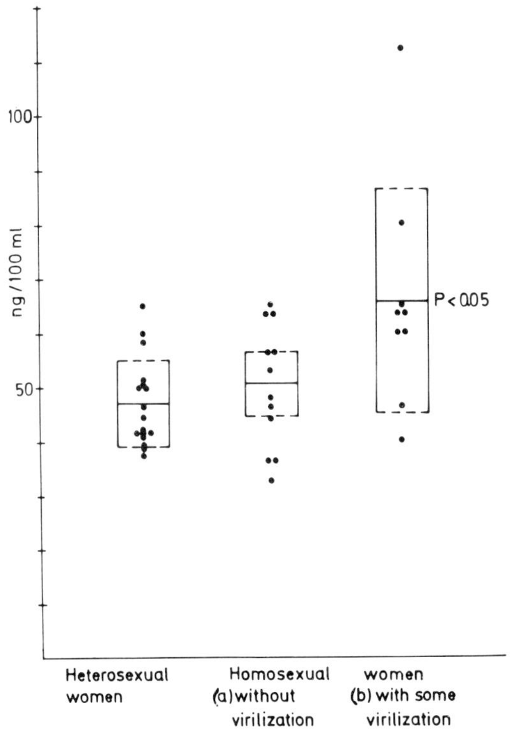

FIG. 7. Total plasma testosterone concentrations in heterosexual women and homosexual women with or without some virilization.

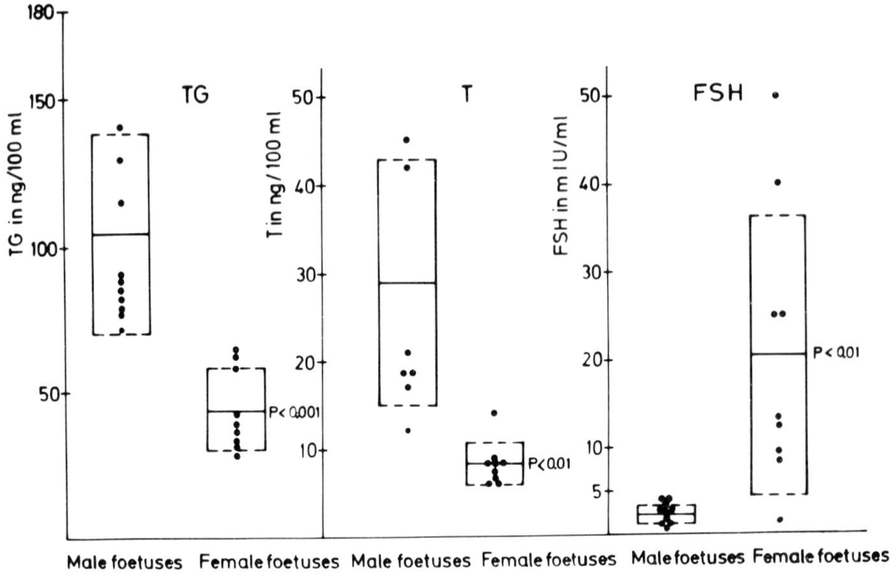

FIG. 8. Testosterone glucuronide (TG), testosterone (T) and FSH levels in amniotic fluids of male and female fetuses between weeks 15 and 26 of pregnancy (means ± S.D.).

organism by acting either locally—that is, as local hormones—or on distant target cells—that is, as blood-borne or systemic hormones. On this definition neurotransmitters may be regarded as local hormones of the brain and a strict differentiation between neurotransmitters and neurohormones appears to be no longer justified.

In recent years it has been demonstrated that neurotransmitters are also responsible for the control of sexual behaviour. Male behaviour was found to be stimulated by acetylcholine and β-adrenergic activators, but inhibited by serotonin and α-adrenergic activators (Gessa & Tagliamonte 1975; Soulairac & Soulairac 1975). On the other hand, female behaviour was reported to be stimulated by noradrenaline, but inhibited by serotonin, dopamine and adrenaline (Everitt *et al.* 1975; Crowley *et al.* 1976).

Fascinatingly enough, such neurotransmitters appear to represent not only temporary activators or inhibitors, but also organizers of the brain. Most recently, we have obtained some experimental data suggesting that the quantity of neurotransmitters and/or their turnover rate during brain differentiation is able to predetermine the quality—that is, the reactivity—of central nervous controllers throughout life (Dörner 1976*a*; Dörner *et al.* 1976, 1977*a, c*).

Rats were treated with the monoamine oxidase inhibitor pargyline, the monoamine depletor reserpine or the acetylcholine esterase inhibitor pyridostigmine during the first two weeks of life. These animals showed significant permanent changes, not only in their sexual behaviour but also in conditioned avoidance behaviour, emotional reactivity and exploratory activity, throughout life.

As demonstrated in Fig. 9, male sexual activity was permanently decreased in males treated neonatally with pargyline or reserpine, but permanently increased in those treated with pyridostigmine. Male sexual activity was also increased in adult male rats treated neonatally with *p*-chlorophenylalanine (unpublished data).

Females treated neonatally with pargyline also showed a permanent decrease, and those given pyridostigmine a permanent significant increase, in male mounting behaviour (Fig. 10).

The permanent behavioural changes produced by psychotropic drugs administered during the period of brain differentiation were associated with permanent structural and biochemical changes in specific brain regions (Dörner *et al.* 1977*c*). In the medial and central amygdalar regions, highly significantly increased nuclear volumes of the nerve cells were found in rats treated neonatally with reserpine and even more markedly in adult males treated neonatally with pargyline. Nuclear structures in the pargyline-treated males were more like those of control females than of control males. Furthermore, significantly decreased concentrations of noradrenaline

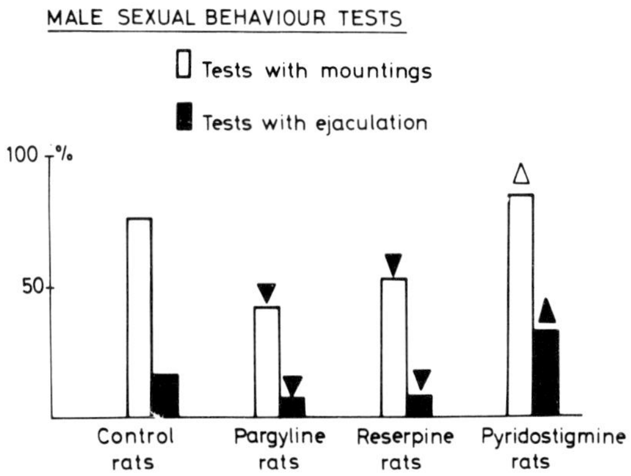

FIG. 9. Male sexual behaviour in juvenile and adult male rats after treatment with pargyline, reserpine or pyridostigmine during the first two weeks of life. Male sexuality was expressed as a percentage of positive tests with mountings and ejaculation on exposure to castrated and oestrogen-treated female rats. ▼, significantly decreased and ▲, significantly increased as compared to the controls (▼ and ▲, $P < 0.001$; Δ, $P < 0.05$).

and dopamine were found in the hypothalamus of adult rats treated neonatally with pargyline.

According to these data, the unphysiological concentrations and/or turnover rates of neurotransmitters apparently produced by psychotropic drugs during brain differentiation can act as teratogens. Similar teratogenic effects may be induced by the unphysiological neurotransmitter concentrations and/or turnover rates produced by abnormal levels of systemic hormones (e.g. sex hormones) as well as by abnormal psychosocial conditions during brain differentiation. Hence, the effects of systemic hormones and psychosocial influences on the differentiation and functioning of the brain appear to represent supplements rather than alternatives, since they are both mediated by neurotransmitters.

As outlined in Fig. 11, neurotransmitters appear to represent common mediators of systemic hormones, of the external environment and of nutritionally dependent metabolic variables equally for the differentiation, maturation and functioning of the brain. Thus psychosomatic interrelationships may become more conceivable and psychosomatic disturbances more accessible to preventive therapy.

Most recently, we have investigated the possible influence of qualitative and

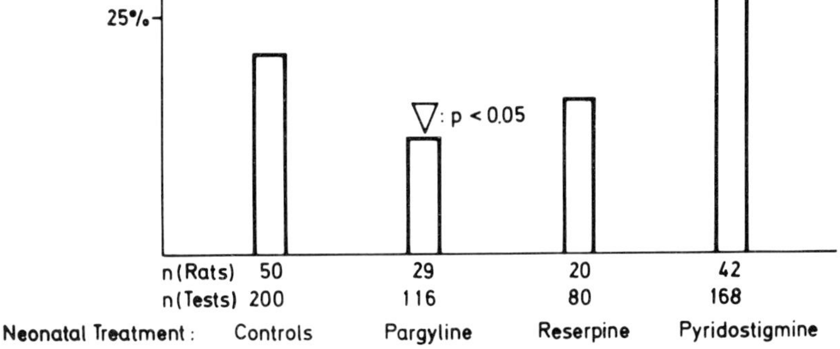

FIG. 10. Male sexual behaviour in adult female rats after treatment with pargyline, reserpine or pyridostigmine during the first two weeks of life. Male sexuality was expressed as a percentage of positive tests with mountings on exposure to castrated and oestrogen-treated female rats.

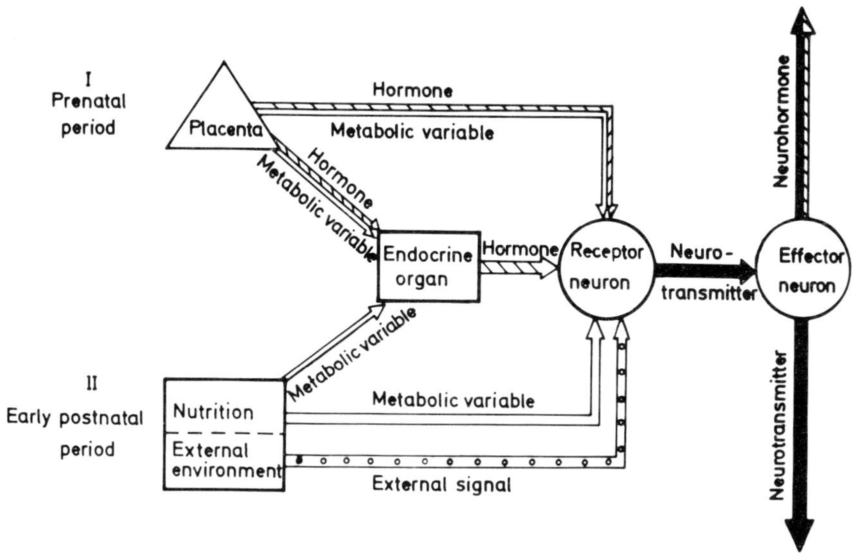

FIG. 11. Schematic representation of possible effects of systemic hormones, metabolic variables and external environmental signals on brain differentiation mediated by neurotransmitters and permanently affecting fundamental processes such as reproduction, metabolism and/or information-processing.

quantitative dysnutrition in early postnatal life on mental, psychic and physical achievements in later life. Some exciting findings have been obtained (Dörner & Grychtolik 1978). Human subjects who were purely bottle-fed during the first three months of life displayed significantly decreased mental, psychic and physical achievements as well as decreased learning capacity and social adaptability at 16 years of age when compared to subjects of similar age who were breast-fed (Fig. 12). Furthermore, boys who were artificially overfed with calorie- and protein-rich formulas during the first three months of life also showed significantly decreased mental, psychic and physical achievements and decreased learning capacity at 16 years of age when compared to boys who were not overfed during the first three months (Fig. 13). Thus, qualitative as well as quantitative dysnutrition in early postnatal life can produce long-lasting ill-effects on the mental, psychic and physical capacities and performance in the human. Similar harmful effects of over-feeding in the perinatal period have been obtained independently in animal experiments (Ryan 1977; Coupain *et al.* 1977).

In my opinion, many diseases affecting fundamental processes such as reproduction, metabolism and information-processing, previously called idiopathic, primary, essential, cryptogenic, endogenous or genuine, are based on environment-dependent disturbances of the differentiation and maturation of the neuroendocrine system. Such adaptational diseases can be prevented, at least in part, by improving the external and or internal environment, particularly during critical differentiation and maturation phases of the neuroendocrine system. Hence, I suggest that teratomorphology, which was founded in the last century, must now be supplemented by teratophysiology and teratopsychology.

Neurotransmitters may thus represent the key factors for the environment-dependent organization of the brain. The quantity of neurotransmitters, and/or their turnover rate during brain differentiation, appear to affect the quality – that is, the set points and tolerance ranges – of neuroendocrine feedback control systems regulating information-processing, metabolism and reproduction throughout life.

As demonstrated in Fig. 14, psychosomatic interrelationships are mediated by neurotransmitters in the brain. Thus psychosocial influences as well as

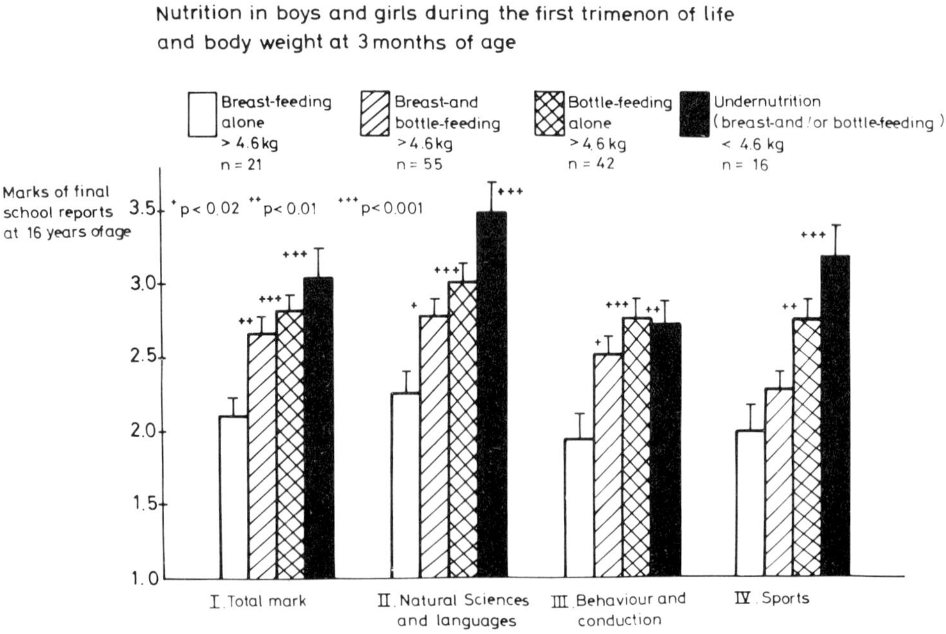

FIG. 12. The influence of breast-and bottle-feeding during the first three months of life on mental, psychic and physical achievements at 16 years of age (means ± S.E.M. of school marks: 1, very good; 2, good; 3, satisfactory; 4, pass; 5, unsatisfactory).

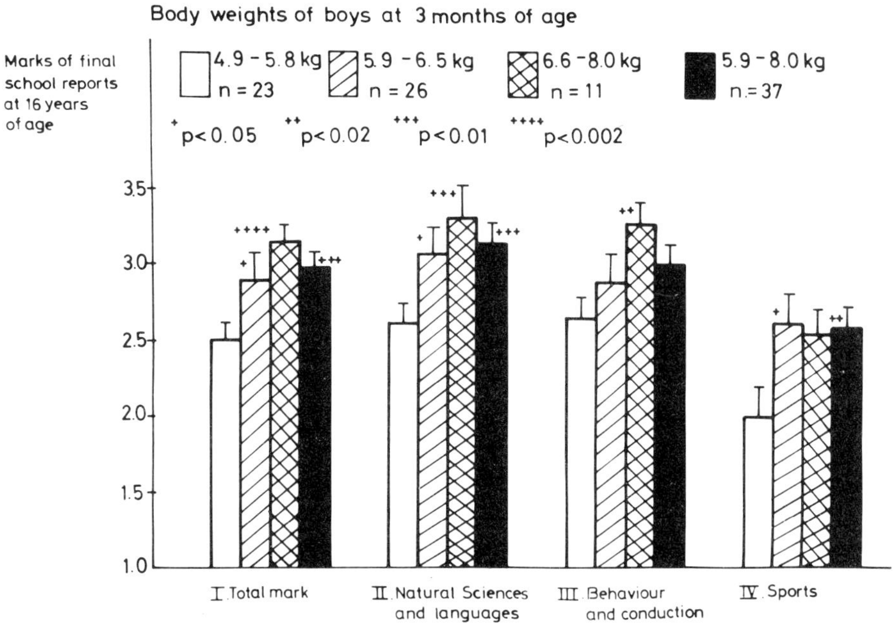

FIG. 13. The influence of perinatal over-nutrition in boys on mental, psychic and physical achievements at 16 years of age (means ± S.E.M. of school marks: 1, very good; 2, good; 3, satisfactory; 4, pass; 5, unsatisfactory).

nutritionally dependent metabolic variables or hormones can affect neurotransmitter metabolism, resulting in alterations in information-processing, metabolism and/or reproduction. These fundamental processes of life influence, in turn, psychosocial conditions and the concentrations of metabolic variables and hormones. Hence, psychosomatic interrelationships are controlled by closed-loop neuroendocrine systems that are combined with each other by neurotransmitter metabolism in the brain. Thus it is also conceivable that changes in the external environment, particularly in psychosocial conditions, as well as changes in the internal environment—that is, in metabolic variables and hormones—can produce alterations in information-processing, metabolism and reproduction as well. That is to say, 'crossing-over' reactions between these systems are possible. Such environmentally dependent effects on fundamental processes are mostly reversible when they take place during adulthood by temporarily affecting gene expression in neurons, but are more or less irreversible when they occur during critical differentiation and maturation periods of the brain by affecting gene expressibility in neurons for the entire life of the individual.

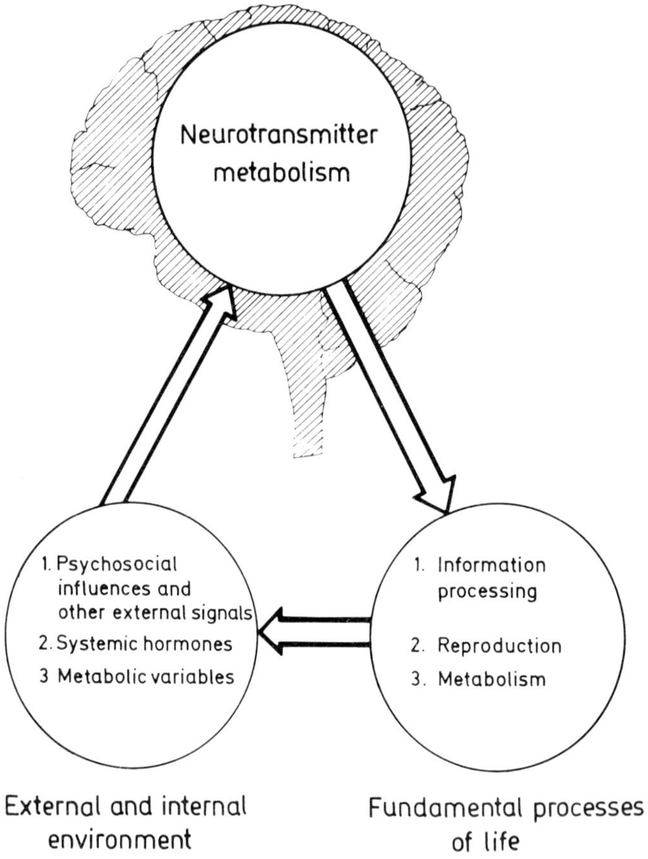

FIG. 14. Psychosomatic interrelationships mediated by neurotransmitters in the brain.

References

ASCHHEIM, S. & ZONDEK, B. (1927) Hypophysenvorderlappenhormon und Schwangerenhormon im Harm von Schwangeren. *Klin. Wochenschr. 6,* 1322

ASCHNER, B. (1912) Über die Beziehungen zwischen Hypophysis und Genitale. *Arch. Gynäkol. 97,* 200-228

BARFIELD, R. J. & CHEN, J. J. (1977) Activation of estrous behaviour in ovariectomized rats by intracerebral implants of estradiol benzoate. *Endocrinology, 101,* 1716–1725

BARRACLOUGH, C. A. & GORSKI, R. A. (1961) Evidence that the hypothalamus is responsible for androgen-induced sterility in the female rat. *Endocrinology 68,* 68–70

BROOKHART, J. M. & DEY, F. L. (1941) Reduction of sexual behaviour in male guinea pigs by hypothalamic lesions. *Am. J. Physiol. 133,* 551–554

CARRER, H., ASCH, G. & ARON, C. (1973/74) New facts concerning the role played by the ventromedial nucleus in the control of estrous cycle duration and sexual receptivity in the rat. *Neuroendocrinology 13,* 129–138

CARTER, C. S., CLEMENS, L. G. & HOEKEMA, D. J. (1972) Neonatal androgen and adult sexual behaviour in the golden hamster. *Physiol. Behav. 9,* 89–95

CLEMENTS, J. A., REYES, F. I., WINTER, J. S. D. & FAIMAN, C. (1976) Studies on human sexual development. III. Fetal pituitary and serum, and amniotic fluid concentrations of LH, CG, and FSH. *J. Clin. Endocrinol. Metab. 42,* 9–19

COUPAIN, J. G., TYSBIR, R. S. & BEECHER, G. R. (1977) Influence of altering dietary protein levels during early development of the rat on the activity of several brain enzymes. *J. Nutr. 107,* 1102–1113

CROWLEY, W. R., FEDER, H. H. & MORIN, L. P. (1976) Role of monoamines in sexual behaviour of the female guinea pig. *Pharmacol. Biochem. Behav. 4,* 67–71

DANTCHAKOFF, V. (1938) Rôle des hormones dans la manifestation des instincts sexuels. *C. R. Hebd. Séances Acad. Sci. (Paris) 206,* 945–947

DIECKMANN, G. & HASSLER, R. (1975) Unilateral hypothalamotomy in sexual delinquents. Report on six cases. *Confinia Neurologica 37,* 177–186

DÖCKE, F. & DÖRNER, G. (1966) Tierexperimentelle Untersuchungen zur Ovulationsauslösung mit Gonadotropinen und Östrogenen. 4. Mittl., Zur neurohormonalen Regulation der Ovulation. *Zbl. Gynäkol. 88,* 273–282

DÖCKE, F., SMOLLICH, A., ROHDE, W., OKRASA, R. & DÖRNER, G. (1975) Studies on extrahypophyseal sites of estrogen action in the induction of ovulation in rats. *Endokrinologie 65,* 274–287

DÖRNER, G. (1967) Tierexperimentelle Untersuchungen zur Frage einer hormonalen Pathogenese der Homosexualität. *Acta Biol. Med. Ger. 19,* 569–584

DÖRNER, G. (1968) Hormonal induction and prevention of female homosexuality. *J. Endocrinol. 42,* 163–164

DÖRNER, G. (1969) Zur Frage einer neuroendokrinen Pathogenese, Prophylaxe und Therapie angeborener Sexualdeviationen. *Dtsch. Med. Wochenschr. 94,* 390–396

DÖRNER, G. (1970) The influence of sex hormones during the hypothalamic differentiation and maturation phases on gonadal function and sexual behaviour during the hypothalamic functional phase. *Endokrinologie 56,* 280–291

DÖRNER, G. (1972) *Sexualhormonabhängige Gehirndifferenzierung und Sexualität,* Gustav Fischer, Jena and Springer, Vienna & New York

DÖRNER, G. (1976*a*) *Hormones and Brain Differentiation,* Elsevier, Amsterdam, Oxford & New York

DÖRNER, G. (1976*b*) Further evidence of permanent behavioural changes in rats treated neonatally with neurodrugs. *Endokrinologie 68,* 345–348

DÖRNER, G. & DÖCKE, F. (1964) Sex-specific reaction of the hypothalamo-hypophysial system of rats. *J. Endocrinol. 30,* 265–266

DÖRNER, G. & HINZ, G. (1972) Neuroendokrin bedingte Prädisposition für weibliche Homosexualität bei erhaltener zyklischer Ovarialfunktion. *Endokrinologie 59,* 48–52

DÖRNER, G. & GRYCHTOLIK, H. (1978) Long-lasting ill-effects of neonatal qualitative and/or quantitative dysnutrition in the human. *Endokrinologie 71,* 81–88

DÖRNER, G. & STAUDT, J. (1968) Structural changes in the preoptic anterior hypothalamic area of the male rat, following neonatal castration and androgen substitution. *Neuroendocrinology 3,* 136–140

DÖRNER, G. & STAUDT, J. (1969) Structural changes in the hypothalamic ventromedial nucleus of the male rat, following neonatal castration and androgen treatment. *Neuroendocrinology 4,* 278–281

DÖRNER, G. & STAUDT, J. (1972) Vergleichende morphologische Untersuchungen der Hypothalamusdifferenzierung bei Ratte und Mensch. *Endokrinologie 59,* 152–155

DÖRNER, G., DÖCKE, F. & MOUSTAFA, S. (1968*a*) Differential localization of a male and a female hypothalamic mating centre. *J. Reprod. Fertil. 17,* 583–586

DÖRNER, G., DÖCKE, F. & HINZ, G. (1968*b*) Entwicklung und Rückbildung neuroendokrin bedingter männlicher Homosexualität. *Acta Biol. Med. Ger. 21,* 577–580

DÖRNER, G., DÖCKE, F. & HINZ, G. (1969) Homo- and hypersexuality in rats with hypothalamic lesions. *Neuroendocrinology 4,* 20–24

DÖRNER, G., DÖCKE, F. & HINZ, G. (1971*a*) Paradoxical effects of estrogen on brain differentiation. *Neuroendocrinology 7,* 146–155

DÖRNER, G., ROHDE, W. & BAUMGARTEN, G. (1971*b*) Bestimmung des genetischen Geschlechts des Foeten durch fluoreszenzmikroskopischen Nachweis des Y-Chromosoms in Fruchtwasserzellen. *Acta Biol. Med. Ger. 26,* 1095–1098

DÖRNER, G., ROHDE, W. & KRELL, L. (1972) Auslösung eines positiven Östrogenfeedback-Effect bei homosexuellen Männern. *Endokrinologie 60,* 297–301

DÖRNER, G., DÖCKE, F. & GÖTZ, F. (1975*a*) Male-like sexual behaviour of female rats with unilateral lesions in the hypothalamic ventromedial nuclear region. *Endokrinologie 65,* 133 –137

DÖRNER, G., ROHDE, W. & SCHNORR, D. (1975*b*) Evocability of a slight positive oestrogen feedback action on LH secretion in castrated and oestrogen-primed men. *Endokrinologie 66,* 373–376

DÖRNER, G., ROHDE, W., STAHL, F., KRELL, L. & MASIUS, W. (1975*c*) Neuroendocrine conditioned predisposition for homosexuality in men. *Arch. Sex. Behav. 4,* 1–8

DÖRNER, G., HECHT, K. & HINZ, G. (1976) Teratopsychogenetic effects apparently produced by nonphysiological neurotransmitter concentrations during brain differentiation. *Endokrinologie 68,* 1–5

DÖRNER, G., HINZ, G., DÖCKE, F. & TÖNJES, R. (1977*a*) Effects of psychotropic drugs on brain differentiation in female rats. *Endokrinologie 70,* 113–123

DÖRNER, G., STAHL, F., ROHDE, W., GÖRETZLEHNER, G., WITKOWSKI, R. & SAFFERT, H. (1977*b*) Sex-specific testosterone and FSH concentrations in amniotic fluids of mid-pregnancy. *Endokrinologie 70,* 86–88

DÖRNER, G., STAUDT, J., WENZEL, J., KVETNANSKÝ, R. & MURGAS, K. (1977*c*) Further evidence of teratogenic effects apparently produced by neurotransmitters during brain differentiation. *Endokrinologie 70,* 326–330

EATON, G. G., GOY, R. W. & PHOENIX, C. H. 1973) Effects of testosterone treatment in adulthood on sexual behaviour of female pseudohermaphrodite Rhesus monkeys. *Nature (New Biol.) 242,* 119–120

EVERITT, B. J., FUXE, K., HÖKFELT, T. & JONSSON, G. (1975) Role of monoamines in the control by hormones of sexual receptivity in the female rat. *J. Comp. Physiol. Psychol. 89,* 556–572

GESSA, G. L. & TAGLIAMONTE, A. (1975) Role of brain serotonin and dopamine in male sexual behaviour, in *Sexual Behaviour: Pharmacology and Biochemistry* (Sandler, M. & Gessa, G. L., eds.), Raven Press, New York

GRADY, K. L. & PHOENIX, C. H. (1963) Hormonal determinants of mating behaviour: the display of feminine behaviour by adult male rats castrated neonatally. *Am. Zool. 3,* 482–483

GRIFFITH, P. D., MERRY, J., BROWNING, M. C. K., EISINGER, A. H., HUNTSMAN, R. G., LORD, E., JENNY, A., POLANI, P. E., TANNER, J. M. & WHITEHOUSE, R. H. (1974) Homosexual women: an endocrine and psychological study. *J. Endocrinol. 63,* 549–556

HARRIS, G. W. (1964) Sex hormones, brain development and brain function. *Endocrinology 75,* 627–648

HOHLWEG, W. & JUNKMANN, K. (1932) Die hormonal nervöse Regulierung der Funktion des Hypophysenvorderlappens. *Klin. Wochenschr. 11,* 321–323

KAMBERI, I. (1974) Catecholaminergic, indolaminergic and cholinergic pathways and the hypothalamic hypophysiotropic neurohormones involved in control of gonadotropin secretion, in *Endocrinology of Sex* (Dörner, G., ed.), pp. 166–184, J. A. Barth, Leipzig

KAWAKAMI, M. & TERASAWA, E. (1974) Role of limbic forebrain structures on reproductive cycles, in *Biological Rhythms in Neuroendocrine Activity* (Kawakami, M., ed.), pp. 197–219, Igaku Shoin, Tokyo

KNOBIL, E. (1974) On the control of gonadotropin secretion in the rhesus monkey. *Recent Prog. Horm. Res. 30,* 1–46

MONEY, J. & SCHWARTZ, M. (1977) Dating, romantic and non-romantic friendship, and sexuality in 17 early-treated adrenogenital females, aged 16–25, in *Congenital Adrenal Hyperplasia* (Lee, P. A., Plotnick, L. P., Kowarski, A. A. & Migeon, C. J., eds.), pp. 419–451, University Park Press, Baltimore

MÜLLER, D., ORTHNER, H., ROEDER, F., KÖNIG, A., BOSSE, K. & KLOOS, G. (1974) The effects of hypothalamic lesions on sex behaviour and gonadotropic functions in the human, in *Endocrinology of Sex* (Dörner, G., ed.), pp. 80–105, J. A. Barth, Leipzig

NADLER, R. D. (1972) Intrahypothalamic exploration of androgen-sensitive brain loci in neonatal female rats. *Trans. N.Y. Acad. Sci. Ser. II 34,* 572–581

NEUMANN, F., ELGER, W. & von BERSWORDT-WALLRABE, R. (1967) Intersexualität männlicher Feten und Hemmung androgenabhängiger Funktionen bei erwachsenen Tieren durch Testosteronblocker. *Dtsch. Med. Wochenschr. 92,* 360–366

PFEIFFER, C. A. (1936) Sexual differences of the hypophyses and their determination by the gonads. *Am. J. Anat. 58,* 195–225

PHOENIX, C. H., GOY, R. W., GERALL, A. A. & YOUNG, W. C. (1959) Organizing action of prenatally administered testosterone propionate on the tissues mediating mating behaviour in the female guinea pig. *Endocrinology 65,* 369–382

POWERS, J. B. (1972) Facilitation of lordosis in ovariectomized rats by intracerebral progesterone implants. *Brain Res. 48,* 311–325

POWERS, J. B. & VALENSTEIN, E. S. (1972) Sexual receptivity facilitation by medial preoptic lesions in female rats. *Science (Wash. D.C.) 175,* 1003–1005

RAISMAN, G. & FIELD, P. M. (1971) Sexual dimorphism in the neuropil of the preoptic area of the rat and its dependence on neonatal androgen. *Brain Res. 54,* 1–29

REDDY, V. V. R., NAFTOLIN, F. & RYAN, K.J. (1974) Conversion of androstenedione to estrone by neural tissues from fetal and neonatal rats. *Endocrinology 94,* 117–121

ROEDER, F. & MÜLLER, D. (1969) Zur stereotaktischen Heilung der pädophilen Homosexualität. *Dtsch. Med. Wochenschr. 94,* 409–415

ROHDE, W., STAHL, F. & DÖRNER, G. (1977) Plasma basal levels of FSH, LH and testosterone in homosexual men. *Endokrinologie 70,* 241–248

RYAN, V. S. (1977) *Effect of Prenatal and Postnatal Nutrition on Development, Behaviour and Physiology of the Rat.* Ph. D. Thesis, Wayne State University. (Abstract in *Diss. Abstr. Int. B Sci. Eng. 37,* 5875)

SACHS, B. D. & POLLAK, E. I.(1973) Sexual behaviour: normal male patterning in androgenized female rats. *Science (Wash. D.C.) 181,* 770–772

SAWYER, Ch. H. (1975) Some recent developments in brain-pituitary-ovarian physiology. *Neuroendocrinology 17,* 97–124

SCHALLY, A. V., KASTIN, A. J. & ARIMURA, A. (1971) Hypothalamic follicle stimulating hormone (FSH) and luteinizing hormone (LH)-regulating hormone: Structure, physiology and clinical studies. *Fertil. Steril. 22,* 703–721

SMITH, P. E. & ENGLE, E. J. (1927) Experimental evidence regarding the role of the anterior pituitary in the development and regulation of the genital system. *Am. J. Anat. 40,* 159–217

SOULAIRAC, M. L. & SOULAIRAC, A. (1975) Monoaminergic and cholinergic control of sexual behaviour in the male rat, in *Sexual Behavior: Pharmacology and Biochemistry* (Sandler, M. & Gessa, G. L., eds.), Raven Press, New York

STAUDT, J. & DÖRNER, G. (1976) Structural changes in the medial and central amygdala of the male rat, following neonatal castration and androgen treatment. *Endokrinologie 67,* 296–300

SWANSON, H., BRAYSHAW, J. S. & PAYNE, A. P. (1974) Effects of neonatal androgenization on sexual and aggressive behaviour in the golden hamster, in *Endocrinology of Sex* (Dörner, G., ed.), pp. 61–74, J. A. Barth, Leipzig

WARD, I. L. (1969) Differential effect of pre- and postnatal androgen on the sexual behavior of intact and spayed female rats. *Horm. Behav. 1,* 25–36

Discussion

Sachar: The issue of testosterone function in homosexuals has been much studied in the US. The original report by Kolodny *et al.* (1971) suggested that testosterone secretion was reduced in Kinsey 5 or 6 homosexuals, but this could not be replicated by other laboratories (Rose 1978) and it seems that the first experiment had failed to control the drug history of the subjects. Alcohol intake, narcotic intake and marihuana smoking all depress testosterone levels (Rose 1978; Mirin *et al.* 1976). The control groups were all-American boys who didn't touch any of those drugs, whereas the homosexuals came from a more free-living population. Did you take account of these variables in your studies? Did you have rigorous control of alcohol and narcotic intake and marihuana smoking among your homosexuals?

Dörner: Marihuana smoking is not possible in our country, and the intake of large amounts of alcohol and narcotics can also largely be excluded in our cases. Huttunen *et al.* (1976) have found normal testosterone concentrations in 17 hospitalized alcoholics after a large dose of alcohol. In effeminate homosexuals, we only found some decrease in the free testosterone level because of increased sex-hormone-binding capacity. Several authors have measured total testosterone concentrations and have also not found any difference between homosexual and heterosexual males (Birk *et al.* 1973; Barlow *et al.* 1974; Pillard *et al.* 1974; Tourney *et al.* 1975).

Sachar: You also found differences in LH and FSH concentrations which were not found in the American investigations.

Dörner: Our findings of increased LH values in homosexual males are in agreement with those of Kolodny *et al.* (1972) and Doerr *et al.* (1976), and do not agree with the data of Parks *et al.* (1974) and Tourney *et al.* (1975). Higher FSH values in homosexual males were also found by Kolodny's and Tourney's groups, but the values did not differ significantly from those of heterosexual males. However, none of these authors have differentiated between effeminate and non-effeminate homosexual males. We only found significantly increased FSH levels in the effeminate ones. In five out of six transsexual men we also found significantly higher FSH levels than in 25 heterosexual men.

Sachar: My point was that the same high LH concentrations are found in men with high alcohol levels (Rose 1978).

Pirke: We have studied a group of about 40 homosexual men and have compared them with age-matched control groups (Doerr *et al.* 1973, 1976). We observed small but significant elevations in the concentrations of LH, free i.e. not protein-bound testosterone, oestradiol and oestrone in peripheral plasma. The total plasma testosterone concentration was normal. We do not know how to interpret these data. The small increase in plasma testosterone certainly does not cause homosexuality and is seen in other pathological and physiological conditions, such as liver disease and old age (Pirke & Doerr 1973). It would be helpful if other groups would study plasma oestrogens in male homosexuals; we could thus learn whether the increase in oestrogen concentrations was just an accidental finding in the homosexuals we studied or a characteristic finding in homosexuality.

Dörner: Dr Pirke finds elevated oestradiol and oestrone levels but normal testosterone and, in contrast to us, increased free testosterone levels due to decreased sex-hormone-binding capacity (Doerr *et al.* 1976). However, a decreased sex-hormone-binding capacity appears to be incompatible with a significantly increased oestrogen plasma level (Stahl *et al.* 1975).

Nieschlag: We should be aware of the limited value of a single hormone determination. Most hormones show considerable fluctuations in blood, some predictable, some not. The point that particularly interested me, Dr Dörner, was on FSH, because this is a hormone shown to fluctuate very little. Your homosexual subjects had an increased FSH concentration. Since we know that increased FSH usually reflects a defect in spermatogenesis, have you investigated their ejaculates?

Dörner: No, we haven't studied that. It has been shown, however, that oligospermia or azoospermia is not more typical of homosexuals than of heterosexuals (Parr & Swyer 1960; Doerr *et al.* 1973). As you know, it is particularly difficult to get sperm samples from transsexual men.

Pirke: We have studied the ejaculates of homosexual men (Doerr *et al.* 1973) and have found them to be normal.

Dörner: I would like to repeat that we observed a rise in FSH levels only in effeminate homosexual and transsexual males. But I would never consider homosexual behaviour to be a direct consequence of increased FSH levels or decreased free testosterone levels in adulthood. However, these findings may indicate that there might have been hormonal abnormalities, particularly androgen deficiency, in prenatal life, giving rise to female differentiation of the brain and to homosexual behaviour in adulthood. In this context, Gupta *et al.* (1976) have given testosterone antiserum to male rats during brain differentiation and have found increased female-like and decreased male-like sexual behaviour, combined with decreased testosterone and increased FSH levels, in adult animals.

Nieschlag: Clinically the fertility of patients with high FSH levels is decreased. If we extrapolate this to your subjects we should find a higher incidence of infertility in homosexuals. However, Dr Pirke found no abnormal ejaculates, indicating undisturbed fertility in his homosexual subjects. These findings are at variance with your elevated FSH levels.

Dörner: I agree that patients with clear-cut disorders of spermatogenesis have high FSH levels. But I don't agree that all males with increased FSH levels must also display disorders of spermatogenesis. In other words, spermatogenetic defects generally result in increased FSH levels, but increased FSH levels need not result in spermatogenetic defects.

Green: How do you define 'effeminate' and 'non-effeminate' homosexuals and 'virile' lesbians as against 'non-virile' lesbians? What were your behavioural or other criteria?

Dörner: Effeminate and non-effeminate homosexual males were characterized on the basis of their general behavioural patterns, including sex-specific gestures, the use of perfume and ornaments, and a sex-specific manner of walking. On the other hand, virile and non-virile lesbians were differentiated by the presence or absence of virilism, particularly hirsutism.

Bancroft: As a general point, many of the comments being made seem to be based on the assumption that homosexuals are a homogeneous group, whereas from the point of view of many characteristics which may be relevant to hormones, they are extremely heterogeneous. If one really wants to use hormone levels or positive feedback or anything else to show the determination of homosexual preference *per se,* one must control these other factors. An example of this in Dr Dörner's study is the pattern of sexual activity in the effeminate men. It may be that many of them are relatively inactive in their pattern of sexual arousal or frequency of orgasm. Their principal homosexual role may be as relatively passive partners with active homosexual males. If you compared them with a group of heterosexual males who were equally inactive, you might find a very similar endocrine picture. It is surely crucial, if one wants to say anything about homosexual preferences as such, to control for these other behavioural variables which can also be relevant to the endocrine factors.

Sachar: Are you suggesting that the amount of successful sexual activity can also have an influence on testosterone levels?

Bancroft: I think it can, but I think it also works the other way round, that if people have relatively low testosterone levels they may have low sexual activity. It is a two-way process.

Keverne: In other words, plasma testosterone may be a reflection of the behaviour rather than a determinant of it?

Bancroft: I think both are true.

Dörner: The plasma free testosterone level in 35 male homosexuals was significantly lower ($P < 0.01$) than in 38 male heterosexuals of similar age. However, nine out of the 35 male homosexuals showed particularly high sexual activity, and the mean free plasma testosterone level of those nine subjects was not significantly different from that of the male heterosexuals (Stahl *et al.* 1976).

Besser: There is another possible explanation of Dr Dörner's results in the homosexuals besides the ones that Dr Sachar suggested. It is becoming clear that homosexuals are carriers of Australia antigen-positive subclinical hepatitis (Catterall & Dane 1977) transmitted among them by direct person-to-person transfer. Such hepatic disease could produce precisely the biochemical changes that you have shown, Dr Dörner, namely increased levels of sex-hormone-binding globulin, a reduction in free testosterone, raised LH concentrations and oligospermia, and hence the high FSH concentration. I agree with Dr Nieschlag that one cannot explain the changes in FSH level purely on testosterone. One has to evoke some other effect on spermatogenesis. All of it could occur with hepatitis.

Dörner: Dr Besser, thank you for the suggestion. I cannot believe, however, that only the effeminate homosexual males as well as the transsexual males are carriers of Australia antigen hepatitis. Promiscuous anal intercourse was clearly denied by the transsexuals.

Crown: I am unhappy about Dr Bancroft's implied equation of 'masculine' and 'feminine' homosexuality with active and passive types. The evidence, both from Kinsey and clinical evidence, is that individuals cannot be classified in this way. They practise both modes.

Bancroft: That is true for the majority of homosexuals, but there are some men who play only a passive role in sexual intercourse with a male partner and who often are not orgasmic themselves. That may be the group studied by Dr Dörner; we don't know because we lack that information. This must be controlled in such studies.

Dörner: I agree with Dr Crown. We were unable to differentiate clearly between homosexual males playing a passive role and those playing an active role. On the other hand, we were able to differentiate between effeminate and non-effeminate homosexual males.

Green: Dr Dörner, do you know whether any of the transsexuals you studied had been taking sex steroids, as transsexuals frequently do? They typically lie about it, too. Do you have good drug histories for your transsexual patients?

Dörner: The transsexual males were under careful psychiatric observation, which confirmed that they were not taking sex hormones.

Herbert: We have been focusing on the interchange between laboratory and clinical work, and to me the most interesting feature of Dr Dörner's paper was the fact that we have here an example of a direct extrapolation from laboratory experiments to clinical practice. I want to take up two aspects of his work: firstly, the hypothalamic lesions made in male homosexuals, and secondly the idea of diagnosing homosexuality before birth by looking at androgen levels in the amniotic fluid. It seems to me that your model demonstrates both the strengths and weaknesses of such extrapolations, Dr Dörner. I don't understand, for example, why you equate female sexual behaviour in rats, which is a *behaviour pattern,* with paedophilic homosexuality in man, which is an *erotic preference;* and I am not convinced that paedophilic homosexuality is the same thing as female sexual behaviour. I wonder how you made the jump between these behaviours in rats and humans?

Dörner: I have never equated female sexual behaviour in male rats with homosexuality in man. We have only cautiously compared male rats, castrated at birth and given androgen replacement in adult life, with homosexual men. Both show a permanent and significant sexual preference for partners of the same sex. We have tested male rats, castrated on the first day of life and given androgens or reimplanted with testes in adulthood, for their preference for male or female partners. These males, androgen-deficient during the period of brain differentiation in neonatal life but with normal or approximately normal androgen levels in adulthood, showed a clear-cut preference for partners of the same sex. In contrast, normal intact male rats or males castrated on the 14th day of life, with androgen replaced in adulthood, displayed a clear-cut sexual preference for partners of the opposite sex.

According to these findings the androgen level during brain differentiation appears to determine the preference for partners of the same or the opposite sex – that is, 'homophilic or heterophilic eroticism'. In other words, irrespective of genetic sex, the higher the androgen level during brain differentiation, the higher the sexual responsiveness to partners of the female sex and the lower the responsiveness to partners of the male sex in adulthood.

Regarding the effects of hypothalamic lesions, neuroendocrine-conditioned homosexual behaviour in male rats – that is, the preference for partners of the same sex in neonatally castrated males given androgens in adulthood – could be suppressed by stereotaxic lesions of the so-called female mating centre in the hypothalamic ventromedial nuclear region (Dörner *et al.* 1968). Hence the conclusion was drawn in this paper: 'If our data can be confirmed in other species, a destruction of the so-called hypothalamic female mating centre could be considered as a means for suppressing homosexuality in human males'. Soon after this, Roeder & Müller (1969) reported that they had succeeded in suppressing homosexual behaviour in men by stereotaxic lesion of the hypothalamic ventromedial nucleus. This treatment was resorted to in paedophilic homosexual men, because they had been repeatedly detained for this act.

Brawer: With respect to your particular model in which male rats were castrated neonatally and later given androgen, and they showed lordosis when put with males, it seems to me that basically you have made a female hypothalamus by gonadectomizing the true male, and then at a later date you have given the animal androgen which is aromatized in the rat hypothalamus. This is equivalent to giving an injection of oestrogen and makes the model inapplicable to the human.

You have essentially made a female hypothalamus and then stimulated it with a hormone that ordinarily stimulates the female hypothalamus.

Sachar: You mean you would get the same results with oestrogen?

Brawer: Yes, you would.

Dörner: That's true in rats, and the effect would be even stronger, because in rats oestrogen is the most effective hormone for activating the sexual response to the masculine stimuli of male partners in the female-differentiated brain of homosexual males as well as of heterosexual females. In the human, on the other hand, androgen is the most effective hormone for activating the sexual response to the masculine stimuli of male partners in the female-differentiated brain of homosexual men and heterosexual women. Therefore, the experimental model of homosexual behaviour in male rats produced by androgen deficiency during brain differentiation followed by high androgen levels during brain activation appears to be particularly applicable to the human.

Ehrhardt: My feeling about your study, Dr Dörner, is that if you want to extrapolate to human beings from your data on rats you must define human behaviour more precisely. If you were to collaborate with psychiatrists and psychologists who define effeminacy, who take drug histories, and who record health states, then you and your colleagues should be able to define the human behavioural side very clearly. Without this, it is difficult to discuss your findings, because we lack the crucial information in the human homosexuality work; especially in view of the fact that intervening variables such as health state and degree and type of homosexuality may have a profound influence on the hormonal differences you find.

Dörner: But you can't expect to obtain more information about the behavioural side in homosexuals from endocrinologists than is generally given by psychologists and sexologists. In this context, I should add that all the homosexual men we studied showed clearly predominantly or even exclusively homosexual behaviour which rated 5 or 6 on the Kinsey rating scale.

Hertoft: The social conditions of the homosexuals should also be specified. From animal studies we know that sex-hormone levels are influenced by stress factors—noise, warmth, crowding and so on. In most societies homosexuals live under very stressing conditions and are forced to hide their homosexuality to a greater or lesser extent and to accept a life on heterosexual premises. We do not know how this stressing life influences their hormonal pattern—what is cause and what is effect.

Short: I would like to take up Dr Dörner's point about the use of positive feedback as a diagnostic tool for brain sex. This is actually deceptive. If one looks for positive feedback in normal men and women, men are not capable of discharging LH in response to ethinyl oestradiol, whereas normal women show the characteristic positive feedback response of LH secretion in response to ethinyl oestradiol. Dr David Baird has studied two intact testicular feminization patients, and although they have a female habitus and normal female sexual behaviour they appear to have a male hypothalamus, as shown by the absence of positive feedback. So I don't think that one can use the presence or absence of positive feedback as a predictive index of sexual behaviour (Van Look *et al.* 1977; Aono *et al.* 1978).

Dörner: Leyendecker *et al.* (1971) showed a positive oestrogen feedback effect in a genetic male with gonadal dysgenesis. On the other hand, Aono *et al.* (1978) did not demonstrate a positive feedback action of oestrogen on LH release in patients with the testicular feminization syndrome, as you say. I agree with these authors when they write: 'It could be assumed that the androgen insensitivity of the hypothalamus during foetal life in TSF patients might cause cyclic gonadotrophin secretory conditions. But the present patients with TFS displayed no LH release after oestrogen administration. The discrepancy between this hypothesis and the present findings could be explained by the following mechanism: testosterone secreted from the testes of TFS patients can be readily converted to oestradiol in the hypothalamus and this oestrogen may induce a male type gonadotrophin secretion.' In view of these findings, during brain differentiation androgen itself may be responsible for the masculinizing organizational effect on sexual behaviour, whereas oestrogen converted from androgen in the brain may be responsible for the masculinizing organizational effect on gonadotropin secretion.

Short: There are also problems of interpretation of apparent positive feedback effects, since one can get a rebound of LH levels in men because ethinyl oestradiol depresses the testosterone level, so when you stop giving the ethinyl oestradiol the LH levels rise slightly. But this is not to be confused with the pronounced LH elevation seen in positive feedback in women.

Green: I am intrigued by the feedback (Hohlweg) effect that Dr Dörner reported (Dörner *et al.* 1975). We published this study in the *Archives of Sexual Behavior* because we thought it was provocative, and I am disappointed that no one has either replicated or failed to replicate it. It is one of the few studies that attempts to address central nervous system mechanisms. Dr L. E. Seyler has since reported a differential effect on LH release between men and women after priming with oestrogens and giving LH-RH (Seyler *et al.* 1978). He has tested female-to-male transsexuals – women who want to become men – who have normal menstrual histories. More recently he has tested female homosexuals. He states that both groups show a typical male response rather than a typical female response. So this is a second study which purports to find a differential central nervous system mechanism, a hypothalamic–pituitary axis mechanism. These are attempts to get at basic mechanisms. They probably have a better chance of success than single determinations of hormones in plasma, which are vulnerable to so many confounding factors. I hope someone will try to replicate your original study, Dr Dörner, and also Dr Seyler's work.

Bancroft: Do the endocrinologists accept Dr Seyler's procedure as a test of positive feedback – measuring a response to LH-RH after priming with diethylstilboestrol, in quite high dose? He claims a reduced response in the normal male and an enhanced response to LH-RH in the normal female, with the female transsexual showing a pattern more similar to the male than the female pattern.

Goy: Does it matter at what stage of the cycle the woman is tested?

Bancroft: The priming is supposed to take care of that.

Besser: Superficially one would have to accept the data, and in fact the positive feedback effect in the normal female occurs both at pituitary level and at hypothalamic level. In a gonadotropin-deficient woman you can get normal cycling and show positive feedback pituitary effects, by just giving LH-RH, so it may be a purely pituitary effect; but there is in addition an augmenting effect via the hypothalamus because LH-RH secretion is increased at the time of the oestradiol surge at mid-cycle (Mortimer *et al.* 1975; Nillius & Wide 1975; Mortimer 1977).

So there is no doubt that both pituitary and hypothalamic effects exist. Presumably the increased secretion of gonadotropin from the pituitary is partly a making available of releasable stores of gonadotropin, and in addition a result of the increased priming from the hypothalamus. I couldn't comment on the particular experiments without knowing the precise protocol, but certainly one can demonstrate both positive and negative feedback in women by giving oestrogen, whereas in men one can only demonstrate negative feedback, in terms of LH-RH response.

Goy: You are not dealing with castrated individuals? What is the nature of the sex difference in castrated men?

Besser: We have tested castrated men and they do have an altered response – they have a high basal level of LH and an excessive response to LH-RH. I don't think one can demonstrate positive feedback effects in castrated men.

Goy: This has been done in the rhesus monkey. Positive feedback was found in castrated males (Knobil 1974).

Herbert: One has to be careful about defining positive feedback. Positive feedback to oestrogen is one thing, but a response to LH-RH is a different story.

In one case you are assessing pituitary response to increased LH-RH, which can be altered by oestradiol, certainly; in the second case the LH-RH levels may be changed by oestrogen but you are essentially dealing with the effect of oestrogen directly on a neural system.

Besser: But where is the site of action of gonadal steroids on positive feedback?

Herbert: This is what is disputed. Some people say it is largely hypothalamic. Knobil says that the effects are all in the pituitary (Krey *et al.* 1975).

Besser: This phenomenon was demonstrated in the human first, and Knobil has confirmed this in non-human primates (as yet unpublished, I believe).

The findings are that you can administer to gonadotropin-deficient female patients long-term LH-RH, and produce normal cyclicity of gonadotropins, positive feedback effects at mid-cycle, normal oestradiol responses, normal progesterone secretion, and a normal menstrual cycle. You can give LH-RH for two years to a woman who has never gone through puberty and produce normal puberty with normal cycles, and that is purely at the pituitary level, with positive and negative feedback working there (Mortimer *et al.* 1975; Nillius & Wide 1975; Mortimer 1977).

Herbert: This is surely an assumption? It may be that giving LH-RH, which we know has neural interactions, enables the brain to respond to oestrogen; moreover, the term 'positive feedback' refers to an effect of oestrogen, not to LH-RH. The LH-RH may simply make it possible.

References

Aono, T., Miyake, A., Kinugasa, T., Kurachi, K. & Matsumoto, K. (1978) Absence of positive feedback effect of oestrogen on LH release in patients with testicular feminization syndrome. *Acta Endocrinol. 87,* 259–267

Barlow, D. H., Abel, G. G., Blanchard, B. B. & Mavissakalian, M. (1974 Plasma testosterone levels and male homosexuality: a failure to replicate. *Arch. Sex. Behav. 3,* 571–575

Birk, L., Williams, G. D., Charsin, M. & Rose, L. I. (1973) Serum testosterone levels in homosexual men. *N. Engl. J. Med. 289,* 1236–1238

Catterall, R. D. & Dane, D. S. (1977) Hepatitis B as a sexually transmitted disease, in *Advanced Medicine,* vol. 13 (Besser, G. M., ed.), Pitman Medical, Tunbridge Wells

Doerr, P., Kockott, G., Vogt, H. J., Pirke, K. M. & Dittmar, F. (1973) Plasma testosterone, estradiol, and semen analysis in male homosexuals. *Arch. Gen. Psychiatr. 29,* 829–833

Doerr, P., Pirke, K. M., Kockott, G. & Dittmar, F. (1976) Further studies on sex hormones in male homosexuals. *Arch. Gen. Psychiatr. 33,* 611–614

Dörner, G., Döcke, F. & Hinz, G. (1968) Entwicklung und Rückbildung neuroendokrin bedingter männlicher Homosexualität. *Acta Biol. Med. Ger. 21,* 577–580

Dörner, G., Rohde, W., Stahl, F., Krell, L. & Masius, W. (1975) Neuroendocrine conditioned predisposition for homosexuality in men. *Arch. Sex. Behav. 4,* 1–8

Gupta, D., Keyes, D. & Eichner, M. (1976) Testosterone antisera-modulated sex behaviour in the rat, in *The Laboratory Animal in the Study of Reproduction* (Antikatzides, T. *et al.,* eds.), pp. 131–139, Gustav Fischer, Stuttgart

Huttunen, M. O., Harkonen, M. & Niskanen, P. (1976) Plasma testosterone concentrations in alcoholics. *J. Stud. Alcohol 37,* 1165–1177

Knobil, E. (1974) On the control of gonadotropin secretion in the rhesus monkey. *Recent Prog. Horm. Res. 30,* 1–46

Kolodny, R. C., Jacobs, L. S., Masters, W. H., Hendryx, J., *et al.* (1971) Plasma testosterone and semen analysis in male homosexuals. *N. Engl. J. Med. 285,* 1170–1174

Kolodny, R. C., Jacobs, L. S., Masters, W. H., Toro, G. & Daughaday, W. H. (1972) Plasma gonadotrophins and prolactin in male homosexuals. *Lancet 2,* 18–20

Krey, L. C., Butler, W. R. & Knobil, E. (1975) Surgical disconnection of the medial basal hypothalamus and pituitary function in the rhesus monkey. I. Gonadotropin secretion. *Endocrinology 96,* 1073–1087

Leyendecker, G., Wardlaw, S., Leffek, B, & Nocke, W. (1971) Studies on the function of the hypothalamic sexual centre in the human: presence of a cyclic centre in a genetic male. *Acta Endocrinol.* Suppl. 155, 36

Mirin, S. M., Mendelson, J. H., Eingboe, J. & Meyer, R. (1976) Acute effect of heroin and naltrexone on testosterone and gonadotropin secretion. *Psychoneuroendocrinology 1,* 359–369

Mortimer, C. H. (1977) Gonadotropin-releasing hormone, in *Clinical Neuroendocrinology* (Martini, L. & Besser, G. M., eds.), Academic Press, New York

Mortimer, C. H., Besser, G. M. & McNeilly, A. S. (1975) in *Hypothalamic Hormones; Chemistry, Physiology, Pharmacology, and Clinical Uses* (Motta, M., Crosignani, P. G. & Martini, L., eds.), Academic Press, New York

Nillius, S. J. & Wide, L. (1975) Gonadotrophin-releasing hormone treatment for induction of follicular maturation and ovulation in amenorrhoeic women with anorexia nervosa. *Br. Med. J. 3,* 405–408

Parks, G. A., Karth-Schütz, S., Panny, R., Hilding, R. F., Dumars, K. W., Frasier, S. D. & New, M. I. (1974) Variation in pituitary-gonadal function in adolescent male homosexuals and heterosexuals. *J. Clin. Endocrin. Metab. 39,* 796–801

Parr, D. & Swyer, G. I. M. (1960) Seminal analysis in 22 homosexuals. *Br. Med. J. 2,* 1359–1361

Pillard, R. C., Rose, R. M. & Sherwood, M. (1974) Plasma testosterone levels in homosexual men. *Arch. Sex. Behav. 3,* 453–457

Pirke, K. M. & Doerr, P. (1973) Age related changes and interrelationships between plasma testosterone, oestradiol and testosterone-binding globulin in normal adult males. *Acta Endocrinol. 74,* 792

Roeder, F. & Müller, D. (1969) Zur stereotaktischen Heilung der pädophilen Homosexualität. *Dtsch. Med. Wochenschr. 94,* 409–415

Rose, R. M. (1978) Neuroendocrine correlates of sexual and aggressive behavior in humans, in *Psychopharmacology. A Generation of Progress* (Lipton, M., DiMascio, A. & Kiliam, K., eds.), pp. 541–552, Raven Press, New York

SEYLER, L. E., CANALIS, E., SPARE, S. & REICHLIN, S. (1978) Abnormal gonadotropin secretory responses to LRH in transsexual women after diethylstilboestrol priming. *J. Clin. Endocrinol. Metab. 47,* 176–183

STAHL, F., DÖRNER, G., KNAPPE, G. & SCHNORR, D. (1975) Total and free testosterone in plasma of hypo- and agonadal men. *Endokrinologie 66,* 152–157

STAHL, F., DÖRNER, G., AHRENS, L. & GRAUDENZ, W. (1976) Significantly decreased apparently free testosterone levels in plasma of male homosexuals. *Endokrinologie 68,* 115–117

TOURNEY, G., PETRILLY, A. J. & HATFIELD, L. M. (1975) Hormonal relationships in homosexual men. *Am. J. Psychiatr. 132,* 288–290

VAN LOOK, P. F. A., HUNTER, W. M., CORKER, C. S. & BAIRD, D. T.(1977) Failure of positive feedback in normal men and subjects with testicular feminisation. *Clin. Endocrinol. 7,* 353–366

Animal models for human sexuality

FRANK A. BEACH

Department of Psychology, University of California, Berkeley

Abstract The value of animal models in biomedical research is firmly established, and many basic principles of human psychology have been explicated as the result of comparative studies. There is pressing need for non-human models in the behavioural sciences as represented by psychiatry, psychology and ethology; and such models should be constructed, provided their validity can be assured. Valid models cannot be based exclusively on similarity in the formal properties of behaviour. Commonality of descriptive terms as applied to different species does not guarantee identity of the concepts to which the terms apply. Model builders must evaluate interspecific similarities and differences in the *causes, mediating mechanisms* and *functional outcomes* of behaviour. The validity of interspecific generalization can never exceed the reliability of intraspecific analysis; and the latter is an indispensable antecedent of the former. Existing and potential models for homosexuality and other psychosexual characteristics of human beings are evaluated within the perspective provided by the foregoing generalizations.

The construction of animal models for human behaviour can be a seductive pastime or a serious scientific enterprise. Valid models may increase our understanding of animal and man, but invalid ones lead to theoretical confusion, and their practical application may have undesirable social consequences. Over a span of 40 years I have proposed some models of sexual behaviour whose superficiality astonishes and embarrasses me today (Beach 1950). Their weaknesses reflect failure to obey two cardinal rules that should govern not only the construction of animal models for human behaviour, but all interspecific comparisons regardless of the behaviour and the species involved.

The first rule is that meaningful comparisons are based not upon the formal characteristics of behaviour, but upon its causal mechanisms and functional outcomes. It is a fact that male rats mount other males in copulatory fashion; just as it is a fact that human males engage in homosexual relations. But considered at the phenomenological level neither fact helps us to understand the other. Only comparative study can discover whether similar causes are involved, and similar functions are served; and only at this level of commonality can we find the proper foundations for a valid behavioural model.

The second rule is that the validity of interspecific generalization cannot exceed the reliability of intraspecific analysis. Significant comparison of a particular type of behaviour in two different species is impossible unless and until the behaviour has been adequately analysed in each species by itself. Only after independent, intraspecific analysis is achieved can we properly interpret the nature and degree of interspecific similarities and differences. Comparisons between mounting behaviour of male rats and homosexual behaviour of men will remain scientifically meaningless until both phenomena have been examined by a common analytical procedure and in terms of similar dimensions.

MATING BEHAVIOUR IN RATS

If we are to use copulatory behaviour of male and female rats as a model for human homosexuality (Dörner 1968; Dörner & Hinz 1968; Rasmussen 1955) we must begin with separate analyses of the behaviour involved in each species.

Stimulus-response analysis of reflexes involved in heterosexual copulation

The copulatory performance of male and female rats consists of stereotyped motor patterns that normally are elicited by specific forms of stimulation and can be adequately described within a relatively simple S-R paradigm. The only essential response of the female, termed *lordosis*, consists of concave arching of the back coupled with simultaneous elevation of the head and hind-quarters. The full sexual repertoire of the receptive female includes other components (Beach 1976), but it is the execution of lordosis that figures most prominently in discussions of homosexual behaviour.

The male's copulatory reactions start with mounting the female *a posteriori* with his forelegs clasping her flanks. In this position he executes a series of very rapid pelvic thrusts culminating in momentary intromission, and then dismounts. A single 'copulatory' bout consists of 8–12 mounts and intromissions during the last of which the male ejaculates intravaginally. Most descriptions of homosexual behaviour emphasize the occurrence of the mounting and thrusting response, but tend to omit discussion of intromission and ejaculation.

I shall refer to the female's display of lordosis, and to the male's execution of mounting and thrusting, as *homotypical* behaviour. In contrast, lordosis by males and mounting by females will be termed *heterotypical.* The next stage in analysis involves identification of the stimuli that elicit homotypical mating responses. These have been exhaustively described in the case of lordosis, which depends upon peripheral receptors for touch and light pressure located in the skin and subcutaneous tissues of the dorsolateral and perivaginal areas (Komisaruk *et al.* 1972; Pfaff *et al.* 1973). Neuroanatomical mapping studies have identified the ascending and descending spinal pathways and major muscle groups involved in the behaviour. Integrative centres in the brain stem and facilitatory diencephalic mechanisms have been localized. It is clear that lordosis is a supraspinal reflex dependent on stimulation of specific somatosensory receptors and subject both to facilitatory and inhibitory modulation by oestrogen-sensitive neurons in the preoptic–anterohypothalamic region of the brain (Modianos & Pfaff 1977). The reflex is readily elicited in oestrous females by mechanical stimulation of the appropriate flank areas, and can even be evoked in the dioestrous and hypophysectomized animal by a combination of deep vaginal probing and manual stimulation of the flank (Komisaruk & Diakow 1973; Rodriguez-Sierra *et al.* 1977).

The male rat's homotypical mating pattern involves more complex sensory-motor coordination than the lordosis reflex, and consequently its stimulus control is less completely known. It is nonetheless correctly defined as a concatenated series of reflexive responses, the initiation and orientation of which depend on a multisensory pattern of visual, olfactory and somatosensory stimuli. Coordination of sequential elements in the pattern is mediated by an epigenetically organized neural programme within the CNS. The programme is activated by specific stimuli normally associated with the oestrous female (Beach 1942), and experience is not necessary for effective execution of heterosexual copulation (Beach 1958).

Bisexual representation of mediating mechanisms

It is evident that peripheral receptors and effectors necessary for the homotypical response of females and males are present in both sexes. The same is true of the central integrating mechanisms involved; for male rats obviously are capable of arching their backs just as females are capable of mounting and thrusting. For these reasons there is nothing remarkable in the observation that male and female rats do in fact exhibit heterotypical as well as homotypical copulatory responses. When we examine such behaviour closely we discover a principle of fundamental importance. There exists a constant and complementary relation between 'sex' of stimulus pattern and 'sex' of response pattern, so that ♂S→♀R, and ♀S→♂R.

The most significant feature of this *Principle of S–R Complementarity* is that it is independent of genetic sex. As a consequence, female-associated stimuli tend to evoke masculine responses *in both males and females;* and in both sexes feminine responses tend to be evoked by male-associated stimuli.

The indicated conclusion is that epigenetically programmed bisexual organization of the CNS provides not only for the execution of both homo- and heterotypical mating reactions, but also for transduction of homotypical stimuli into heterotypical responses, as well as heterotypical stimuli into homotypical behaviour.

The putative mechanisms for the mediation of complementary relations between stimulus and response patterns are schematically represented in Fig. 1. As a working hypothesis it is proposed that the basic features of this plan are present in both males and females, although it is not supposed that different S–R combinations will occur with equal probability, nor that all possible combinations have been included. Full discussion of all implications of this model would go beyond the bounds and necessity of the present paper. Its significance here is limited to our consideration of homosexual behaviour.

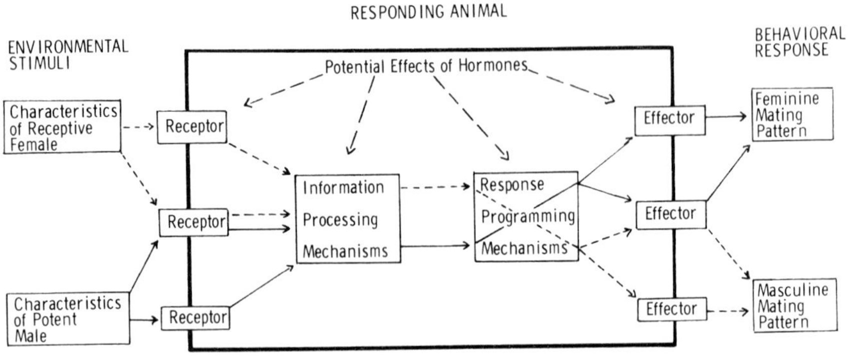

FIG. 1. Model of relations between stimulus and response patterns in behaviour.
Sensory stimuli associated with a sexually receptive female or with a sexually potent male activate different combinations of peripheral receptors. The resulting information is centrally processed (perception) and transmitted to other mechanisms within which patterns of motor output are organized. Relations between processing and programming are genetically determined to maintain a basic S–R complementarity so that ♂S→♀R, and ♀S→♂R. Gonadal hormones can modify S–R relations at any or all of four stages in the model.

'Homosexual' behaviour

Eight different patterns of behaviour commonly or occasionally displayed by male and female mammals of various species are listed in Table 1. As indicated in the column 'Term for behaviour', the designation 'homosexual' is commonly applied to males when they exhibit homotypical mating responses to other males, and to females when they display heterotypical responses to other females.

TABLE 1
Types of copulatory and quasi-copulatory relationships observed in some species of mammals

	Initiator of mount. activity		*Recipient of mounting activity*		
Pattern	*Genetic sex*	*Term for behaviour*	*Genetic sex*	*Behavioural response*	*Term for behaviour*
1	Male	Normal	Female	Cooperative*	Normal (receptive)
2	Male	Normal	Female	Resistant or passive	Normal (unreceptive)
3	Male	Homosexual	Male	Resistant or passive*	Normal (or homosex.)
4	Male	Homosexual	Male	Cooperative	Homosexual
5	Female	Homosexual	Female	Resistant or passive	Normal
6	Female	Homosexual	Female	Cooperative	Homosexual
7	Female	None	Male	Resistant or passive	None
8	Female	None	Male	Cooperative	None

* 'Cooperative' implies full display of the feminine pattern of receptivity regardless of the sex of the responding individual. Sometimes the importance of a positive response is overlooked so that a passive individual that is mounted by another of the same sex and fails to exhibit active resistance is labelled 'homosexual'.

Instead of labelling certain responses 'homosexual' it is more illuminating first to consider independently the 'sex' of the motor pattern and the 'sex' of the evoking stimulus pattern, and then to examine relations between the two. When this is done the patterns of interaction summarized in Table 1 can be classified in three major categories.

A. No sexual response (no need for classification)
   1. Female recipient 2 and 5.
   2. Male recipient 3 and 7.

B. Homotypical response to heterosexual stimulus (S-R complementarity)
   1. Male initiator 1 and 4.
   2. Female initiator 6 and 8.
   3. Male recipient 4 and 8.
   4. Female recipient 1 and 6.

C. Homotypical response without heterotypical stimulus (Perceptual deficit?)
   1. Male initiator 2 and 3.
   2. Female initiator 5 and 7.

Section B of this outline shows that eight of the 16 patterns can be interpreted as manifestations of the principle of S–R complementarity, which in turn reflects a bisexually programmed CNS. The four patterns listed under C are less easily explained, but all four involve violation of the complementarity principle. In terms of the diagram in Fig. 1 these violations might reflect errors in information processing, which could be described psychologically as defective perception. An alternative or supplementary explanation involves the effect of varying levels of 'drive' or 'response probability' (Beach 1971), which leads to an examination of the role of gonadal hormones as modulators of mating behaviour.

Effects of gonadal hormones

These are divisible into two major categories: (1) organizing effects on embryonic development, and (2) facilitating and inhibiting effects on adult behaviour. The conventional working hypothesis is that during a 'critical period' of organogenesis and embryonic differentiation, endogenously produced testosterone exerts 'masculinizing' effects on the functional organization of CNS mechanisms destined to mediate male behaviour in postnatal life. If androgen is absent during the critical period, 'masculine' mechanisms do not differentiate completely, but the alternate mechanisms associated with female behaviour do become organized. This of course describes the normal course of events in the development of the female. In terms of the model presented in Fig. 1, the presence or absence of androgen during development could affect CNS mechanisms that process incoming information, others that programme outgoing motor patterns, or both. Current theories make no distinction, although they focus on overt mating reactions. It is my belief that the possibility of permanent modification of perceptual functions deserves equal attention.

There is considerable experimental evidence in favour of the brain modification hypothesis, but there are other ways of dealing with the behavioural evidence (Beach 1971). We have neither the space nor the need to examine them here, where it is sufficient to emphasize that as far as mating behaviour of rats is concerned the only proven effects of manipulating the normal endocrine balance during development are to modify the influence of gonadal hormones on adult behaviour. To state the case more explicitly, hypothecated brain mechanisms are heuristically useful, but the basic data with which we must deal consist of overt responses to environmental stimuli. In the final analysis we study effects of hormones upon organismic behaviour. Our primary measurements reflect a pattern of S–R contingencies, and the most parsimonious initial interpretations of hormonal effects are framed, not in terms of putative events within the CNS, but in terms of *response probabilities;* that is, the probability that S_1 will elicit R_1 (Beach 1971). Neurophysiological explanations can be of great value, but their validity must be assessed in terms of agreement with facts provided by systematic behavioural analysis.

In terms of behavioural analysis the primary effect of testosterone on mating in adult rats can be expressed as follows: T ↑ Pr ♀S → ♂R, or testosterone increases the probability that the feminine stimulus pattern will elicit the masculine response pattern. The analogous formula for oestrogen would be: O ↑ Pr ♂S → ♀R. Both formulae are equally applicable in male and female animals, although a genetically or developmentally determined bias produces a stronger response to androgen in males and to oestrogen in females. In large measure the crucial developmental effects of androgen on adult mating behaviour in rats can be interpreted as a re-setting of this sex-linked bias.

1. For *males,* withdrawal of testosterone during the sensitive phase of development affects adult mating behaviour in two ways.
   (a) The function T ↑ Pr ♀S → ♂R is decreased.
   (b) The function O ↑ Pr ♂S → ♀R is increased.
2. For *females,* addition of testosterone during the sensitive phase of development affects adult mating behaviour in two ways.
   (a) The function O ↑ Pr ♂S → ♀R is decreased.
   (b) The function T ↑ Pr ♀S → ♂R is increased.

The results of these changes will be that the experimentally treated males show less masculine behaviour toward receptive females, and more feminine behaviour in response to normal males (thereby eliciting more mounting by the latter), and will consequently be described as 'homosexual'. Fetally androgenized females will display less receptive behaviour to normal males, and more mounting responses to oestrous females (thereby inducing more lordosis behaviour in the latter), and will also be designated as 'homosexual'. What has actually been measured is a change in S−R contingencies rather than any modification of brain mechanisms. Direct search for CNS changes is of course an essential next step, but for the time being the foregoing analysis will have to serve as our causal explanation of the observed behaviour. Whether or not the term 'homosexuality' is an appropriate designation depends in part on functional aspects of the S−R relations.

Functional considerations

Behaviour patterns characteristic of a species living in its natural environment can generally be assumed to serve some adaptive function even if that function is not immediately apparent. This assumption is based upon the fact that species-specific repertoires represent evolutionary products of natural selection, which would scarcely facilitate the dispersal of genes that induced maladaptive behaviour tendencies. Laboratory rats are domestic descendants of the wild brown rat, *Rattus norvegicus.* Various strains have been selectively bred over hundreds of generations until the wild genotype has been considerably modified, as shown by numerous differences from the wild type in physiology and behaviour (Donaldson 1924; Calhoun 1962; Barnett 1975). For this reason alone we cannot take it for granted that all behaviour typical of laboratory strains necessarily fulfils the criterion of adaptive function.

Conditions under which domestic rats customarily are bred and reared often are such as to prevent, attenuate or redirect the natural course of behavioural development. For example, rats are usually reared in sex-segregated groups, confined in small metal cages, fed a standard and constant diet, kept in a reasonably constant temperature and often maintained under a reversed light-dark rhythm. Furthermore, specific experiments on behaviour, including all of those alluded to in this chapter, involve the study of relatively small groups of subjects, often no more than 10–20, taken from a single strain and studied for a few days, weeks or at most a few months. For good reasons behaviour is usually observed under conditions calculated to produce responses in which the investigator is interested, and therefore to minimize the appearance of competing or alternative reaction patterns.

Most of the strictures mentioned are imposed deliberately with the commendable intention of reducing unwanted variance and maximizing the effect of independent variables. One inevitable consequence is a corresponding reduction in the spontaneity and richness of the behaviour that is allowed to occur. Another possible though less predictable effect is the manifestation of behaviour that is not a feature of the normal species repertoire, and therefore cannot be assumed *a priori* to subserve an adaptive function.

It is my opinion that the homosexual activities which occur in laboratory rats should be classified as adventitious responses without functional significance. Female mounting and male lordosis are properly viewed as epiphenomenal manifestations of a bisexually organized CNS. Such responses, together with male-male mounting, constitute reactions to stimulus situations that do not exist in the natural environment of *Rattus norvegicus*; and in fact homosexual behaviour of the type discussed here has never been seen in natural populations (Calhoun 1962). Finally, even when it is evoked in the laboratory, this behaviour usually depends upon contrived experimental situations and the creation of an abnormal endocrine balance.

In the light of these restrictions it is difficult to understand why such behaviour would be chosen as a model for human homosexuality, unless it were explicitly or implicitly assumed that homosexuality itself is somehow abnormal or pathological. If such an assumption is indeed involved, then the validity of the model becomes a problem of considerable social as well as scientific significance.

COMPARISONS OF RATS AND HUMAN BEINGS

As just intimated, the selection of a specific animal model for any aspect of human behaviour inevitably reflects an explicit or implicit interpretation of the original phenomenon. One widely accepted view is that the persistent and exclusive practice of homosexual behaviour is 'abnormal' or 'pathological'. Acceptance of this interpretation by some experimentalists can be inferred from their choice of terms, e.g. 'the aetiopathogenesis of genuine homosexuality [as] an inborn deviation of sex drive' (Dörner 1976, p. 199). This is not the place to discuss alternative interpretations, but it is necessary to emphasize that those who arbitrarily classify any behaviour as 'abnormal' must accept the responsibility for defining precisely and, in so far as possible quantitatively, the characteristics and dimensions of normality.

To put the case more explicitly, a reasonably complete understanding of *heterosexuality* is an essential prerequisite to the effective analysis of homosexuality. I have tried to show that homosexual behaviour in rats can tentatively be explained using concepts derived from the study of heterosexual copulation. Can the elucidation of human homosexuality be achieved in similar fashion? The problem is a difficult one because sexual relations between men and women are traditionally described in psychological terms, and simple S–R functions rarely are even mentioned. Nevertheless there is some evidence worthy of serious examination.

Heterosexual interactions

Human coitus involves a number of component responses that almost certainly are programmed in genetically organized reflexive circuits. Obvious examples are penile erection and the ejaculatory pattern. In some paraplegic men erection, ejaculation and convulsive thrusting of the pelvic region can be elicited by somatosensory stimulation of the genitals or cutaneous surfaces of the inner thigh and perineal regions (Riddoch 1917; Munro *et al.* 1948; Zeitlin *et al.* 1957). The reactions are not always evoked, and they are lacking entirely in some individuals, but their occurrence in some spinal patients suffering total loss of voluntary control and sensory feedback to the brain argues for the involvement of preorganized spinal circuits in the coital performance of normal males. This interpretation is consonant with descriptions of similar reactions to genital stimulation shown by the male fetus at 18.5 weeks (Humphrey & Hooker 1961).

Reports of sexual reflexes in paraplegic women have not come to my attention. However, it is well established that many normal women respond to mechanical stimulation of the genitals with clitoral erection, vaginal 'sweating', convulsive contraction of vaginal and uterine muscles, tachycardia, hyperventilation and widespread vasomotor changes (Masters & Johnson 1965). Each of these phenomena can properly be described as reflexive, and although we cannot be certain that they are organized in the spinal cord and brain stem, the possibility may be seriously entertained.

In anticipation of the following analysis of homosexual behaviour it is important to emphasize the impressive similarity between the responses of men and women to sexual stimulation that results in orgasm. Details are summarized in Table 2.

Human coital patterns are of course more than simple concatenations of

TABLE 2
Responses associated with orgasm in men and women

Men	*Women*
Excitement phase	
Nipple erection (30%)	Nipple erection
	Sex-tension flush (25%)
Plateau phase	
Sex-tension flush (25%)	Sex-tension flush (75%)
Carpopedal spasm	Carpopedal spasm
Generalized skeletal muscl e tension	Generalized skeletal muscle tension
Hyperventilation	Hyperventilation
Tachycardia (100 to 160/min)	Tachycardia (100 to 160/min)
Orgasmic phase	
Specific skeletal muscle contractions	Specific skeletal muscle contractions
Hyperventilation	Hyperventilation
Tachycardia (100 to 180/min)	Tachycardia (110 to 180/min)
Resolution phase	
Sweating reaction (30 to 40%)	Sweating reaction (30 to 40%)
Hyperventilation	Hyperventilation
Tachycardia (150 to 80/min)	Tachycardia (150 to 80/min)

(From Masters & Johnson 1965)

reflexes, and they differ in many ways from rat copulation. They are less stereotyped, are to some extent culturally patterned, and at the same time are idiosyncratic within every society (Ford & Beach 1951). The 'stimulus basis' for sexual attraction and erotic arousal is even more variable from culture to culture, and from individual to individual, than are modes of intercourse. Except for direct contact with the genitals and other primary erogenous zones such as the breasts, there are few if any culturally universal forms of sexual stimulation. For example, practices highly effective in different societies range from biting off bits of the partner's eyebrows to poking him or her in the eye (Ford & Beach 1951). Furthermore, the traditional 'erotic code' of every culture is subject to extensive individual differences (Davenport 1977). In American society, for instance, some heterosexual and homosexual women derive no gratification from clitoral stimulation; and some heterosexual and homosexual men prefer oral intercourse above any other source of arousal and satisfaction.

Individual experience and learning play the principal role in determining such preferences and practices, and this justifies the assumption that they are mediated chiefly by cerebral mechanisms whose functional characteristics depend on personal history. This is a basic difference between people and rats, and it has extremely important implications for any analysis of human homosexuality.

Homosexual relations

In comparing homo- and heterosexual behaviour it is illuminating to begin with similarities instead of differences; and we should note at the outset that *the basic consummatory reflexes are identical,* because the neuromuscular, vascular and glandular components of the orgastic pattern are the same whether stimulation is provided by a heterosexual or homosexual partner. In addition to this, no useful distinction between concepts of heterosexual and homosexual can be made in terms of the kinds of inter-individual behaviour that occur, unless 'heterosexual' behaviour is defined exclusively as vaginal intercourse. Homosexual men engage in anal intercourse, but so do heterosexual couples. Homosexual men and homosexual women achieve orgasm by mutual masturbation and by oral-genital stimulation, but so do heterosexual partners. The once popular psychoanalytic distinctions between participants in a homosexual interaction in terms of 'active' and 'passive', or 'insertor' and 'insertee', are no longer considered 'operationally useful' (Hooker 1965), nor analogous to masculine and feminine heterosexual roles (Hoffman 1977).

If homosexuality in men and women cannot be distinguished from heterosexuality by the kinds of behaviour involved, in the same manner that lordosis in male rats and mounting in females are designated as homosexual, can we nevertheless make a valid distinction among human beings on the basis of the kinds of sexual partners that are preferred? A direct, affirmative and simplistic answer to this question is embodied in the popular stereotype of 'the homosexual' – a stereotype that unfortunately is accepted uncritically by many physicians and scientists.

It is a common misconception that male homosexuals invariably prefer effeminate male partners, and that homosexual women are attracted predominantly to other women possessing chiefly masculine traits. This myth reflects an extremely strong, culturally induced conviction that men and women are by nature heterosexual, that this is the only 'normal' condition, and that the innate tendency is too strong to be denied even within an exclusively homosexual relationship. The unconscious insistence that a masculine-feminine polarity must exist between homosexuals may be some heterosexuals' way of asserting their own normality and protecting their own gender identity. There are, of course, marked differences of object choice among homosexuals, just as there are among heterosexuals, and in some cases the preferred partner may indeed be one with personality traits or behavioural tendencies characteristic of the opposite sex. More often, however, the opposite is true, and like attracts like. Martin Hoffman, who has studied the male homosexual community in great detail, has reached the following conclusion.

> 'Male homosexuals are most attracted by masculine partners and not by effeminate ones. It is clear to any student of the homosexual world that effeminate men are held in much lower esteem than are the masculine-looking homosexuals, and it is masculinity rather than girlishness which is most desired in the sexual partners of most male homosexuals' (Hoffman 1977, p. 178).

Del Martin and Phyllis Lyon, founders of Daughters of Bilitis, the first international organization of lesbians, have thus described the psychology of the female homosexual (Martin & Lyon 1972).

> 'Lesbians are women who are attracted to *women* (p. 22). Lesbianism is not a matter of gender-role designation, but contains within it elements of psychological, emotional, and spiritual involvement between two *women* (p. 23). At least three-fourths of the Lesbians we have known have had heterosexual intercourse more than once.... For the majority of these women the experience was good, erotically; that is, orgasm was achieved and there was a pleasurable feeling. But there was not the emotional

involvement which was present in a Lesbian sexual relationship. And that is what makes the difference (p. 84). In order to understand the Lesbian, it is therefore necessary that you think of her as ... a woman. The only thing that distinguishes her as a Lesbian is her choice of another woman as her sex, love or life partner' (p. 19).

Effects of gonadal hormones

Taking a cue from the earlier discussion of rat mating, we can ask two questions about possible relations between gonadal hormones and human sexuality. *(a)* Are there any effects on behaviour of hormones secreted in adulthood, and *(b)* are there any effects of androgen on brain organization during prenatal development?

To the first question the reply must be that hormonal effects almost certainly exist, but their precise nature and extent are difficult to evaluate, because human sexual responses are influenced by so many variables that any hormonal contributions tend to be modulated or masked by the impact of other determinants.

Reflexes of the male genital system are certainly affected by testosterone, and there is no doubt that castration impairs potency (Bremer 1959), or that androgen therapy may compensate in some measure for hypogonadism (Miller *et al.* 1938). At the same time potency often declines despite normal androgen levels, and may recover after psychotherapy. The erotic responsiveness of some women fluctuates with the natural endocrine rhythm of the menstrual cycle, but other individuals experience no regular psychological changes (Melges & Hamburg 1977). A number of experimentalists and clinicians are persuaded that androgenic hormone facilitates feminine sexual response, and such may indeed be the case although many authorities remain to be convinced.

One point which seems quite clear is that gonadal hormones secreted in adulthood almost certainly do not control the direction of object choice. It seems to me most unlikely that preference for male or female sex partners is determined by the plasma concentrations of androgen or oestrogen, or by the balance or ratio between them. This opinion directly contradicts the results of a number of reports dating back nearly 40 years (Glass *et al.* 1940), and continuing to the present; but the results are themselves contradictory. For example, Kolodny *et al.* (1971) reported average plasma levels of testosterone of 264 ± 15 ng/100ml for one group of homosexual men, as compared to 689 ± 26 ng/100ml for a group of heterosexuals. In contrast, Brodie *et al.* (1974) found comparable values to be 605 ± 178 ng/100ml for heterosexual, and 800

± 191 ng/ml for homosexual subjects. It is reported that homosexual men become less active when treated with so-called 'antiandrogens', but this reflects an overall reduction in sexual responsiveness and potency rather than redirection of sexual interest into heterosexual channels (Money 1970).

The theory that 'genuine', 'inborn homosexuality' in men is due to a 'predominantly female-differentiated brain' has been advanced by Dörner (1976), and somewhat similar views have been expressed by some American workers (Diamond 1977). Dörner explains the putative brain anomalies as follows:

> '...it may be concluded that primary, hypo-, bi- or homosexuality can be based on different degrees of androgen deficiency in males and androgen or oestrogen overdosage in females during the critical period of sex-specific brain differentiation' (1976, p. 207).

The hypothesis that sex steroids influence brain differentiation in the human fetus may well be correct. It may also be true that such differentiation permanently affects neuroendocrine functions of the hypothalamus. What remains to be proved is that the hypothesized sex differences in diencephalic nuclei have anything whatsoever to do with choice of sexual partners by adult men and women. It would be foolish to deny the possibility, but proof will not come from experiments on mating in rats.

Functional considerations

Whereas the homosexual behaviour of laboratory rats lacks any obvious adaptive function, quite the opposite may be true of human homosexuality. Within the limits allowed by the prevailing social system, homosexual alliances can serve most of the major functions to which permanent heterosexual unions are oriented. Reproduction alone is excluded, but this is not a primary object in many heterosexual marriages, and is specifically avoided in the increasingly popular heterosexual liaisons without marriage that are rapidly gaining covert acceptance in many Western societies.

The primary functions served by protracted homosexual relations extend well beyond genital gratification, and include the satisfaction of universal needs for companionship, emotional support, mutuality of interests and goals, improved economic security, and division of labour and responsibility. In other words, the mature homosexual needs and seeks affiliative relations and interpersonal bonds for the same reasons they are sought by heterosexuals. The primary difference is that for the homosexual these needs are met most effectively by a like-sexed partner.

Therefore, when homosexuality is understood in all of its dimensions, and is not viewed exclusively in terms of genitally oriented behaviour, it is seen as having positive potential functions for the individual. The extent to which these are realized depends in part upon attitudes of society, and in part on the characteristics of the man or woman involved. Both qualifications are applicable to a heterosexual life as well, but successful homosexual adjustment meets with many more serious social obstacles.

ALTERNATIVE ANIMAL MODELS

A city dweller lost in the country asked a farmer's child, 'If you wanted to get to Kansas City which way would you go?' The little boy replied, 'If I wanted to go to Kansas City I wouldn't start from here!' The moral is that selection of an appropriate point of departure constitutes the first step of a successful journey.

I fear that theorists who hope to improve our understanding of human homosexuality by starting from the 'rat copulation model' are unlikely to reach their goal. One reason is that they have chosen an inappropriate point of departure. The other reason is that they misconstrue certain important features of the very phenomenon the model is intended to explain. Allegiance to the 'illness theory' of human homosexuality has dictated a strictly physiological model, and simultaneously has diverted attention from the importance of functional analysis. It is possible that consideration of a more balanced interpretation would facilitate discovery of a more effective model. Instead of relying on the conventional medical view of homosexual behaviour as the manifestation of physiological or psychogenic pathology, we might be better advised to concentrate on its ontogenetic causes and functional outcomes, and then to seek other species in which similar causes-and-effects could conceivably be operative.

An obvious beginning is to examine the evidence pertaining to other primate species (Goy & Goldfoot 1975; Meyer-Bahlburg 1977). This choice is dictated by three principal considerations. (1) Monkeys and apes are man's nearest living relatives and are likely to share more of his characteristics than are shared by non-primate mammals. It appears, for example, that for primates in general the effects of gonadal hormones on sexual activity are more permissive than obligatory, and this opens up the possibility for modulation of sexual behaviour by other determinants, including learning. (2) Many primates can be and are being studied in nature as well as in the laboratory. We can thereby increase our understanding of the natural causes and functions of behaviour in addition to its physiological control. (3) It is known already that a certain amount of male and female homosexual behaviour occurs in captivity, and also in the natural habitat. (4) There are crucial interspecific similarities which encourage the belief that the causes and functions of such behaviour may be meaningfully related to the causes and functions of human homosexuality.

Widely distributed primate characteristics

Some features of sexual behaviour are present in all primates, whereas others apply to some species and not to others, but the most general and important are as follows: (1) All primates are neotenic and as a result their young mature slowly during a protracted dependency period. Relations between adults, juveniles and infants are continuous and influential in their control of behavioural development. Learning and experience play an essential role in the acquisition of the 'social skills' necessary for successful interaction with other individuals and with social groups. (2) As mentioned earlier, sexual behaviour is not rigidly governed by the endocrine system, and sexual interaction occurs in non-reproductive contexts. It is influenced by experience and by idiosyncratic variables leading to individual differences in sexual styles, preferences and modes of expression (Goy & Goldfoot 1975). (3) With few exceptions primates spend their entire lives as members of socially structured groups in which behaviour between two individuals is to some degree affected by the presence and attitudes of conspecifics not directly involved in the immediate, dyadic exchange. Social inhibition and facilitation of individual behaviour are commonplace. (4) Subgroups may exist within a troop and maintain their functional integrity despite integration in the larger population. These may be male–female pairs, mothers and offspring, or unisexual groups of juvenile and subadult males. (5) Non-reproductive dyadic affiliations are common, as between two females or two males. The interaction may never include any sexual expression, but positive social valence is reflected in the frequency of association and the mutuality of oriented activities.

Descriptions of homosexual behaviour

The most commonly reported form of homosexual interaction consists of one male monkey mounting another and executing pelvic thrusts. We have no way of estimating its normal incidence, but this type of behaviour has been observed in the male rhesus macaque, *Macaca mulatta* (Kempf 1917; Harlow 1965; Erwin & Maple 1976), stumptail macaque, *M. arctoides* (Chevalier-Skolnikoff 1976), and Japanese macaque, *M. fuscata* (Hanby & Brown 1974). Its display is not confined to caged individuals but occurs as well within mixed groups of males, adult females and juveniles living in large, outdoor compounds.

Several observers of different species have been able to observe directly the occurrence of full anal penetration with thrusting, but most authorities agree that during such interaction ejaculation occurs very rarely if at all. In addition to anal intercourse, sexual relations between captive stumptail males have been reported to include unilateral and mutual oral–genital contact as well as manual stimulation of the penis (Chevalier-Skolnikoff 1976).

Goy & Goldfoot (1975) believe that occasions for homosexual behaviour may be particularly prevalent within the groups of 'peripheralized males' characteristic of free-living troops of rhesus monkeys and some species of baboons. It has been suggested that such a phenomenon might resemble facultative homosexuality among human prisoners and other sexually segregated male groups.

At the same time there are reports of preferential response in which two rhesus males with a long homosexual relationship repeatedly engaged in anal intercourse while avoiding or attacking a receptive female (Erwin & Maple 1976). The relations of this particular pair included complete assumption of the feminine role by the mounted individual who 'lip-smacked', presented, and reached back to support the mounting male with one hand. Both males copulated normally to ejaculation when paired alone with a receptive female.

Female homosexual behaviour is less common than male, but has been observed in captive and free-living animals. Japanese macaque females living in heterosexual groups in a two-acre corral have occasionally been seen to mount each other, but only during the breeding season (Hanby & Brown 1974). Prolonged observation of 150 free-living rhesus females revealed that eight individuals in oestrus mounted other females on one or more occasions (Carpenter 1942).

The most extensive description of female homosexuality in monkeys is based on observation of a small number of stumptail macaques maintained in rather crowded conditions with adult males and infants (Chevalier-Skolnikoff 1976). On a few occasions one female mounted another, and while thrusting against her back showed behavioural reactions interpreted by the observer as indication of orgasm.

Hypothesized functions

We have no direct evidence to indicate how or why homosexual behaviour develops in these non-human primates, but the possibilities for experimental investigation of its ontogeny are obvious, and should be explored if the behaviour is to be studied as a model for the human condition. One very important feature mentioned by several observers is that homosexual interaction most commonly (invariably?) involves two animals with a long history of previous association. In other words, strangers rarely or never are involved. Another noteworthy feature is the absence of threats or other agonistic antecedents to the homosexual encounters here described. Finally, it may be significant that ejaculation by males is rare or totally lacking, and that only one account of female behaviour refers to sexual climax.

Different authorities have suggested different functional interpretations. Carpenter (1942) believed that homosexual mounting by free-living rhesus females represents a substitute for heterosexual copulation. Similar behaviour by captive female stumptail macaques was seen by Chevalier-Skolnikoff (1976) as 'fostering general social cohesion' between individuals 'who have strong emotional ties', as well as yielding erotic gratification to the mounting female. Kempf (1917) speculated that male–male mounting in groups of rhesus monkeys or baboons might represent a 'trade off' in which the subordinate animal gains social protection while the dominant achieves sexual gratification. Other writers, notably Maslow (1936), suggested that some forms of homosexual mounting in monkeys constitute behavioural expression of dominant–subordinate relations and should not be classified as sexual behaviour.

A particularly thought-provoking suggestion has been advanced by Erwin and Maple in reference to their observations of repeated anal copulation between two rhesus males, both of whom regularly copulated to ejaculation when placed with a receptive female.

> 'While there was clearly a sexual component in the relationship between these two males... ejaculation was never documented during homosexual coitus. This suggests to us that the bond between these males may have been based more on affection than on sexual fulfillment' (1976, p. 13).

This interpretation is reminiscent of our earlier assessment of the sociopsychological functions of human homosexuality.

No one can tell whether a valid non-human primate model for human homosexuality could be developed. It cannot be accomplished with present evidence alone, but parts of that evidence justify a reasonable degree of optimism. Additional research, both experimental and observational, will have to be done. My own prejudice would dictate beginning with the aim of comparing heterosexual relations rather than concentrating on homosexual interactions. Nonetheless I would agree with other writers (Goy & Goldfoot 1975; Meyer-Bahlburg 1977) in believing that the best model for human sexuality in general almost certainly will be built on some other species of primate.

References

BARNETT, S. A. (1975) *The Rat: a study in Behavior*, University of Chicago Press, Chicago

BEACH, F. A. (1942) Analysis of the stimuli adequate to elicit mating behaviour in the sexually inexperienced male rat. *J. Comp. Psychol. 33*, 163–207

BEACH, F. A. (1950) Commentary on *Corydon* by André Gide, Farrar, Straus & Co, New York

BEACH, F. A. (1958) Normal sexual behavior in male rats isolated at fourteen days of age. *J. Comp. Physiol. Psychol. 51*, 37–38

BEACH, F. A. (1971) Hormonal factors controlling the differentiation, development and display of copulatory behaviour in the ramstergig and related species, in *Biopsychology of Development* (Aronson, L. & Tobach, E., eds.), pp. 249–296, Academic Press, New York

BEACH, F. A. (1976) Sexual attractivity, proceptivity and receptivity in female mammals. *Horm. Behav. 7*, 105–138

BREMER, J. (1959) *Asexualization*, Macmillan, New York

BRODIE, H. K. H., GARTRELL, N., DOERING, C. & RHUE, T. (1974) Plasma testosterone levels in heterosexual and homosexual men. *Am. J. Psychiat. 131*, 82–83

CALHOUN, J. B. (1962) *The Ecology and Sociobiology of the Norway Rat.* U.S. Publ. Health Service Publ. No. 1008, Govt. Printing Office, Washington D.C. (pp. 288)

CARPENTER, C. R. (1942) Sexual behavior of free ranging rhesus monkeys *(Macaca mulatta)*: specimens, procedures and behavioral characteristics in estrus. *J. Comp. Psychol. 33*, 113–162

CHEVALIER-SKOLNIKOFF, S. (1976) Homosexual behavior in a laboratory group of stumptail monkeys *(Macaca arctoides)*: forms, contexts, and possible social functions. *Arch. Sex. Behav. 5*, 511–527

DAVENPORT, W. (1965) Sexual patterns and their regulation in a society of the Southwest Pacific, in *Sex and Behavior* (Beach, F. A., ed.), Wiley, New York

DAVENPORT, W. (1977) Sex in cross-cultural perspective, in *Human Sexuality in Four Perspectives* (Beach, F. A., ed.), The Johns Hopkins University Press, Baltimore

DIAMOND, M. (1977) Human development: biological foundations for social development, in *Human Sexuality in Four Perspectives* (Beach, F. A., ed.), The Johns Hopkins University Press, Baltimore

DONALDSON, H. H. (1924) *The Rat: Data and Reference Tables*, Publ. of the Wistar Institute of Anatomy, Philadelphia

DÖRNER, G. (1968) Hormonal induction and prevention of female homosexuality. *J. Endocrinol. 42*. 163–164

DÖRNER, G. (1976) *Hormones and Brain Differentiation*, Elsevier, Amsterdam, Oxford & New York

DÖRNER, G. & HINZ, G. (1968) Induction and prevention of male homosexuality by androgens. *J. Endocrinol. 40*, 387–388

ERWIN, J. & MAPLE, T. (1976) Ambisexual behaviour with male–male anal penetration in male rhesus monkeys. *Arch. Sex. Behav. 5*, 9–14

FORD, C. S. & BEACH, F. A. (1951) *Patterns of Sexual Behavior*, Harper & Row, New York

GLASS, S. J., DEUEL, H. J. & WRIGHT, C. A. (1940) Sex hormone studies in male homosexuality. *J. Clin. Endocrinol. 4*, 540–544

GOY, R. W. & GOLDFOOT, D. A. (1975) Neuroendocrinology: animal models and problems of human sexuality. *Arch. Sex. Behav. 4*. 405–420

HANBY, J. P. & BROWN, C. E. (1974) Development of sociosexual behaviour in Japanese macaques *(Macaca fuscata). Behaviour 49*, 152–196

HARLOW, H. F. (1965) Sexual behavior in the rhesus monkey, in *Sex and Behavior* (Beach, F. A., ed.), Wiley, New York

HOFFMAN, M. (1977) Homosexuality, in *Human Sexuality in Four Perspectives* (Beach, F. A., ed.), The Johns Hopkins University Press, Baltimore

HOOKER, E. (1965) An empirical study of some relations between sexual patterns and gender identity in male homosexuals, in *Sex Research, New Developments* (Money, J., ed.), Holt, Rinehart & Winston, New York

HUMPHREY, T. & HOOKER, D. (1961) Reflexes elicited by stimulating perineal and adjacent areas of human fetuses. *Transact. Am. Neurol. Assn*

KEMPF, E. J. (1917) The social and sexual behaviour of infrahuman primates with some comparable facts in human behaviour. *Psychoanal. Rev. 4,* 127–154

KOLODNY, R. C., MASTERS, W. H., HENDRYX, J. & TORO, G. (1971) Plasma testosterone and semen analysis in male homosexuals. *N. Engl. J. Med. 439,* 1170–1174

KOMISARUK, B. R. & DIAKOW, C. (1973) Lordosis reflex intensity in rats in relation to the estrous cycle, ovariectomy, estrogen administration and mating behavior. *Endocrinology 93,* 548–557

KOMISARUK, B. R., ADLER, N. T. & HUTCHISON, J. (1972) Genital sensory field: enlargement by estrogen treatment in female rats. *Science (Wash. D.C.) 178,* 1295–1298

MARTIN, D. & LYON, O. (1972) *Lesbian/Woman,* Glide Publications, San Francisco

MASLOW, A. H. (1936) The role of dominance in the social and sexual behavior of infrahuman primates. I. Observations at Villas Park Zoo. *J. Gen. Psychol. 48,* 261–277

MASTERS, W. H. & JOHNSON, V. E. (1965) The sexual response cycles of the human male and female: comparative anatomy and physiology, in *Sex and Behavior* (Beach, F. A., ed.), Wiley, New York

MELGES, F. T. & HAMBURG, D. A. (1977) Psychological effects of hormonal changes in women, in *Human Sexuality in Four Perspectives* (Beach, F. A., ed.), The Johns Hopkins University Press, Baltimore

MEYER-BAHLBURG, H. F. L. (1977) Sex hormones and male homosexuality in comparative perspective. *Arch. Sex. Behav. 6,* 297–325

MILLER, N., HUBERT, G. & HAMILTON, J. B. (1938) Mental and behavioral changes following male hormone treatment of adult castration, hypogonadism and psychic impotence. *Proc. Soc. Exp. Biol. Med. 38,* 538–540

MODIANOS, D. & PFAFF, D. (1977) Steroid and peptide hormones and the neural mechanisms for reproductive behavior, in *Endocrinology* (James, V. H. T., ed.) *(International Congress Series no. 402, vol. 1),* pp. 67–71, Excerpta Medica, Amsterdam

MONEY, J. (1970) Use of an androgen-depleting hormone in the treatment of male sex offenders. *J. Sex Res. 6,* 165–172

MUNRO, D. H., HORNE, H. W. & PAULL, D. P. (1948) The effect of injury to the spinal cord and cauda equina on the sexual potency of men. *N.Engl. J. Med. 239,* 903–911

PFAFF, D., LEWIS, C., DIAKOW, C. & KEINER, M. (1973) Neurophysiological analysis of mating responses as hormone-sensitive reflexes. *Prog. Physiol. Psychol. 5,* 253–297

RASMUSSEN, E. W. (1955) Experimental homosexual behavior in male albino rats. *Acta Psychologica 11,* 303–334

RIDDOCH, G. (1917) The reflex connections of the completely divided spinal cord in man, compared with those associated with less severe lesions. *Brain 16,* 264–402

RODRIGUEZ-SIERRA, J. F., CROWLEY, W. R. & KOMISARUK, B. R. (1977) Induction of lordosis responsiveness by vaginal stimulation in rats is independent of anterior or posterior pituitary hormones. *Horm. Behav. 8,* 348–355

ZEITLIN, A. B., COTTRELL, T. L. & LLOYD, F. A. (1957) Sexology of the paraplegic male. *Fertil. Steril. 8,* 337–345

Discussion

Hutchison: May I mention an example in a different species which lends support to Professor Beach's stimulus-response complementarity model proposed for the rat? In the amphibian *Xenopus*, if you transect the brain of the male at the level of the isthmus and present the appropriate stimuli for sexual clasping behaviour, the male shows complex clasping patterns (Hutchison & Poynton 1963). If you transect the brain of a genetic female and present stimuli for male behaviour, the female shows clasping patterns similar to those of the male (J.B. Hutchison, unpublished data). This illustrates that the particular stimulus pattern elicits male behaviour in these animals irrespective of genetic sex, which would fit in with your complementarity model. It also suggests that even at the level of the hindbrain both male and female have mechanisms which can coordinate sexual behaviour typical of one sex, the male in this species.

My other point also relates to the applicability of the complementarity model to species other than the rat. You mentioned that one difficulty in studying sexual behaviour is that we tend to observe it in the laboratory. This is particularly the case in the rat, where the types of behaviour which the animal can perform are restricted not only by the stimulus conditions that we use but also by the constraints imposed by tests done in laboratory conditions. However, a lot of ethological work, in which animals are observed in their natural environment, suggests that in the early courtship phases of sexual behaviour the animal may express what appears to be conflict between many different motivational systems (see review by Fentress 1978). For example, in territorial birds such as the chaffinch the male may show aggressive behaviour to the female, flight from the female or the beginnings of sexual behaviour in rapid succession during the early phases of the breeding season (Hinde 1970). There appears to be a succession of behaviour patterns which pertain to very different systems. In some ways, it is difficult to relate this sort of observation to the model in terms of stimulus-response complementarity.

Beach: I wouldn't expect the model to apply without modification. For a start I shall be content if my model is valid for rats only, or perhaps for mammals.

Dörner: Dr Beach, scientists such as Aristotle, Galen, Leonardo and Flourens were among the first to extrapolate from animals to man, by trusting in the continuity of biological mechanisms, as Blakemore (1977) points out. It seems that there has always been strong resistance to such extrapolation. On the other hand, there is a German proverb 'Jeder Vergleich hinkt'—every comparison is lame. I think that is also true for models. In my view a model cannot represent reality; it can only approach reality. In the case of your stimulus-response complementarity model, I agree when you say that 'In terms of behavioural analysis the primary effect of testosterone on mating in adult rats can be expressed as follows: T ↑ Pr ♀S → ♂R, or testosterone increases the probability that the masculine stimulus pattern will elicit the feminine response pattern'. But I think that is not the whole truth, because testosterone can also increase the probability that the masculine stimulus pattern will elicit the feminine response pattern. In other words, the responsiveness of a female-differentiated brain to a masculine stimulus pattern is also increased by testosterone in adulthood (Dörner *et al.* 1968; Meyerson *et al.* 1973).

Hence, when we castrate male rats at birth and replace testosterone or reimplant testes in adulthood, these rats with a female-differentiated brain are activated by testosterone, which results in a significant sexual preference for other males. These male rats show clear-cut receptive behavioural responses when sexually approached by other males. On the other hand, when we castrate male rats on the 14th day of life and replace testosterone or reimplant testes in adulthood, we see no such receptive sexual responses in these males. In about 99% of them as well as of normal intact males, unconcern or aversion and rejection is observed when they are sexually approached by other males. I think that is what we also see in adult heterosexual men in general, when they are sexually approached by other men.

Beach: But do you think that the behaviour is comparable as far as function and motivation are concerned?

Dörner: Of course I cannot equate the sexual behaviour of rats with that of humans. But I think we can cautiously compare the preference in sexual responsiveness for partners of the same sex observed in male rats castrated at birth with androgen replaced in adulthood to the preferential sexual responsiveness of homosexual men for other men. I would like to stress once more that we have always tested the preference in sexual responsiveness of animals to the approach of vigorous males or oestrous females. Certain male or female behavioural patterns of males toward other males were never considered as homosexual behaviour (namely, slight lordosis behaviour or mounting behaviour). Only the significant preference of clear-cut receptive sexual responsiveness, including complete lordosis, of males toward other males as compared to mounting behaviour and intromission toward oestrous females was considered as such behaviour.

Beach: There are of course human cultures in which the aversive behaviour you describe would be *abnormal* for males. In my book *Sex and Behavior* William Davenport (1965) describes one society in which exclusive homosexuality is a normal pattern during several years of each man's life.

Dörner: That is true for particular periods of life, but not in adulthood and throughout life.

Beach: Your statements on the behaviour of rats may well be correct. My question is whether we are dealing with comparable phenomena in another species, and I am suggesting that there are certain rules which must be followed in making such comparisons. It seems to me that you are using different rules.

Dörner: I am only claiming that we find more female-like than male-like behaviour in male rats–that is, a significant sexual preference for other males–when there is an androgen deficiency during a critical period of brain differentiation but a normal or approximately normal androgen level in adulthood.

Beach: This is true as far as the rat is concerned.

Dörner: Then there is the question whether the neuroendocrine situation is similar in homosexual men, particularly in effeminate ones, and in transsexual men. We have to investigate this possibility. The only direct evidence for or against this theory will be obtained when we find clear-cut androgen deficiencies in amniotic fluids of genetic males during the critical period of brain differentiation, follow up these cases for many years, and look for sexual deviations. In addition, however, we have obtained some indirect evidence in adults with sexual deviations suggesting that there may have been, in fact, abnormal concentrations of sex hormones in prenatal life, as described in my monograph *Hormones and Brain Differentiation* (Dörner 1976).

Sachar: To turn to another very challenging point, essentially Dr Beach has tried to make a distinction between copulatory behaviour and the inbuilt motor patterns involving copulation, and 'bonding' behaviour. Accordingly, we cannot understand the question of human homosexuality unless we take seriously the fundamental importance of these bonding mechanisms. He has suggested, therefore, that if we want to look at an appropriate animal model in order to understand the psychological and biological matrices that may underpin these kinds of choices and may shift the balance of probabilities toward one direction or the other, we should look for an animal system, probably among the sub-human primates, in which this range of behaviour is available for study. We should look at primates where there is heterosexual bonding with real mates and choices, as well as male bonding behaviour. He suggests that if we found such a system and studied it in a natural setting and *then* tried hormonal manipulations, we should be in a better position to understand the human phenomenon.

Crown: Professor Beach has given us a valuable lead into understanding more about human homosexual behaviour. This is a *spectrum* of behaviour, from that which is very much like copulatory behaviour with mounting and thrusting, right through to a bonding relationship of 30 years which is identical in essence to heterosexual human behaviour. An interesting recent study

(Judson *et al.* 1977) was made by venereologists seeking sources of venereal infection who went to the homophile steam baths in Denver and examined clients. They heard accounts of sexual behaviour at the most promiscuous level – what I would call pure copulatory behaviour. Men went to these baths purely to make sexual contact, with no emotion at all.

Sachar: Like any other bordello?

Crown: Yes. The average number of male contacts per month was 7.9. This seems to me to represent the promiscuous end of the spectrum of homosexual behaviour, which runs on from pure copulatory behaviour through to deep human relationships with the affectional bonds to which you referred.

Herbert: Dr Beach's paper raises a new and important point, namely the social and emotional context in which copulation occurs, which is very badly studied in the laboratory. We pay really no attention to it. This is in contrast to ethologists in the field: those studying sub-human primates consider the social structure of the group to have a very considerable influence on individual behaviour. People working clinically and those working in the laboratory need to develop the same kind of assessment procedures for measuring or in some way determining the emotional context of copulatory behaviour, as for measuring behaviour itself. We have spent much time in developing methods of quantifying sexual behaviour, for example breaking it down into components. Has the time come to widen the analysis to take into account the emotional context and, if so, how do we do it? Is there a relationship between what we in the laboratory can do and what those working with homosexuals, or indeed heterosexuals, can do?

Beach: The point is well taken. Consider only primates for the moment. One simply cannot adequately interpret the effects of testosterone on male copulatory behaviour without first understanding what I have termed the *socio-sexual matrix* in which this normally occurs (Beach 1977). Dr Keverne's socially subordinate male talapoin monkeys, for example, might just as well be castrated when they are confronted with a receptive female in the same social environment with a dominant male (see pp. 271–280). The subordinate male won't even look at the female. Or take the situation that Hans Kummer (1971) has described in the hamadryas baboon. Each dominant male has his own group of females and there is no indication of sexual jealousy or competition for females because of the superordinate importance of the one-male group. My point is that knowledge of factors normally controlling behaviour in nature is essential for understanding behaviour seen in the laboratory. And to this end we need to comprehend the functional significance of naturally occurring behaviour.

In our study of human beings we need to learn much more about the 'aetiology' of *heterosexual* attraction, which is just as much a mystery to me as *homosexual* attraction.

For both animals and human beings it is clear that no valid model is likely to emerge until we grasp the importance of the non-reproductive aspects of sexual activity, and include its relation to the overall social structure of the species involved.

Marteau: I want to thank Professor Beach for this warning from the scientific side of the fence, because I spend a lot of time giving a similar warning on the other side, to theologians and existential psychologists, reminding them that their feet are also bound in clay and that we have to balance both sides in looking at a human being. We need to remember that we are a microcosm of the whole of nature. We are not just the final link in the chain of one or other primate, or one species or another. For me the whole of creation is contained in the human species and some parts may be more relevant in one situation or with one person than with another. We also need to acknowledge the fact that mankind has made a vast leap from the animal world. The reactions of human beings to their world, their society, their situation and choices, and to the way in which their instincts are to some degree under their own control, are fundamentally different from those of the animal kingdom. The animal instincts are specific in their aims and processes, although they can be changed and frustrated by nature or the experimentalist. A human being's instincts would appear to be generic and thus capable of a variety of aims and of taking many forms. For this reason only humans are able to sublimate their lower aims to those of a higher order (Maslow 1968).

This needs to be taken into account when we extrapolate from one situation to another. In recalling the concepts of Abraham Maslow I am reminded that he was concerned that the understanding of human beings had come either from the psychoanalyst, analysing the very sick, or the behaviourists analysing animal behaviour. This he felt left out any examination of those who had produced something positive in their life-style. He therefore proceeded to examine those whose life-styles had given something to society. From this he discovered how important it is for human beings to have a higher value system, and what this does. It was the first attempt to examine human beings without the use of either 'sick' or 'animalistic' categories. The problem has been that if these are your categories, then your final definition will have to be contained within them. If we examine man 'as an animal' we shall reduce him to an animal.

I do not want to belittle the experimental work being done. It is an important step in understanding some aspects of human behaviour, but, as

Professor Beach has reminded us, it is dangerous to extrapolate. We also have to remember that extrapolation can be a two-way process. I fear that some of the descriptions of animal behaviour given here do seem occasionally to be stated in somewhat humanistic terms. If you describe the behaviour in human terms it is not surprising that it seems relevant to the human situation.

Green: Dr Beach underscored a point relevant to the failure of aversion treatment for homosexuality. Obviously, either hetero- or homosexuality is an interaction between erotic attractiveness and an affectional system. This is one reason why simply using aversion treatment to same-sex stimuli is not enough to evolve a heterosexual affectional system.

Secondly, the three non-human primates deemed closest to man are the great apes – the chimpanzee, orang-utan and gorilla. I don't know much about the social matrixes in which these three species develop; it would be interesting to consider which of the three, if it *is* one of those, would serve as the best model.

Goy: I would like to revert to this fundamental issue of homophilia and heterophilia and their origins. As Dr Beach pointed out, it is hard to prove that a rat is homophilic; certainly in natural conditions the probability of the male displaying feminine responses, even with a strong male stimulus, is low. It doesn't occur often. There must be reasons for that, and some of us think part of the reason is the prenatal hormone environment. I would like to contrast that with the primate species that I know well, the rhesus monkey.

If you look at the willingness of the male to display feminine behaviour in response to a male stimulus (regardless of the sex of the animal providing the male stimulus) the probability is very nearly equal to one in normal male monkeys. There is no question in my mind – although I don't know how one can ever prove a function of any behaviour – that mounting behaviour, especially in pre-adolescent monkeys, is a social bonding mechanism. I have no idea why, in heterosexual groups, male monkeys take that as a serious job and do most of the bonding, and females don't, but nevertheless, on the one hand you have a species like the rhesus monkey where homophilia is rampant, and a species like the rat where it is rare. I don't know which is the better model for the human being. I don't think homophilia in humans, especially between human males *is* a very conspicuous feature of life. It is a rare occurrence, at least to the extent that the homophilic bonding is expressed by sexual behaviour.

Green: What about social drinking behaviour – 'pub-crawling'?

Goy: You are saying that one just looks at the species and decides what the bonding behaviour is for that particular species, and that is part of the problem we are talking about. It is not unlikely that human males have some behavioural means for establishing and expressing homophilic bonding. It does not seem likely that sexual behaviour is the common means to this end.

Sachar: Incidentally, in our preoccupation with primates we should not overlook a fascinating species which shows friendship and so on, namely the dolphin.

Bancroft: Dr Beach was distinguishing between what one can call copulatory behaviour, or consummatory behaviour, and affectional, bonding behaviour. For the human at least, we should consider a third component which has to do with arousability and response to stimuli – which persuades a man to go into a steam bath in the first place. In the development of human sexuality it is interesting to look at the way this biological and perhaps relatively undifferentiated sexual responsiveness becomes incorporated into the pattern of affectional bonding, which is often where sex goes wrong and people have problems. One can take men or women into laboratories and show them erotic stimuli and they respond. It has nothing to do with affectional bonds, but with responding to stimuli, and this is where the issue of sexual preferences arises. This aspect *may* be biologically or hormonally determined; I would hope that there is some animal model which would be relevant to the human situation.

Sachar: You are distinguishing between homoerotic and homophilic, and you don't want us to lose sight of the homoerotic?

Bancroft: Yes; there is this purely biological element which we should not forget.

Beach: I also want to know what aspects of human sexual behaviour are hormonally influenced. I therefore ask: what aspects or components of the sexual behaviour of other species can be definitely shown to depend on hormones? I find my best examples in invertebrates with an almost totally preorganized nervous system. Complex patterns of behaviour can be elicited in newly emerged moths simply by applying the appropriate hormone directly to the abdominal ganglia. The pattern is 'turned on' within minutes and is performed perfectly without any afferent input from the environment (Riddiford & Truman 1974). The essential central connections are laid down during embryogenesis and are fully functional as soon as the hormonal stimulus is applied.

The lordosis reflex of the female rat is a beautiful example of an oestrogen-sensitive reflex. Through the work of Donald Pfaff and his collaborators (Modianos & Pfaff 1977) we can even identify the afferent input, the ascending and descending spinal tracts, and the muscle groups involved. It is thus possible to hypothesize just where the hormone has its effect. In the male rat we can trace the efferent pathways for erection and ejaculation and can examine effects of hormones on these mechanisms. This is the first level at which we should search for similarities and differences between rats and people. Does testosterone exert similar effects on simple reflexes? In fact, to what extent are the reflexes similar? What effects, if any, does oestrogen have on the vaginal and uterine reactions associated with orgasm in women? This is the level at which I would start looking for models or even basic similarities between one species or another.

Bancroft: I accept that, in terms of target organ responses. Comparable models would be relatively easy here, but is there anything that animals can tell us about appetitive behaviour and sexual preference? Your experiments on beagles indicate something about the hormonal factors which determine whether an animal will be motivated to go to look for a sexual partner of a particular type.

Beach: In our experiments with beagles we place three males beneath wire cages in a large field which also contains three spayed females, each in a similar cage. The experimental female is then allowed to react to any or all of the caged dogs. If she is in oestrus she visits males much more than she visits females. When she is standing next to a caged male she 'presents', pointing her rear in his direction, deviating her tail and sometimes showing vulvar contractions. Females not in heat show no preference for visiting males (Beach & LeBoeuf 1967). For the oestrous bitch the male's odour is important.

If the female is given a preference test with two samples of urine, one from a dioestrous female, the other from a male, when the female is not in heat she shows a preference for the female urine; but when in heat her preference changes. She now prefers male urine.

Bancroft: Can you say that the preference for the male in that situation is hormonally determined or is learned–reinforced because she gets a better deal from the male when she is sexually aroused?

Beach: This preference is shown by females with no mating experience.

Green: To belabour the obvious and add to the complexity, we have to keep in mind differences in attractiveness between individuals as we build our model. For many heterosexual males there are many females who elicit absolutely no arousal, and equally for many homosexual males there are many males who have no erotic appeal. I don't think we can look on our models, irrespective of species, as being reflexively responsive to individuals of the same or the other anatomical sex.

Beach: Certainly not. We find some female dogs will not allow certain males to copulate, no matter how receptive the same female may be to a different male partner.

Green: The same is seen in non-human primates.

Ehrhardt: Dr Beach, what are your thoughts about considering the evidence from other cultures? There are cultures where males go through a prescribed phase of homosexuality. The same cultures are described as lacking the phenomenon of long-term obligatory homosexuality. Everybody passes through a phase of homosexuality but subsequently everyone gets married and has heterosexual relations (Money & Ehrhardt 1972). Is it perhaps that obligatory homosexuality in our culture is an artifact caused by a strict taboo on bisexual behaviour?

Beach: My working hypothesis is that the human brain is bisexually organized, but the tendency for male or female behaviour is not evenly balanced in the two sexes. There is a sex-related bias, partly caused by prenatal hormones, partly due to other genetically determined factors. However, in the absence of social structuring of sex roles, homosexual behaviour might be much more prevalent than it is.

Hutchison: On the question of what determines sexual preference, it might be possible to distinguish between factors operating in adulthood and those acting in infancy. There are some avian examples which demonstrate clearly the importance of learning in early development. For example, polymorphous snow geese tend to mate preferentially with the colour form to which they were exposed in early life (Cooke *et al.* 1976). There is an indication that sexual imprinting also occurs in mammals (Sembraus & Klee 1975), but as yet there have been few studies in species other than birds.

Goy: We have investigated the question of when the mounting behaviour of rhesus monkeys stops being purely bonding and becomes associated with erotic arousal. I have studied the monkeys for four years of their development. If we plot the percentage of mounts shown by the male monkey to a female partner during development (he lives in a social group containing both males and females), during the first year of life he mounts males and females equally frequently. By the fourth year of life (it is probably puberty but I haven't followed the hormonal profiles or the spermatogenic profiles in these males) the females are already in puberty (they start 6–12 months ahead of the males), so they are now very attractive. If a male at this stage of development achieves an intromission with one of the females in the group, his preference rises to close to 100% of his mounts being directed toward the female from that time on, whether she is receptive or not. His mounting of male partners falls off, although he still obeys the fundamental rule of having to maintain his friendship bonds with the males in the group.

I took the males that had intromissions at 36 months of age and went back retrospectively in the data accumulated on them. When they are taken away from their mothers at the end of the first year, and continued as a group of infants or juveniles, these same males do exactly the same thing as in the *second* year of life, mounting males infrequently and females very frequently. However, they are not having intromissions then. This is an indication on the part of these males, well in advance of the time they will claim those females sexually, of their intention to dominate the group and retain those females as sexual partners when they come of age. It is an interesting phenomenon. I am not sure that it is erotic although in many of the mounts, whether they are homosexual or heterosexual, the mounter gets an erection.

Sachar: Does this high level of mounts to females in the second year fall to the baseline level in the third year of life, and then rise again just before puberty?

Goy: Yes; in the third year they are mounting about 50/50, males/females. So it is a transient period after they are separated from their mothers early, where they make clear their intention to dominate the group.

Abbott: In the marmoset, a monogamous primate, the offspring in the captive family group hardly exhibit any sexual behaviour whatsoever and it is usually exclusively limited to the parents (Rothe 1975; Abbott 1978). In artificially created groups, sexual behaviour occurs most frequently between the breeding pair, the dominant male and female (Rothe 1975; Abbott & Hearn 1978). The dominant animals usually disrupt mating between their partners and subordinates (Epple 1967; Abbott & Hearn 1978) and there is evidence that subordinate males may fail to intromit and ejaculate, and that dominant males fail to intromit and ejaculate when mounting subordinate females (Rothe 1975). However, this may not always be the case with subordinate animals, as sperm have been recovered from the vaginal washings of subordinate females after mating with subordinate males (Abbott & Hearn 1978). Nevertheless, sexual behaviour is not such an obvious feature of group activity in these monogamous primates as in the rhesus monkey and is suppressed to a greater or lesser extent in all but the breeding pair. Furthermore, if the dominant pair of an artificial group is removed, another pair will form and take their place ($n = 3$; D. H. Abbott, unpublished work 1977), and if only one dominant animal is removed, the remaining partner will form another pair with the highest ranking member of the opposite sex left in the group ($n = 2$).

References

ABBOTT, D. H. (1978) The physical, hormonal and behavioural development of the common marmoset, *Callithrix jacchus jacchus*, in *The Biology of the Callitrichidae* (Rothe, H., Wolters, H. J. & Hearn, J. P., eds.), University of Göttingen Press, Göttingen, in press

ABBOTT, D. H. & HEARN, J. P. (1978) Physical, hormonal and behavioural aspects of sexual development in the marmoset monkey, *Callithrix jacchus*. *J. Reprod. Fertil. 53*, 155–166
BEACH, F.A. (1977) Cross-species comparisons and the human heritage, in *Human Sexuality in Four Perspectives* (Beach, F. A.,ed.), pp. 296–316, The Johns Hopkins University Press, Baltimore
BEACH, F. A. & LEBOEUF, B. J. (1967) Coital behaviour in dogs. I. Preferential mating in the bitch. *Anim. Behav. 15*, 546–558
BLAKEMORE, C. (1977) *Mechanics of the Mind*, p. 62, Cambridge University Press, Cambridge
COOKE, F., FINNEY, G. H. & ROCKWELL, R. F. (1976) Assortative mating in lesser snow geese *(Anser caerulescens)*. *Behav. Genet. 6*, 127–140
DAVENPORT, W. (1965) Sexual patterns and their regulation in a society of the Southwest Pacific, in *Sex and Behavior* (Beach, F. A., ed.), Wiley, New York
DÖRNER, G. (1976) *Hormones and Brain Differentiation*, Elsevier, Amsterdam, Oxford & New York
DÖRNER, G., DÖCKE, F. & MOUSTAFA, S. (1968) Homosexuality in female rats following testosterone implantation in the anterior hypothalamus*J. Reprod. Fertil. 17*, 173–175
EPPLE, G. (1967) Vergleichende Untersuchungen über Sexual und Sozialerhalten der Krallenaffen (Hapalidae). *Folia Primatol. 7*, 37–65
FENTRESS, J. C. (1978) Conflict and context in sexual behaviour, in *Biological Determinants of Sexual Behaviour* (Hutchison, J. B. , ed.), pp. 579–615, Wiley, Chichester
HINDE, R. A. (1970) *Animal Behavior: A Synthesis of Ethology and Comparative Psychology* (2nd edn), McGraw-Hill, New York
HUTCHISON, J. B. & POYNTON, J. C. (1963) A neurological study of the clasp reflex in *Xenopus laevis* (Daudin). *Behaviour 22*, 41–63
JUDSON, F. N., MILLER, K. G. & SCHAFFNIT, G. N. (1977) Screening for gonorrhoea and syphilis in the Gay Baths–Denver, Colorado. *Am. J. Public Health 67*, 740–742
KUMMER, H. (1971) *Primate Societies: Group Techniques of Ecological Adaptation*, Aldine, New York
MASLOW, A. (1968) *Toward a Psychology of Being*, Insight Books, New York
MEYERSON, B. J., LINDSTRÖM, L., NORDSTRÖM, E. B. & AGMO, A. (1973) Sexual motivation in the female rat after testosterone treatment. *Physiol. Behav. 11*, 421–428
MODIANOS, D. & PFAFF, D. (1977) Steroid and peptide hormones, and the neural mechanisms for reproductive behaviour, in *Endocrinology* (James, V.H.T., ed.) *(International Congress Series no. 402, vol. 1)*, pp. 67–71, Excerpta Medica, Amsterdam
MONEY, J. & EHRHARDT, A. A. (1972) *Man and Woman, Boy and Girl: The Differentiation and Dimorphism of Gender Identity from Conception to Maturity*, The Johns Hopkins University Press, Baltimore
RIDDIFORD, L. M. & TRUMAN, J. W. (1974) Hormones and insect behavior, in *Experimental Analysis of Insect Behavior* (Barton Browne, L., ed.), pp. 286–296, Springer-Verlag, Berlin
ROTHE, H. (1975) Some aspects of sexuality and reproduction in groups of captive marmosets *(Callithrix jacchus)*. *Z. Tierpsychol. 37*, 255–273
SEMBRAUS, H. H. & KLEE, G. (1975) Die sensible Periode für die sexuelle Prägung beim Kaninchen. *Z. Tierz. Zuechtungsbiol. 92*, 145–152

Male homosexuality: perversion, deviation or variant ?

SIDNEY CROWN

The London Hospital, Whitechapel

Abstract Male homosexuality has complex determinants: biological, psychological, social, cultural and situational factors may be relevant, either inhibiting heterosexuality or leading towards homosexuality. Environmental factors seem paramount, particularly significant early relationships, usually within the family. Especially implicated are the personalities and interaction of the parents, recent interest being especially in the father's role. Also relevant is the family as a complex social system and the modes of communication within it, both verbal and non-verbal. Social research and sociopolitical pressures have helped to liberalize attitudes to homosexually 'deviant' behaviour but have not added significantly to its understanding. Many factors are involved in determining whether homosexual men seek therapy and reach a particular therapist. These factors relate to the patient's and therapist's personalities; to different therapeutic philosophies and therapeutic goals; and to the formal and informal referral networks in society.

THE PRESENT POSITION

I thought that in this paper I would do the opposite of what we normally do to satisfy editorial requirements: start with a series of brief statements which seem to represent accepted knowledge as I read it, indicating areas of potential growth; and then concentrate on what I know best – clinical and therapeutic considerations.

First: homosexuality – either a single act or a pattern of behaviour – may involve biological, psychological, social, cultural or situational factors, together with their interaction.

Second: an important growth area is the delineation, analysis and, if possible, control of the biological factors whether these be physical, chemical or hormonal. That Freud recognized this is interestingly illustrated by the last sentence of his monograph (Freud 1905): 'The unsatisfactory conclusion, however, that emerges from these investigations of the disturbances of sexual life is that we know far too little of the biological processes constituting the essence of sexuality to be able to construct from our fragmentary information a theory adequate to the understanding alike of normal and of pathological conditions'. It seems likely at least in principle that biological factors may account for part of the spectrum of homosexuality: the life-long 'obligatory', essential, idiopathic homosexual compared to the transient, 'facultative', optional or induced homosexual (Money 1970). If biological factors account for 'obligatory' homosexuality, then 'facultative' homosexuality may be left to the environmentalists to diagnose, provide therapy for and, possibly, prevent.

Third: the light cast on homosexuality by sociology (homosexuality as deviance) and from the homophile organizations (homosexuality as variant) has been sociopolitically powerful, but scientifically barren. Social research has modified the climate of acceptance of homosexuality, at least on the surface, but has not significantly added to basic understanding of the phenomenon. In fact, paradoxically the effect of sociopolitical pressure has been to discourage clinicians and therapists from risking social opprobrium by doing research on these problems. The risk is of name-calling, for example 'change-therapist' (Tripp 1977), of being involved in rowdy meetings or of pressure to alter students' required reading lists. Arguments about whether male homosexuality is a normal 'variant', is statistically 'deviant' or is psychopathologically 'perverse' seem empty. Homosexuality is a sexual orientation towards someone of one's own sex. The term should be used without implications just as one might, in other areas, use terms such as 'anxiety', 'paranoid', 'depersonalization' or 'hypochondria'. One may then try to understand its aetiology in a particular person or the common factors involved in its general aetiology. In terms purely of avoidance of 'labelling' individuals (Roman 1971), 'deviance' is probably the word that is most acceptable to the extremes of orthodox medicine on the conservative, and peer-group supports (Robinson & Henry 1977) on the radical ends of the spectrum.

Fourth: within psychology the influential theoretical systems are three. The first is psychoanalysis, in which the emphasis is on understanding (Gillespie 1956). Homosexuality is regarded unequivocally as a perversion because aspects of behaviour appropriate for an earlier developmental period have not been replaced by adult heterosexual responses. The second force is learning theory with its emphasis on manipulation and control of homosexual behaviour in therapy. The 'third force' (Yalom 1975) in current therapies is the humanist-existential approach and the 'new' therapies (Liss 1974). These therapies align themselves with the 'Gay Liberation' homophile philosophy: namely accept it, talk about it ('let it all hang out'), be responsible for yourself, I'm not your keeper, and so on. This approach is not oriented to research, theory or therapy, although it may achieve personal inner peace for selected individuals.

Fifth: these very great differences between the three approaches in their attitude to homosexuality and the place of each in the medico-social system suggest how patients ('clients') of different types of personality with different types of homosexual 'problem' and with different goals in therapy tend to gravitate towards the type of change-agent (or 'no-change' agent) which suits them best. This may explain why the experience of different therapists with male homosexuality seems to differ so much. Thus, for example, the factors in self-selection necessary in today's social climate which take a homosexual to a form of aversion therapy to alter his sexual orientation are certainly different from those that might send an individual who accepts his homosexuality to a psychotherapist for help with a by-product of it, such as the sadness of being childless. Contrast, too, the bravado which encourages a young, extroverted homosexual to give up the idea of 'change' of sexual orientation and to be proud of being 'gay', to 'come out' in the gay world (Dank 1971).

In summary, therefore, it seems to me that where we 'are at' is that advances in developmental neurology and endocrinology may be relevant to a part of the spectrum of homosexual behaviour but sexual orientation is likely to be mainly environmental in its determination; society in both its macro- and micro-aspects guides the majority into heterosexuality, but our need is to understand further the psychological and social forces and their combinations that lead a sizable minority towards a homosexual orientation, if the widely quoted figures of Kinsey *et al.* (1948) are accepted that 4 % of adult males in the USA are solely homosexually orientated and 37 % have had some adult experience of homosexuality.

PSYCHOANALYSIS

Classical psychoanalysis

Freud's monograph *Three Essays on Sexuality* (1905) appears in many authors' reference lists—so many that I thought I ought to re-read it! I commend the exercise to others. Considering the date, it is a remarkably perspicacious work. Obviously there are mistakes in detail and the expression (though not the language) is dated but Freud makes a number of points whose fundamental importance remains: the origins of heterosexuality are as remarkable as those of homosexuality. Innate factors are likely to be relevant (and details of the *Essays* were modified up to 1925 to take account of advances in knowledge). Homosexuality is culturally omnipresent and historically of importance. Normal or supernormal achievement in all other life areas than sexuality is the rule rather than the exception, so that homosexuality can hardly be subsumed under any disease concept.

Freud suggested that man was inherently capable of expressing sexuality in many ways ('polymorphous perversity') and that a bisexual potential was the norm. To explain the fact that a sizable minority turned their sexual orientation towards their own sex, Freud suggested that it was necessary to look at the vicissitudes of life experience, especially within the family. Freud suggested too that there were likely to be types of homosexuality of varying degrees of mutability or immutability. He used the terms 'absolute', 'amphigenic' (bisexual) and 'contingent' (related to external conditions). He differentiated homosexuality with its love for another adult of the same sex from perversions of sexuality which expressed themselves in both a different object (e.g. a child) or in different aims (e.g. masturbation with a fetish object). He attempted to show, from psychoanalytic reconstruction, that normal sexuality included a number of developmental components from early life: thus kissing, sucking, biting, looking, exhibiting, smelling, touching, masturbating, love for the same-sex parent; feelings of possessiveness and jealousy in a three-cornered (oedipal) relation; the appropriate mixture of sexuality and assertiveness—all are components of sexuality and may appear in adult sexual behaviour. If one component dominated so that in the adult this component, for example looking or exhibiting, displaced expression by union of the genitalia then, by definition, this was sexually perverse behaviour—that is, scopophilia or exhibitionism.

The other still-interesting issue Freud attempted to face was why a psychoneurotic symptom (such as an anxiety-phobic state) caused personal suffering (ego dystonic), whereas perversion, the other side of the coin, appeared to be regarded by the individual with equanimity (ego syntonic). Because of his belief in the existence of complex organizations of function within the mind (defences) he made the psychodynamic hypothesis that some kind of internal 'bargain' seemed to be struck so that those areas of the mind responsible for the arousal of guilt (superego), and with which a symptom such as a phobia seemed to represent a compromise formation, for reasons not then—and not now—clear, could allow sexually perverse behaviour to be indulged in without neurotic suffering, as if this behaviour was less guilt-producing than the conflict it was said to disguise—for example, aggressive feelings to the same sex parent in competition for the love of the opposite sex parent.

Recent psychoanalytic developments

Freud's (1905) theory was based on early psychoanalytic ideas about psychosexual development. Gillespie (1956), a distinguished contemporary English psychoanalyst, makes the point that the full role of aggression, the conscience (superego), mechanisms of defence against anxiety, and the importance of social (object) relationships both in their reality (external) representation and their internalized representation (e.g. the model of the punishing parent), need to be taken into account if we are to update Freud's psychosexual theory.

The most authoritative modern representation of psychoanalytic thought on male homosexuality is the research of Bieber (1962). A large team (n = 77) of psychoanalysts, all belonging to one professional organization, drew up, discussed and revised a questionnaire relating to male homosexuality covering the areas felt from the literature and clinical practice to be likely to be relevant. This questionnaire was filled in by the therapists of 106 homosexual male patients and the questionnaire was also filled in for a comparison group of 100 heterosexual male patients. These data were conscientiously sifted and statistically analysed. Despite the obvious methodological limitations this study represents a praiseworthy attempt by a group of psychoanalytically oriented therapists to add some relatively hard data to the previously available soft data derived from individual psychoanalytic reconstruction.

Bieber (1962) considers homosexuality a perversion of the sex drive, the basic orientation of which is towards the opposite sex. Homosexuality develops as a symptom, or inhibition – a fear of the opposite sex – this symptom being particularly accounted for by relations in the family: thus the pathogenic influence of the close-binding intimate mother with homosexual sons. These mothers have seductive, inhibitory, over-controlling attitudes. With the fathers, there was a profound, unremitting interpersonal disturbance of the relationship with the homosexual son: detached, hostile, minimizing, openly rejecting. The attitude of homosexual sons towards their fathers was characterized by hatred and fear. A 'classical', homosexual triangular pattern was noted: the mother, close-binding, dominant and minimizing towards her husband, who was a detached, particularly a hostile-detached, father. Bieber's statistical analyses suggested that this combination is highly pathogenetic of homosexuality or of homosexual problem development.

In a psychoanalytically orientated psychometric study Bene (1965) gave the Bene-Anthony Family Relations Test to 83 male homosexuals and a control group of 84 married men, group-matched on a number of variables. The parents of the subject were alive and their marriage was intact until at least the patient's 14th year; other matching was for age and size of family, and father's occupation (manual or non-manual). The Bene-Anthony Test is semi-projective in type but yields a quantitative score. It is directed towards the evaluation of early family relationships. Careful statistical analyses of test items showed that the homosexuals had a more negative (hostile, affectionless) relation with their fathers than the married men; an interesting and unexplained finding was that the homosexuals expressed more hostility and less affection than the married men to their mothers. Thus the pathogenetic influence of the cold, harsh, rejecting father was confirmed, but not the picture of the close-binding mother.

The changing emphasis in recent psychodynamic studies from the mother to the father seems not only to reflect the likely importance of the same sex parent, but also to be a tacit acknowledgement that fathers have been neglected in much so-called family-oriented research. Certainly the influence of the father on the development of male homosexuality seems highly salient and in need of further study.

Bieber (1962) goes so far as to suggest that if the father is an emotionally positive figure, the development of a male homosexual is virtually inconceivable.

The implication of these recent psychoanalytic studies is to shift interest from the individual to the family. Bene's investigation was an attempt to study family structure via the memories and projections of individuals. The research gap that now needs filling is the direct study of interactions within families containing a homosexual compared to those in families with no homosexual member. Forms of communication in particular need objectifying: verbal, para-linguistic (how things are said), and non-verbal communication. Such studies have been attempted in families containing a schizophrenic member but have been difficult to replicate. Another possible family observation technique that might be adaptable is the use of experimental conflict situations which encourage family cooperation and stress; such methods have been used in the assessment of two-person relationships, especially marriages (Goodrich & Boomer 1963). A third possible method is the use of trained observers to go into families and rate aspects of family interaction. This technique has been used by Kreitman *et al.* (1971).

Latent homosexuality

Freud's idea that man had an inherently bisexual nature allowed for the concept of latent homosexuality—stirrings below the threshold of conscious awareness that a person might be homosexual, leading to anxiety. Bieber

(1962) suggested that men's basic orientation is heterosexual; thus Bieber's epigram that every homosexual is a 'latent heterosexual'. Clinically what is important is that a person may be unaccepting and anxious about his sexual orientation as he perceives it. Homosexuality may of course be expressed in thought and fantasy, in set and attitude, and in physiological arousal, as well as in action-patterns such as role and behaviour. In this sense uncertainty about sexual orientation is a clinical reality, although the term 'latent' may be scientifically unhelpful.

LEARNING

It is not at all easy to determine what part learning theory can play in the systematic understanding of the development of sexual orientation as opposed to the obviously relevant part it plays in devising contingencies of unlearning sexual behaviour. A person's learning (conditioning) history is so infinitely complicated and sexual behaviours are so finite that it seems important to look for common learning elements in people's life patterns. In this, learning theory and psychoanalysis may together return to intra-family learning experiences, although conceptualizing these experiences will be different.

Eysenck (1976) has recently outlined a new approach to the learning theory model of neurosis. Eysenck is dismissive equally of Freud and of Skinner because he regards them as either setting up theoretical hypotheses—one presumes he means those such as 'castration' anxiety or the Oedipus complex—which are non-falsifiable as with Freud, or, with Skinner, as using a basic concept such as operant conditioning which, because it depends at some stage on the occurrence of a chance event which is reinforced and fixed in a behavioural repertoire, equally can never be rigorously falsified. Eysenck prefers to extend a classical conditioning paradigm and he is particularly concerned to face up to the problem of the 'neurotic paradox'—namely that behaviour which is patently non-rewarding is not extinguished. The reasoning in Eysenck's paper (1976) is complicated and I do not regard myself as expert enough to evaluate the arguments of learning theorists, but his suggested model attempts a number of things. It replaces the classical law of extinction by a version which allows for incubation (enhancement) effects of exposure to conditioned stimulus (CS)-only stimuli as well as for extinction effects. Secondly, the importance of individual differences is emphasized and relations are suggested between personality and the conditioning of neurotic behaviour. Thirdly, stress is laid on innate fear patterns and 'preparedness' as factors in the genesis of conditioned fear responses. Fourthly the concept of 'pain' in the classical experimental animal literature and its use in creating models of neurosis is supplemented by other more humanly relevant, cognitive, concepts ('frustrative non-reward'; 'approach-avoidance' conflict). Fifthly, 'traumatic' single-trial conditioning is abandoned as a concept and a new theory based on incubation is proposed.

If it is possible to accept Eysenck's model for neurotic symptoms which are anxiety-based (such as phobias and obsessions) it may prove possible to extend the paradigm to the development of a behavioural–attitudinal complex such as sexual orientation. What is particularly difficult is to understand how a person learns to be heterosexual or to turn away from heterosexuality. If the latter, why towards homosexuality rather than towards sexual dysfunction (impotence; orgasmic dysfunction)? And when one rather than the other?

I think it is interesting that recognition of the complexity of human behaviour has brought the two major approaches to behaviour, psychoanalysis and learning theory, closer together. 'Pure' behaviourism stresses learning principles which are essentially environmentally controlled; 'pure' psychoanalysis emphasizes the importance of the person's inner world, of conflict, fantasy, stratagems, plans, hopes and fears. Cognitive psychology has tended to act as a theoretical bridge, in part acceptable to both approaches, so that behaviourism has become more intra-psychic and psychoanalysis more behavioural. It is of course arbitrary whether a theoretical analysis of behaviour is conceptualized in one terminology rather than another. This area was explored in a previous Ciba Foundation symposium, *The Role of Learning in Psychotherapy* (Ciba Foundation 1968)–to my mind a much under-rated book.

To summarize at this point, homosexuality is produced neither just by individual intra-psychic nor family pathology nor by societal forces. The aetiology is complex, multifactorial and interactional, with biological potential interacting with psychological, social, cultural and situational forces to produce the condition.

THERAPY

It seems clear from the most reliable descriptive studies of male homosexuals that the majority of them in the community are seen neither by psychotherapists nor by behaviour therapists. Saghir *et al.* (1969) made a study of remarkable care in the size and selection of their sample and in the thoroughness of data collection. Eighty-nine men (age range 19–70, average 35 years) were interviewed through the cooperation of homophile organizations in two large US cities. Regarding treatment history, 74 % had never had psychotherapy, suggesting that, at that time at least, the majority of homosexuals did not become involved in psychotherapy. While a sample gathered through homophile organizations is of course to an unknown extent a selected sample, and possibly one biased against treatment, it would still seem likely that the majority of male homosexuals do not enter therapy. Saghir *et al.* (1969) suggest that they make the necessary adjustments and compromises on their own. Possibly with changes in society more use is made of self-help groups such as Gay Liberation. The increased availability of behaviour therapy techniques in the last ten years or so may also have altered the situation. Therapists of both major approaches therefore see highly selected samples of homosexuals. The selective factors include type of therapy and therapeutic philosophy, as well as the personality of the client and the complicated mechanisms existing in society for referral, both formal (general practitioner, counsellor, etc.) and informal (spouse, friends, etc.).

Psychoanalysts show a mixed (ambivalent) attitude towards the results of therapy. On the one hand, psychoanalysis has always tended to see therapy as influencing the whole person rather than being mainly symptom-oriented. On the other hand, therapeutic enthusiasm is obvious from the section on therapeutic results in Bieber's study (1962). The patients were rated at a final follow-up enquiry in 1960 and judgements were made of change or lack of it during the course of treatment. They do not include, therefore, a significant follow-up period. The patients being evaluated had had at least 150 hours of psychoanalysis. Of the total homosexual group (n = 106), 29 (27 %) had become exclusively heterosexual. What is of particular interest, however, is that of 76 patients exclusively homosexual or sexually inactive at the start of treatment only 14 (19 %) had become exclusively heterosexual. Of 30 initially bisexual patients 15 (50 %) became exclusively heterosexual. The difference in outcome between those starting as exclusively homosexual and those initially bisexual was statistically highly significant. Factors particularly affecting the outcome of treatment were initial bisexuality, staying in treatment longer, stating a desire to change sexual orientation at the outset, age under 35 years, and less severe father-son psychopathology.

These results may be compared with the results of several trials of behaviour therapy by McConaghy (1976) under the title 'Is homosexual orientation irreversible?'. McConaghy draws the interesting distinction between sexual behaviour as it might present before or develop after treatment and 'true' sexual orientation, which he sees as something the client may not be consciously aware of but is reflected through autonomic arousal to homosexual or heterosexual stimulation measured by penile plethysmography. In four studies homosexual patients were randomly allocated to receive either different forms of aversive therapy or a positive conditioning procedure. Before and after therapy the patients' sexual orientation was determined by penile volume responses. The aversive techniques were effective in reducing homosexual and increasing heterosexual behaviour. With all forms of aversive treatment about one-quarter of the patients reported an increase in heterosexual feelings and heterosexual intercourse at follow-up. About one-quarter of the patients reported a reduction in homosexual feelings at follow-up. A similar percentage reported no homosexual physical encounters since receiving treatment. However, changes in autonomic arousal (penile plethysmography) were not concordant with changes in feeling and behaviour, and McConaghy concluded that while present treatments may reduce or eliminate patients' homosexual behaviour and awareness of homosexual feelings, they do not alter their sexual orientation.

It is interesting to contrast the studies of Bieber and McConaghy in the light of considerations discussed in this paper. The actual therapeutic results seem not dissimilar—perhaps one-quarter of homosexual patients treated will be helped to alter their overt sexual behaviour and subjective sexual experience. Both studies show how selected are the patients seen—Bieber's from those who wanted and could afford psychoanalysis; while McConaghy makes it clear that the patients in all his samples were referred for behaviour therapy. Both investigators emphasized the importance for therapy of factors such as relative youth and previous heterosexual experience. Thus, over 15 % of McConaghy's clients were married and approximately half had had previous heterosexual intercourse (McConaghy 1976, Table 1, p. 558).

PSYCHOPHYSIOLOGY OF HOMOSEXUALITY

The cognitive components of male sexual deviance (attitude, fantasy) may be differentiated from sexual behaviour and from the psychophysiological dimension reflected in penile erection. McConaghy (1976) has suggested that penile responsivity may reflect true sexual orientation and notes that this may not co-vary with attitude and behaviour. A study by Bancroft (1969) of 10 male homosexuals treated with aversion therapy seems to confirm this. Modification of erectile responses endured after therapy in only one subject.

Many people, scientific and lay, consider that homosexuality may be fundamentally different from other sexual deviations. There is a relationship to a whole person, rather than to a part of a person, such as a piece of clothing, or to an isolated piece of a person's behaviour such as cruelty. Could this be what is being reflected physiologically? It seems possible that sexual deviations such as fetishism, transvestism, or sado-masochism may resemble neurotic symptoms, and, as with phobias, be capable of modification at all levels – attitude, behaviour and physiology. Homosexuality may reflect the whole personality, modifiable in socially mediated areas such as attitude and behaviour, but not at the level of basic physiology. Confirmation of this possibility awaits further comparative studies.

CONCLUSION

It seems likely that basic sexual orientation is laid down in the early years of life. Biological factors may be relevant but probably more important are complicated learning experiences with early caretaking figures, usually the parents. With male homosexuality the indications are that the father may be the more relevant parent. This learning may be conceptualized in terms of psychoanalytic or conditioning models. Most homosexually oriented men live with their sexuality, with or without peer group support. Those who come for therapy to the two main modalities of treatment, psychotherapy or behaviour therapy, are already highly selected, either self-selected or selected as a result of the complexities of the informal referral network, or general practitioners' or psychiatrists' habits of patient selection. Of those reaching therapy about 25 % benefit in terms of less homosexual fantasy and behaviour. Relative youth and evidence of previous heterosexual behaviour are important factors in patient selection as well as motivation for change sufficient for the client to complete a course of whatever treatment has been selected. Whether basic sexual orientation, once laid down, can be altered is an interesting, open question.

References

BANCROFT, J. (1969) Aversion therapy for homosexuality. A pilot study of 10 cases. *Br. J. Psychiatr. 115,* 1417–1431

BENE, E. (1965) On the genesis of male homosexuality: an attempt at clarifying the role of parents. *Br. J. Psychiatr. 111,* 803–813

BIEBER, I. (1962) *Homosexuality. A Psychoanalytic Study,* Basic Books, New York

CIBA FOUNDATION (1968) *The Role of Learning in Psychotherapy (Ciba Found. Symp.),* Churchill, London

DANK, B.M. (1971) Coming out in the Gay World. *Psychiatry 34,* 180–197

EYSENCK, H.J. (1976) The learning theory model of neurosis - a new approach. *Behav. Res. Ther. 14,* 251–267

FREUD, S. (1905) *Three Essays on the Theory of Sexuality,* The Hogarth Press, London

GILLESPIE, W.H. (1956) The general theory of sexual perversion. *Int. J. Psychoanal. 37,* 1–8

GOODRICH, D.W. & BOOMER, D.S. (1963) Experimental assessment of modes of conflict resolution. *Family Process 2,* 15–24
KINSEY, A.C., POMEROY, W.B. & MARTIN, C.E. (1948) *Sexual Behaviour in the Human Male,* Saunders, Philadelphia
KREITMAN, N., COLLINS, J., NELSON, B. & TROOP, J. (1971) Neurosis and marital interaction. IV. Manifest psychological interaction. *Br. J. Psychiatr. 119,* 243–252
LISS, J. (1974) *Free to Feel,* Wildwood House, London
MCCONAGHY, N. (1976) Is a homosexual orientation irreversible? *Br. J. Psychiatr. 129,* 556–563
MONEY, J. (1970) Sexual dimorphism and homosexual gender identity. *Psychol. Bull. 74,* 425–440
ROBINSON, D. & HENRY, S. (1977) *Self Help and Health. Mutual Aid for Modern Problems,* Martin Roberts, London,
ROMAN, P.M. (1971) Labeling theory and community psychiatry. *Psychiatry 34,* 378–390
SAGHIR, M.J., ROBINS, E. & WALBRAN, B. (1969) Homosexuality. II. Sexual behaviour of the male homosexual. *Arch. Gen. Psychiatr. 21,* 219–229
TRIPP, C.A. (1977) *The Homosexual Matrix,* Quartet Books, London
YALOM, I.D. (1975) *The Theory and Practice of Group Psychotherapy,* Basic Books, New York

Discussion

Bancroft: I have to reject the idea (McConaghy 1976) that recording erections in response to erotic stimuli in the laboratory is in any sense measuring a 'core' homosexual tendency, whereas looking at behaviour isn't. The data simply show that aversive techniques are not successful in altering people's ability to respond to erotic stimuli, at least over a period of time. Treatment in general, aversion therapy or anything else, in people who are highly motivated to change, may well lead to their trying out alternative patterns of behaviour–particularly heterosexual behaviour–so that the changes that endure after a course of treatment of whatever kind are likely to be types of behaviour that weren't there before, and there is no particular reason why the responsiveness to homosexual stimuli should not remain, and often does remain. My own work with aversion therapy (Bancroft 1974) was a series of studies which served to show that aversion therapy is ineffective in changing sexual preferences, and that if one is going to help people with a homosexual orientation who want to change their behaviour one should look towards helping them establish new forms of behaviour, or helping them to become happier with their homosexual pattern of behaviour.

The fundamental difference between my point of view and that of the majority of psychoanalysts is that I am unable to find any use in regarding homosexuality as a disease or illness. I don't believe we understand why people develop heterosexual or homosexual preferences, and we certainly have no reason to conclude that homosexual preferences are necessarily pathological or disadvantageous. They are often a handicap in our present society, but it is possible to have extremely valuable and acceptable homosexual relationships, and there are some awful heterosexual ones!

Sachar: The American Psychiatric Association's new diagnostic system does not list homosexuality *per se* as a mental disorder. This created controversy in some quarters. An analytic group was upset by this, but less so when it was pointed out that their formulations about the particular neurotic constellation in homosexuals and their families were drawn exclusively from the patients who came to them for extensive treatment. As we have heard, only a relatively small proportion of homosexuals come for treatment. A group at Washington University made an effort to get a broader selection of homosexuals and on their personality test measures they could not distinguish a homosexual group from a matched normal control population. So the decision of the American Psychiatric Association task force, ratified by the organization's membership, is to list as suffering from a mental disorder those people who are exceedingly uncomfortable or who experience homosexuality as a symptom but not to classify homosexuality *per se* as a mental disorder.

Green: Homosexuality may be the sole condition which is a mental disorder only if you go to a psychiatrist for it!

Bancroft: The treatment is then to get rid of all psychiatrists?

Green: One of the good points that Dr Crown made was in talking of the homosexual*ities*, in the way many people now refer to the schizophren*ias*. Those of us who are unhappy enough to be looking for either a psychogenic or a biochemical final answer to aetiology sometimes ignore the fact that there may be many homosexualities and that we may not find a unitary early life experience or neuroendocrine aetiology of the homosexualities (or of the heterosexual*ities*).

You referred to the study by Bieber (1962). One should point out a double confounding in those data, demonstrated by Marvin Siegelman (1972, 1974). About one-third of the homosexuals in Bieber's sample had been 'feminine' as young children and showed a high degree of femininity in adult life. If you eliminate femininity as a factor in analysing the psychological status of male homosexuals you also cancel out differences in neuroticism scores between homosexuals and heterosexuals. If you cancel neuroticism differences, then the family constellation that Bieber found vanishes. So there is a 'double confound' that may contribute to Bieber's finding of a close-binding intimate mother, namely 'femininity' differences between samples and psychiatric patient status.

Finally, a clinical point that I have uncovered among the boys I have been following, whom I described earlier (p. 60), is that a homosexual orientation can appear very early in life. Boys of 7 or 8 years tell me that when they look at another boy undressed, or at a picture of a nude male, they get erections, and they don't get erections when they look at nude females or pictures of nude females. So the capacity for homosexual arousal can be present very early in life, well before puberty. I don't know whether this points towards a psychogenic or a biological influence. However, it may point against its accessibility to any kind of intervention. I am not surprised that therapists, using the best techniques they have, with a very selected group of highly motivated patients, fail to re-orientate three-quarters of their patients to heterosexuality.

Crown: It would be unfair to dismiss Bieber's study completely. It was a careful study. West (1960), an authority in the UK on homosexuality and not a psychoanalyst, has summarized a number of studies, clinical and psychometric, showing in the background of homosexuals over-close relations with the mother and a negative relationship with the father.

Green: When Siegelman parcels out neuroticism scores, those kinds of family patterns disappear. Such family patterns are correlated more with general levels of neuroticism than with sexual orientation. Unless one controls for that, it confounds the results.

Bancroft: There is an exception to that; this is Siegelman's 1972 study when he looked at homosexuals who are anxious about their gender identity.

Green: Yes—they are more neurotic. Femininity is a confound for neuroticism, and neuroticism is a confound for the finding of a close-binding intimate mother and detached father.

Crown: Do you feel that this relationship isn't relevant at all?

Green: You can find it, but you also find this pattern in control families with masculine boys, and in families of drug addicts, or delinquents, and in pre-schizophrenic families. It appears in many psychiatric situations and is not specific to homosexuality.

Sachar: In another context Ovesey (1969) described three syndromes of male homosexuality, one of which involved an intense tie with the mother and an intense identification with her. In the second syndrome there was a very nurturing father and an oral yearning for him which the patient went on to try to recapture in his relations with men. Thirdly there was essentially a phobia of the female genitals—in recoiling, the subject turned away from women and towards men. So Ovesey has described in his clinical papers something like the homosexuali*ties* to which Dr Green referred.

Beach: Dr Crown has expressed cautious hope that people working on the physiology and behaviour of animals would be able to come up with something that would increase our understanding of human psychology. I would like to make a point here, as important as it is obvious.

Data or concepts in physiology are no more objective, 'scientific' or valuable than data or concepts in psychology, and evidence relating to rats or rhesus monkeys has no special value that gives it greater scientific respectability than data on human beings. Problems that are defined at one level—let us say, the human psychological level—have to be dealt with and conceptualized at that level. We cannot reduce them to 'lower' levels, although we may think we do so when we talk about plasma levels of testosterone and in the same breath mention a psychological construct such as homosexuality. We are moving from one level to another, dealing with disparate entities, like apples and oranges. I particularly distrust the implication that we are being more hard-headed and scientific when we move from a more complex level to what we think of as a simpler one. One hopes that models can be used, and in some cases we know they can, but they prove effective when we already know that mechanisms involved are identical or very similar. We can deal with cross-species models of infectious disease, dietary deficiencies, and certain aspects of endocrinology because we already know that the mechanisms and phenomena are the same. But we cannot *assume* that they are the same. Certainly many behavioural or psychological concepts are not transferable without modification.

Marteau: May I take up the point that the aetiology of homosexuality may vary? In many of the groups with which I deal there is a tremendous overlay of religious guilt, and especially in the area of homosexuality. If a boy, in a family where sex is never spoken about, has one homosexual experience as part of his growing up process, an experience he has come to regard as a grave matter, he becomes convinced he is homosexual. He then begins a pattern of homosexuality, becomes frightened about women, and becomes tied into the situation. This is one pattern we often see. Such boys may now be convinced that they are homosexual, although their first sexual orientation can be discovered in short-term therapy. True, they are only a small part of the whole spectrum, yet at the present time this group appears to be on the increase because of the cultural atmosphere and the labelling it makes possible. This may be atypical but it demonstrates that there is no point in looking for a single cause for homosexuality. Homosexuality is one expression of an individual's being, one piece of behaviour, and a very important one, and is characteristic of the individual's response to relationships in both the sexual and non-sexual fields. It may be that this particular piece of behaviour has been consciously or unconsciously chosen to demonstrate something about the whole of that individual's personality, or problem of relating. It is a handy thing to hang out, if you need to hang out something.

Crown: Professor Beach emphasized the dangers of generalizing across species which one recognizes even in general medicine where, for example, certain species may develop arthritis and others do not. There are major differences between human and non-human primates in their capacities for verbalization, symbolization and conceptualization. Thus Father Marteau's subgroup of homosexuals may conceptualize their problem in a different way from the homosexuals who come to me for psychotherapy or go to John Bancroft for aversion therapy.

Bancroft: I have heard Bieber speak of what he called the 'eroticization of the threatening object', and he directly tried to link this to some observations on primates. It ties in with the idea of the negative relationship with the father, that if a young male is frightened of an older male, like the father, one way of relating to the older male is to sexualize the relationship or to make erotic approaches or genital displays.

Sachar: Essentially 'presenting'? Do you see this much in primate colonies as one dimension of relating to a threatening male, by adopting the feminine posture?

Keverne: We refer to the 'presentation posture' by male monkeys as being non-sexual because of the context in which it occurs. It is more likely to occur in aggressive encounters than in a sexual context.

Sachar: And the dominant male doesn't follow it up in a sexual way?

Keverne: He may mount the other male but I have never seen such presentations responded to with both mounting and intromission in monkeys. It is what we might call a dominance–subordination interaction.

Herbert: The earliest observation of this was made by Kempf (1917). He described what he called homosexual behaviour in monkeys, and he related it to the dominance hierarchy.

Brawer: I am confused by this discussion and would like to know to what purpose psychiatrists want to understand homosexuality. If we were discussing the schizophrenias the purpose would be clear. One would want to extrapolate from the laboratory to the clinic in order to understand and better treat the condition, because schizophrenia is 'bad'. But why are you clinicians anxious to have something applicable from the laboratory if, after all, homosexuality is simply an interesting piece of behaviour which is neither bad nor good? One could simply discuss it as an academic point.

Bancroft: It is a huge social problem. This is one reason. Homosexuals suffer because they are stigmatized by the heterosexual majority, and the stigma is often reinforced by assumptions about the determination of this behaviour.

Crown: A major interest of psychiatry is to understand human behaviour. In this sense homosexuality is not only a social phenomenon but an important psychological phenomenon, just as heterosexuality is.

Brawer: Then you are looking at it as something to be treated, as you would treat a disease.

Crown: No, I simply want to understand it, just as I want to understand heterosexuality, or schizophrenia. It is of academic, clinical and social interest.

Marteau: It is more than that for me, because the gay scene is not really so 'gay'. A large number of such people feel they are being 'robbed'—severely robbed—first, of the family, and second, of being accepted in their society or subculture. They suffer deprivation and want to do something about it. Of course, a great number of people equally have problems in heterosexuality. We are also concerned with these in marital therapy, not because we see marriage as a disease, but because we want to try to help people enjoy it better. But the homosexual is in a different position. Those who are unhappy really want to be heterosexual and therefore they want some change agent. The reason a person is labelled a 'psychiatric patient' is because he goes to a psychiatrist, and it has been suggested that you could cure all psychiatric disease if you closed psychiatric hospitals! Those who come to psychotherapy centres often do so because in that setting they are not called patients and are not made into patients. There are many social deprivations in the UK which arise from being labelled as a psychiatric patient. It is impossible to obtain certain jobs, or to emigrate. These deprivations do not arise if such people go to a private physician or psychiatrist or to psychiatric clinics.

Brawer: Do you then regard homosexuality as something to be reversed? If not, perhaps you should be treating everyone who is not homosexual, in order to create an atmosphere that they can live in?

Marteau: No. I see my work as a psychotherapist as helping people who are *sad,* and if they are sad about this, I am there to help them. If they are sad about something else, I am there to help them also. I do not label them as mentally diseased or as deviants: I call them 'sad'. If they wish to do something about it, it is my task to help them uncover the roots of their sadness and work through them. I do not label homosexuality or bereavement or depression as mental disease. Sometimes people have a right to be sad. To call it 'depression' is not to do anything with it except to deny it and push it away. Sometimes merely to tell someone 'you have a perfect right to be sad' is what is needed, rather than to label them as depressive, give them drugs and send them off with a label.

We are concerned with trying to help people understand themselves. You as experimentalists pay tribute to the fact that animal behaviour has meaning and spend a great deal of effort trying to uncover just what it means. I believe that all human behaviour, even the most bizarre, also has meaning. It may be confusing to me, and even more to the one afflicted, but I do not look on it as crazy, merely in need of understanding.

Sachar: It is reasonable for us as scientists, in a symposium on sex, hormones and behaviour, as we look at the role of sex hormones in the regulation of sexual behaviour in animals (and there is some evidence for a role in human beings as well), to try to account for the certain percentage of the population who are homosexual and to raise the question of whether alterations in hormonal state either prenatally or postnatally help to account for why some people make this choice rather than another, without making value judgements on that choice. To return to Dr Crown's question, which is a legitimate question, if we see homosexuals as a heterogeneous group, is it possible that a subgroup exists—perhaps a small fraction, if psychosocial variables may account for 90 % of the variance—in which some small part of the variance can be related to a biological predisposition, and among all the possible biological predispositions, might hormones play a role? We have heard a mixture of evidence on this point. Follow-up studies have been described of children exposed to one or another kind of hormonal influence; interesting things happen to them but homosexuality does not seem to be one of the outcomes. On the other hand, there is a scattering of data suggesting that among some homosexuals of extreme type—perhaps the obligatory type, the feminine type, and perhaps among some transsexuals—there may be evidence for altered neuroendocrine regulation. Again, the data are scattered and from different laboratories, and it remains an open question at present.

In terms of trying to ask questions amenable to research, it may be too much to tackle the problem of homosexuality, with all its variations and social pressures. We have a more homogeneous, stereotyped group in the transsexuals, who from age 2–4 years are convinced that they have the wrong body; there is very little apparent relation to parental and family constellations; and the group is totally resistant to any psychotherapeutic intervention. I don't know of even one reported case of successful psychotherapeutic treatment of a transsexual. These are people with true conviction, normal in most other respects, who from their earliest childhood memories have it firmly in their minds that they have the wrong body and are determined to be operated on. If one wants to tackle any problem, this group, from the neuroendocrine point of view, might be more amenable than the broad spectrum of the homosexualities.

Goy: We are not likely to have an animal model for it; that is the problem!

Bancroft: There is a fundamental question here relevant to animal work. Is there any evidence for a hormonal determination of sexual *preferences,* rather than particular types of behaviour, in animals?

Hutchison: There is some evidence that androgens play a part in determining sexual preference in rodents. For example, androgens administered soon after birth to female rats (Meyerson & Lindström 1973) or gerbils (Holman 1977) induce a preference, as measured in adulthood by a choice test, for the oestrous female. However, preference for the opposite sex is only part of the problem. An equally important question concerns the type of partner chosen. Why should one sexual partner of the opposite sex be chosen rather than another? There is clear evidence that mating preferences, particularly in birds, are acquired through a process of learning, termed 'sexual imprinting', relatively early in development (reviewed by Bateson 1978). Sexual imprinting begins at a specific stage in development when the animal is particularly sensitive to certain classes of stimuli such as adult plumage coloration. Whether hormones are involved in the learning process is still a matter for speculation. It seems likely that sexual imprinting can be distinguished from early 'filial imprinting', in which birds form an attachment for their mother early in life. The latter process occurs soon after hatching, whereas some evidence suggests that sexual imprinting comes later, when adult plumage develops.

Ehrhardt: If we include birds, we should mention studies by Schutz (1965) on male ducks who were raised only with other males. Later they typically preferred males as mating partners.

Hutchison: There is no evidence for any hormonal role yet. But this is an interesting point, because one can also ask how early-learning processes involved in mate selection relate to the early effects of hormones on the sexual differentiation of brain mechanisms of behaviour. This problem has not, as far as I know, been studied yet.

Jost: In the ring dove, testosterone does not stimulate mounting-copulation behaviour in males out of season unless the males have cohabited with females for some time. They must be familiar with the female, and *then* hormones become active. So this is taking the thing the other way, in that we have a kind of psychological effect permitting the hormonal effect.

Herbert: It is extraordinarily important to distinguish between behavioural role and behavioural pattern. By this I mean not just looking at the way an animal responds to being mounted or to mounting, but whether it prefers either a female or another male. Nearly all the animal work has been done on behavioural pattern rather than preference. Recent work, including that of B.J. Meyerson in Sweden (unpublished), points to *preference* being affected in the same sort of way as *role* by the same sort of hormone, in both beagles and rats.

Keverne: You are talking about an early differentiating effect of hormones on sexual preference: but certainly in the adult rhesus monkey, hormonal state can influence preference behaviour without necessarily involving an early action of the hormone on the CNS. Hormones activate behaviour towards a preferred object but the hormone isn't known to determine that preference in the first place.

Jost: We have discussed sexual inversion or abnormality or whatever one likes to call it, and we have discussed the role of hormones in this situation, but we still need studies of the *normal* situation. For example, I should like to know if a hormonal threshold for sexual interest or sexual appetite can be defined, quite apart from the choice of partner; we know that sexual interest or sexual appetite does not appear in subjects castrated in early infancy. The second point concerns the choice of partner. Is it conceivable that once the hormonal threshold for having sexual appetite or interest is attained, the selection of the partner depends on a little more testosterone, or a little less? Does such a concept not implicitly underlie the hormonal studies of homosexuality?

Sachar: We can't answer these interesting questions yet, unfortunately.

References

BANCROFT, J.H.J. (1974) *Deviant Sexual Behaviour: Modification and Assessment,* Oxford University Press, London

BATESON, P.P.G. (1978) Early experience and sexual preferences, in *Biological Determinants of Sexual Behaviour* (Hutchison, J.B. ed.), pp. 29–55, Wiley, Chichester

BIEBER, I. (1962) *Homosexuality. A Psychoanalytic Study,* Basic Books, New York

HOLMAN, S.D. (1977) *Developmental Influences of Hormones on Sexual Behaviour in the Mongolian Gerbil.* Ph.D. Thesis, University of Cambridge

KEMPF, E.J. (1917) The social and sexual behaviour of infra-human primates with some comparable facts in human behaviour. *Psychoanal. Rev. 4,* 127–154

MCCONAGHY, N. (1976) Is a homosexual orientation irreversible? *Br. J. Psychiatr. 129,* 556–563

MEYERSON, B.J. & LINDSTRÖM, L. (1973) Sexual motivation in the neonatally androgen-treated female rat, in *Hormones and Brain Function* (Lissak, K., ed.), pp. 443–448, Plenum Press, New York

OVESEY, L. (1969) *Homosexuality and Pseudohomosexuality,* Science House, New York

SCHUTZ, F. (1965) Homosexualität und Prägung. Eine experimentelle Untersuchung an Enten. *Psychol. Forsch. 28,* 439–463

SIEGELMAN, M. (1972) Adjustment of male homosexuals and heterosexuals. *Arch. Sex. Behav. 2,* 9–25

SIEGELMAN, M. (1974) Parental background of male homosexuals and heterosexuals. *Arch. Sex. Behav. 3,* 3–18

WEST, D.J. (1960) *Homosexuality (2nd edn),* Pelican Books, London

Transsexuality: some remarks based on clinical experience

PREBEN HERTOFT and THORKIL SØRENSEN

The University Clinic of Psychiatry, The Sexological Research Unit, Rigshospitalet, Copenhagen

Abstract People with severe gender identity problems have always existed. Some hope to find a solution to their deep intrapersonal conflicts in a so-called sex transformation. The term 'transsexual' was coined by Cauldwell in 1949 and since then an unknown number of people all over the world, probably more biological men than women, have undergone a hormonal and surgical sex-transformation procedure. In this chapter we discuss the impossibility of real sex change from man to woman and vice versa. We briefly touch on two classical cases of sex transformation with some connection with Denmark: the Lili Elbe case of 1930 and the famous Chris Jorgensen case from the early fifties. We discuss the incidence of transsexuality and follow-up studies of patients, and give preliminary results from a Danish study of 110 people (81 men and 29 women) who during the past 25 years have applied for a sex-change operation. Of these, 56 individuals (42 men and 14 women) have had such operations. These are minimum figures since some transsexuals are known to have had operations in other countries but have not contacted Danish hospitals or health personnel.

I

If you are born as a man, but want to be a woman – or born as a woman but want to be a man – you are demanding something impossible. But nowadays this is not a rare wish and we call such people transsexuals. So-called transsexual people have existed at all times; only the term is new, coined by Cauldwell in 1949 but especially known through Benjamin's (1966) work. In *Metamorphoses* by Ovid we hear about Tiresias, who lived seven years as a woman but changed back to man again. It is hardly casually that the magical events of Tiresias are told in the beginning of Ovid's version of the myth of Narcissus and Echo. As we know, Narcissus was lost (Echo, who loved him, was reduced to her voice), but Tiresias was not, maybe because Tiresias had the chance to change back to his original sex.

The difference between the past and the present is—among other things—that what was possible in the old days only through magic and the intervention of gods is now possible through hormonal and surgical procedures. Or is it? Personally, we dislike some of the vocabulary used in this connection, but we have been unable to produce any new terms. But it is our impression that many doctors and psychologists are using words like 'sex change' or 'sex transformation' without any reservations, though they sound like advertisements promising unhappy people something which cannot be delivered. What is called a sex transformation or sex change is only a change, more or less successful, from male to female appearance or vice versa. It would be preferable if we were to avoid as much as possible terms like sex change or sex transformation, because these terms are seductive, and certainly transsexuals are easily seduced at the stage before they are operated on.

People suffering from severe intrapersonal conflicts are in need of help. But it is not always possible to offer them real relief, and both patients and the medical profession have to accept this fact. Some people are so lucky as to be able to handle their inner conflicts in a flexible way; others are more rigid in their search for solutions. 'Sex change' (and from now on we shall stop putting this and similar terms in quotation marks, although to us they are still there) is always a rigid attempt to get out of a deep conflict—often a bad solution or no solution at all. Therefore, it is often a sad experience to meet people who want to change sex. Sad, because these people are victims of early rejection, but longing for love, acceptance and dignity, and believe that a sex transformation will bring them what they are so intensely seeking. Sad, because we know that they will not understand possible reservations to their wish, but will minimize the warnings, doubt the motives behind them and maybe believe that the doctor does not wish to see them happy. And the patient will seek new doctors until he finds one who 'understands' him; that is, one who accepts what the patient requests. Unfortunately, many more people seek sex transformation than those few who have a chance to profit from this procedure.

Personally we are convinced that even those few who profit from an operation, and feel they live a better life postoperatively, deep in their minds are well aware that they have not changed sex. But, contrary to the story of Tiresias, there is no way back.

It is, of course, the medical and psychological professions' obligation to devote time (often much) to this problem and to this group of patients in spite of personal feelings and uneasiness.

But let us not fool ourselves into believing we change people. We do not.

The word 'uneasiness' is not used with any moral connotations and not at random. We use it as Robert Stoller does in his chapter 'Male transsexualism: uneasiness'. We agree mostly with his attitude to sex transformation, but look forward to further confirmation of his aetiological theories. Stoller (1975) writes: 'First let me express the opinion, in disagreement with those who feel that "sex transformation" is never indicated, that there are extremely feminine males who can effortlessly pass undetected in society as females, for whom there is no known treatment that would render them masculine in behaviour and appearance. In the absence of any such treatment, we have three choices: (1) insist nonetheless that they be treated by some method that does not work (e.g. psychoanalysis); (2) do nothing, with or without moral exhortation; (3) provide them with 'sex transformation'. I have been in favor of the third for these patients'. And Stoller continues: 'But the issue is complicated, more so than is usually acknowledged. Some years ago, positions were polarized: a small number of physicians favored helping patients to change sex role while a majority of people particularly in the medical profession, including psychiatrists, were opposed. Now, publicity and showmanship have reversed opinion, with much of the public and the medical profession comfortably—and unthinkingly—accepting the treatment. Here is the first complication: The patients themselves announce the diagnosis of transsexualism and expect us simply to perform the mechanics necessary for altering their bodies. This is odd, but more distressing are the referrals from medical colleagues who fail their responsibility to make their own diagnosis and accept the patient as a transsexual simply *because the patient has requested* "sex transformation" '.

II

It is often said that the first sex-change operation was performed in Denmark, the famous Chris Jorgensen case of 1951–1953, and that the background for the operation was the specially liberal and 'understanding' attitude of the Danish authorities. This, however, is not quite true. It was not the first published sex-change operation. And the original intention of the medical team was not to change a man into a woman, but to help a man who suffered from his homosexual impulses.

As early as 1930 a sex-change operation had been done in Germany, yet a Dane was also involved in that case, this time as a patient. In 1931 a book was published in Danish about this case; the book was translated into English and published in New York in 1933 under the vivid title *Man into Woman. An Authentic Story of the Miraculous Transformation of the Danish Painter Einar Wegener (Andreas Sparre)* (Hoyer 1933). The book is interesting as a psychological document but the medical information is sparse. We are told that the patient underwent two operations in a German public, reputable clinic. The first was probably an amputation of the external genitalia including the testes: the second operation, performed a year later, was possibly an implantation of an ovary. He died some weeks later, still in hospital (from an autoimmunization process?). Since both operations were done in Dresden, through which the river Elbe flows, the patient took the name Lili Elbe.

But let us go back to Chris Jorgensen for a moment. We have studied the files and interviewed Dr Georg Stürup, the psychiatrist in the team. From these sources it is clear that Chris Jorgensen, who had Danish ancestors, wanted to change sex, but the medical team did not originally intend to perform a sex-change operation; it only moved in that direction.

To understand this it is necessary to realize that in the thirties and forties medical authorities in Denmark as well as in many other countries regarded sexual minorities as suffering people, because their sex drive was not 'normal'. Many deviant people also accepted this attitude. Sometimes, if the deviant person was in psychological or social trouble because of this 'abnormal drive' (or the society's attitude towards deviation), castration was advised (and often accepted). The philosophy was that the reduction of libido usually following castration would calm the person down and he would feel more at ease. And the Danish team regarded Chris Jorgensen as a homosexual man suffering from his homosexuality and since he himself asked for castration, they would not deny him this operation. Not until afterwards, when the press published the case, did the team behind the procedure accept it as a sex change. The rest of the story is well known.

III

We do not know the total number of transsexuals in the world or how many people have had a so-called sex transformation. Probably the proportion of people with severe gender identity problems differs from one culture to another. Further, in some countries sex transformations are not accepted and it is impossible to get a sex-change operation; in others the only condition is that the person involved can pay for the operation and medical care; in other countries again the treatment as such is free of charge (for example in Denmark and Sweden) but permission from the forensic authorities is required before the castration can be done.

Some American research workers estimate a prevalence of 1 : 100 000 men and 1 : 400 000 women, but these figures are probably too low. The Swedish psychiatrist Wålinder, who has studied transsexuality for many years, stated in 1967 a prevalence in Sweden of 1 : 37 000 men and 1 : 103 000 women. But in a later study (1971) he mentions that the ratio between men and women approaches 1 : 1. Personally we doubt whether the ratio of male to female will be 1:1, but we need further studies to elucidate this.

Follow-up studies of transsexuals are rather few. In many countries it is nearly impossible to follow most of the patients, for many reasons. However, Randell (1969), Money & Ehrhardt (1970), Hoenig *et al.* (1971) and Wålinder & Thuwe (1975) have published follow-up studies. These give information about the patients' functioning in their new sex role, how they are accepted by society and their surroundings, and about their social status, sexual and marital life and whether they regret the sex change or not. Most of the follow-up studies are rather optimistic in their evaluation of the results, which seems reasonable, since the cases operated on are very strictly selected. But we do not hear much about these patients' inner life and psychodynamics.

Since the Swedish study by Wålinder & Thuwe (1975) is among the newest and most comprehensive we shall mention a few of the results here, which are very similar to those of other follow-up studies.

In the period 1962–1974 92 patients (58 men and 34 women) who wanted a sex transformation were referred to St. Jörgen Mental Hospital, Gothenburg. Twenty-six men (45%) and 26 women (74%) were accepted after an in-depth examination over one or more years (for details, see the original paper). Psychotics, patients living in very special social conditions and patients not considered to be transsexuals were not accepted for operation. The follow-up study includes 24 people (13 men and 11 women) with a postoperative observation period of at least three years. We shall not describe the results in detail, but they can be summarized by saying that females changing sex have a better prognosis than males, individuals who are socially well adjusted before the operation usually are also well adjusted afterwards, but people with previous bad social adjustment are seldom better adjusted after the sex transformation (though they often claim preoperatively that afterwards they will manage much better). Regarding their sexual life, most biological males but only a few biological females had some problems in their new sex role. Only two biological men, and no women, regretted the operation; one biological man committed suicide shortly after the operation. Wålinder & Thuwe conclude that the results are good for 80% of the patients both from a subjective and an objective point of view, and that these 80% have a much better life now than before.

We do not doubt these or other optimistic evaluations, especially since we know how severe the problems were. But sex transformation is always a palliative treatment only, and we believe that if one looks at transsexuals from some other viewpoints, one may not find 80% comfortable in their new situation, but possibly 20%. Both therapists and patients know that after the operation a change back is impossible. The patient often feels real gratitude to the therapist and will not disappoint him, and the therapist dare not ask questions, which can disturb a fragile situation. Further, some therapists are more interested in external adaptation than in psychological subtleties and it is easier to publish tables and curves on external adaptation than to describe psychological factors. No wonder most follow-up studies throw only limited light on a very complicated matter.

IV

In Denmark 110 people – 81 biological men and 29 biological women – have asked for sex transformation since the days of Chris Jorgensen. Among them we know that 56 – 42 men and 14 women – have had a sex-change operation in Denmark, and some transsexuals, probably not more than 20, have had operations abroad, mostly men. We have some information about at least 10 of them; some of them were later treated in Danish hospitals. Of course, patients operated on outside Denmark are offered the same after-care programme as the rest of the patients.

It is necessary to stress that only people settled in Denmark can have the surgical procedure in this country, since we still receive letters from many foreigners requesting operations in Denmark.

A total of 110 evaluations and 56 sex-change transformations may not seem much. But this is a very time-consuming group of patients and a well-functioning, highly specialized team has to be established if the group is to be handled as well as possible. We have therefore centralized the treatment in two places in Denmark, the Psychiatric Hospital, Risskov and the Rigshospitalet, Copenhagen and, since Danish transsexuals have a tendency to move to Copenhagen, most of the patients are seen at the Rigshopitalet.

Our Gender Identity Clinic is part of the psychiatric department. A team of psychiatrists, clinical psychologists and social workers follows the patients during all phases – the phase of evaluation, the phase of surgical treatment and the after-care phase –, and is responsible for contact and coordination with the other departments involved, such as the chromosome laboratory, the hormonal unit and gynaecological department, the department of plastic surgery, the dermatological department (for epilation of the beard etc.) and the speech unit. We also assist the patients in their contacts with civil, forensic and social authorities and with their employers and families. It is our intention to observe each patient for one year before the beginning of hormonal treatment and another year before the surgical procedures are carried out, and to follow the patient after the operation as long as necessary, usually for several years. An after-care programme is as essential as the earlier phases of the programme, since many patients get into difficulties afterwards and need as much support in this phase as before operation. Most of our patients accept the after-care programme with gratitude; some of them are so lonely that our staff seems to provide their closest human relationships.

We have just started a follow-up study of 39 patients, 29 men-to-women and 10 women-to-men. We have no results yet from this study, but we expect that our results on social outcome and so on will not differ much from those of other studies. But we hope also to be able to contribute something to the psychodynamic description of transsexuals.

It is sometimes claimed that transsexualism is a kind of repressed homosexuality. The transsexual seeks, through a sex change, to establish an alibi for his repressed homosexual impulses. But this point of view is in our opinion not very informative and, further, it is necessary to distinguish between transsexual men and women.

What is identical in transsexual men and women is, among other things, a marked narcissism; they live more in a world of fantasies than realities and their ability to establish genuine, mutual relationships is rather limited. Therefore they often appear rigid and stereotyped. But in their sexual expression and their defence mechanisms there are distinct differences between transsexual men and women.

Wilhelm Reich (originally 1922; 1975) has described two narcissistic types, one characterized by a submissive, pseudofeminine appearance, the other by a phallic, pseudomasculine appearance. Reich explains: 'The first narcissistic type, with manifest feelings of inferiority and latent narcissism, may be contrasted to the second type with manifest and compensative narcissism and latent feelings of inferiority', and it was his impression that the second type is more sparsely represented than the first. He drew up a list which 'may serve to clarify the differences and similarities of the two types':

First type	*Second type*
Manifest feelings of inferiority	Latent feelings of inferiority
Latent narcissism	Manifest compensative narcissism
Anal - urethral disposition	Anal - urethral disposition
Strong, lasting incestuous attachment	Short incestuous attachment with subsequent alienation
Overidealization of women	Undervaluation of women
Passive - feminine	Active homosexual (latent or manifest)

Latent sadism, manifest masochism	Overt sadism
Exhibitionist tendencies repressed; modesty	Unrepressed exhibitionism transferred from the genital to sexual and other feats
Satisfaction through ego ideal	Satisfaction through overvaluation of real ego

(A few items relating to transference and prognosis are omitted here.)

Reich comments that 'the two types are polarized in regard to the dynamics of the unconscious and the conduct of partial drives. They share in common an anal-urethral disposition, intense incestuous desire in childhood, and a severe castration complex'. Reich hardly had transsexual men and women in his mind when he, 25 years old, described these two narcissistic types, but it is striking how much the first type has in common with transsexual men and how much the second type includes traits typical of many transsexual women.

On sexual behaviour and attitude, the transsexual men in our sample, as in all other samples, usually dislike their genitals, hide them from their partner and do not seek genital satisfaction, while the women are highly clitorally fixated. The men show a low genital activity in both heterosexual and homosexual relationships; the women have high genital and sexual activity. On defence mechanisms, the men particularly use denial, idealization and repression, and the women denial, projection and reaction formations. These and several other characteristics correspond very much to Reich's two types. For example, the core group of transsexual men, as we see them, have a tendency to autoplastic reactions and the transsexual women to alloplastic reactions. The transsexual man is in many ways different from the homosexual man, while the transsexual woman in many ways is similar to certain types of homosexual woman.

In our final study we shall elaborate and support our viewpoints in more detail.

V

Different forms of non-surgical treatment have been given to transsexuals—psychotherapy of different kinds as well as pharmacological treatment—but without success. People with severe gender identity conflicts, especially so-called transsexuals, suffer very much. Some of them are so damaged that no help is possible. But for some of them a hormonal and surgical sex transformation is a relief and opens up possibilities of a better life. One of the present problems is that we need better directives on who can profit from sex-change operations, since our indications are very broad, not to say inaccurate. Let us hope that follow-up studies can help us to establish better indications for so-called sex transformations and to reserve hormonal and surgical treatment for those few who have a chance to profit from it.

References

BENJAMIN, H. (1966) *The Transsexual Phenomenon,* The Julian Press, New York

CAULDWELL, D. (1949) Psychopathia transsexualis. *Sexology 16,* 274–280

HOENIG, J., KENNA, J. C. & YOUD, ANN (1971) Surgical treatment for transsexualism. *Acta Psychiatr. Scand. 47,* 106–133

HOYER, N. (ed.) (1933) *Man into Woman. An Authentic Story of a Change of Sex. The True Story of the Miraculous Transformation of the Danish Painter Einar Wegener (Andreas Sparre),* Dutton, New York

MONEY, J. & EHRHARDT, A. A. (1975) Transsexuelle nach Geschlechtswechsel, in *Tendenzen der Sexualforschung* (Schmidt, G., Sigusch, S. & Schorsch, E., eds.) *(Beiträge zur Sexualforschung, 49),* Ferdinand Enke Verlag, Stuttgart

RANDELL, J. (1969) Preoperative and postoperative status of male and female transsexuals, in *Transsexualism and Sex Reassignment* (Green, R. & Money, J., eds.). The Johns Hopkins University Press, Baltimore

REICH, WILHELM (1975) Two narcissistic types, in *Early Writings,* vol. 1, Farrar, Straus & Giroux, New York

STOLLER, R. J. (1975) *The Transsexual Experiment,* Hogarth Press, London

WÅLINDER, J. (1967) *Transsexualism. A Study of Forty-three Cases,* Akademiförlaget, Göteborg

WÅLINDER, J. (1971) Incidence and sex ratio of transsexualism in Sweden. *Br. J. Psychiat. 119,* 195–196

WÅLINDER, J. & THUWE, I. (1975) *A Social Psychiatric Follow-up Study of 24 Sex-reassigned Transsexuals,* Scandinavian University Books, Göteborg

Discussion

Ehrhardt: The situation in the United States has changed very much since the middle sixties when the first official gender identity clinic was started at the Johns Hopkins Medical School. Money and I did our first follow-up study then. As it turned out, we were dealing with a highly selected sample, since the patients who presented at Johns Hopkins had usually lived for many years in the desired sex role (Money & Ehrhardt 1970). Since then, a number of gender identity clinics in the States and Canada have opened their doors to transsexuals. The general consensus is that about one out of 10 self-declared transsexuals is a good candidate for sex-reassignment surgery.

The problem remains of how to deal with the other nine. They are suffering people who also have a gender identity problem, and hormones and surgery do not seem to help their dilemma.

The probationary period of someone living in the desired role before hormonal and surgical treatment seems to be one of the best predictors of outcome. The best university team in the States is the Stanford group. They recently increased the probationary time from one to two years. In general they have been successful with their patients. In addition to academic departments, private surgeons have offered operations to transsexuals. And since we are dealing with desperate people, many of them are willing to pay a lot of money if they can circumvent thorough evaluation and a probationary waiting period. Unfortunately, no follow-up studies on those patients exist. They could teach us a lot: namely, whether the criteria and team evaluations which most people feel are necessary are, indeed, the best predictors for ultimate outcome in adjustment.

My own interest has been particularly centred on female transsexuals. I have worked especially with adolescent female transsexuals. In a follow-up study on female transsexuals, three out of 20 have become homosexuals and have totally given up their transsexual wish (McCauley & Ehrhardt 1978). If you work with adolescents the patients have to wait until age 21 anyway before an operation can be done. This compulsory waiting period makes it more likely that transsexuals will agree to non-surgical treatment. The interesting thing was that these three who changed their mind about sex reassignment were in no way different from the rest of the group. They were as desperate; they also said that if they were unable to receive hormone treatment they would commit suicide; and they showed the same typical behaviour pattern in other respects. With encouragement to explore a homosexual life-style, especially since they had to wait until age 21 anyway, all three found their niche among homosexuals and seemed to have made an adequate adjustment. Although I agree that transsexualism is a different behaviour pattern from homosexuality, sometimes it appears that the edges are blurred. If one has the opportunity (often one does not, since the transsexual will not cooperate), I would encourage all female transsexuals to try out a homosexual life-style first. Any other treatment approach is preferable to sex reassignment, which after all is a major intervention.

Hertoft: Often that would be a much better solution, but many transsexuals do not accept such advice and regard it as an insult.

Sachar: Those three cases are very important, because according to the literature the results of offering any solution other than surgery and hormones have been terrible.

Beach: Do you believe this solution would be effective for male transsexuals?

Ehrhardt: I don 't know. I think female transsexuals are different from male transsexuals in many ways.

Hertoft: I agree; transsexual women are very much like some kinds of homosexual women, but transsexual men differ in many ways from most homosexual men. We sometimes see that women who start as transsexuals live a much happier life as lesbians, and it is also easier to motivate them to live as lesbians than it is to motivate transsexual men to live as homosexuals, because the men know they are not homosexual and do not want this.

Ehrhardt: In our group of 20 women, 17 were not motivated at all to associate with lesbians. However, sometimes you can motivate a patient to try lesbianism. Therefore, this alternative should at least be suggested to any patient.

Hertoft: I agree. Some transsexual women react with resentment if you suggest that they live as lesbians. I know your study very well and the other excellent studies and, coming from a small homogeneous society as I do, it is easy to criticize what is happening in much bigger, more heterogeneous societies. In many ways Denmark can be looked at as a laboratory with special advantages. We are able to find most people again, we have few gender identity clinics, and these clinics are in close contact with one another. We have nearly no private clinics or hospitals offering sex change to patients who have been refused by the public clinics. And, furthermore, most of our patients have no money for operations outside Denmark. This gives us different conditions from those in the US and also an obligation to set up careful and in-depth studies.

Green: Just as we talked about the homosexuali*ties*, we also have to talk about the transsexuali*ties*. The Stanford group have done the best job of delineating three subgroups of males requesting sex-change who cross-sectionally look the same but have very different autobiographies. One subgroup fits the classic description of transsexualism: that is, a cross-sex identity from very early childhood, no erotic arousal from cross-dressing, and very little experience with penile eroticism; the so-called 'true' transsexual. Another group seems to come from more of a transvestite background in which there has been repeated erotic arousal to cross-dressing, perhaps with some heterosexuality as well, and the somewhat later onset of the wish to be women. The third group seems to have been actively involved in the homosexual subculture. The Stanford group in their follow-up studies are trying to see whether there are disparate outcomes from these three groups after sex change. They are beginning to see some differences. They are finding that those from the primarily homosexual background aren't doing as well as those in the other two groups. I wonder whether you are seeing any differences among the three types of people who present as transsexuals?

Hertoft: Some very effeminate homosexuals are satisfied with a homosexual life-style when young, but as they grow older they want to shift over and live the rest of their lives as 'real women'. Some of them have a Mae West or Marlene Dietrich idea of what it is to live as a woman. And often they succeed, in a modest way, in living that way—woman as vamp, seducing and controlling men. We do not know much of what is going on in their minds and some of them are not very interested in telling us about it, maybe because they live as prostitutes or semi-prostitutes, supported by men. Some of them get married, often to young men of foreign nationality. This type and their life-style is very different from what is called the core group of transsexuals, but I am not sure they are more unhappy than other so-called transsexuals. They really react alloplastically and might have psychopathic traits and they are very different from the examples mentioned by Dick Green who wear women's shoes at 1½ years old and grow up to be extremely feminine.

The story of transvestites is different and sometimes more sad. Paradoxically, some transvestites pay a price for the fact that many Western societies nowadays are more 'liberal' and less restrictive than before. A coin always has two sides. In a restrictive society these people remain transvestites and accept that there are no other possibilities, but in a 'liberal' society some of them get the idea that they will be happier if they change sex. Too late they realize that the operation was a mistake. I imagine one finds some of these cases among those mentioned by Dr Ehrhardt. That is the reverse side of what I call a pseudo-liberal acceptance by the surroundings. And I see no solution of this conflict, since it is no solution to go back to the restrictive days. Somebody always pays a price for changes in society. The only possible solution is information, information and information. And this is not always enough.

Crown: You mentioned a prevalence of approximately 4:1 in favour of male transsexuals, Dr Hertoft. It is interesting that this ratio is found in all the sexual deviancies—homosexuality, sadomasochism, fetishism. Sexual deviance was considered a male middle-class activity by Kinsey, and although the class relationship seems to be changing, it is still very much male-oriented. I wonder whether this is, as people rather glibly say, a social phenomenon (women have always been allowed to cross-dress and therefore it is all right), or whether there is some biological significance. Dr Beach has pointed out (1976) that masturbation is more common in male animals and has suggested that this might have evolutionary significance. Can this argument be made for male homosexuality in the human? If as many women were homosexual as men, damage might be done to the species.

Beach: I would rephrase the issue this way: in mammalian evolution the female makes the largest investment in reproduction. My suspicion is that the human female, heterosexual or homosexual, has a greater need for the bonding aspect of the relationship—a much stronger need than the male has. It may be that many of the men Dr Dörner is studying are individuals who are involved primarily or exclusively in the genital aspects of sexual interaction and that for them the interpersonal relationship is of minimal importance. Such men have a larger number of different partners, shorter periods of impersonal interaction, no bonding, and so on. But that is part of being a *male,* and similarly lesbianism is part of being a *female,* before either men or women are homosexual. Human beings are male or female long before they are homosexual, so to speak. Differences between male and female human homosexuals are reflections of underlying, basic masculinity and femininity, and those differences can be traced back to evolutionary factors in terms of sex differences in investment in reproduction.

Sachar: Dr Hertoft, your transsexuals have a period of massive hormone therapy long before the operation. The men receive oestrogens in high doses; the women receive androgens. Oestrogens reduce libido in men. What is their experience of that change in libido and could you tease apart any psychological changes occurring during this long period of purely hormonal therapy? The women are given androgens well before the operation; what happens to their libido and their psychic experiences?

Hertoft: Differences are shown. Most of the men dislike their genitals and don't want to use them; they don't want to masturbate; they don't want a partner to touch their genitals. Most of them don't want erections either, and therefore I think they are telling the truth when they say that it's a lovely effect to have no or rare erections. They are given large doses of oestrogens; after castration the doses are lower. Some go to Germany to get oestrogens on the black market because they want more than the doctors give them. That is one of the problems in this field, that you can't always believe that they do what you want them to do.

Sachar: Is there any impression that these massive doses of oestrogen in men reduce libido below what the ordinary woman would experience?

Ehrhardt: My observation has been that many of the transsexual men become totally asexual during that time. They have no erections and claim to have no libido and very little sexual fantasy. In general they see the massive doses of oestrogen as having a tranquillizing effect. Of course, this may be largely a psychological effect, since they are not particularly motivated to engage in sexual activities as long as they still have a penis.

Hertoft: Their breasts often grow bigger, which satisfies them very much.

Sachar: The dose of oestrogen is reduced after the operation; what happens to libido then?

Hertoft: It is difficult to say. Often their libido is low, but they want to have sexual intercourse with a (heterosexual) man and to use their new vagina. It is difficult to know the degree of sexual satisfaction. Some of them claim they get it, and I suppose some are telling the truth; others are not. Some tell us they get no orgasm as such but feel a psychological and bodily satisfaction during the sexual contact with a partner.

Ehrhardt: The Minnesota group came up with a figure of about a 60–70% rate of orgasm with male-to-female transsexuals after the patients received a new vagina.

Sachar: But an orgasm *where?*

Hertoft: Most heterosexual men do not know much about their own anatomy and physiological reactions during sexual excitement and orgasm. Further, because of different taboos, they do not allow themselves to accept the pleasures of anal stimulation, not to say anal intercourse. Therefore they often do not register the orgasmic contractions in the perineal and perianal muscles. Some of our male-to-female transsexuals describe orgastic reactions which seem to be contractions in the perineal and perianal muscles, and since these muscles are still intact after the sex-change operation, and since orgasm is also something happening in your mind, not only in your genitals, I see no reason not to believe in the possibility of an orgasm after a sex-change operation which has removed the penis.

Sachar: The women who take androgens are an interesting group in that they are not medically ill, whereas women who receive hormones usually are. What do they experience?

Hertoft: Usually they are sexually very interested and active. Androgens, you know, develop a bigger clitoris and a higher libido. Often they prefer heterosexual female partners, not lesbians, because, as they claim, they are not lesbians themselves. They also accept androgens, because they masculinize them, producing a beard and so on. What they dislike is their breasts and, if still present, their menstruations.

Sachar: It used to be claimed that the increase in libido in women on androgens could be entirely accounted for by clitoral oedema and local irritation. Do you believe that from your observations?

Hertoft: No.

Everitt: This kind of explanation has been around in the literature for many years and although it may be partly true it is most unlikely to be the whole story. Some years ago we demonstrated that the decreased sexual activity which followed removal of adrenal androgens in female rhesus monkeys could be completely reversed by placing small amounts of testosterone directly into the anterior hypothalamus (Everitt & Herbert 1975). The change in behaviour, therefore, was due to the action of the hormones on the brain and not the clitoris, and I feel sure that this is the case in women as well.

Nieschlag: I would like to extend the question of oestrogen treatment to another aspect. There are diseases whose incidence is sex-linked and which are claimed to be correlated with sex steroid levels. You have a beautiful experimental group where you have treated each sex with the opposite sex hormone; do you find different incidences of, say, atherosclerosis, coronary artery disease and thrombosis in these experimental groups, compared to normal people, especially in men treated with high doses of oestrogens?

Hertoft: Our experience is too brief. We shall have to wait 10–20 years before we can answer that question.

Ehrhardt: In the follow-up study, with Money, some of the patients were followed for 10 years, but the group was too small for us to draw any firm conclusions (Money & Ehrhardt 1970).

Hertoft: In Göteborg they started this form of treatment in 1962 but were only able to find 25 persons with a three-year observation period: we still need 20 years before we can answer this question.

Nieschlag: Massive doses of oestrogens should induce thrombosis very quickly, so even three years should be a good period. I would strongly suggest that you follow up this aspect.

Hertoft: We do warn the patients, but they don't listen; they are not interested. It is a problem, of course.

Goy: Do transsexual males, after the surgery and readjustment, masturbate and, if so, how?

Hertoft: No. Some say that they had hoped to develop a clitoris but they don't. Most of them don't masturbate. They are not very genitally active.

Ehrhardt: May I add to that and to the question of orgasm. One can have an orgasm over the whole perineal area. We know this from girls born without a vagina who later have an artificial vagina surgically created. They are often orgasmic.

Green: There is also penile thrusting across the prostate where the new vaginal canal is placed. That is erotically arousing to many male-to-female transsexuals after operation.

Herbert: I am not sure that those of us who work on monkeys or any primates accept the idea of 'opposite' hormones, implying a 'male' hormone and 'female' hormone. But isn't there a case, from the results on male-to-female transsexuals, for treating them after the operation not only with oestrogen but with small amounts of androgen too, because their low genital activity and low libido could be due to their low levels of androgen?

Ehrhardt: We found in individual male transsexuals that they complained about low libido if they were treated only with Premarin, which is oestrogen. Provera was sometimes added for five days during the month. This is medroxyprogesterone acetate and is not androgenic. In male transsexuals the combination of oestrogen and progesterone seems to increase libido sometimes.

Hertoft: I rarely hear that complaint; they have complaints, but not usually about their libido. Some of them are tired.

Sachar: Has that hormone combination been tried in animals?

Ehrhardt: No. That would be very interesting, because the effect has been observed clinically also in patients with Turner's syndrome. It would be interesting if in primates the combination of oestrogen and progesterone could be shown to affect libido.

Green: I would like to abort some of your enthusiasm, Dr Sachar (p. 162), for studying transsexuals, on the basis of my experience. Some are classic fabricators. Others are concerned with their phobia about being homosexual, with what they think men and women are meant to be like, and whether or not they are supposed to be sexual. There is the permission-giving quality of cross-dressing and the destigmatization of not being homosexual now that they have other hormones in their body. All of these things are so confounding that one cannot give much scientific credence to their reports of sexual activity as a function of what hormones they are getting. They are not a good model.

Ehrhardt: But a systematic study of patients with Turner's syndrome on various treatment regimens and the effects on libido might be worthwhile.

Hertoft: I would like to tell a little story. One day I met a female physician. I knew she worked in a mother's aid institution and often found her work very burdensome, since she mostly met women having trouble with their pregnancies, wanting abortions and so on. But that day she felt very much at ease and said, smiling: 'That is because at last I have met a pregnant woman who was happy about her pregnancy. It was in a grocer's shop'—in other words, outside her office, outside her consulting room. But many of us working with sexual minority groups only get our knowledge from contact with people having trouble and needing our help. If you want to get a realistic, all-round impression of the lives of transsexuals, transvestites, homosexuals and so on, you have to go out in society and find out what the subcultures are like. And, if you dare, it is often very easy to be accepted by certain sexual subcultures. Not all of them: it can be difficult to enter a sadomasochistic or paedophilic subculture. But in many countries it is easy to meet homosexuals, transvestites and transsexuals. And you will find that many people belonging to a minority group live a daily life not very different from other people; this is especially the case with many homosexuals.

But in this discussion I have the feeling that some participants know a lot about animals but don't know much about how their neighbours live. And that is, of course, necessary too. I would be interested to know, for example, from Professor Dörner, how homosexuals are living and treated in his country. This is important to know as a background not only for this discussion but also for understanding his own research.

Dörner: In our country homosexuals have similar rights and duties as heterosexuals. Furthermore, we try to teach heterosexuals that they should understand homosexuals. In Berlin/GDR we have also a group of experts, including a psychiatrist, a gynaecologist, a colleague from forensic medicine, a surgeon and an endocrinologist, and we decide whether to recommend a change of Christian name or surgical transformation in transsexual men or women.

Green: Has your own work generated any opposition from homosexual organizations in East Germany? Do they see it as 'anti-homosexual' in tendency?

Dörner Not at all! On the contrary, I have received letters from homosexuals acknowledging our work and I have even been consulted by homosexuals from other countries. When the law for the prosecution of homosexuals was abolished many years ago in the German Democratic Republic it was still in operation in the Federal Republic of Germany. At that time I also received letters from lawyers of homosexual men living in the Federal Republic, asking me to act as an expert witness in court. In their opinion their homosexual clients could not be prosecuted when there were findings suggesting that the origin of homosexual behaviour might be a biological one. Shortly afterwards, this inhumane law was also abolished in the Federal Republic.

References

BEACH, F. A. (1976) Cross-species comparisons and the human heritage. *Arch. Sex. Behav. 5,* 469–485

EVERITT, B. J. & HERBERT, J. (1975) The effects of implanting testosterone propionate into the central nervous system on the sexual behaviour of adrenalectomized female rhesus monkeys. *Brain Res. 86,* 109–120

McCAULEY, E. A. & EHRHARDT, A. A. (1978) Role expectations and definitions: a comparison of female transsexuals and lesbians. *J. Homosexual. 3,* 137–147

MONEY, J. & EHRHARDT, A. A. (1970) Transsexuelle nach Geschlechtswechsel, in *Tendenzen der Sexualforschung* (Schmidt, G., Sigusch, S. & Schorsch, E., eds.) *(Beiträge zur Sexualforschung, 49),* Ferdinand Enke Verlag, Stuttgart

The endocrine function of the human testis in regard to sexuality

EBERHARD NIESCHLAG

Abteilung Experimentelle Endokrinologie, Universitäts-Frauenklinik, Münster

Abstract It is well known that the testes play a determining role in male sexuality. However, the exact interrelations between endocrine testicular function and sexual behaviour are not well understood. If these interrelations are to be investigated a number of factors influencing testicular function have to be considered: circadian and seasonal variations, age-related changes, body constitution, physical activity and drug interactions, as well as the influence of endocrine and non-endocrine diseases. The paper emphasizes the complexity of the field and warns against seeing correlations between single random plasma sex hormone determinations and sexual behaviour.

A relationship between the male reproductive functions including sexual behaviour and the testes in humans has been known since antiquity—that is, ever since written or figurative documents have been available. Likewise, treatment for sexual dysfunction with ingested testes or testicular extracts (although pharmacologically ineffective) has been practised since ancient times and is still performed, even by cultures well beyond the stage of primitive medicine. However, our scientific knowledge correlating endocrine function and human sexuality is still very scanty. It is largely anecdotal and based predominantly on unsatisfactorily documented clinical experience, which is inadequate to deal with the complexity of the field.

This field of research suffered for long periods from restrictions due to social taboos. The interdisciplinary cooperation between endocrinologists, psychologists and psychiatrists necessary for approaching this complex area was also lacking until recently. In addition, the endocrinological methodology was relatively crude by comparison with the subtle problems of sexual behaviour. Until a few years ago sex hormones were measured mainly in urine samples, and the hormone determinations were done on metabolic end-products which only poorly and indirectly reflect events at the target organ level. The techniques now available facilitating frequent and serial hormone determinations in blood provide a more direct approach. Nevertheless, measurements at the target organ level will have to be developed in the future, if endocrinological and behavioural interrelations are to be further clarified.

Yet our understanding of the physiology of testicular functions has leapt forward considerably in recent years. This paper aims to point out some aspects of normal and pathological testicular function which may be relevant to sexuality and which should be considered when interactions between hormones and behaviour are studied. It also offers a word of caution to those hoping for simple correlations between hormones in blood and behaviour, although such hormone measurements today provide the most feasible approach for studying this field.

NORMAL TESTICULAR FUNCTION

We shall first consider endocrine testicular function in the healthy adult man with clear male gender identity and heterosexual orientation, usually referred to as 'normal' man.

Steroid secretion from the testis

The testis of the healthy adult man produces a variety of steroids (Fig. 1). Of these testosterone is produced in largest concentrations (about 7 mg/day). Although dihydrotestosterone proved to be about twice as effective in some biological tests (Liao & Fang 1969), testosterone is quantitatively

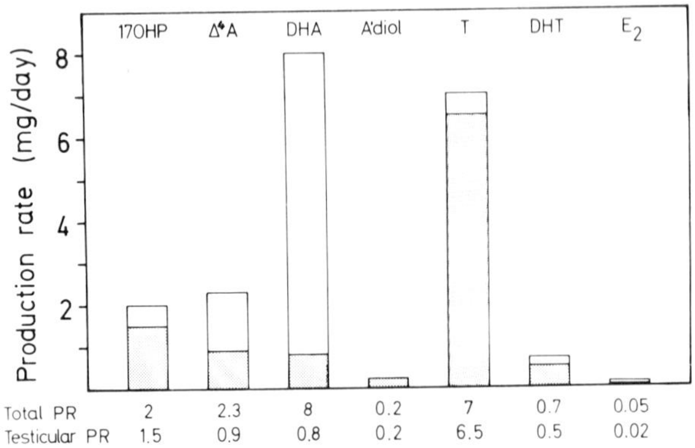

FIG. 1. Daily rates of production of steroids in adult men. Grey parts of the columns, testicular production; white parts, adrenal and/or peripheral production. 17OHP, 17-hydroxyprogesterone; Δ^4A, androstenedione; DHA, dehydroepiandrosterone; A'diol, androstenediol; T, testosterone; DHT, dihydrotestosterone; E_2, oestradiol.

the most potent androgen in circulation. In blood testosterone is bound to sex-hormone-binding globulin and only the small free fraction is available to receptors and thus biologically active. In order to exert its effects testosterone needs to be converted into dihydrotestosterone in some target tissues; in others it works directly and in hypothalamic areas aromatization to oestrogens may be required. From animal experiments, clinical experience and substitution therapy it is known that testosterone is required for the maintenance of the secondary male sex characteristics including the accessory reproductive glands, beard growth, body hair distribution, muscle strength, and for normal sexual functions, libido and potency.

Circadian rhythm

Testosterone is not secreted in a constant flow from the testes but rather in short secretory spikes, 6–7 usually occurring during the day, preceded by luteinizing hormone (LH) peaks three hours earlier (Vigersky *et al.* 1976). In addition, the mean testosterone concentration shows a clear diurnal variation with high concentration in the morning and on average 25% lower values in the evening (Nieschlag 1974).

It has been found that the rise in testosterone concentration during sleep occurs in synchrony with REM phases (rapid eye movement, or active, sleep) (Evans *et al.* 1971) and that morning erections occur at the hours when plasma testosterone concentrations are highest. However, whether these correlations are merely coincidental or interdependent remains to be clarified.

From the short-term and diurnal variations in plasma testosterone occurring in normal men it can be concluded that single plasma testosterone determinations can be rather misleading when one is investigating correlations between sexual behaviour and plasma androgens. It is necessary to base such studies on multiple samples rather than on single determinations. Obtaining two samples during the day, one in the morning and one in the evening, as we formerly recommended for clinical purposes (Nieschlag 1974), does not appear to be sufficient for behavioural studies. Three samples during one hour (Goldzieher *et al.* 1976) or samples obtained using a constant-withdrawal pump over longer periods (Lacerda *et al.* 1973) provide a better basis. It should be pointed out that hardly any of the studies on behavioural aspects done so far fulfil these requirements.

Seasonal variations

Seasonal variations in reproductive functions in various mammalian species are well documented. Some non-human primates, especially the rhesus monkey, also show a distinct circannual pattern of conception rates and deliveries, which persists under strictly controlled laboratory conditions excluding exogenous stimuli from temperature, humidity, diet and natural light (i.e. photoperiods) which are considered the strongest signals for seasonality. This holds true as much for the menstrual cycle in the female (Keverne & Michael 1970) as for testosterone production, testicular size and sperm production in the male rhesus monkey (Robinson *et al.* 1975; Wickings & Nieschlag 1977).

In general, circannual cyclic phenomena are much less obvious in humans than in animals, probably because humans are exposed to about the same amount of light, although of different quality, all year round from artificial light sources. Nevertheless some circannual rhythmicity of reproduction persists in humans. Thus we have found that the highest conception rates in our area (Münster) occur in summer and the lowest in winter (R. Overhage & E. Nieschlag, unpublished work). A similar pattern was described for Finland between 1960 and 1954 (Timonen & Carpen 1968).

The contributions of men and women to this seasonality are not clearly known. It has been found, however, that plasma testosterone concentrations in men show seasonal variations with the lowest concentrations in spring, increases during the summer and peak values in September (Reinberg *et al.* 1975; Smals *et al.* 1976). The frequency of sexual activity followed the pattern of plasma testosterone concentrations (Reinberg *et al.* 1978). Thus, a correlation between plasma testosterone and sexual activity in men depending on the season has been demonstrated.

Age-related changes

The testosterone concentration in blood from fetal life to senescence shows a characteristic profile with a first peak at about week 12 of gestation (Reyes *et al.* 1974), a second peak shortly after birth and finally a sharp increase to adult levels during puberty (Forest *et al.* 1976). While the fetal peak is related to the sexual differentiation and masculinization of the genitalia and thus to problems of gender identity, the peak after birth may be of importance in programming hypothalamo-pituitary centres participating in gonadal feedback control. Among the earliest clinical signs of puberty are ejaculation and masturbation, which indicates that even with relatively low circulating androgen concentrations sexual activity can be initiated.

Plasma testosterone levels remain constant from the completion of puberty to about 50–55 years of age and decrease slowly thereafter (Nieschlag *et al.*

1973; Vermeulen *et al.* 1972; Stearns *et al.* 1974). At the same time the percentage binding of testosterone to sex-hormone-binding globulin increases so that the biologically active, free fraction decreases to a greater degree than the total plasma testosterone concentrations (Pirke & Doerr 1973). This increase in concentration of the sex-hormone-binding globulin is most likely due to the increased oestrogen levels in advancing age, which induce the hepatic synthesis of this protein (Kley *et al.* 1974).

More drastic than the decrease in total and free testosterone levels in plasma is the diminishing response of the testes to stimulation by human chorionic gonadotropin (hCG) (Nieschlag *et al.* 1973). While the increase in basal levels of testosterone in the Leydig cell function test in healthy men before the age of 55 is 2–2.5-fold, the response in older men becomes smaller and, in some cases, the testes fail to respond with any measurable testosterone increase at all. This indicates that hypogonadism in advancing age is primarily of testicular origin, since pituitary LH secretion increases adequately to the lower testosterone plasma concentration and a strong correlation between LH and the degree of stimulatory response to hCG can be demonstrated (Nieschlag *et al.* 1973).

A decrease in sexual activity has been documented parallel to the age-related decrease in endocrine testicular function (Kinsey *et al.* 1953), suggesting a correlation between the two variables. However, the populations in which sexual activity was studied were not the same as those in which endocrine factors were studied so that, to the best of my knowledge, no clear documentation of sexual activity and endocrine testicular capacity in single individuals exists. The fact that testosterone substitution in men with low androgen concentrations in the syndrome of the male climacteric often restores sexual activity further supports the hypothesis that declining testosterone production is at least one causative factor in the decreasing sexual activity of advancing age.

Body constitution

Investigations of male singers revealed a correlation between vocal register, body constitution and sex steroid concentrations in plasma (Meuser & Nieschlag 1977). Basses had a higher incidence of athletic body build, they were taller and heavier and had larger feet than tenors, who were characterized by a preponderance of pyknic and leptosomatic constitutions. Basses also showed higher plasma testosterone and lower oestradiol concentrations than tenors, clearly reflected in the molar ratios of the two steroids (Fig. 2). The sexual activity of the entire group of subjects investigated, as evidenced by the

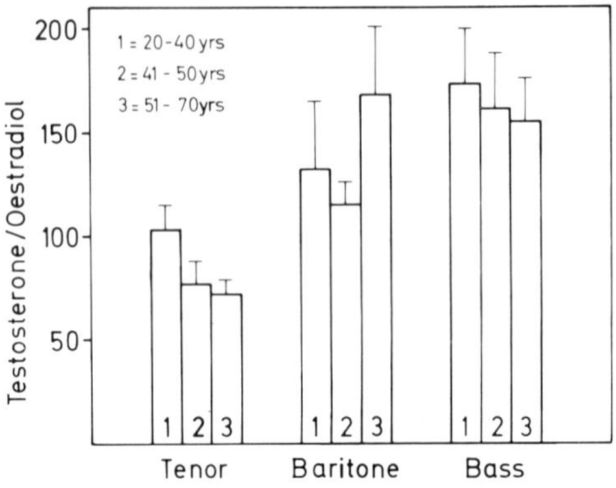

FIG. 2. Molar ratios of testosterone to oestradiol in plasma of male singers.

number of ejaculations per week, showed the familiar age-related decrease.

In keeping with the higher testosterone/oestradiol ratios, the sexual activity of basses in the 20–40 years age group was higher than that of baritones and tenors (Fig. 3).

This study was based on only one blood sample per subject, so the results can only be viewed as preliminary. The correlation indicated between body characteristics, sex hormones and sexual activity, however, is intriguing and merits more detailed investigation. It should be mentioned in this context

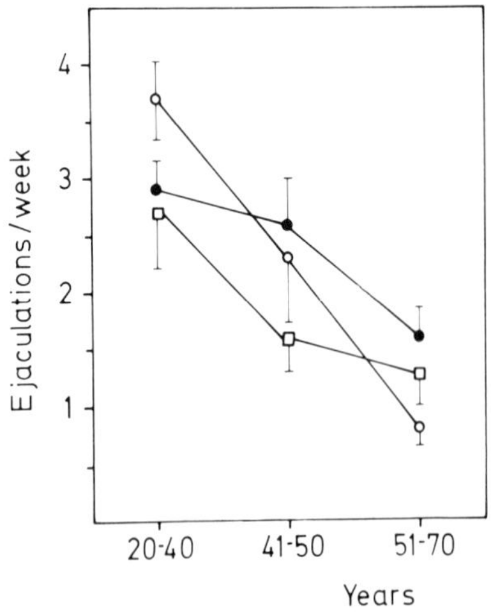

FIG. 3. Sexual activity (ejaculations per week) of male singers (●, tenor; □, baritone; ○, bass).

that a positive correlation between physical height and frequency of sexual intercourse was found in a study on the life-styles of executives (Johnson 1974). On the other hand, exhibitionists with markedly increased sexual activity (Schott & Seidel 1976) and a group of violent rapists (Rada *et al.* 1976) showed increased plasma testosterone concentrations when compared to normal men.

Acute effects of physical and sexual activity

Physical exercise and stress over hours or days such as mountain climbing (Vermeulen 1973), marathon running (Dessypris *et al.* 1976) and combat training (Aakvaag *et al.* 1978) reduce plasma testosterone significantly and drastically. This decrease under natural conditions can be confirmed in the laboratory. When six young men were subjected to a three-hour endurance training on a bicycle ergometer with their heart rate adjusted to 110 per minute, a 25% decrease in plasma testosterone occurred which was higher than would have been expected from normal diurnal variations. In contrast, short-term exhausting exercise (30 minutes with the bicycle adjusted so that a constant heart rate of 160–170 per minute resulted) produced a 30% increase in plasma testosterone, measured at the end of the 30-minute period (Fig. 4) (Berchthold *et al.* 1978). Thus, exercise produces alterations in plasma testosterone concentration, the pattern depending on the type of exercise. Finally, Kreuz *et al.* (1972) emphasized that prolonged psychological stress alone may also suppress plasma testosterone concentrations.

These findings have to be borne in mind when one is investigating correlations between sexual intercourse and plasma hormone concentrations. When higher testosterone concentrations in blood are reported during and after intercourse than when at rest (Fox *et al.* 1972), the effects may be brought about by the physical part of sexual activity. That other authors (Stearns *et al.* 1973) have not seen such increases during coitus could perhaps be explained by the great individual differences in physical involvement during intercourse. Similary, Fox *et al.* (1972) did not find that masturbation had an effect on plasma testosterone concentrations. It has also been shown that viewing a pornographic film independent of physical activity may result in increased plasma testosterone levels (Pirke *et al.* 1974).

In conclusion, it is fair to state that the available data on correlations between plasma testosterone and actual sexual intercourse are still very scanty and that no clear picture has yet emerged.

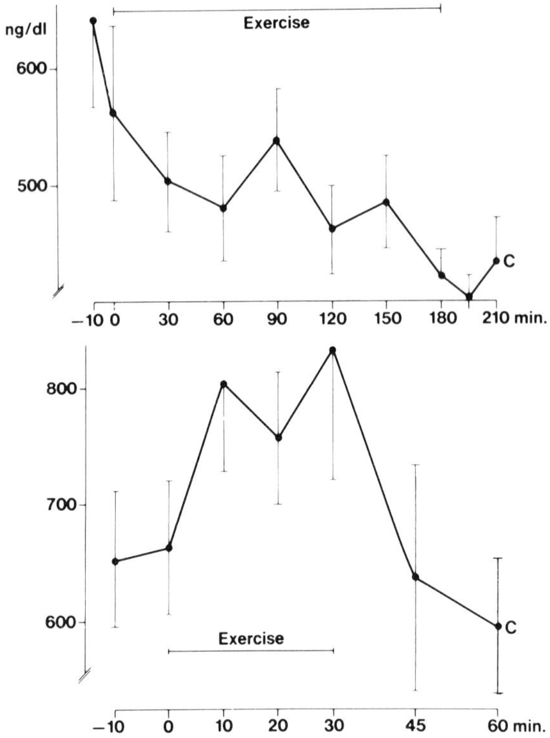

FIG. 4. Effect of physical exercise on plasma testosterone. *Upper panel:* endurance training over three hours with the bicycle ergometer adjusted to result in a pulse rate of 110 per minute. *Lower panel:* exhaustive training for 30 minutes with the ergometer adjusted to result in a pulse rate of 160–170 per minute.

HOMOSEXUAL ORIENTATION

In this section the hormone pattern in blood of adult men with a homosexual orientation will be summarized. Loraine *et al.* (1970) reported lower urinary excretion of testosterone in homosexual than in heterosexual men. As I pointed out above (p. 183), urinary testosterone represents only a small fraction of the steroid secreted by the testes and is an end-product of androgen metabolism rather than the actual hormone reaching the target organs. Hence this may not be a very good variable to study. Later, Kolodny *et al.* (1971) described lower plasma testosterone concentrations in a group of 30 homosexuals than in a heterosexual group. The selection of subjects was objectionable since almost half of them were chronic marihuana smokers, in whom low testosterone values have been found to be due to drug consumption (Mendelson *et al.* 1974). In other studies, Pillard *et al.* (1974) also found lower plasma testosterone concentrations in homosexual men, Brodie *et al.* (1974) even found elevated levels and Doerr *et al.* (1973) found normal plasma testosterone levels. The latter authors assured the integrity of the reproductive functions of their subjects, as semen analysis was always normal. Yet they found elevated oestradiol levels and, in a later study (Doerr *et al.* (1976), also elevated oestrone and percentage free testosterone. These differences were minute but significant.

Of the pituitary hormones, the prolactin concentration was found to be unaltered (Friedman & Frantz 1977) while LH was increased (Doerr *et al.* 1976). In evaluating neuroendocrine functions in homosexuals, Dörner *et al.* (1975) found a positive feedback of exogenous oestrogens on LH secretion in homosexuals, normally only observed in the female. No clear picture has yet emerged from an evaluation of plasma concentrations which would describe and explain the endocrine situation in homosexuality. At present, investigating the fetal or perinatal period appears to provide a better lead than hormone measurements in adult subjects (see also Dörner, this volume).

PATHOLOGICAL TESTICULAR FUNCTION

Endocrine dysfunction

As shown in Table 1, the causes of hypogonadism are manifold and can be located in the hypothalamus, the pituitary, the testes themselves or in the target organs. The clinical appearance of a patient and his sexual problems are determined by the onset of testosterone deficiency. Lack of androgen action during fetal life leads to problems of gender identity, onset during childhood or puberty to disturbed pubertal development, and onset after completion of puberty to a loss of secondary sex characteristics, libido and potency. There have been substantial investigations of the psychology of patients with gender identity problems (for review see Money & Ehrhardt 1972). There is, however, very little information beyond clinical observations on the relation between endocrine testicular function and sexual behaviour in patients with hypogonadism arising during adulthood, although endocrine alterations are well recognized.

We know that loss of libido and potency is one of the earliest signs of a pituitary tumour and is a common complaint in patients with Klinefelter's

TABLE 1

Survey of male hypogonadism and affected aspects of sexuality

Localization of disorder	*Cause*	*Syndrome*	*Aspect of sexuality affected*
Hypothalamus	LH-RH deficiency	Kallman's syndrome (hypogonadotrophic eunuchoidism) Prader-Labhart-Willi syndrome Pubertas tarda	Pubertal development + sexual activity
Pituitary	LH + FSH deficiency	Pituitary insufficiency	Sexual activity
	LH deficiency	Fertile eunuch	–
	Prolactin overproduction	Gynaecomastia/impotence/oligospermia	Sexual activity
Testes	Lack of or decreased testosterone synthesis	Anorchia Castration Klinefelter's syndrome Cryptorchism	Pubertal development + sexual activity
	Oestrogen overproduction	Leydig cell tumours	Sexual activity
	Precursor deficiency	Hypogonadism in Addison's disease	Sexual activity
	Enzyme block	Pseudohermaphroditismus masculinus	Gender identity
	?	Infertility	–
Target organs	Lack of receptors	Testicular feminization	Gender identity
	Steroid α-reductase deficiency	Imperato-McGinley syndrome	Gender identity

syndrome. We know that in hypogonadal men on hormone substitution therapy, sexual activities somehow correlate with the dose and spacing of the testosterone treatment. Yet there is a dearth of exact information correlating the circulating plasma testosterone concentrations with sexual behavioural parameters in these patients. In men with Leydig cell tumours impotence and gynaecomastia are the leading symptoms, resulting from an overproduction of oestrogens. Again, in this interesting experiment of nature, endocrine–behavioural interrelations have not been established. Since the study of Bremer (1959) revealing the great variability in sexual behaviour after castration there has been little attempt to elucidate these phenomena further with modern endocrinological methods.

Non-endocrine diseases

A number of primarily non-endocrine diseases such as liver cirrhosis, renal insufficiency and atherosclerosis are associated with disturbances of libido and potency, secondary to involvement of the testes. The endocrine defects in these systemic diseases have been quite well established, as they result in decreased circulating total testosterone concentrations, decreases in the free testosterone fraction, increases in plasma oestrogens, and an impaired endocrine capacity of the testes as revealed by stimulation with hCG. Nevertheless, exact relations between hormonal and behavioural factors have not been established.

Drug interactions

Several widely used drugs such as digitalis and spironolactone interfere with sexual functions, causing loss of potency and sometimes gynaecomastia. These drugs appear to act at the receptor site in the target organs (Pita *et al.* 1975), so that alterations in plasma hormone concentrations may not be found (Stripp *et al.* 1975; Caminos-Torres *et al.* 1977).

Alcohol is known to interfere with sexual behaviour, and the interference with testosterone metabolism and the lowering of plasma testosterone concentrations have been well documented after acute (Ylikarhi *et al.* 1974) and chronic ethanol consumption (Gordon *et al.* 1976). Hallucinatory drugs such as heroin, marihuana and methadone are often associated with sexual dysfunction and decreased plasma testosterone concentrations have been demonstrated after the use of these drugs (Azizi *et al.* 1973; Mendelson *et al.* 1974) which persist even during withdrawal therapy (Kley *et al.* 1977).

IMPOTENCE

Since the necessity of androgens for normal sexual functions is established, it is fair to suspect endocrine alterations even in men with 'psychogenic' impotence in whom organic lesions and overt hypogonadism cannot be diagnosed. Cooper *et al.* (1970) described a lower urinary testosterone excretion in patients with psychogenic impotence than in normal men, and attempted to divide the disorder into 'psychogenic' and 'constitutional' on the grounds of androgen excretion. In studies based on plasma testosterone estimations, no significant differences from normal men could be detected (e.g. Nieschlag *et al.* 1971; Delitala *et al.* 1977). However, Leydig cell function tests (maximal hCG stimulation over three days) revealed an impaired endocrine capacity of the testes in patients (Fig. 5) (Nieschlag *et al.* 1971). Since such an impaired capacity is also found in other primary non-endocrine diseases, this reaction may be a consequence of impotence rather than a cause. Abnormalities in the pituitary function, investigated by LH-RH (LH releasing hormone) stimulation, could not be detected (Delitala *et al.* 1977). The therapeutic regimens with androgens or LH-RH were not convincingly demonstrated to be superior to placebo, so that the concept of endocrine causes of psychogenic impotence remains questionable.

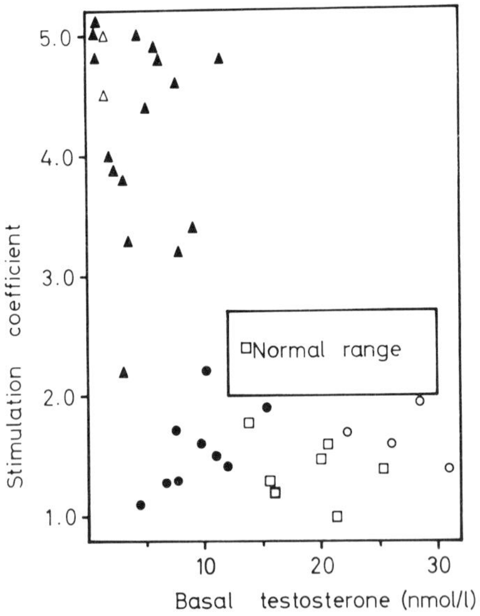

FIG.. 5. Results of Leydig cell function tests in normal hypogonadal and psychogenically impotent men. ▲, pituitary tumours; Δ, Kallman's syndrome; ●, Klinefelter's syndrome; O, Addison's disease; □, impotentia coeundi.

CONCLUSIONS

There are many endogenous and exogenous factors that influence the endocrine testicular function and the concentration of testosterone in plasma in physiological and pathological conditions. All these factors have to be considered when correlating endocrine testicular function and sexual behaviour. It is now clear that single determinations of sex hormones in plasma provide very little information and may even be misleading. Although the endocrine alterations underlying male hypogonadism are well documented, sexual behavioural aspects of these disorders remain ill-defined. Future research in this field may profit from the investigation of sexual behaviour in hypogonadism and in replacement therapy.

References

AAKVAAG, A., BENTDAL, O., QUIGSTAD, K., WALSTAD, P., RONNINGEN, H. & FONNUM, F. (1978) Testosterone and testosterone binding globulin (TeBG) in young men during prolonged stress. *Int. J. Andrology 1,* 22

AZIZI, F., VAGENAKIS, A. G., LONGCOPE, C., INGBAI, S. H. & BRAVERMANN, L. E. (1973) Decreased serum testosterone concentration in male heroin and methadone addicts. *Steroids 22,* 467

BERCHTHOLD, P., BERGER, R., CÜPPERS, H. J., HERRMANN, J., NIESCHLAG, E., RUDORFF, K., ZIMMERMANN, H. & KRÜSKEMPER, H. L. (1978) Non-glucoregulatory hormones (T_4, T_3, rT_3, TSH, testosterone) during physical exercise in juvenile-type diabetics. *Horm. Metab. Res., 10,* 263

BREMER, J. (1959) *Asexualisation: A Follow-up Study of 244 Cases,* Macmillan, New York

BRODIE, H. K. H., GARTWELL, N., DOERING, C. & RHUE, T. (1974) Plasma testosterone levels in heterosexual and homosexual men. *Am. J. Psychiatr. 131,* 82

CAMINOS-TORRES, R., MA, L. & SNYDER, P. J. (1977) Gynecomastia and semen abnormalities induced by spironolactone in normal men. *J. Clin. Endocrinol. Metab. 45,* 255

COOPER, A. J., ISMAIL, A. A. A., SMITH, C. G. & LORAINE, J. A. (1970) Androgen function in 'psychogenic' and 'constitutional' types of impotence. *Br. Med. J. 3,* 17

DELITALA, G., MASALA, A., ALGNA, S. & LOTTI, G. (1977) Luteinizing hormone, follicle stimulating hormone and testosterone in normal and impotent men following LH-RH and hCG stimulation. *Clin. Endocrinol. 6,* 11

DESSYPRIS, A., KUOPPASALMI, K. & ADLERCREUTZ, H. (1976) Plasma cortisol, testosterone, androstenedione and luteinizing hormone (LH) in a non-competitive marathon run. *J. Steroid Biochem. 7,* 33

DÖRNER, G., ROHDE, W., STAHL, F., KRELL, L. & MASINS, W. G. (1975) A neuroendocrine predisposition for homosexuality in men. *Arch. Sex. Behav. 4,* 1

DOERR, P., KOCKOTT, G., VOGT, H. J., PIRKE, K. M. & DITTMAR, F. (1973) Plasma testosterone, estradiol and semen analysis in male homosexuals. *Arch. Gen. Psychiatr. 29,* 829

DOERR, P., PIRKE, K. M., KOCKOTT, G. & DITTMAR, F. (1976) Further studies on sex hormones in male homosexuals. *Arch. Gen. Psychiatr. 33,* 611

EVANS, J. I., MACLEAN, A. W., ISMAIL, A. A. A. & LOVE, D. (1971) Concentrations of plasma testosterone in normal men during sleep. *Nature (Lond.) 229,* 261

FOREST, M. G., PERETTI, E. & BERTRAND, J. (1976) Hypothalamic pituitary-gonadal relationships in man from birth to puberty. *Clin. Endocrinol. 5,* 551

FOX, C. A., ISMAIL, A. A. A., LOVE, D. N., KIRKHAM, K. E. & LORAINE, J. A. (1972) Studies on the relationship between plasma testosterone levels and human sexual activity. *J. Endocrinol. 52,* 51

FRIEDMAN, R. C. & FRANTZ, A. G. (1977) Plasma prolactin levels in male homosexuals. *Horm. Behav. 9,* 19

GOLDZIEHER, J. W., DOZIER, T. S., SMITH, K. D. & STEINBERGER, E. (1976) Improving the diagnostic reliability of rapidly fluctuating plasma hormone levels by optimized multiple-sampling techniques. *J. Clin. Endocrinol. Metab. 43,* 824

GORDON, G. G., ALTMAN, K., SOUTHREN, A. L., RUBIN, E. & LIEBER, C. S. (1976) Effect of alcohol (Ethanol) administration on sex-hormone-metabolism in normal men. *N. Engl. J. Med. 295,* 793

JOHNSON, H. J. (1974) *Executive Life Styles,* Crowell, New York

KEVERNE, E. B. & MICHAEL, R. P. (1970) Annual changes in the menstruation of rhesus monkeys. *J. Endocrinol. 48,* 669

KINSEY, A. C., POMEROY, W. B., MARTIN, C. E. & GEBHARD, P. H. (1953) *Sexual Behavior in the Human Female,* Saunders, Philadelphia

KLEY, H. K., NIESCHLAG, E., BIDLINGMAIER, F. & KRÜSKEMPER, N. H. L. (1974) Possible age-dependent influence of estrogens on the binding of testosterone in plasma of adult men. *Horm. Metab. Res. 6,* 213

KLEY, H.K., OELLERICH, M., WIEGELMANN, W., HERRMANN, J., RUDORFF, K. H., NIESCHLAG, E. & KRÜSKEMPER, H. L. (1977) The effect of methadone on hypophyseal and peripheral glandular hormones during withdrawal. *Horm. Metab. Res. 9,* 484

KOLODNY, R.C., MASTERS, W. H., HENDRYX, B. S. & TORO, G. (1971) Plasma testosterone and semen analysis in male homosexuals. *N. Engl. J. Med. 285,* 1170

KREUZ, L. E., ROSE, R. M. & JENNINGS, J. R. (1972) Suppression of plasma testosterone levels and psychological stress. *Arch. Gen. Psychiatr. 26,* 479

LACERDA, L., KOWARSKI, A., JOHANSON, A. J., ATHANASION, R. & MIGEON, C. J. (1973) Integrated concentrations and circadian variation of plasma testosterone in normal men. *J. Clin. Endocrinol. 37,* 366

LIAO, S. & FANG, S. (1969) Receptor proteins for androgens and the mode of action of androgens on gene transcription in ventral prostate. *Vitam. Horm. 27,* 17

LORAINE, J. A., ISMAIL, A. A. A., ADAMOPOULOS, D. A. & DOVE, G. A. (1970) Endocrine function in male and female homosexuals. *Br. Med. J. 4,* 406

MENDELSON, J. H., KUEHNLE, J., ELLINGBOE, J. & BARBOR, T. F. (1974) Testosterone levels before, during and after chronic marihuana smoking. *N. Engl. J. Med. 290,* 1051

MEUSER, W. & NIESCHLAG, E. (1977) Sexualhormone und Stimmlage des Mannes. *Dtsch. Med. Wochenschr. 102,* 261

MONEY, J. & EHRHARDT, A. A. (1972) *Man and Woman, Boy and Girl; The Differentiation and Dimorphism of Gender Identity from Conception to Maturity,* The Johns Hopkins University Press, Baltimore

NIESCHLAG, E. (1974) Circadian rhythm of plasma testosterone, in *Chronobiological Aspects of Endocrinology* (Aschoff, J., Ceresa, F. & Halberg, F., eds.), p. 117, Schattauer-Verlag, Stuttgart & New York

NIESCHLAG, E., ROHR, M., WOMBACHER, H. & OVERZIER, C. (1971) Leydig-Zell-Funktionstest. *Klin. Wochenschr. 49,* 91

NIESCHLAG, E., KLEY, H. K., WIEGELMANN, W., SOLBACH, H. G. & KRÜSKEMPER, H. L. (1973) Lebensalter und endokrine Funktion der Testes des erwachsenen Mannes. *Dtsch. Med. Wochenschr. 26,* 1281

PILLARD, R. C., ROSE, R. M. & SHERWOOD, M. (1974) Plasma testosterone levels in homosexual men. *Arch. Sex. Behav. 3,* 453

PIRKE, K. M. & DOERR, P. (1973) Age related changes and interrelationships between plasma testosterone, oestradiol and testosterone-binding globulin in normal adult males. *Acta Endocrinol. 74,* 792

PIRKE, K. M., KOCKOTT, G. & DITTMAR, F. (1974) Psychosexual stimulation and plasma testosterone in man. *Arch. Sex. Behav. 3,* 577

PITA, J. C. Jr., LIPPMAN, M. E., THOMPSON, E. B. & LORIAUX, D. L. (1975) Interaction of spironolactone and digitalis with the 5α-dihydrotestosterone (DHT) receptor of rat ventral prostate. *Endocrinology 97,* 1521

RADA, R. T., LAWS, D. R. & KELLNER, R. (1976) Plasma testosterone levels in the rapist. *Psychosom. Med. 38,* 257

REINBERG, A., LAGOGUEY, M., CHAUFFOURNIER, J. M. & CESSELIN, F. (1975) Circannual and circadian rhythms in plasma testosterone in five healthy young Parisian males. *Acta Endocrinol. 80,* 732

REINBERG, A., LAGOGUEY, M., CESSELIN, F., TOUITOU, Y., LEGRAND, J. C., DELASSALLE, A., ANTREASSIAN, J. & LAGOGUEY, A. (1978) Circadian and circannual rhythms in plasma hormones and other variables of five healthy young human males. *Acta Endocrinol., 88,* 417-427

REYES, F. I., BORODITSKY, A. S., WINTER, J. S. D. & FAIMAN, C. (1974) Studies on human sexual development. II. Fetal and maternal serum gonadotropin and sex steroid concentrations. *J. Clin. Endocrinol. 38,* 612

ROBINSON, J. A., SCHEFFLER, G., EISELE, S. G. & GOY, R. W. (1975) Effects of age and season on sexual behaviour and plasma testosterone and dihydrotestosterone concentrations of laboratory-housed male rhesus monkeys *(Macaca mulatta). Biol. Reprod. 13,* 202

SCHOTT, G. & SEIDEL, K. (1976) Über Beziehungen zwischen freiem Testosteron und sexueller Überaktivität bei Exhibitionisten. *Dtsch. Gesundheitswes. 31,* 541

SMALS, A. G. H., KLOPPENBORG, P. W. C. & BENRAAD, Th. J. (1976) Circannual cycle in plasma testosterone levels in man. *J. Clin. Endocrinol. Metab. 42,* 979

STEARNS, E. L., WINTER, J. S.D. & FAIMAN, C. (1973) Effects of coitus on gonadotropins, prolactin and sex steroid levels in man. *J. Clin. Endocrinol. Metab. 37,* 687

STEARNS, E. L., MACDONNELL, J. A., KAUFMAN, B. J., PADUA, R., LUCMAN, T. S., WINTER, J. S. D. & FAIMAN, C. (1974) Declining testicular function with age. *Am. J. Med. 57,* 761

STRIPP, B., TAYLOR, A. A., BARTTER, F. C., GILLETTE, J. R., LORIAUX, D. L., EASLEY, R. & MENARD, R. H. (1975) Effect of spironolactone on sex hormones in man. *J. Clin. Endocrinol. Metab. 41,* 777

TIMONEN, S. & CARPEN, E. (1968) Multiple pregnancies and photoperiodicity. *Ann. Chir. Gynaecol. Fenn. 57,* 135

VERMEULEN, A., RUBENS, R. & VERDONCK, L. (1972) Testosterone secretion and metabolism in male senescence. *J. Clin. Endocrinol. Metab. 34,* 730

VERMEULEN, A. (1973) Testosterone in plasma. A physiopathological study. *Verh. K. Vlaam. Acad. Geneeskd. Belg. 35,* 95-150

VIGERSKY, R. A., EASLEY, R. B. & LORIAUX, D. L. (1976) Effect of fluoxymesterone on the pituitary-gonadal axis: the role of testosterone-estradiol-binding globulin. *J. Clin. Endocrinol. Metab. 43,* 1

WICKINGS, E. J. & NIESCHLAG, E. (1977) Testosterone production and metabolism in laboratory-maintained male rhesus monkeys. *Int. J. Fertil. 22,* 56

YLIKARHI, R., HUTTUNEN, M., HARKONEN, M., SEUDERLING, U., OMIKKI, F., KARONEN, F. L. & ADLERKREUTZ, H. (1974) Low plasma testosterone values in men during hangover. *J. Steroid Biochem. 5,* 655

Discussion

Pirke: I should like to comment on the age-dependence of sexual activity and of plasma testosterone levels in men. As Dr Nieschlag has shown, the frequency of sexual activity decreases much earlier than does the level of plasma testosterone. The decrease in sexual activity is probably more dependent on social, psychological and other factors than on testosterone, as Verwoerdt *et al.* (1969) have demonstrated.

Nieschlag: There seems to be a certain testosterone level above which sexual activity is independent of the absolute concentration of the hormone. About

300ng/100 ml (12nmol/l) is roughly the level below which sexual activity decreases drastically. But you may find someone with very high levels of testosterone and rare sexual activity, or someone with lower values who is sexually rather active.

Ehrhardt: Am I correct in assuming, then, that you think that only a critical level of testosterone is needed for sexual arousal with no correlation between intensity of sexual behaviour and higher levels of testosterone?

Nieschlag: That seems to be the case.

Bancroft: Raboch has reported most data on the relationship between testosterone levels and sexual activity, and his work supports this view. In comparing groups of men with Klinefelter's syndrome, those with varicocoele and normals, he found fairly marked differences in testosterone levels with only slight differences in sexual behaviour between the groups (Raboch & Starka 1972, 1973).

Can I ask you about the effect of sexual activity on testosterone levels? You mentioned the study by Fox *et al.*(1972) in which testosterone levels were raised before sexual activity. This suggests that the increase in testosterone reflects anticipatory sexual arousal, which might account for the absence of a rise in testosterone concentrations in studies on masturbation made in fertility clinics where patients are producing semen samples. Gerald Lincoln (1974) has suggested that the increase might be due to increased blood flow through the testis. Masters & Johnson (1966) have observed that the testis enlarges in size during sexual arousal. Could this influence the circulating hormone levels? If so, perhaps the testosterone rise is not dependent on LH stimulation, but is just extra release from the testis.

Nieschlag: Fox *et al.* (1972) showed an increase in circulating testosterone in anticipation of intercourse and also a further increase after intercourse. Blood flow through the testis, especially in the human, has not been thoroughly studied. It is possible that blood flow alone regulates peripheral testosterone concentrations. There are, however, no methods available for measuring blood flow through the human testis. There have been experiments with isotopes in patients before castration for prostatic cancer, but such methods cannot be applied to healthy men.

Bancroft: You could measure temperature change.

Nieschlag: This is a very indirect measure of blood flow.

Dörner: Blood flow in the gonads appears to be regulated by gonadotropins (Götz & Dörner 1974).

Crown: I would like to plead with our endocrinological colleagues that where they enter the psychological and social areas they should use the same degree of sophistication as they use in their physiological work. It is mainly a question of cooperation with other departments. This relates to several points in your very interesting paper, Dr Nieschlag.

You mentioned opera singers' personalities. Basses, tenors and baritones see themselves in certain ways, and it is difficult to rely on some of their own estimations of, for example, their sexual activity. You mentioned impotence, which is also complex. Erectile impotence must be separated from ejaculatory problems, for example.

One needs to know more about what you mean by impotence in your study.

The same applies to masturbation. This can be regular and intense, or occasional; it can be the only sexual outlet of a person, and so on. These differences need to be distinguished. Finally, the validity of questionnaires sent through the post is dubious. One must try to make a relationship with the subjects first; one is then much more likely to get valid answers to a questionnaire, for example, about frequency of intercourse.

Nieschlag: I agree with what you say, and I feel that we do these psychological studies rather like amateurs. I would like to have behavioural scientists to assist me, but this is difficult to accomplish.

On the specific point of opera singers and their self-rating, I should point out that there were very few solo singers in the study but rather chorus singers. The latter are probably more modest in this sort of self-assessment.

Concerning masturbation, we must take account of the circumstances in which it occurs. The patient who comes to the infertility clinic is not sexually aroused. We have the impression from such patients that they have *depressed* testosterone levels, probably due to the stress of being investigated for fertility.

Hertoft: Men with erectile failure are often impotent only with a partner, not during masturbation or when left alone. I had a patient who in safe 'company' with women often had good erections, when dancing, in a taxi and so on, but as soon as he was left alone with his partner and she wanted to have sexual intercourse, he lost his erection. I can't imagine how this failure can be explained as an effect of low testosterone values. But I would not be surprised if impotent men often had lower values of testosterone before a treatment than after, and that a successful treatment is followed by higher hormonal levels. But we need studies to elucidate this hypothesis.

Sachar: An approach to the differential diagnosis of psychogenic and organic impotence being used in the US, particularly by Fisher, is by studying REM sleep-related erections (Fisher *et al.* 1975). Men with psychogenic impotence have normal erections during REM sleep.

Bancroft: Alternatively, it could be said that the impotence of men who have normal erections during REM sleep is psychogenic. That is an *assumption,* in other words. They are *testing* the use of sleep erections to distinguish between organic and psychogenic factors, and there is a long way to go before they have validated it.

Could I add something else about impotence, to take up Preben Hertoft's point about defining the situation? There are various types of impotence, and failure of erection may not always be the primary problem; to define impotence as failure of erection of the penis is as misleading as to describe female unresponsiveness as a dry vagina. In some men the problem is localized to the ability to get an erection and their appetite and desire for sex is normal; but other men have as their primary problem a lack of interest in sexual matters. We are currently studying the treatment of 'erectile impotence', so-called, and the men coming into the study fall into two groups. One group has as the primary difficulty a low interest in sex, assessed by self-rating of how often they think about sex (a subjective but nevertheless relevant assessment), and the other group has a relatively high interest in sex but inability to get an erection. We are measuring testosterone concentrations in these two groups but as yet have no results.

Nieschlag: In this context, an observation in patients with pituitary tumours may be of interest. In these patients loss of libido and potency occur relatively early during the course of the disease. However, these men rarely consult a doctor because of the impotence, since the loss of libido occurs simultaneously; they come later for other complaints and then impotence is also revealed. Thus potency problems due to a definite endocrine disorder may only rarely be the first symptom encountered by the physician.

Bancroft: We found that cyproterone acetate and ethinyl oestradiol in male sexual offenders produced greater effect on self-ratings of sexual interest and frequency of masturbation than on their ability to produce erections in response to erotic stimuli in the laboratory. So these hormones may have more effect on central factors to do with sexual interest than on erection *per se* (Bancroft *et al.* 1974).

Sachar: I studied men during depressive episodes in which there was characteristically a major loss of libido and sexual interest, yet testosterone levels did not differ from those of age-matched normals during that period and did not change with clinical recovery, either (Sachar *et al.* 1973).

Besser: I must take issue with Dr Nieschlag's suggestion that patients with pituitary problems may not present primarily with symptoms related to their sex function. That is not entirely true. The condition of hyperprolactinaemia has recently become very commonly recognized in the population at large, perhaps not quite as common in men as in women. We have to be aware that hyperprolactinaemia in the male may present with no other sign or symptom than a decrease of interest in sex and in erectile potency. Treatment of the hyperprolactinaemia corrects both the impotence and the lack of libido (Thorner *et al.* 1977). *Some* of these patients have evidence of microadenomas which otherwise would not be suspected.

While everyone is aware that it may be difficult to distinguish organic and non-organic causes, I would suggest that it is essential to do at least two prolactin measurements on all impotent male patients who would otherwise be called psychogenic. Only 10% of our male hyperprolactinaemia patients have galactorrhoea, and gynaecomastia if present is minimal. Testicular size is not decreased. Testosterone levels are usually in the lower 20% of the normal range, and are not always low. Sometimes we find the cause, and sometimes it is microadenoma. If it is important to make more than one testosterone measurement, it is even more important to measure more than one pituitary hormone, because pituitary hormones are secreted in brief pulsatile bursts, whereas the bursts of testosterone secretion have a slower cycle. Patients who generally run high prolactin levels may on occasions have levels within the normal range at the troughs of the pulsatile pattern.

Sachar: Why should elevated prolactin levels have anything to do with potency?

Besser: We wish we knew. There is evidence that hyperprolactinaemia interferes with the actions of gonadotropins on the gonad in the male as well as the female.

Sachar: Tiny doses of phenothiazines raise prolactin concentrations tremendously without interfering with libido.

Besser: They may interfere with sexual performance, however. The drug metoclopramide, frequently used in the UK (and the equivalent drug sulpiride used on the Continent) for dyspepsia and also as a minor tranquillizer, commonly produces hyperprolactinaemia and impotence. Certainly male patients taking phenothiazines may become impotent and women commonly have oligomenorrhoea or amenorrhoea. It has been questioned whether the hypogonadism of schizophrenia is the result at least in part of phenothiazine medication. Many other psychotropic drugs (haloperidol, pimozide) also raise prolactin concentrations.

Goy: They also raise cortisol levels.

Besser: Not in humans.

Sachar: High doses of phenothiazines impair sexual performance. Because the prolactin response is so sensitive, however even small subtherapeutic doses of phenothiazines raise prolactin concentrations to a maximum. If prolactin itself were the culprit, one would expect very small doses of phenothiazines to disturb sexual performance, which is not the case.

Besser: We frequently see such cases; reserpine and methyl dopa given for hypertension also raise prolactin levels and produce impotence. If the prolactin level is lowered with bromocriptine the impotence is corrected.

Bancroft: Aren't you unlikely to find a high level of prolactin associated with impotence and a normal testosterone level?

Besser: Most people dealing with males and hyperprolactinaemia agree that a proportion of impotent male patients with hyperprolactinaemia have testosterone values in the normal range.

Goy: Dr Nieschlag has reported the decline with ageing of peripheral levels of testosterone; it seems to me that investigators tend to approach the older age group as if it were uniform, whereas clearly it isn't. Depression is common, senile dementia is becoming more common and likely to be more so; there are changes in sleep patterns in older people. I just wonder if the finding is not an artifact and that the circadian rhythm might be shifted, or that the series includes individuals who are under stress, and things of that sort. If you could control those factors you might not find a decline.

Nieschlag: In ageing men there is great variation in the testosterone values, and we only find the decrease by taking the statistical mean of large numbers of individuals. There is considerable inter-individual variation.

Dörner: In our institute a clear-cut fall in plasma free testosterone levels was found with ageing, as described by Vermeulen *et al.* (1972) as well as by Pirke & Doerr (1975). This fall was associated with a parallel fall in urinary testosterone excretion (F. Stahl, unpublished work).

Nieschlag: The mean urinary testosterone values agree better with the age-related decline in activity than the plasma values. Urinary values start to decrease from the age of 40, while total plasma testosterone begins to fall 10–15 years later.

Besser: The amount of sex-hormone-binding globulin increases from about the age of 50 (Anderson 1974; Vermeulen *et al.* 1972). A point which Dr Nieschlag made needs repeating, namely that although *total* plasma testosterone begins to fall after the decrease in sexual activity starts, *free* testosterone falls much earlier and that seems to parallel the decline in sexual activity, because the binding protein for testosterone increases much earlier and shows a better relation with age. So you cannot interpret testosterone values without measuring the concentration of sex-hormone-binding globulin, as Anderson (1974) showed. The alteration is secondary to ischaemic change in the testis; it needs more LH to keep the testosterone level up; and when you overstimulate the testis with LH it makes relatively more oestrogen. The increase in oestrogen seems to be greater than the increase in testosterone. This increased oestrogen increases the binding protein for testosterone and thereby reduces the free testosterone even more for a given total steroid concentration, so though the total value doesn't fall early, the free level does, and that is presumably why the urinary figures reflect it better.

Jost: If we have to consider testosterone as a kind of prohormone, which is transformed into dihydrotestosterone in certain organs and aromatized in other organs, measuring plasma testosterone is only one point in the whole system and to obtain a better idea of how it works we should discover the rate of conversion in different people. Is the proportion of testosterone which is converted to the active components the same in different situations? Before we start going into too much detail it is important to take into account the fact that testosterone must be converted before it can act on different structures.

Nieschlag: I agree. Our studies so far are mainly pilot studies and we should now try to study the underlying physiological phenomena in more depth.

Pirke: We have measured dihydrotestosterone (DHT) in old men (Pirke & Doerr 1975). There is a fall in free, not protein-bound DHT while the concentration of total DHT remains unchanged.

Nieschlag: But you did not correlate this with the sexual activity of your subjects?

Pirke: No. I would like to comment on the literature on impotence. The results reported are contradictory. Ismail *et al.* (1970), Legros *et al.* (1973) and Raboch *et al.* (1975) reported low plasma testosterone concentrations in patients suffering from 'psychogenic impotence', while Lawrence *et al.* (1974), Comhaire & Vermeulen (1975) and our group (Pirke *et al.* 1978) found no difference between impotent and normal men. I believe that these discrepancies are caused by the fact that the patients studied by different groups belonged to different subgroups of 'impotence'. I think it is important whether patients complain about loss of libido or not. Hormonal findings in impotent men can only be compared when the patients studied are described exactly. We have observed that impotent patients who do not complain about decreasing libido usually have normal LH and testosterone values.

Green: On the ageing phenomenon, Solnick & Birren (1977) studied latency to erection. Erotic slides were shown to men aged 20–30 years and men aged 50–60 years. The time to full erection was six times longer in the older men. There were no hormone studies.

The work of Raboch *et al.* (1977) has been mentioned. In one study they compared chromatin-positive Klinefelter syndrome males, men with cryptorchism, men with varicocoeles, and a group of medically normal men. In all three pathological groups testosterone levels were significantly lower, yet they found no differences in reported coital frequencies between the four groups.

A report by Kraemer *et al.* (1976) describes a unique relationship between testosterone levels and sexual activity. Men with high and low plasma testosterone levels showed no differences in reported coital frequency or masturbation. When individual subjects were examined, however, they found that as an individual's testosterone level fell, this was associated with renewed sexual activity, which then raised the hormone levels. They suggested that coital activity may be a homeostatic device which keeps the testosterone level within the normal range! In other words, intercourse was driving testosterone rather than testosterone driving sexual intercourse.

To conclude with a question: how can we explain the high rates of erection and masturbation of many prepubertal boys when their testosterone levels are so low?

Nieschlag: This last point illustrates very well the fact that testosterone may not be the only factor influencing sexual activity, because we know that other androgens besides testosterone, such as dehydroepiandrosterone, increase in boys from the age of eight years onwards. This steroid is mainly of adrenal origin but it has androgenic activity. We don't know its role in sexual function. We may have to study the role of other steroids to explain these phenomena.

On the other hand, your observation emphasizes how little testosterone is required for sexual activity.

Bancroft: The rate of sexual activity in boys goes up enormously when testosterone levels rise at puberty, of course.

Green: Yes, but erection, masturbation and orgasm do occur, without ejaculation, before puberty.

Nieschlag: These are the early signs of puberty, however.

Bancroft: We know nothing about the *incidence* of prepubertal masturbation and orgasm.

Sachar: We have focused on the declining part of the curve here (for whatever reasons !), but a very studiable topic would be the sharp rise in sex hormones over a period of months associated with the onset of puberty. One could observe the secretion of these hormones coming in sequentially and assess the behavioural changes as they occur. Dr Ehrhardt is in fact starting such a study of the entrance into puberty.

Herbert: We know that the behavioural response to testosterone is a slow one, in marked contrast to the response to oestrogen. Do you think, Dr Nieschlag, that the *shape* of the diurnal rhythm, or even of rhythms longer than diurnal ones, is important? For example, what the brain 'sees' of testosterone may relate to an integrated action over a long period, so that in attempting to correlate levels of testosterone with sexual activity we should not only be interested in getting as accurate a picture of the levels as we can, but also in the shape of the output. We know that for cortisol, also, there are daily fluctuations such that for some parts of the day we are effectively adrenalectomized, and yet we go on living. Furthermore, if the rhythm changes this may have important consequences on the brain and target tissues.

The question of combinations of hormones has been raised and prolactin has been discussed. There are other relevant hormones too—for example, cortisol and oestrogen. Is there any evidence that oestrogen, given to a man in whom testosterone is maintained, produces impotence, or is its effect simply due to decreased testosterone?

Finally, we are all making an assumption about free and bound testosterone. We are assuming that what matters in the brain is the level of free testosterone. But if blood flows past a steroid-binding neuron which removes a proportion of the free testosterone, what happens to the bound fraction? Are we sure we should ignore the bound fraction?

Nieschlag: On the relation between the diurnal rhythm of testosterone and sexual activity, I am not aware of any conclusive study. Hypogonadal patients are usually given injections of long-acting testosterone esters. A supranormal peak of plasma testosterone develops a few hours after the injection and slowly declines over a fortnight to the previous subnormal testosterone concentrations. There are no diurnal variations during this fortnight, but the patients report that they feel perfectly well and have satisfactory sexual activity. So I don't know what the physiological significance of the diurnal rhythm of testosterone really is, especially in regard to sexual activity.

Our knowledge of the role of oestradiol mainly derives from men castrated for prostatic cancer or from patients with testicular tumours (Leydig cell tumours). In these patients exposed to high oestrogen doses, impotence is clearly a consequence. What has not been tried is to give very low doses of oestrogens to normal men and impotent men. This is an area which could and should be investigated.

On the question of free and bound testosterone, the assumption is that the bound hormone serves as a pool for the free, and as soon as the free hormone is used up by the receptors or by the cells, more comes from the bound pool to fill up the free pool. The 'bound' pool acts as a reservoir.

Sachar: I believe Dr Herbert is asking why if the brain has a high affinity for testosterone and is peeling off the testosterone easily from the binding proteins, the fraction of free hormone in the plasma at any particular point is of any great physiological significance.

Bancroft: Presumably if normal feedback is operating, the free hormone will be kept at a steady state?

Besser: Our knowledge here really derives from cortisol and cortisol-binding globulin, and we have extrapolated to testosterone and testosterone-binding globulin. Dr Herbert's point is well made, because the binding constants that make the steroid bind to the protein may be variable. For example, in human pregnancy where oestrogen concentrations are high the free levels of cortisol are actually higher than in the non-pregnant state, so something has altered. The feedback is still there but something has changed in the equilibrium. It is even more complex with testosterone because you have the effect of albumin, which binds a lot of oestrogen and only a little testosterone, but oestrogen controls the sex-hormone-binding globulin levels, and there is a complex see-saw relationship between oestrogen, its binding to albumin, and its effect on liver production of sex-hormone-binding globulin. When you increase oestrogen a little there is a whole sequence of changes, a cascade effect; Burke & Anderson (1972) have proposed a hypothesis about this. So the constants that control the binding affinity to sex-hormone-binding globulin may be highly relevant and may be variable.

Sachar: Studies of psychotropic drugs show the bound and free fractions to be very important. The concentration of the free fraction seems to be better correlated with clinical response. (J. M. Davis, unpublished paper, Psychiatric Research, Rochester N.Y, October 1977). Perhaps testosterone as a psychoactive agent behaves similarly.

Goy: If the binding proteins are made in the liver, if you hepatectomized an animal and kept it alive with silastic capsules you could test the effects of oestradiol as against testosterone, because oestrogen stimulates the synthesis of the binding protein.

Nieschlag: You don't need to hepatectomize an animal; there are species with no binding proteins, like the rat.

Goy: This is a model for the rat!

Short: Could I take up Dr Sachar's plea that we focus attention on puberty? Dr Nieschlag gave us a particularly good paper, and I liked the way he used pitch of voice as a bioassay of androgen. I was intrigued by the recent study of Daw (1970) showing that one can use the age at which boys' voices break from treble to alto to get historical demographic data on the time of puberty. An analysis of the age of boys singing in J. S. Bach's choir in Leipzig in the middle of the 18th century showed that the age at which they switched from treble to alto was between 17 and 17¼ years, whereas in London today the average age at which boys' voices switch from treble to alto is 13.3 years. So there has been the same advancement of puberty in boys as there has been in girls. We should pay more attention to the pitch of the human voice because it is such an easy clinical end-point to use.

Another clinical observation that should be exploited more, in relation to bioassaying the effects of androgen, is the age at which the prepuce separates from the glans, because this is an androgen-dependent effect (Hunter 1935; Gairdner 1949). If we want to look at the degree of androgenization that has occurred in boys during fetal life, along the lines of Dr Dörner's work, the degree of separation of prepuce from glans at birth may give us a valuable clue.

Finally, we have recently tried to establish the time at which spermatozoa are first formed in boys, by simply looking for sperm in the urine. To our surprise, spermatozoa first appeared in the urine of 53 boys at an average age of 13.3 years (± S.E. 0.12), so that boys become presumptively 'fertile' (we don't know if they actually are fertile), at about Tanner stage 2–3 of puberty, sometimes even before the first pubic hair appears. In other words, all boys pass through the phase of being fertile 'eunuchs'. So the first stage of puberty, the enlargement of the testis, coincides with the completion of spermatogenesis and precedes enlargement of the penis, development of pubic hair and the other male secondary sexual characteristics (Richardson & Short 1978).

References

ANDERSON, D. C. (1974) Sex-hormone-binding globulin. *Clin. Endocrinol. 3,* 69–96

BANCROFT, J. H. J., TENNENT, T. G., LOUCAS, K. & CASS, J. (1974) Control of deviant sexual behaviour by drugs: behavioural effects of oestrogen and antiandrogen. *Br. J. Psychiatr. 125,* 310–315

BURKE, C. W. & ANDERSON, D. C. (1972) Sex-hormone-binding globulin is an oestrogen amplifier. *Nature (Lond.) 240,* 38–40

COMHAIRE, F. & VERMEULEN, A. (1975) Plasma testosterone in patients with varicocoele and sexual inadequacy. *J. Clin. Endocrinol. 40,* 824

DAW, S. F. (1970) Age of boys' puberty in Leipzig, 1729–49, as indicated by voice breaking in J .S. Bach's choir members. *Hum. Biol. 42,* 87–89

FISHER, C., SCHIAVI, R. & LEAR, H. (1975) Assessment of nocturnal REM erection in the differential diagnosis of sexual impotence. *J. Sex Marital Ther. 4,* 277–289

FOX, C. A., ISMAIL, A. A. A., LOVE, D. N., KIRKHAM, K. E. & LORAINE, J. A. (1972) Studies on the relationship between plasma testosterone levels and human sexual activity. *J. Endocrinol. 52,* 51

GAIRDNER, D. (1949) The fate of the foreskin. A study of circumcision. *Br. Med. J. 2,* 1433–1437

GÖTZ, H. G. & DÖRNER, G. (1974) Effect of testosterone and FSH on the testicular function of hypophysectomized immature rats, in *Endocrinology of Sex* (Dörner, G., ed.), pp. 258–261, J. A. Barth, Leipzig

HUNTER, R. H. (1935) Notes on the development of the prepuce. *J. Anat. 70,* 68–75

ISMAIL, A. A. A., DAVIDSON, D. W., LORAINE, J. A., CULLEN, D. R., IRVINE, W. J., COOPER, A. J. & SMITH, C. G. (1970) Assessment of gonadal function in impotent men, in *Reproductive Endocrinology* (Irvine, W. J., ed.), Livingstone, Edinburgh

KRAEMER, M., BECKER, H., BRODIE, M., DOERING, C., MOOS, R. & HAMBURG, D. (1976) Orgasmic frequency and plasma testosterone levels in normal human males. *Arch. Sex. Behav. 5,* 125–132

LAWRENCE, D. M. & SWYER, G. I. M. (1974) Plasma testosterone and testosterone binding affinities in men with impotence, oligospermia, azoospermia, and hypogonadism. *Br. Med. J. 1,* 349

LEGROS, J. J., FRANCHIMONT, P., PALEMVLIERS, M. & SERVAIS, J. (1973) FSH, LH and testosterone blood levels in patients with psychogenic impotence. *Endocrinol. Exp. 7,* 59

LINCOLN, G. A. (1974) Luteinising hormone and testosterone in man. *Nature (Lond.) 252,* 232–233

MASTERS, W. H. & JOHNSON, V. E. (1966) *Human Sexual Response,* Churchill, London

PIRKE, K. M. & DOERR, P. (1975) Age related changes in free plasma testosterone, dihydrotestosterone and oestradiol. *Acta Endocrinol. 80,* 171–178

PIRKE, K. M., KOCKOTT, G., ALDENHOFF, J., BESINGER, U. & FEIL, W. (1978) Function of the pituitary gonadal system in patients with erectile impotence and premature ejaculation. *Arch. Sex. Behav.,* in press

RABOCH, J. & STARKA, L. (1972) Coital activity of men and levels of plasmatic testosterone. *J. Sex Res. 8,* 219–224

RABOCH, J. & STARKA, L. (1973) Reported coital activity of men and levels of plasma testosterone. *Arch. Sex. Behav. 2,* 309–316

RABOCH, J., MELLAN, J. & STARKA, L. (1975) Plasma testosterone in male patients with sexual dysfunction. *Arch. Sex. Behav. 4,* 541

RABOCH, J., MELLAN, J. & STARKA, L. (1977) Adult cryptorchids: sexual development and activity. *Arch. Sex. Behav. 6,* 413–419

RICHARDSON, D. W. & SHORT, R. V. (1978) The time of onset of sperm production in boys. *(I.P.P.F. 7th Biomedical Workshop on Fertility Regulation during Adolescence), J. Biosoc. Sci.,* in press

SACHAR, E. J., HALPERN, F. S., ROSENFELD, R., GALLAGHER, T. & HELLMAN, L. (1973) Plasma and urinary testosterone in depressed men. *Arch. Gen. Psychiatr. 28,* 15–18

SOLNICK, R. & BIRREN, J. (1977) Age and male erectile responsiveness. *Arch. Sex. Behav. 6,* 1–9

THORNER, M. O., EDWARDS, C. R. W., HANKER, J. P., ABRAHAM, G. & BESSER, G. M. (1977) Prolactin and gonadotrophin interaction in the male, in *The Testis in Normal and Infertile Men* (Troen, P. & Nankin, H., eds.), Raven Press, New York

VERMEULEN, A., RUBENS, R. & VERDONCK, L. (1972) Testosterone secretion and metabolism in male senescence. *J. Clin. Endocrinol. Metab. 34,* 730–735

VERWOERDT, A., PFEIFFER, E. & WANG, H. S. (1969) Sexual behaviour in senescence – changes in sexual activity and interest of aging men and women. *J. Geriatr. Psychiatr. 2,* 163

Androgens and human sexual behaviour

JOHN BANCROFT and NIELS E. SKAKKEBAEK

MRC Reproductive Biology Unit, Edinburgh, and Fertility Clinic and Laboratory of Reproductive Biology, University Hospital, Copenhagen

Abstract Androgens are generally believed to be necessary for normal sexual responsiveness in the human male and female. The evidence for this is limited and sometimes conflicting. This paper considers evidence from experiments in which exogenous androgens are given to people with impaired sexual response. Results from a study in which testosterone was given to unresponsive women are reported, together with the preliminary results of giving androstenedione to sexually unresponsive women taking oral contraceptives and giving testosterone undecanoate to hypogonadal males.

In the first study, when testosterone was combined with counselling, significant effects were produced by the addition of testosterone. In the androstenedione study, where no counselling was given, beneficial effects of the androgen have been unusual.

Examples of the evaluation of androgen replacement in hypogonadal males are also presented. Finally, some methodological problems of evaluating the effects of exogenous hormone in human sexual behaviour are briefly discussed.

There is fairly general agreement that androgens are necessary for normal human male sexual responsiveness and drive, but this is based to a large extent on uncontrolled studies or anecdotal clinical data. The apparently variable response to castration (Bremer 1959), particularly in the timing of behavioural effects, underlines our relative ignorance of the role of androgens in human male sexuality. In women we again have only clinical impressions accumulated over many years that androgens can enhance sexual response, but whether they are necessary in this respect is still uncertain (Bancroft 1978).

We have embarked on a series of studies that aim to clarify the role of androgens in the sexual behaviour of both the human male and female. This work is at an early stage and the problem must be seen as a jig-saw puzzle for which we have as yet only a few of the pieces. In this paper I hope to persuade you, first, that androgens are relevant to both sexes but, secondly, that in studying this relevance there are considerable methodological problems.

There are three principal ways of studying the relationship between hormones and behaviour in humans: (1) by studying the sexual behaviour of individuals with abnormally high or low endogenous androgen levels, or naturally varying levels, as during the menstrual cycle; (2) by manipulating levels of endogenous androgens by means of antiandrogens; and (3) by giving exogenous androgens and observing their effects on behaviour.

Although we are using all three approaches we shall concentrate here on the third—the effect of exogenous androgens—and will illustrate our methodological approach by examples from three such studies, while pointing out the problems in interpreting circulating plasma levels of androgens during exogenous administration.

Let us first consider the male, in particular the hypogonadal male, where the relevance of androgens is perhaps most easily demonstrated. We have been studying a group of 12 hypogonadal Danish men, six with hypergonadotrophic hypogonadism, mainly castrates, and six with hypogonadotrophic hypogonadism, mainly Kallman's syndrome. Most of these men have been on androgen replacement therapy previously, either suppositories or by injection, and we have used the availability of a new oral androgen, testosterone undecanoate (TU) (Coert *et al.* 1975) as the reason for changing their treatment regime and thus being able to study their response to androgens in a controlled fashion. Testosterone undecanoate (17β-hydroxy-4-androsten-3-one 17β-undecanoate; $C_{30}H_{48}O_3$), being fat soluble, is absorbed to a considerable extent via the lymphatics and largely avoids breakdown in the liver. It therefore promises to be superior to previous oral androgens without any apparent toxicity. We used a double-blind cross-over design measuring behavioural and endocrine variables during the original replacement therapy, during a period with no treatment, and then while the patient was receiving placebo or testosterone undecanoate for a period of eight weeks each. Sexual activity and ejaculation were recorded by means of diaries, frequency of sexual thoughts by weekly self-rating scales, and mood and energy by weekly Lorr & McNair mood check lists. Sexual attitudes were recorded monthly by means of the semantic differential (Whitehead & Mathews 1977).

This study is not yet finished, though seven of the 12 men have completed the trial and all seven have shown fairly convincing and rapid responses to the new androgen. We shall illustrate this with two cases. The first (Fig. 1) is a married man of 40 castrated because of bilateral testicular tumours at the age of 39. He had been maintained since castration on testosterone supposit-

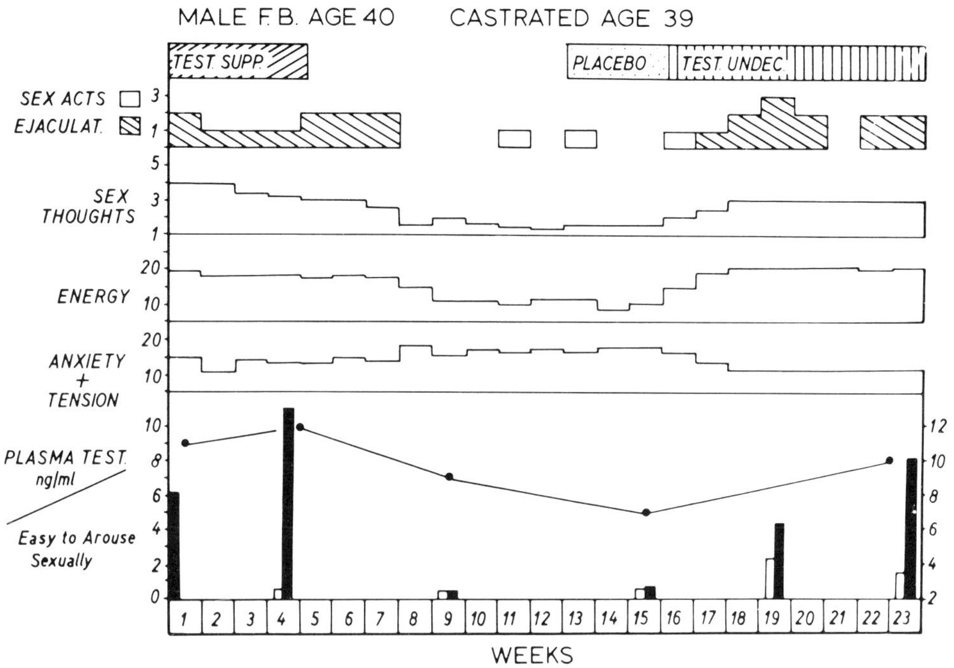

FIG. 1. Effects of testosterone undecanoate and placebo on a castrated hypogonadal man. *Left-hand scale:* plasma testosterone (ng/ml). □, early-morning pretreatment level, ■, 4 h after morning dose. *Right-hand scale:* 'easy to arouse sexually' (Semantic Differential) (● —— ●).

ories, 40 mg twice daily. When this regime was stopped there was little measurable change in sexual behaviour for the first two to three weeks. After this there was a definite decline in sexual interest and activity and general energy. Sexual activity almost ceased and when attempted, he could not ejaculate.

He was started on the first treatment regime (placebo) but because he complained of lack of effect, he was moved on to the second regime (TU, 80 mg twice daily) after three weeks. Within three to four days he felt an effect on his sexual interest and within a week was able to ejaculate again. These changes were also reflected in his semantic differential self-ratings of how easy he was to arouse sexually. Also noticed was a very rapid and considerable increase in his self-ratings of energy.

The second case is a 37-year-old married man with hypogonadotrophic hypogonadism (Fig. 2). He had had a brief two-month period of treatment

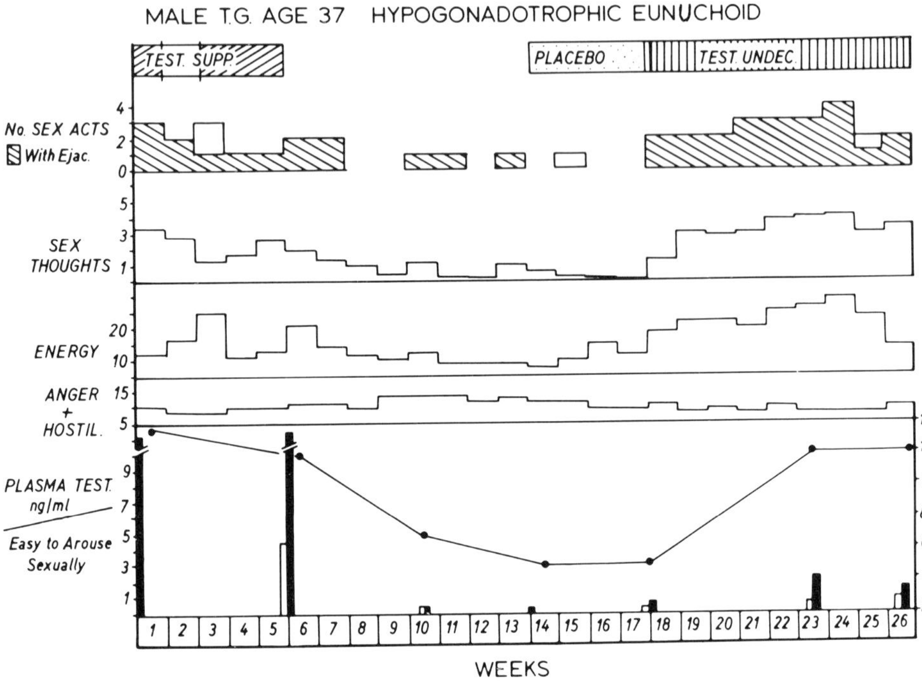

FIG. 2. Effects of testosterone undecanoate and placebo on a hypogonadal man with Kallman's syndrome. For details of plasma testosterone concentration and 'easy to arouse sexually' see Fig. 1.

with human chorionic gonadotropin (hCG) for delayed puberty at the age of 15, and then no further treatment until the age of 34; since that time he had been maintained mainly on testosterone suppositories. Again he showed no obvious decline sexually or in his energy levels until he had been without treatment for two weeks, and he continued to have occasional sexual acts with ejaculation until the tenth week, when he became unable to ejaculate during sexual intercourse. He responded sexually and with increased energy during the first week on testosterone undecanoate, having failed to show any response during the period on placebo.

In both cases, the decline in activity on stopping exogenous androgens is rather more gradual than the increase on re-starting them, and the mechanism underlying this difference is a matter of some interest and as yet not fully understood.

The relationship between exogenous androgens and behaviour in these cases is obviously convincing—not surprisingly, perhaps, in the case of the castrated man, who was sexually experienced at the time of castration, but remarkable in the hypogonadotrophic man, who had been hypogonadal since birth. It remains a possibility that his very brief period of hCG treatment at the age of 15 in some way sensitized him to later androgen therapy, but it seems more likely that this brief episode was irrelevant and he would have responded to his more recent treatment in the same way, even without that earlier episode.

Blood was sampled in those men at monthly intervals, two samples being taken on each occasion, one first thing in the morning before the first dose of androgen and the other four hours later. In the first case very high levels of testosterone were being obtained with the original testosterone suppositories (11.5 ng/ml), though baseline levels were falling very low before the next suppository (0.5 ng/ml) (Fig. 1). Very low levels were also obtained during the 'no treatment' period, whereas levels within the normal range were obtained when he was taking testosterone undecanoate. In the second case (Fig. 2) we again found very high blood levels with the testosterone suppositories (15.0, 12.8 ng/ml). But the levels found during the period on testosterone undecanoate, though higher than during the period of no treatment, were still below the normal range (2.0, 1.0 ng/ml)—yet the behavioural effects were convincing. The plasma testosterone concentration reaches a peak 4–5 hours after oral administration (Nieschlag *et al.* 1975), so we should have been close to the peak with our sampling.

When we consider the human female, we have no directly comparable paradigm of hypo-androgenicity. Women who undergo both oophorectomy and adrenalectomy do describe loss of sexual response (Waxenburg *et al.* 1959) which can probably be restored with exogenous androgens. But such cases, because of the pathology associated with these operative procedures, are much more complex to analyse and seldom occur nowadays.

In our first study of women, done in Oxford (Carney *et al.* 1978), we evaluated the effects of androgens in the intact but sexually unresponsive woman. We considered it unlikely in such cases that hormones alone would be sufficient, but that if combined with counselling they might give better results than would counselling alone. In this study, which involved 32 couples, we compared the effect of testosterone, 10 mg daily taken sublingually, with that of a tranquillizer, diazepam (10 mg daily), both combined with our usual method of counselling. A factorial design was used in this double-blind study: half the women had relatively low anxiety about sex, half had relatively high anxiety; half of them received testosterone plus counselling, half, diazepam plus counselling (Fig. 3). We postulated that the low anxiety group would do better with testosterone, and the high anxiety group with diaze-

	High anxiety	*Low anxiety*
Testosterone plus counselling	n = 8	n = 8
Diazepam plus counselling	n = 8	n = 8

FIG. 3. Factorial design of double-blind (Oxford) study of the effects of androgens on sexually unresponsive women.

pam. There was a further factor in the 2 × 2 × 2 design, a variation in the counselling regime, which is not relevant to this discussion.

Behavioural assessment was by means of diaries, self-rating questionnaires and interview ratings by a 'blind' assessor. These procedures were carried out before treatment, for a month after treatment, and six months later. The women receiving testosterone did significantly better than those receiving diazepam on a number of variables, including the subjective quality of sexual intercourse, pleasant feelings associated with sex, frequency of sexually exciting thoughts, frequency of orgasm, and several others, including an increase in the perceived sexual attractiveness of their male partners. These changes were to a large extent maintained at the end of the follow-up period when the women had not been taking androgens for six months (Table 1).

These results strongly support a role for androgens in the woman, though we are left uncertain on a number of points. We still lack good indicators for the use of androgen therapy, as our hypothesis that the women with low anxiety would do better with testosterone was only weakly supported. We were not in a position to make any endocrine assessment of these women and it remains uncertain whether the improvement was due to a pharmacological or a physiological effect of the hormone, though the dose used was a fairly modest one and there were no virilizing effects. We are also uncertain whether androgens would be effective without the counselling in such women.

In the next study, now in progress in Edinburgh, we are pursuing these questions further. We took a group of women who attributed a loss of sexual responsiveness to their use of oral contraceptives. Would exogenous andro-

TABLE 1

Effects of androgens on female unresponsiveness: measures showing the superiority of testosterone to diazepam

Self ratings	*One-month follow-up*	*Six-month follow-up*
Diary: enjoyment of sexual intercourse		+
Sexual thoughts with excitement		+
Pleasant sexual feelings	+	++
Sexual attraction of male partner	+	+
Frequency of orgasm	+	
Vaginal lubrication		+
Vaginal discomfort	+	

+, $P = <0.05$; ++, $P = <0.01$.
(From Carney *et al.* 1978)

gens help these women? The evidence for an effect of oral contraceptives on androgen levels is sparse, and to some extent conflicting. Mostly it suggests that testosterone concentrations are normal or are raised, presumably due to an increase in sex-hormone-binding globulin (SHBG) provoked by the oestrogen in the pill (Easterling *et al.* 1974; Kjeld *et al.* 1976). On the other hand, there is good reason to believe that androstenedione, the principal circulating androgen in women, will be reduced by oral contraceptives because of the considerable suppression of its ovarian production from the Graafian follicle, which normally accounts for approximately half the available androstenedione (Baird *et al.* 1974). Androstenedione can be considered as a 'prehormone' since it is probably the main source of testosterone in the woman (Baird *et al.* 1968), the testosterone being formed by extra-glandular conversion.

Androstenedione has also been shown to restore receptivity in rhesus monkeys treated with dexamethasone (Everitt & Herbert 1971), though this could be due to its conversion to testosterone. Nevertheless, because of the relatively high blood levels of androstenedione present in normal women, and the good absorption after its oral administration (Horton & Tait 1966), we decided to investigate the effects of this androgen, given orally 20 mg daily, on the sexual behaviour of the women in our study. We used a double-blind cross-over design similar to that used with the hypogonadal males, comparing androstenedione with placebo, each for two months after a one-month baseline period (Fig. 4). Fifteen women have been involved; again the study is not quite complete, but this time the results are fairly conclusive in a negative direction. Of the first 14 women, only one has shown a convincing behavioural response to androstenedione, with one other woman showing a modest response which could have been due to other factors.

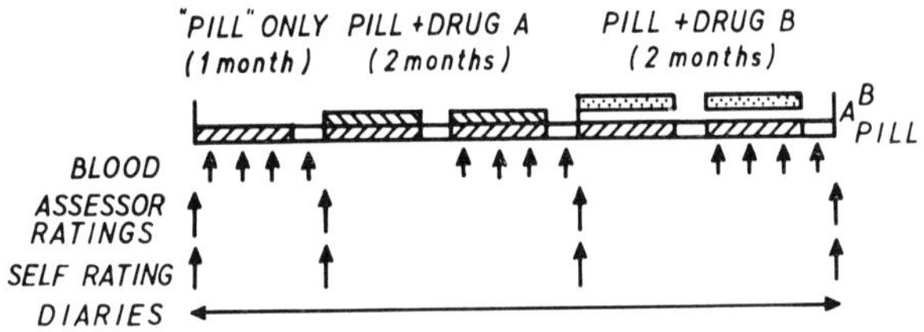

FIG. 4. Design of a double-blind study of the effects of androstenedione (20 mg/day) and placebo on sexual responsiveness in women taking oral contraceptives.

There are three obvious possible explanations for these predominantly negative findings. Either

(i) Androgens are not relevant to the problem in these women, or

(ii) Androgens will only help if combined with counselling, or

(iii) The dose of androstenedione was insufficient.

The dose of androstenedione used in the study was chosen to provide approximately the equivalent of the normal daily production of testosterone (0.34 mg/day; Horton & Tait 1966) and hence we were looking for a physiological rather than a pharmacological effect.

In this study we were in a position to make some endocrine assessment, and in the course of doing so we have again encountered some of the methodological complexities of monitoring and evaluating the administration of exogenous androgens.

First, as we anticipated, the initial androgen levels in these women were low. The mean levels for four weekly blood samples for each woman during the baseline month showed that in nine of the first 14 cases the androstenedione levels were below the normal range (mean 998 pg/ml, S.D. 320) and all but one of the testosterone levels were below normal (mean 246 pg/ml, S.D. 63) (Fig. 5). The apparent contrast with previous findings (e.g. Kjeld *et al.* 1976) raises the interesting possibility that women who are sexually unresponsive while taking oral contraceptives may differ from others in having relativ-

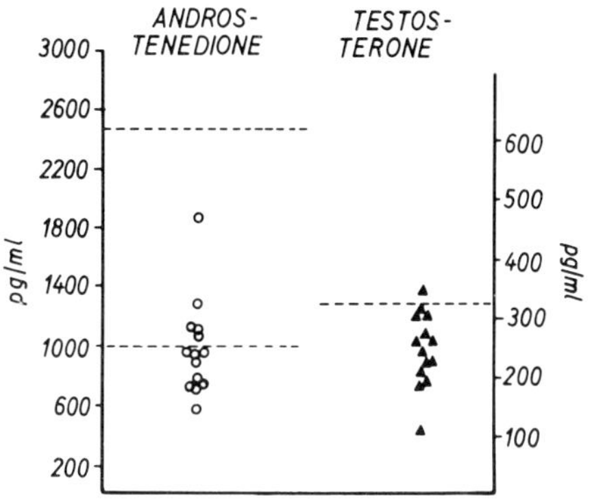

FIG. 5. Mean blood levels of androgens in sexually unresponsive women taking oral contraceptives. Baseline concentrations before administration of androstenedione.

ely low androgen levels. Remarkably, there are no other available data on hormone levels of any kind in sexually unresponsive women, whether taking oral contraceptives or not. Our next step is therefore to compare the baseline hormonal and behavioural data in this group of women with data in a group of pill users free from sexual difficulties and matched for the type of oral contraceptive. But even if we were to find a difference, this would still not account for the lack of response to androstenedione in this study, unless we were giving insufficient amounts or the wrong androgen.

The next question therefore is 'What were the blood levels of androgen in these women while they were taking the oral androstenedione?'. Absorption studies in three of the women in the study showed a fairly rapid absorption of oral androstenedione, blood levels reaching a peak within 1–2 hours and levelling off after 4–5 hours (Fig. 6). It will also be seen that the plasma testosterone levels increased quickly, the testosterone curve being very similar to that for androstenedione.

Our use of one daily dose of androstenedione was the same as in the previous study, where we used a daily sublingual dose of testosterone. There are no data on the absorption of sublingually administered testosterone in women, but data from men suggest a similar absorption curve to that for androstenedione, though with a more rapid return to baseline levels (data supplied by Organon Ltd). We aimed for an approximately 12-hour interval between giving the androstenedione orally and blood sampling, well past the 'half-life' of the oral dose, and were interested to see whether the levels would still be elevated.

For androstenedione this was not so. In fact, there were changes in levels

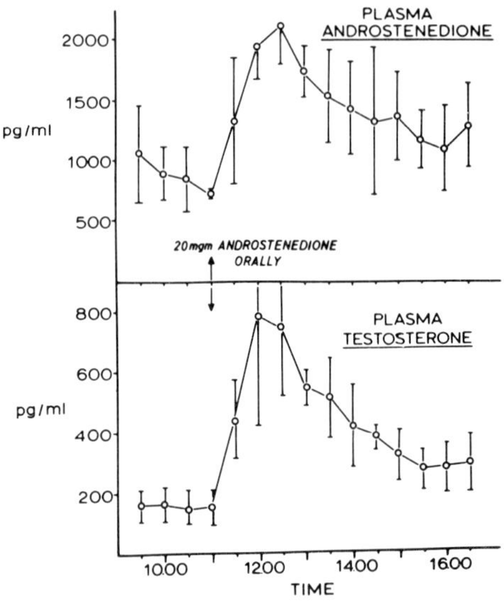

FIG. 6. Plasma levels of androstenedione and testosterone after oral administration of androstenedione (20 mg) in three women taking oral contraceptives.

over time, possibly related to the stress of venepuncture and gradual adaptation to it, thus confounding any effect of the oral androstenedione on baseline blood levels. The testosterone concentrations were, however, significantly increased during the period on oral androstenedione, though the majority were still below the normal range (mean for placebo period, 232 pg/ml, S.D. 77.2; for androstenedione period, 288 pg/ml, S.D. 75; $t = 3.81$, $P = < 0.01$). This may have been the result of conversion of some of the androstenedione to oestrogen and a consequent increase in sex-hormone-binding globulin (SHBG). Measurements of both oestrogen and SHBG concentrations are now being made, and it will obviously be important to see whether oestrogen levels are raised as a result of the androstenedione.

When we look at the one individual who showed a definite behavioural response we find that her androgen levels behaved almost the same as the means for the group as a whole. Her mean testosterone levels for the baseline period, the placebo period and the androstenedione period respectively were as follows: 264, 253 and 294 pg/ml. Her levels therefore remained low. This brings us to a very fundamental question. What is the relationship between circulating levels of androgens and their activity at the target organ site? The answer seems to be that we do not yet know, and until we do, the measurement of such levels will add very little to such an investigation.

There is good reason to believe that the level of unbound or 'free' testosterone is more relevant than the 'total' amount (Anderson 1974) and our measurement of the amount of binding may throw further light on this question. Of greater relevance, however, is the probability that the biologically active testosterone is that bound to the receptor of the target organ—something that we have no way of measuring. But the relevance of a change in circulating testosterone will presumably depend on the scope for additional binding at these target organ sites.

CONCLUSIONS

1. The evidence so far indicates the necessity of androgens for male sexual responsiveness. In the female, the necessity for androgens is a distinct possibility but further work is needed to establish this.
2. In further studies on the role of androgens in human sexual behaviour the exogenous administration of the hormone in 'double-blind' controlled conditions and with appropriate measurement of its behavioural effects will continue to be the most feasible approach. The ephemeral nature of the blood hormone level, and the fact that it will be influenced by the time of hormone administration and only remotely related to the 'bio-availability' of the hormone at the target tissue receptor, means that blood hormone levels may not be a particularly helpful way of monitoring the effectiveness of therapy.

ACKNOWLEDGEMENTS

This study was supported in part by a grant from the Danish Medical Research Council to Niels E. Skakkebaek.

We are grateful to Organon Ltd for their supply of Testoral, androstenedione and testosterone undecanoate used in these studies.

References

ANDERSON, D. C. (1974) Sex-hormone-binding globulin (review article). *Clin. Endocrinol. 3*, 69–96

BAIRD, D. T., HORTON, R., LONGCOPE, C. & TAIT, J. F. (1968) Steroid prehormones. *Perspect. Biol. Med. 11*, 384–421

BAIRD, D. T., BURGER, P. E., HEAVON-JONES, G. D. & SCARAMUZZI, R. J. (1974) The site of secretion of androstenedione in non-pregnant women. *J. Endocrinol. 63*, 201–212

BANCROFT, J. (1978) The relationship between hormones and sexual behaviour in humans, in *Biological Determinants of Sexual Behaviour* (Hutchison, J.B., ed.), Wiley, Chichester & New York

BREMER, J. (1959) *Asexualisation: A Follow-up Study of 244 Cases*, Macmillan, New York

CARNEY, P. A., BANCROFT, J. & MATHEWS, A. (1978) The combination of hormone and counselling in the treatment of female sexual unresponsiveness. *Br. J. Psychiatr., 133*, 339–346

COERT, A., GEELER, J., DE VISSER, J. & VAN DER VIES, J. (1975) The pharmacology and metabolism of testosterone undecanoate (T.U.), a new orally active androgen. *Acta Endocrinol. 79*, 789–800

EASTERLING, W. E., TALBERT, L. M. & POTTER, H. D. (1974) Serum testosterone levels in the polycystic ovary syndrome. *Am. J. Obstet. Gynecol. 120*, 385–389

EVERITT, B. J. & HERBERT, J. (1971) The effects of dexamethasone and androgens on sexual receptivity of female rhesus monkeys. *J. Endocrinol. 51*, 575–588

HORTON, R. & TAIT, J. F. (1966) Androstenedione production and interconversion rates measured in peripheral blood and studies on the possible sites of its conversion to testosterone. *J. Clin. Invest. 45*, 301–313

KJELD, J. M., PUAH, C. M. & JOPLIN, G. F. (1976) Changed levels of endogenous sex steroids in women on oral contraceptives. *Br. Med. J. 2*, 1354–1356

NIESCHLAG, E., MAUSS, J., COERT, A. & KICOVIC, P. (1975) Plasma androgen levels in men after oral administration of testosterone or testosterone undecanoate. *Acta Endocrinol. 79*, 366–374

WAXENBURG, S. E., DRELLICH, M. G. & SUTHERLAND, A. M. (1959) The role of hormones in human behaviour. I. Changes in female sexuality after adrenalectomy. *J. Clin. Endocrinol. Metab. 19*, 193–202

WHITEHEAD, A. & MATHEWS, A. (1977) Attitude change during behavioural treatment of sexual inadequacy. *Br. J. Soc. Clin. Psychol. 16*, 275–281

Discussion

Sachar: If the contraceptive pill is affecting the binding globulin (and there is evidence that oestrogens do affect it), the amount of free testosterone available will be markedly reduced and a modest dose of androstenedione, by the time it is converted to testosterone, may be so mopped up by the binding globulin as to have a relatively trivial effect. You shouldn't give up this approach, therefore. A somewhat higher dose of testosterone might work in these unresponsive women.

Besser: One has to be very careful in studying the effects of oral contraceptives. Measurements of sex-hormone-binding globulin (SHBG) levels in women who are taking oral contraceptives show a very varied pattern. We have compared the use of different combinations of oestrogen and progestagens in the management of hairy women, who often have normal total testosterone levels but very low levels of SHBG, with a view to increasing the binding protein. Different oral contraceptives have totally different effects on SHGB. It depends on the androgenic activity of the progesterone-like component. Some combinations are dominantly oestrogenic and produce large increases in SHBG. Others push SHBG down to low levels. Some oral contraceptives produce a dramatic fall in SHBG between Days 21 and 28 of the cycle, from the withdrawal of the oestrogenic effect. One cannot equate different studies on 'the' oral contraceptive, therefore. The therapy is entirely different, depending on the brand chosen, and indeed we choose as part of the therapeutic programme different types of oestrogen: progesterone combination, depending on the precise ratio of total testosterone to SHBG in the blood. When some people find high levels of testosterone and others, low levels, it may depend on the pill being used or the time of sampling within the cycle. Did your patients all take the same oral contraceptive?

Another factor is that some women with sexual response problems while taking oral contraceptives actually have hyperprolactinaemia. The low-oestrogen pill does not usually raise prolactin concentrations, unlike the high dose pill (> 50 μg of ethinyl oestradiol), unless the women is predisposed. When that happens she develops dramatic hyperprolactinaemia. She may get problems after ceasing to take the pill, too, such as oligomenorrhoea or amenorrhoea, or galactorrhoea.

Bancroft: I accept all you say. In a further study now in progress we are matching the groups for the same oral contraceptives. So far, half have been taking pills containing 50 μg oestrogen and half, those containing 30 μg, and they are using a variety of brands.

Sachar: One approach might be to change the type of pill being taken to one that would reduce or at least not raise the concentration of binding globulin?

Besser: Yes, if one wanted to examine the importance of androgens. I would ask, very simply, what happens to sexual drive in women with the polycystic ovary syndrome, who have high levels of adrenal androgens and testosterone. It is not my impression that they are highly sexed women—quite the converse; but then there are social aspects, such as the acne and development of facial hair.

Bancroft: We are starting a study of hirsute women using cyproterone acetate. In an earlier study recently completed (unpublished), which didn't include behavioural assessment, some women complained of impaired sexual response. This could be another model for pursuing this relationship. I can't find any behavioural data on women with polycystic ovaries.

Ehrhardt: In your first study of sexual unresponsiveness in women, why didn't you have a third control group receiving counselling alone and no drugs, to see whether you got the same kind of effect?

Bancroft: That would have to involve the use of a placebo control to be useful. I regret in retrospect that in that study we didn't use placebo rather than diazepam as a control. That study is being repeated in London by

Dr A. Mathews, who is comparing placebo with sublingually administered testosterone. The point is that in controlled clinical studies of this kind one has to be modest in the design and in the numbers involved, or the study breaks down. At the same time, such studies are difficult to do and one naturally tries to get as much useful information as is reasonable. We had hoped to show a role for diazepam in certain cases.

We are doing another similar study of couples where the man is sexually unresponsive and comparing testosterone undecanoate plus counselling with placebo plus counselling.

Hertoft: You refer to counselling almost as if it was a drug itself! Can you explain what kind of counselling you use?

Bancroft: The counselling we use is based on the Masters & Johnson (1966) approach, which we use normally in our sexual problems clinic, and on the whole it is effective. We work with the couple. They are sent home with fairly precise behavioural assignments: then they come back to us and discuss their problems in carrying out their assignments. Then we deal with interpersonal issues, such as resentment, and lead on to the next behavioural step.

Sachar: Turning to the testosterone levels achieved in the men, there is a threshold, perhaps, and as long as one gets above that threshold, one may have sufficient hormonal priming for sexual activity?

Bancroft: I am not sure. Perhaps a certain amount of testosterone is needed in the *tissues,* and when you have that, it doesn't matter what concentration is in the blood.

Nieschlag: You didn't measure any other metabolites, such as dihydrotestosterone? That may be important. There is evidence that dihydrotestosterone may increase proportionally more than testosterone after testosterone undecanoate treatment (A. Vermeulen, personal communication).

As a separate point, I gather that you wanted to learn something about the role of androgens in females by giving them androstenedione. This androgen is readily metabolized to oestrogens, so it may not be the right compound for such studies. The oestradiol values in your women may be higher than normal. You should probably use another androgen which is not so easily converted.

Bancroft: The lower levels of testosterone, in other words, may be due to a rise in SHBG provoked by oestrogen formed from the androstenedione! We shall be measuring dihydrotestosterone levels in both studies but these results are not yet available.

Nieschlag: When you give 10 mg of free testosterone sublingually to women over four months, do you see any virilization?

Bancroft: No. Clitoral size was not measured but no-one has commented on her clitoris. Each week, including a month before starting giving the androgen, I asked the subjects to check off any changes in body hair growth, oiliness of the skin or voice change; no effects have been reported in either study. Two women taking testosterone sublingually said their head hair was healthier when they were on the drug; one other woman said that her nails, which previously were always cracking, were much better when she was taking testosterone. Those were the only effects, both desirable ones.

Nieschlag: A good parameter to follow may be the voice, because this may provide an early sign of virilization.

Bancroft: Bear in mind that the women are taking androstenedione in one study for only two months and in the other study for four months.

Nieschlag: That can be long enough for subtle changes in the voice.

Green: On the subject of testosterone levels and human female sex drive, Persky *et al.* (1977) have evidence suggesting that at ovulation there is a surge in plasma testosterone in the woman with a smaller surge about eight days after ovulation. If that is a valid phenomenon, perhaps these women on the pill, who are not ovulating, are experiencing diminished sex drive because they are not having one or two bursts of testosterone during the cycle.

Bancroft: The balance of several studies suggests that both androstenedione and testosterone have a peak similar to the oestrogen peak during the menstrual cycle but without the mid-cycle dip. In other words, it is a more gradual change, reaching its height round ovulation. One would expect it to be much less on the pill, although there is evidence that adrenal androgens vary during the menstrual cycle as well (Genazzani *et al.* 1977).

Green: I am suggesting that it could be testosterone rather than oestradiol.

Bancroft: Yes. Although androstenedione might be having some androgenic behavioural effect in its own right, we were assuming that if it has an effect it would mainly be by conversion to testosterone.

Hutchison: I realize that your samples are small, but is there evidence of a relationship in the hypogonadal men between the period of androgen deficit and the effectiveness of the exogenous hormone? Although not many species have been studied yet, work in animals suggests that long-term castrates may be less sensitive to systemically administered androgen than short-term castrates. In the male Barbary dove (Hutchison 1969), and in rats (Davidson & Bloch 1969), significantly more androgen is required to initiate sexual behaviour in long-term than in short-term castrates. This suggests a reduced sensitivity to the steroid in conditions of prolonged hormone deficit.

Bancroft: This is an important point which may be relevant to the experimental method one uses in this type of research. One may get different effects depending on how long a period the person is on and off such hormones; the number of times that the androgen is removed and replaced may also influence its effects. We should keep an open mind on this point.

Hutchison: Differences in the effectiveness of androgen could be related to peripheral rather than central factors. I think it is important to distinguish between factors influencing the effectiveness of androgen that directly involve the brain and those that are a consequence of plasma binding or metabolism of the steroid before it reaches the brain. It can be argued that systemically injected androgen reaches the brain of long-term castrates in much lower concentrations due, for example, to changes in the amount of SHBG. To resolve this issue, animal work is required which tests the effectiveness of androgen applied directly to the brain. So far as I know this has only been done in one species so far, the Barbary dove. Crystalline implants of androgen, sited in the anterior hypothalamus of the long-term castrate, are far less effective in restoring pre-copulatory courtship than similar implants in short-term castrates. This suggests that a decline in effectiveness of androgen may be related to a change in the hormone sensitivity of the brain (Hutchison 1974). What happens to SHBG in men with long-term androgen deficits?

Besser: The production of SHBG is a result of the interplay between oestrogen and androgen, so castrated males tend to have higher than normal levels of SHBG because of the lack of androgen and the unopposed oestrogen (resulting from conversion of adrenal androgen). When you give testosterone it will be largely bound, so it will be relatively less effective. After a while the level of SHBG falls. The normal male has low levels of SHBG; the normale female has higher levels.

Nieschlag: Studies in castrated men show just what you say, that the SHBG is influenced by the balance of testosterone and oestradiol. After castration the concentrations of both hormones fall and you don't see a change in SHBG in the castrated men. The same is true in men treated with cyproterone acetate. Both testosterone and oestradiol concentrations fall and the SHBG level stays the same (Bartsch *et al.* 1977).

Besser: Are you suggesting that giving androgen to a male does *not* result in the lowering of an abnormally high SHBG level?

Nieschlag: In the hypogonadal man, with an increase in oestradiol relative to testosterone (which is specifically true of Klinefelter's syndrome where high oestrogen, low testosterone and high SHBG levels are found), when testosterone is given the SHBG level immediately falls. In castrated men it is different. I think this is a technical problem and is not so relevant.

I want to make one point which stresses the importance of androgen in females. In women with Addison's disease one can replace gluco- and mineralocorticosteroids but some of these patients still don't feel well. If they receive small doses of androgens some of these women are normalized. This is an indication clinically that women require androgens. However, I have no controlled data to support this clinical impression.

Everitt: In your study of women, Dr Bancroft, you referred to changes in mood and, indeed, you were using a mood-altering drug, diazepam. What do you see as the relationship between mood and sexual activity and how might they both be affected by hormones?

Bancroft: We have some data on mood in that first study which we haven't analysed yet. Mood obviously is important, but I don't know what the relationship is. The clinical data on sexual changes in people who are depressed, or on mood changes in people who have sexual difficulties, are appallingly inadequate. This is a difficult area to investigate. There is likely to be an important relationship and there may be some common mediating factors which are related to steroids and monoamines in the CNS. It is an important area which needs to be grappled with.

Ehrhardt: Several studies have looked at mood over the menstrual cycle, or at sexual activity over the menstrual cycle (see review by McCauley & Ehrhardt 1976). I am not aware of any study of mood and sexual activity in the same women.

Bancroft: There is one valid study of the effects of the pill on mood and sexual behaviour, by Cullberg (1973). But even in that study the assessment of sexual behaviour was extremely superficial. He concluded that the sexual changes in women taking the pill were usually secondary to mood changes. Most of the studies where mood and sexual behaviour have been examined in the same women have been inadequate. I would accept some of the data on the menstrual cycle, although I can't accept that they convincingly show a mid-cycle change in sexual behaviour.

Green: You showed a beautiful correlation between energy level and the return of sexual interest and behaviour in men. I wonder if any pharmacological agent would have a comparable effect on energy level, and not be an androgenic compound?

Bancroft: What about amphetamines? This brings us back to the issue of cerebral monoamines.

Everitt: The fact that energy level and sexual activity are correlated does not, of course, mean that the former underlies the latter. From what I know of a rather poor literature, most of the psychostimulant drugs of abuse, such as amphetamines, eventually impair sexual activity and may result in impotence (e.g. Gossop *et al.* 1974). This is also true of opiates and, according to some workers, marihuana as well (Hollister 1975).

References

BARTSCH, W., HORST, H. J., BECKER, H. & NEHSE, G. (1977) Sex hormone binding globulin capacity, testosterone, 5α-dihydrotestosterone, oestradiol and prolactin in plasma of patients with prostatic carcinoma under various types of hormonal treatment. *Acta Endocrinol. 85,* 650–659

CULLBERG, J. (1973) Mood changes and menstrual symptoms with different gestagen/estrogen combinations. *Acta Psychiatr. Scand.,* Suppl. 236

DAVIDSON, J. M. & BLOCH, G. H. (1969) Neuroendocrine aspects of male reproduction. *Biol. Reprod. 1,* 67–92

GENAZZANI, A. R., MAGRINI, G., FACCHINETTI, F., ROMAGUINO, S., PINTOR, C., FELBER, J. P. & FIORETTI, P. (1977) Behaviour and origin of plasma androgens throughout the menstrual cycle, in *Androgens and Antiandrogens* (Martini, L. & Motta, M., eds.), Raven Press, New York

GOSSOP, M. R., STERN, R. & CONNELL, P. H. (1974) Drug dependence and sexual function: a comparison of intravenous users of narcotics and oral users of amphetamines. *Br. J. Psychiatr. 124,* 431–434

HOLLISTER, L. E. (1975) The mystique of social drugs and sex, in *Sexual Behaviour: Pharmacology and Biochemistry* (Sandler, M. & Gessa, G.L., eds.), pp. 85–92, Raven Press, New York

HUTCHISON, J. B. (1969) Changes in hypothalamic responsiveness to testosterone in male Barbary doves *(Streptopelia risoria). Nature (Lond.) 222,* 176–177

HUTCHISON, J. B. (1974) Post-castration decline in behavioural responsiveness to intrahypothalamic androgen in doves. *Brain Res. 80,* 1–10

MCCAULEY, E. A. & EHRHARDT, A. A. (1976) Female sexual response: hormonal and behavioral interactions, in *Health Care for Women. I. Current Social and Behavioral Issues* (Youngs, D. D. & Ehrhardt, A. A., eds.), pp. 455–476, Saunders, Philadelphia

MASTERS, W. H. & JOHNSON, V. E. (1966) *Human Sexual Response,* Churchill, London

PERSKY, H., LIEF, H., O'BRIEN, C., STRAUSS, D. & MILLER, W. (1977) Reproductive hormone levels and sexual behaviours of young couples during the menstrual cycle, in *Progress in Sexology* (Gemme, R. & Wheeler, C., eds.), Plenum Publishing Corporation, New York

Sexual compatibility in rhesus monkeys: predicting sexual performance of oppositely sexed pairs of adults

R. W. GOY

Department of Psychology and Wisconsin Regional Primate Research Center, University of Wisconsin-Madison

Abstract The percentage of male rhesus monkeys that display ejaculation in standardized daily 12-minute tests varies with the ovarian cycle of the female partner. In a study of 18 oppositely sexed pairs, ejaculation by males occurred on about 40% of the tests given early in the follicular phase, on about 85% of the tests given near the time of the female's oestradiol surge, and on about 40% of tests given during the mid-luteal phase. These overall changes were not characteristic of all pairs studied. Male partners in some pairs ejaculated on nearly all luteal tests whereas others ejaculated on only a few or not at all.

Two subsequent studies provided evidence that the *latency to ejaculation* characteristic of a particular pair during follicular tests accurately predicted the percentage of tests on which ejaculation occurred during the luteal phase. When the same male was tested with two different female partners, differences in the frequency of ejaculation during luteal tests were inversely related to latency to ejaculation measured during follicular tests. In the second study, when two different males were tested daily with the same female during the same cycle, the male with the shorter latency to ejaculation during follicular tests showed the higher frequency of ejaculation in luteal tests.

The frequency of ejaculation is as variable among pairs early in the follicular phase as it is among pairs tested during the mid-luteal phase. The early follicular phase is characterized by insufficient or suboptimal oestrogenization of the female. In order to test the possibility that the latency to ejaculation characteristic of a pair might be related to frequency of ejaculation during states of suboptimal oestrogenization, spayed females were given optimal amounts of exogenous oestradiol and the average latency to ejaculation of their male partners was measured. Latencies to ejaculation measured when females were given optimal amounts of oestradiol were inversely related to the frequency of ejaculation when the same pairs were tested after administration of suboptimal doses of oestrogen to the females.

A final experiment showed that the particular latency to ejaculation that characterizes a female in her sexual interactions with different males influences the retention of copulation by males after they are castrated. Eight females tested eight times with each of nine males had significantly different average latencies to ejaculation which provided a basis for ranking the females as typically producing short or long latencies to ejaculation by male partners. When these same females were used as partners for 10 recently castrated males, the frequency of ejaculation was significantly greater on tests with the four females having the lowest ranks than on tests with the four females having the highest ranks.

The suggestion is made that this behavioural measure, *latency to ejaculation*, can be used as an index of pair compatibility. Relationships between the concept of pair compatibility and current concepts of sexual attractiveness, proceptivity and receptivity are discussed.

Despite the obvious fact that intravaginal deposition of the ejaculate during coitus is one of the most fundamental requirements for reproduction, efforts to predict accurately whether or not it will occur when oppositely sexed adult rhesus monkeys are paired have not been very successful. Recent efforts in this direction have focused attention on aspects of the female partner and her behaviour during pairing. Concepts of attractiveness and receptivity have been operationalized (Herbert 1968; Michael 1973) and, although there are some logical difficulties (Goldfoot 1977), these variables have been shown to influence ejaculatory performance by the male. When consideration is given to the interactive nature of mating behaviour, however, it is clear that measurement of attractiveness, receptivity and even proceptivity will not provide complete predictability of coital ejaculatory performance if these properties are measured in the female alone (Beach 1976). Intuitively, how attractive the female is to the male is only part of the predictive equation. Probably of equal importance is the question of how attractive the male is to the female. The same egalitarian status applies to whatever characteristics of the male correspond conceptually to the female's receptivity and proceptivity.

The quantitative state of each of these traits as well as how they are specifically combined for the male and the female as partners may be able to provide investigators with an accurate predictive schema. When the balance among them is optimal, pairs of individuals can be characterized as highly compatible and the probability of ejaculation will be high. When the balance is less optimal, pairs can be regarded as less compatible and the probability of ejaculation occurring will be correspondingly reduced.

While it is premature at this time to quantitatively measure each of those traits in both partners or to determine the essential nature of the balance among them, the phenomenon of 'pair compatibility' has already been described (Goy & Goldfoot 1975; Phoenix 1973). To recapitulate briefly, nine male rhesus monkeys were paired with eight oestrogen-primed females such that every possible pair had at least eight standardized time-limited tests. Both the frequency of ejaculation and the latency to ejaculation depended partly on the particular male, partly on the particular female, and partly on the specific pair. The variance in ejaculatory measures attributable to the specific pair was conceptualized as 'pair compatibility'. When frequency was used as the measure of compatibility, high compatibility was estimated by the occurrence of ejaculation on nearly every test of a pair; low compatibility was inferred from the absence or near absence of ejaculations, and the 72 unique pairs studied represented a reasonable continuum from low to high compatibility.

The hypothetical continuum is perhaps better represented by using latency to ejaculation, defined as the time elapsed from putting the pair in the same cage to the occurrence of ejaculation by the male, than by using frequency of ejaculation. In addition to being a physical measure, latency has the advantage over frequency of eliminating ties and ceiling effects. For example, for many of the 72 pairs studied ejaculation occurred on 100% of their tests, but average latency discriminated among these tied pairs. The principal disadvantage of latency to ejaculation as a measure is that no satisfactory estimate exists for pairs that fail to ejaculate on any test. Nevertheless, the two measures are significantly correlated ($r = -0.51$, $P < 0.01$, based on data for the 67 of the 72 pairs that ejaculated on at least one of their eight tests), and which of the two is selected for use as an indicator of pair compatibility has to depend partly on the needs of the specific study.

In the original demonstration the notion of pair compatibility was not set out as an explanatory concept, and its functions or possible effects were not suggested. It is the purpose of this chapter to examine the effects of variation in pair compatibility on the sexual behaviour of selected pairs in standardized testing situations. For this purpose the measurement of latency to ejaculation of a particular pair will be used as the index of pair compatibility. Inasmuch as this measure of pair compatibility is to be used to account for variance in frequency of ejaculation, and these two measures are correlated when the data for each are obtained from the same test, the predictive value of the independent variable will be tested trans-situationally. That is, latency data collected from one set of tests will be used to predict frequency of ejaculation in a different set of tests. The nature of the prediction itself is simple, the hypothesis being that pairs identified as having shorter latencies to ejaculation under one set of conditions will show a higher frequency of ejaculation under a different set of conditions than pairs having longer latencies to ejaculation.

EXPERIMENTS AND RESULTS

The ovarian cycle and its associated endocrine cycle in the female rhesus monkey provides a convenient and natural situation for testing this hypothesis. A number of published reports have shown that when pairs of oppositely sexed rhesus are selected randomly and tested daily throughout the menstrual cycle of the female, the frequency of ejaculation by the male partner varies predictably with the endocrine changes occurring in the female (Czaja *et al.* 1975; Goy & Resko 1972; Michael & Bonsall 1977).

An example of this cyclical variation in male ejaculatory performance is illustrated in Fig. 1. Results are based on data from 18 females and 18 males randomly selected from the Wisconsin Primate Center breeding colony and

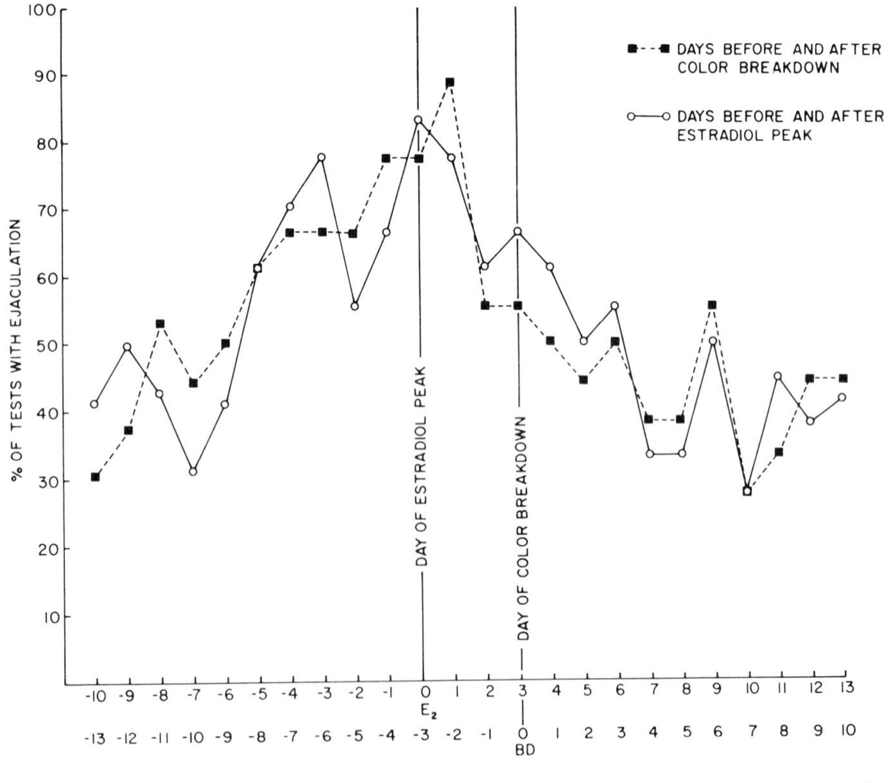

FIG. 1. Changes in the percentage of tests on which ejaculation occurred as a function of the female partner's ovarian cycle. Data obtained from 18 oppositely sexed pairs of rhesus tested daily for 12 min. The cycle is plotted in terms of days before and after both the occurrence of the females' oestradiol peak and day of colour breakdown.

randomly paired. Each pair was tested daily, starting on the first day of menstruation and ending on the first day of the succeeding menstruation. The percentage of pairs that copulated to ejaculation during a standardized 12-minute test conducted on each day of the females' cycle is shown in Fig. 1. Only 24 days of the cycle are represented, and the data are plotted according to two different cyclical events: (1) the day of maximum concentration of oestradiol in the peripheral circulation as measured by radioimmunoassay, and (2) the day of colour breakdown, defined as the first day that the gradual trend of increasing intensity of sexual skin reddening is suddenly reversed. Either method of defining the cycle is valid for present purposes, but the ease with which the reddening of the sexual skin can be read by a trained observer and the non-invasive nature of such observations make this method of defining the cycle the one of choice for the experiments to be described. Regardless of the method used, the cycle for randomized pairs is characterized by ejaculation on about 40% of the tests early in the follicular phase, 80–90% of the tests near the time of the oestradiol surge or 2–4 days before colour breakdown, and on only about 40% of the tests given during the middle of the luteal phase on Days 6–10 after the oestradiol surge.

Data of the sort shown in Fig. 1, or those based on the average frequency of display of specific behaviour, can mask large differences between individual pairs (Rowell 1963). For example, Michael & Welegalla (1968) estimated that although on average the variation in the display of behaviour corresponded to cyclical changes in female endocrine condition, nearly 50% of the pairs they studied showed little or no measurable cyclical variation. The possibility that pairs that show cyclical variation in the frequency of ejaculation might differ in latency to ejaculation from pairs that do not show cyclical variation was examined in the following experiments done by Kim Wallen and myself.

Nine females were tested daily throughout one complete menstrual cycle. Each day, a female was paired successively for 12 minutes with two males, and the daily order of presenting each male to the female was alternated. Thus, 18 males were used as partners for the nine females, providing a total of 18 possible pairs.

Daily observations were made of sex-skin coloration of the females. The occurrence of colour breakdown was noted, and tests for 10 days before the day of breakdown (follicular tests) provide data on the average latency to ejaculation characterizing each pair. In the calculation of average latency for a given pair, only tests on which ejaculation occurred were used. That is, arbitrary and artificial 'estimates' of latency to ejaculation were not used. Tests given on the 10 days after the day of colour breakdown (luteal tests) provided data on the frequency of ejaculation characteristic of each pair. These two sets of data from the follicular and luteal tests were used to test the hypothesis that shorter latencies to ejaculation during follicular tests would be associated with higher frequencies of ejaculation during luteal tests for the same pair.

Results of this study showed, as expected, that the average latencies to ejaculation on follicular tests varied significantly according to the particular pair ($F = 8.56$, 17 and 122 df, $P < 0.001$) and also according to the particular female ($F = 7.77$, 8 and 131 df, $P < 0.001$) (Table 1). For individual pairs,

TABLE 1
Average frequency and latency to ejaculation during the follicular phase

Pairs — *Females*	*Males*	*No. of tests*	*No. of tests with ejaculation*	*Average latency for pairs (min)*	*S.D.*	*Average latency for females (min)*	*S.D.*
720	544	10	7	4.67	3.16	2.95	2.46
	1155	10	10	1.75	0.47		
1256	1618	9	6	3.54	2.69	2.98	2.00
	826	9	9	2.61	0.60		
1437	1517	10	9	4.02	1.47	3.59	1.34
	526	10	10	3.20	1.15		
1765	1547	10	10	6.40	3.23	4.21	3.28
	1152	10	10	2.02	1.10		
1370	714	10	4	6.81	2.93	4.62	2.36
	1304	10	10	3.75	1.49		
1499	1355	10	10	6.59	2.81	5.93	1.89
	438	10	9	5.22	0.65		
1250	4845	10	5	9.20	1.69	6.19	2.95
	1518	10	8	4.31	1.69		
1225	987	10	10	7.77	3.09	7.22	3.00
	1623	10	9	6.61	2.96		
1648	1621	10	3	9.66	2.84	9.31	2.42
	1622	10	1	8.25	--------		--------
				$F = 8.56$		$F = 7.77$	
				17 & 122 df		8 & 131 df	
				$P < 0.001$		$P < 0.001$	

average latencies varied from as short as 2.02 to as long as 9.66 minutes of the 12-minute testing period. (Variance among pairs includes the contribution made by specific males, but no estimate of variation among males independent of the specific female partner is available.) Latencies varied among females as partners between 2.98 and 9.31 minutes. The influence of the particular female was substantial, as shown not only by the significant F-ratio, but also by the fact that the latencies to ejaculation shown by the two males paired with the same female were significantly correlated ($r = +0.75$, $P < 0.01$). The correlation, as well as the significant F-ratio for the effect of the particular female, indicates that, on average, there was less variance between males with the same partner than there was among males with different partners.

The male that had the shorter latency during follicular tests with the female had the higher frequency of ejaculation with that female during luteal tests. This relationship between latency and frequency is illustrated in Fig. 2. Here the 18 males were divided into two equal groups: one including the male partners having the shorter latency (mean 4.19 min), and the other including the male partners having the longer latency (mean 6.38 min) with each female during the 10 follicular tests before breakdown of the sex-skin coloration.

The percentage of tests on which ejaculation occurred did not differ greatly between shorter and longer latency males during the females' follicular phase, but did differ markedly during the luteal phase (10 daily tests after colour breakdown).

TABLE 2

Comparison of ejaculation frequencies for males with the shorter follicular latency and males with the longer latency when paired with the same female

		% of tests with ejaculation			
	N	*Follicular phase*		*Luteal phase*	
			NS		
Males with shorter follicular latency ($\bar{X}$ = 4.19 min)	9	85.4		83.3	
			NS		$t_d = 4.46$, 8df, $P < 0.005$
Males with longer follicular latency ($\bar{X}$ = 6.52 min)	9	71.9		43.3	
			$t_d = 3.24$, 8df, $P < 0.01$		

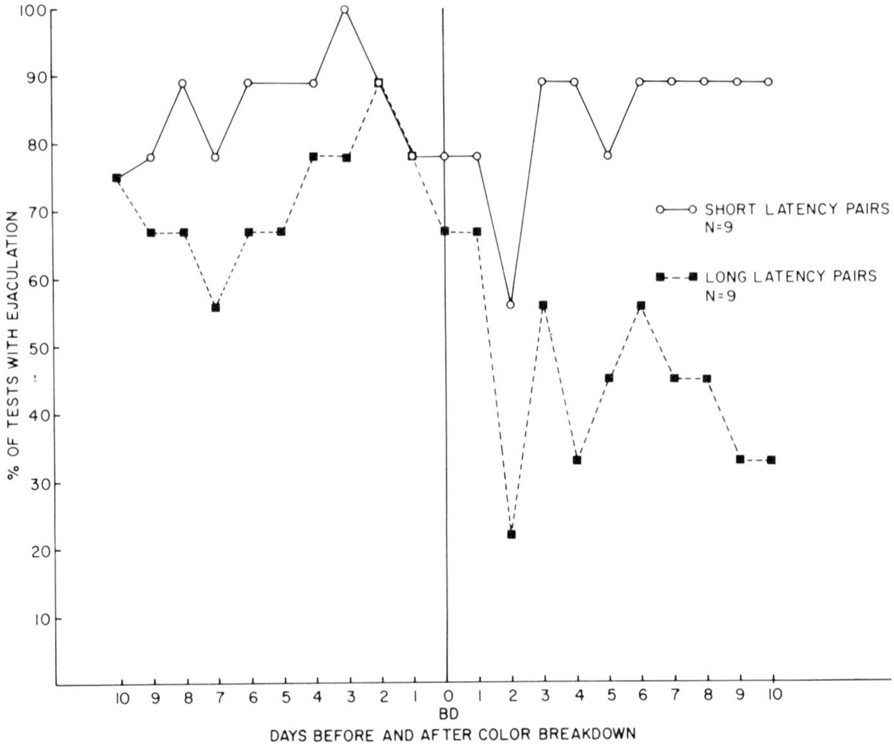

FIG. 2. Differences between two groups of males (one with shorter latencies to ejaculation and the other with longer latencies) in the percentage of tests on which ejaculation occurred with the same female partner. Data were obtained by successively pairing two males with a single female daily throughout one cycle of changes in coloration of sexual skin.

Alternatively stated, pairs characterized by short ejaculation latencies during the follicular tests did not show cyclical variation in the frequency of ejaculation, and the so-called 'luteal inhibition' of copulation was not observed. In contrast, pairs showing longer latencies to ejaculation during follicular tests displayed cyclical variation in the frequency of ejaculation, and ejaculation occurred on only 43.3% of the tests given during the luteal phase of the females' cycle (Table 2). The difference between these two groups in cyclical and non-cyclical patterns of copulation to ejaculation, or the difference between them with respect to the presence or absence of 'luteal inhibition', cannot be accounted for by systematic differences in the female cycle. Clearly, for every male that showed a high frequency of copulation to ejaculation during a female's luteal phase, a corresponding male paired with the same female in the same luteal phase showed infrequent ejaculation. The difference in their performances during the luteal phase cannot be explained by the simple-minded notion that the time-limit for the test (12 min) prevented the display of ejaculation by males with the longer follicular latencies. Their average follicular latency was substantially less than this time limit, and their frequency of ejaculation during the follicular phase did not differ from that of the males with the shorter latencies.

The average latency to ejaculation characterizing the individual pairs during the 10 days before colour breakdown was not necessarily representative of the pair during their initial ejaculatory encounter. The female's follicular phase usually lasts longer than 10 days before colour breakdown, and for these particular females the duration of this phase varied between 13 and 15 days and initial ejaculations of their male partners varied between 15 and 3 days before breakdown. Males that had shorter average latencies during the 10 days before breakdown ('fast' males) did not differ significantly from the males with longer average latencies ('slow' males) in terms of their latencies on the initial ejaculation (means and standard deviations were 7.25 ± 2.95 min and 7.63 ± 3.84 min respectively). However, 'fast' males showed statistically significant reductions in latency to ejaculation after the initial ejaculation with the female whereas 'slow' males did not (Table 3). In addition, the 'fast' males' average latencies with the females during the 10 days before breakdown were significantly correlated with their latencies to the initial ejaculation ($r = +0.731$, $P < 0.01$).

TABLE 3

Changes in latency to ejaculation for males with shorter and males with longer average follicular latencies

	N	*Mean latency (min) on initial ejaculation*	*Mean of individual mean latency (min) on later ejaculations*
Males with shorter follicular latency ('fast' males)	9	7.25 ± 2.95	4.9 ± 2.7
Males with longer follicular latency ('slow' males)	9	7.63 ± 3.84	6.52 ± 2.15

'Fast' males, 7.25 ± 2.95 vs 4.9 ± 2.7: $t_d = 4.55$, 8df, $P < 0.01$

Initial ejaculation, 7.25 ± 2.95 vs 7.63 ± 3.84: NS

Later ejaculations, 4.9 ± 2.7 vs 6.52 ± 2.15: $t_d = 2.28$, 16 df, $P < 0.025$

'Slow' males, 7.63 ± 3.84 vs 6.52 ± 2.15: NS

The results of the experiment just described can be briefly summarized in the following way. When two randomly selected males are paired successively with the same female during the same menstrual cycle, the male having the shorter latency to ejaculation on follicular tests will be less likely to decrease his frequency of ejaculation with the female during luteal tests than the male having the longer follicular latency. However, this experiment does not answer the question of whether this relationship between follicular latency to ejaculation and luteal frequency of ejaculation will be similar when the same male is tested with two different females. That is, can the measurement of average latency during follicular tests accurately predict how a male will behave with each of two females during their luteal phases? The following experiment shows that it can.

Twelve randomly selected males were tested daily throughout one complete menstrual cycle with either two or three female partners. Cycles of the female partners were not concurrent, and two or more months characteristically elapsed between the different testing series for each pair. Whether a female was paired first or last with the male had no effect on outcomes, and accordingly this factor is ignored here. Data on latency to ejaculation obtained from tests conducted during the 10 days before colour breakdown (follicular phase) were used to calculate the average follicular latency for each pair. Data on the frequency of ejaculation were obtained from tests given during the 10 days after breakdown (luteal phase) for each pair. The males and females used in the study provided a total of 26 pairs.

Average latencies to ejaculation during follicular tests for individual pairs varied from 1.58 ± 0.53 to 9.62 ± 1.61 minutes and the mean and standard deviation of the individual pair averages were 6.69 ± 2.14 minutes. This relatively higher value for the mean of the individual pair averages is evidence that the random selection procedures used for pairing resulted in a sample that was slightly biased toward less compatible pairs. Note that the overall mean in this sample (6.69 min) was slightly greater than the mean for the 'slow males' in the previous experiment (6.52 min). One consequence of this bias is that relatively few of the males showed average follicular latencies that differed statistically significantly according to the female partner used. Only five of the 12 males studied did so, and two of these five were tested with three different females. Thus, for only 14 of the 26 pairs were the latencies to ejaculation during follicular tests significantly different for the same male with two different females. The seven possible paired comparisons are shown in Table 4, and in six of the seven cases the pair with the shorter follicular latency had a significantly higher frequency of ejaculation on luteal tests. In the seventh case the male (1304) failed to ejaculate with either of the female

TABLE 4

Relationship between latency to ejaculation during follicular tests and frequency of ejaculation during luteal tests of pairs of rhesus monkeys

Pairs		*Average latency (min) to ejaculation in follicular tests (Mean ± S.D.)*		*% of luteal tests with ejaculation*	
Males	*Females*				
523	1233	7.92 ± 1.88	$t = 3.88$ 11df, $P < 0.005$	0	$P < 0.005$
	1370	4.18 ± 1.38		100	
544	1231	8.89 ± 1.62	$t = 8.29$ 15df, $P < 0.001$	11	$P < 0.005$
	1426	3.95 ± 0.82		100	
1304	1515	9.50 ± 2.90	$t = 2.28$ 11df, $P < 0.025$	0	NS
	570	6.17 ± 2.29		0	
987	341	8.40 ± 2.02	$t \pm 2.83$ 8df, $P < 0.025$	0	$P < 0.005$
	688	5.65 ± 0.80		100	
987	341	8.40 ± 2.02	$t = 2.42$ 11df, $P < 0.025$	0	$P < 0.005$
	1242	6.12 ± 1.39		90	
1520	571	7.31 ± 2.40	$t = 5.88$ 12df, $P < 0.005$	10	$P < 0.005$
	868	2.00 ± 1.20		90	
1520	571	7.31 ± 2.40	$t = 7.50$ 11 df, $P < 0.005$	10	$P < 0.05$
	1247	1.58 ± 0.53		60	

partners during the luteal phase tests, and readers may note that his follicular latency averages with each female, though significantly different, were both as long as or longer than the average latency characteristic of 'slow' males in the first experiment.

Of the remaining seven males and 14 females used in this study (not shown in Table 4), two males showed significantly higher frequencies of ejaculation during the luteal phase with one partner than with the other, but they failed to show a corresponding significant difference in average follicular latency to ejaculation. For both males, however, the differences in latency that were found were in the expected direction. That is, the shorter average latency during follicular tests was associated with the higher frequency of ejaculation during luteal tests. The remaining five males did not show significant differences in either latency to or frequency of ejaculation between their two female partners.

This experiment demonstrates that the latency to ejaculation during the follicular phase is not a characteristic of an individual male, but rather of an individual pair. The measure thus reflects some quality of the interaction of that pair, and that quality provides the basis for determining whether the luteal phase of the female partner's cycle will be characterized by a high or low frequency of copulation to ejaculation.

The reader's attention is again directed to Fig. 1 (p. 230), in which it can be seen that the luteal phase of the female's cycle is not the only time in the cycle when a low frequency of ejaculation can be expected for randomly paired individuals. Early in the follicular phase (Days 10–13 before colour breakdown) the percentage of pairings that are associated with ejaculation by the male partner can be as low as that found during the luteal phase. This low frequency of copulation to ejaculation early in the follicular phase has never been fully explained, but it may be related to the circumstance that the probability of ejaculation is more adversely affected by incomplete oestrogenization of the female in some pairs than in others. Moreover, it seems likely that when males do ejaculate with their female partners early in the follicular phase, their performance is attributable to a special quality of their relationship to the female, and that this quality might not be different from that already shown to influence ejaculatory performance in the luteal phase. Difficulties arise in adequately testing this possibility in the intact female because of uncertainties about the onset and duration of the early follicular period, especially if its essential characteristic is that of incomplete or insufficient oestrogenization. Moreover, if the onset of menstruation is regarded as the first day of the follicular phase, then this early period of incomplete oestrogenization is confounded with possible effects on behaviour of the bloody vaginal discharge. An alternative approach to this same question is to use spayed females injected with known quantities of oestradiol for controlled periods of time. This is the approach I have adopted here, and the data were obtained in a study done by John Czaja and myself for originally quite different purposes. The results of that study will be published in an article dealing with parametric relations between dosage of oestradiol and mating behaviour of rhesus females. For present purposes the important item is that the dosages of oestradiol injected can be divided into those associated with ejaculation during more than 40 % of the tests and those associated with ejaculation during less than 40 % of the time. For convenience, these can be referred to respectively as high and low oestrogen treatments.

Fifteen adult females spayed for more than a year and nine adult intact males were used in this study. Each female was tested eight times after low oestrogen treatment and four times after high oestrogen treatment. The order of administration of the treatments was random, and two weeks (on average) elapsed between successive treatments. Each test consisted of pairing the female with each of three males successively for 12 minutes. The three males used for any given female were always the same for each of the eight low and four high oestrogen treatment tests. Altogether the nine males and 15 females were combined in a manner that provided data on 45 individual pairs. This was done by using the same three of nine males with the same five of 15 females in all tests.

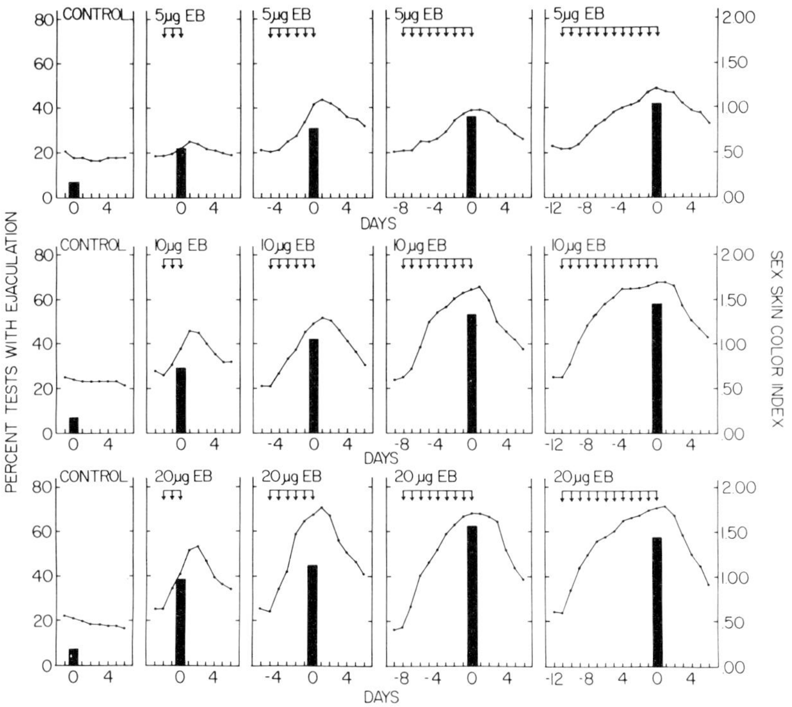

FIG. 3. Effects of different dosages of oestradiol-17β benzoate (EB) on the percentage of tests with ejaculation (solid bar) and on coloration (continuous curve) of the females' sexual skin.

The number and kinds of oestrogen treatments given to the spayed females are shown in Fig. 3, which identifies the specific treatments with oestradiol benzoate and also shows the effects of the treatments on sex-skin coloration and on the frequency of ejaculation. Each small graph depicts an independent treatment and its effects. Both in terms of sex-skin coloration and percentage of tests with ejaculation, only four of the treatments meet the arbitrary criterion of complete oestrogenization (high oestrogen tests, 10 μg oestradiol benzoate for 9 and 12 days before testing and 20 μg for 9 and 12 days before testing). The remaining eight (excluding the no-hormone or control tests) are regarded as treatments involving incomplete oestrogenization (low oestrogen tests).

The results indicated that the latencies to ejaculation during tests after treatment with high dosages of oestradiol could predict with reasonable accuracy the frequency of ejaculation on tests after low-dosage oestrogen treatments. This relationship between measurements of latency and frequency was supported by three different analyses of the data. First, of the 45 pairs studied, male partners in 38 of these pairs ejaculated during the four tests after high dosages of oestrogen given to their female partners. The mean of the individual mean latencies during these tests was 5.68 ± 2.68 minutes. In these same 38 pairs, males ejaculated on 41.4 % of the eight tests given after low oestrogen treatment of their female partners. The correlation between individual mean latency during high oestrogen tests and the percentage of the low oestrogen tests on which ejaculation occurred was -0.437, $P < 0.01$. Interpretation of this correlation, as well as its probability estimate, is hampered by the circumstance that 15 females and nine males do not in fact provide 38 independent pairs. However, a second type of evidence supporting the prediction was obtained in the following comparison.

Since each female was tested with the same three males under each testing condition it was possible to rank the males from longest to shortest average latency with a particular female during tests after high oestrogen dosages. Then, after low oestrogen dosages, the percentage of tests on which the male with the shortest average latency ejaculated with the female was compared to the percentage ejaculation of the male with the longest average latency. This analysis showed (Table 5) that males with the shortest latency to ejaculation (mean, 3.96 ± 1.86 min) with their partner ejaculated on average in 58.3 ± 27.8 % of the tests given during low oestrogen treatments. Males with the longest latencies (mean, 7.13 ± 2.64 min) ejaculated during only 30.2 ± 35.1 % of these tests with the same female. The difference was statistically significant ($t_{dep} = 2.82$, 11df, $P < 0.01$). When males were matched according to the particular female with which they were tested, the correlation between their average latencies during high oestrogen treatments was + 0.74, $N = 12, P < 0.01$. This correlation indicates the degree to which a particular female influenced the latencies of both her male partners. In addition, that the female contributed to their relative rankings is shown by the fact that the same male might have the shortest latency with one female and the longest latency with another (see, for example, males 1694 and 1701 in Table 5). Three females had to be dropped from this analysis because two of their three male partners failed to ejaculate with them on any test.

TABLE 5

Relation between latency to ejaculation on tests during high oestrogen and frequency of ejaculation on tests during low oestrogen

Females	*Males*	*Latency*[a] *(min)*	*% of tests with ejaculation*	*Females*	*Males*	*Latency (min)*	*% of tests with ejaculation*
322	1691	2.25 ± 0.43	12.5	1082	1689	6.67 ± 2.01	62.5
	1692	5.25 ± 1.06	0		1694	11.75 ± - - -[b]	0
542	1692	6.13 ± 3.36	62.5	1348	1548	2.81 ± 1.51	87.5
	1691	11.50 ± 0.35	0		1688	4.00 ± - - -[b]	12.5
1484	1546	5.62 ± 1.74	62.5	891	1701	5.25 ± 2.38	25.0
	1691	6.38 ± 0.88	50.0		1548	9.50 ± 0.35	0
332	1694	3.75 ± 0.35	25.0	1448	1548	2.19 ± 0.31	62.5
	1698	6.67 ± 4.94	62.5		1701	5.00 ± 1.40	62.5
1468	1698	2.44 ± 0.13	37.5	1148	1688	6.25 ± 2.57	87.5
	1694	6.38 ± 3.36	12.5		1701	7.08 ± 3.88	62.5
1333	1698	2.42 ± 1.18	75.0	669	1548	1.81 ± 0.75	100
	1694	8.25 ± 0.18	5		1701	4.00 ± 1.26	100

[a] Mean ± S.D.
[b] Ejaculation occurred only once.

The third and final analysis was done in the following way. Seven of the nine males provided estimates of latency to ejaculation with each of their respective five female partners during tests with high oestrogen. Thus, it was possible to rank the five average latencies to ejaculation obtained for each male with the different partners from shortest (1) to longest (5). Table 6 shows the percentage of low oestrogen tests on which ejaculation occurred for

TABLE 6

Relation between latency to ejaculation on tests during high oestrogen treatment and percentage ejaculation on tests during low oestrogen treatment of spayed rhesus monkeys

Male	Rank of the pair for average latency to ejaculation during high oestrogen (Shortest) 1	2	3	4	5 (Longest)
	% ejaculation on tests during low oestrogen				
1548	100	62.5	87.5	50	0
1688	12.5	100	12.5	0	50
1689	37.5	62.5	62.5	37.5	0
1691	12.5	50	0	0	0
1694	25	12.5	0	0	0
1698	75	37.5	37.5	62.5	0
1701	12.5	100	62.5	25	62.5
Mean	39.2	46.4	37.5	25.0	16.0

each male when that male's pairings were ranked according to his average latency to ejaculation on tests after high oestrogen treatment. The Friedman two-way analysis of variance by ranks yielded a significant Chi-square χ^2_r = 12.70, 4df, $P < 0.02$.

Although females in this experiment were tested with their male partners without being given exogenous oestradiol (see Fig. 3, control tests) no attempt was made to assess whether ejaculations that occurred on these tests were related to ejaculatory latencies for the pairs during hormonal treatments. There are two reasons why that relationship was not evaluated: (1) the findings would not be strictly relevant to the hypothesis originally advanced, which is concerned with low oestrogenization, and (2) the frequency of ejaculation during no-hormone tests was very low and most of the ejaculations that did occur were displayed by the male partners of a single female. The fact that singular female rhesus monkeys continue to be receptive and engage in frequent copulation after bilateral ovariectomy has been noted in other studies as well (Everitt *et al.* 1972; Goldfoot *et al.* 1976).

Each of the three types of analysis made on these data supports the general notion that some factor represented by the latency to ejaculation that characterizes a pair when the female is given adequate oestrogen also influences the frequency with which that pair will copulate to ejaculation when the female is insufficiently oestrogenized. In the experiment described above, 'memory' is not a likely explanation of the influence demonstrated. There were twice as many low oestrogen as high oestrogen tests, and all tests were given in random order. Thus, low oestrogen tests preceded high oestrogen tests twice as often as they followed them, thereby minimizing contributions of 'memory' to this effect. Moreover, memory cannot account for copulation in the early stages of the follicular phase since, in the experimental designs usually employed, tests during that period precede tests given at later stages of the cycle. To the extent that these artificial treatments with exogenous oestradiol benzoate represent the hormonal states that prevail during different stages of the follicular phase of the intact cycle, the results may provide some insight into solving the question of why some pairs copulate during the early part of the follicular phase and others do not.

Throughout the results obtained in the experiments so far described, one recurrent finding has been the influence of the female on the latency to ejaculation by her male partner. This influence is substantial enough that (1) males tested with the same female show correlated latencies to ejaculation and less variance exists between their latencies than among males tested with different female partners, and (2) the same male tested with different female partners can have significantly different latencies to ejaculation. The fact that this influence of the particular female is so readily demonstrable implies that her effect on the male's latency is a trait that she brings to the pairing situation and that males generally recognize and respond to this trait. In this discussion caution is of value, since it is evident from what has already been presented that there are exceptions to the generalized influence of this characteristic of the female. Obviously, two males tested with the same female can have significantly different latencies to ejaculation, and their ejaculatory performances with her can be very different. Nevertheless, it seems quite likely that if a female were tested with a sufficiently large number of males a useful generalizable estimate of her degree of influence might be obtained.

Finally, I shall present some evidence supporting the notion that the influence of the female on the performance of males is generalizable. For this purpose a retrospective reanalysis of data collected several years ago is presented. The data were obtained in a study concerned with the effects of castration on the sexual behaviour of adult male rhesus (Phoenix *et al.* 1973). In that study eight spayed females were used as partners for nine control males (Group I) that were left intact throughout the study and 10 other males (Group II) that were castrated after a period of baseline tests. The performance of the females with the intact control males has already been referred to (p. 228), and the analysis of those results provided the empirical basis for the concept of pair compatibility (Phoenix 1973). In the present context, the data from tests of the females with the nine intact males (Group I) will be used to obtain a measure of the females' influence on latency to ejaculation by a relatively large sample of males. The nature of this influence is shown in Table 7, which shows the average latency to ejaculation from eight separate tests for each of the 72 pairs made possible by combining every male in Group I with each female. In addition, the table shows the average latency to ejaculation for all males in Group I with each female partner, and the average rank for each female's influence on ejaculation latency. The question to be examined is whether these estimates of ejaculation latency obtained by using males in Group I as partners will predict the ejaculatory performance of males in Group II with the same eight females.

TABLE 7

Average latency[a] in minutes to ejaculation for each male from Group I paired with each female

Group I males	*Females*								
	2227	*2221*	*2214*	*2229*	*2224*	*2203*	*472*	*2220*	$\bar{X}$
58	0.7	0.6	1.2	1.6	1.0	1.6	0.6	1.8	1.1
30	1.4	1.7	3.2	1.6	3.9	2.3	2.1	2.9	2.3
91	3.9	1.6	2.5	1.2	2.7	3.5	—	4.2	2.8
00	1.8	3.3	1.7	3.2	3.5	1.6	4.0	6.9	3.2
35	3.4	2.4	3.7	6.1	3.0	4.5	1.9	4.3	3.6
56	3.5	5.8	4.2	3.1	—	5.6	—	—	4.4
27	2.3	3.7	3.3	2.4	5.3	4.8	8.2	6.5	4.5
73	3.5	3.0	3.0	4.8	3.2	5.0	7.0	9.9	4.9
50	3.6	4.3	4.7	4.8	7.5	6.8	7.0	—	5.5
$\bar{X}$	2.6	2.9	3.0	3.2	3.7	3.9	4.3	5.2	
Average rank	2.8	2.9	3.7	3.7	5.0	5.1	4.8	7.1	

(Data taken partly from Phoenix *et al.* (1973) and partly from Phoenix (1973).

[a]Only positive tests were used in calculating average latency for each pair.

Although before castration males in Group II were tested only once on average with each of the eight females (hence the results are less reliable than if they were based on a larger number of tests), the percentage of tests on which ejaculation occurred for each female was significantly correlated with her average latency with males in Group I ($r = -0.77$, $P < 0.025$; Table 8).

TABLE 8

Relation between average latency to ejaculation for males in group I ($N = 9$) and frequency of ejaculation by males in Group II ($N = 10$) with the same females

Males	*Measure*	*Females*							
		2227	*2221*	*2214*	*2229*	*2224*	*2203*	*472*	*2220*
Group I	Average latency (min)	2.6	2.9	3.0	3.2	3.7	3.9	4.3	5.2
Group II before castration	% of tests with ejaculation	100.0	87.5	64.2	70.0	66.7	81.2	57.1	50.0
Group II after castration	% of tests with ejaculation	32.5	40.0	18.0	27.5	16.0	13.3	12.5	4.4

The correlation between Group I average latency and Group II ejaculation frequency persisted even after the males in Group II had been castrated ($r = -0.86$, $P < 0.01$). The fact that this correlation is higher after castration than before is unimportant and probably merely reflects the increased reliability of the estimate of ejaculation frequency, since each male in Group II was tested at least 40 times with each female after castration. Of considerable importance, however, in my opinion, was the finding that this generalizable quality of the female could function to retard the decline in frequency of ejaculation after castration (Fig. 4). Postcastrational tests for each male were separated into those with the four of the eight females that had the shorter latencies to ejaculation as independently rated ('optimal females') and those with the four females that had the longer latencies ('suboptimal females'). Frequencies of ejaculation by the castrated males were consistently higher with the 'optimal' than with the 'suboptimal' females.

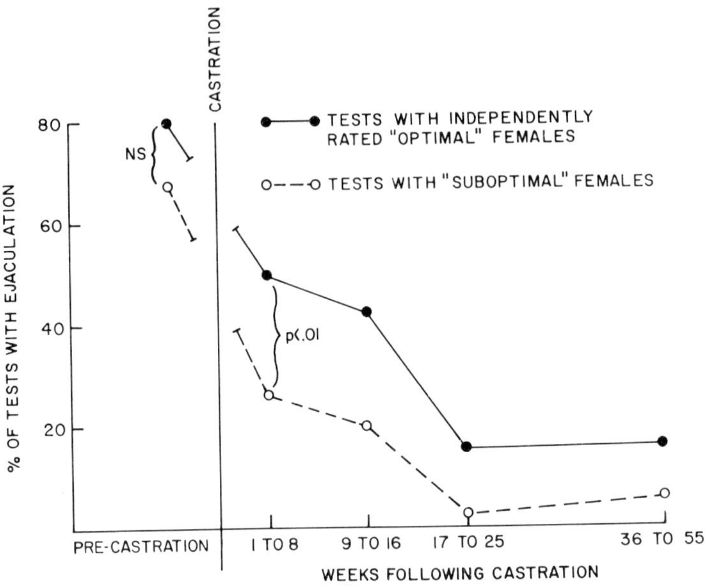

FIG. 4. Differential decline of male rhesus sexual behaviour after castration, tested with two different classes of female partners. 'Optimal' females are those with which an independent group of intact males had short latencies to ejaculation. 'Suboptimal' females are those with which the independent group of males had longer latencies.

DISCUSSION

The results presented here have been aimed primarily at demonstrating that the ejaculatory latency characteristic of a pair predicts reasonably well how frequently that pair will engage in copulation. Ejaculatory latency not only predicts how frequently a pair will copulate; it also predicts which pairs will copulate more often than others, and in that sense it serves as an operational statement of pair compatibility. It is not my intention to promulgate the notion that speed of mating is the appropriate empirical measure of pair compatibility in every species, or that it is either the best or only measure for the rhesus monkey. Indeed, as Hediger (1965) has shown, the speed of mating varies greatly among different mammalian species, and rapid mating is adaptive in a number of ecological circumstances, one of which is high predator intensity. And in terms of the rhesus monkey, one might hope that pair compatibility could be operationalized along some continuum of partner preference rather than ejaculatory latency. These highly social animals which, in the wild, form and maintain bonds between individuals for long periods of time (even for life), may display kinds of behaviour that are in greater concert with other preconceived ideas about compatibility than mere speed of mating, which does not distinguish between rape and more positive affections.

For purposes of prediction, however, it matters little what empirically observable behaviour is used as an index of pair compatibility. As long as the concept is based on observed responses, its nature as a predictor of other responses by the same animal in the same situation is inescapably circular. If it is defined in behavioural terms it suffers the same limitation as the concept of social dominance (Gartlan 1978; Hinde 1976), and the responses it 'predicts' serve equally well as alternative definers. This unfortunate circularity is a property of most uniformities between responses, or response–response laws as they have sometimes been called, although in this study circularity was at least partly avoided by measuring the two responses in different situations. Identifying the stimulus parameters of pair compatibility would eliminate circularity and permit greater experimental control, but we are more likely to be able to delineate the parameters if the trait is generalizable than if it is a sole manifestation of processes unique to a particular pair. The results reported here indicate that, at least for the influence the female brings to the pairing situation, the trait is generalizable from one sample of male partners to another. Although the point cannot be made on the basis of present data there is reason to think that the influence on pair compatibility attributable to a particular male is also generalizable (Phoenix 1973). Moreover, the influence each animal exerts on the mating situation seems strongly linked to its incentive as a sexual partner. In short, mutual sexual attractiveness is probably at the core of pair compatibility.

Most investigators of primate sexual behaviour have been aware of the importance of non-hormonal factors, and significant efforts have been made to identify the bases of sexual attractiveness. The effort has been largely limited to the attractiveness of the female (Michael & Keverne 1968; Keverne 1974). The generalizability of these early findings was questioned by Goldfoot *et al.* (1976), and later studies by Michael *et al.* (1977) showed that attempts to vary female attractiveness independently produced reliable changes in copulation to ejaculation only in specific pairs. Which pairs copulated and how frequently could not be predicted. A related phenomenon seems to exist in the single study that tried to vary male sexual attractiveness (Eaton 1973). In that study, when females controlled which of several males could enter the testing chamber, the frequency with which they released individual males did not correlate with frequency of copulation to ejaculation. These studies on the female and on the male do not predict the copulatory frequency of individual pairs precisely because the approach excludes the phenomenon of pair compatibility and mutual sexual attractiveness. Without being unduly optimistic, I venture to hope that the approaches to sexual attractiveness represented by this study and our earlier ones will greatly increase the predictability of the frequency with which individual pairs display ejaculation.

ACKNOWLEDGEMENTS

This is publication No. 17-036 of the Wisconsin Regional Primate Research Center, supported by grants RR00167 and MH21312 from the National Institutes of Health. I gratefully acknowledge the help of Kim Wallen and John Czaja in the collection and analysis of data used in this chapter and of Barbara Brenz and John Wolf for their help in preparing the manuscript. My special thanks go to Stephen Eisele, who was responsible for daily estimates of the cyclical changes in coloration of the sexual skin of the females used as subjects for the various experiments.

References

BEACH, F.A. (1976) Sexual attractivity, proceptivity and receptivity in female mammals. *Horm. Behav. 7,* 105–138

CZAJA, J.A., EISELE, S.G. & GOY, R.W. (1975) Cyclical changes in the sexual skin of female rhesus: relationships to mating behavior and successful artificial insemination. *Fed. Proc. 34,* 1680–1684

EATON, G.G. (1973) Social and endocrine determinants of sexual behavior in simian and prosimian females, in *Primate Reproductive Behavior* (Phoenix, C.H., ed.) *(Symposia of the IVth International Congress of Primatology, vol. 2),* pp. 20–35, Karger, Basle

EVERITT, B.J., HERBERT, J. & HAMER, J. D. (1972) Sexual receptivity of bilaterally adrenalectomised female rhesus monkeys. *Physiol. Behav. 8,* 409–415

GARTLAN, J.S. (1978) Aggression and submission in monkey societies: a reply. *Anim. Behav.,* in press

GOLDFOOT, D. A., (1977) Sociosexual behaviors of nonhuman primates during development and maturity: social and hormonal relationships, in *Behavioral Primatology: Advances in Research and Theory,* vol. 1 (Schrier, A.M., ed.), pp. 139–184, Lawrence Erlbaum Associates, Hillsdale, New Jersey

GOLDFOOT, D.A., KRAVETZ, M. A., GOY, R.W. & FREEMAN, S. K. (1976) Lack of effect of vaginal lavages and aliphatic acids on ejaculatory responses in rhesus monkeys: behavioral and chemical analyses. *Horm. Behav. 7,* 1–27

GOY, R.W. & GOLDFOOT, D.A. (1975) Neuroendocrinology: animal models and problems of human sexuality. *Arch. Sex. Behav. 4,* 405–420

GOY, R.W. & RESKO, J. A. (1972) Gonadal hormones and behaviour of normal and pseudohermaphroditic nonhuman female primates. *Recent Prog. Horm. Res. 28,* 707–733

HEDIGER, H. (1965) Environmental factors influencing the reproduction of zoo animals, in *Sex and Behavior* (Beach, F. A., ed.), pp. 319–354, Wiley, New York

HERBERT, J. (1968) Sexual preference in the rhesus monkey, *Macaca mulatta,* in the laboratory. *Anim. Behav. 16,* 120–128

HINDE, R.A. (1976) Interactions, relationships and social structure. *Man (N.S.) 11,* 1–17

KEVERNE, E.B. (1974) Sex attractants in primates. *New Sci. 61,* 22–24

MICHAEL, R.P. (1973) The effects of hormones on sexual behavior in female cat and rhesus monkey, in *Handbook of Physiology*, Section 7: *Endocrinology*, vol. 2, part 1 (Greep, R.O., ed.), pp. 187–221, Williams & Wilkins, Baltimore

MICHAEL, R.P. & BONSALL, R.W. (1977) Peri-ovulatory synchronisation of behaviour in male and female rhesus monkeys. *Nature (Lond.) 265*, 463–465

MICHAEL, R.P. & KEVERNE, E.B. (1968) Pheromones in the communication of sexual status in primates. *Nature (Lond.) 218*, 746–749

MICHAEL, R. P. & WELEGALLA, J. (1968) Ovarian hormones and the sexual behaviour of the female rhesus monkey *(Macaca mulatta)* under laboratory conditions. *J. Endocrinol. 41*, 407–420

MICHAEL, R.P., ZUMPE, D., RICHTER, M. & BONSALL, R.W. (1977) Behavioural effects of a synthetic mixture of aliphatic acids in rhesus monkeys *(Macaca mulatta)*. *Horm. Behav. 9*, 296–308

PHOENIX, C.H. (1973) Ejaculation by male rhesus as a function of the female partner. *Horm. Behav. 4*, 365–370

PHOENIX, C. H., SLOB, A.K. & GOY, R.W. (1973) Effects of castration and replacement therapy on the sexual behavior of adult male rhesus. *J. Comp. Physiol. Psychol. 84*, 472–481

ROWELL, T.E. (1963) Behaviour and female reproductive cycles of rhesus macaques. *J. Reprod. Fertil. 6*, 192–203

Discussion

Keverne: You have been looking at the behavioural interaction purely from the point of view of the male, which to my mind brings into issue your definition of a compatible pair. I would prefer to define a compatible pair as one in which the male synchronizes his behaviour with the female's endocrine state. In other words, I would suggest that a male that responds appropriately to female proceptive behaviour, *or* to female unreceptiveness, is the male that is compatible with that female. In the luteal phase of the menstrual cycle, where the female monkey shows decreased proceptivity and possibly increased unreceptiveness, a male monkey whose sexual interest likewise declines (i.e. one that does *not* show mounts or ejaculations) is surely more compatible than one who persists in mounting against the female's inclinations?

To illustrate this I should like to take up the case for liberating the female rhesus monkey—that is, permitting the female to determine the degree of sexual interaction with the male. In other words, we allow a female to press a lever to get access to an operantly naive male. We then see quite a different picture from the one you have given us (Keverne 1976). For example, consider two male monkeys, one a sexually potent male who mounts and ejaculates with the female throughout the menstrual cycle. Another male mounts and ejaculates particularly in the follicular phase and loses sexual interest in that female in the luteal phase. If we look at that female's lever pressing for access to each of these males, she presses faster and more regularly for the sexually potent male in the follicular phase of the cycle; at mid-cycle she doesn't distinguish between them; but in the luteal phase she now prefers the male who is less sexually potent—in other words, the male who synchronizes his behaviour with her endocrine state. I would suggest that the latter combination is the more compatible pair, at least in the luteal phase of the female's menstrual cycle.

Goy: I do feel a little awkward about saying 'the faster, the better' and using a measure for pair compatibility that doesn't really discriminate rape from love! However, I am only presenting this work as a beginning, and I don't think your criticism is entirely justified. It really does take two to tango, and I have shown that the female does in general very much influence the latency of the males. I refuse to believe that she is doing it to get it over with. That is not the nature of the effect. In the study by Eaton (1973), for example, where female pigtail monkeys selected males from a cafeteria of males, the proof that it takes two for this interaction is that the female's willingness to release a male as possible sexual partner couldn't predict whether copulation or ejaculation would occur. I am sure the same would happen with the rhesus monkey. It isn't just a matter of how interested the female is in the male; the interest has to be mutual. The facilitation of ejaculatory latency depends on mutuality. The female has many techniques with which to alter latency, by refusal, by cold-shouldering, by not being provocative, by not being vaginally lubricated. Any of these variables can be studied as potential specific measures of pair compatibility. I don't think any of them can be studied with lever pressing.

Short: I would like to continue Dr Keverne's point, because I agree completely with him. In talking about compatible pairs you have put a human value judgement on primate behaviour, Dr Goy, and you are assuming that it is desirable for the monkey to have sexual intercourse very frequently throughout the cycle. But from an evolutionary point of view it is desirable to have intercourse only at the time of ovulation. Surely, your phrase 'most compatible' could also be interpreted as 'least discriminating'?

Goy: I disagree that it is desirable from an evolutionary point of view to copulate *only* at ovulation. On the contrary, in species in which the highest degree of affiliative bonding is demonstrated through sexuality and free sexual expression, maximum rates of copulation are the most important manifestation of friendship, and friendship is important to survival.

Beach: You are thinking in terms of reproduction only, Dr Short?

Short: Yes. We can only make inferences about the social significance of sexual behaviour by studying what actually happens in the wild. So far as I am aware, the copulatory frequencies of rhesus monkeys in the wild, outside the oestrous period, are rather low.

Goy: That may or may not be true; the evidence is not good on that point. Field workers never follow their animals into the bushes, and they only see the copulations they see!

Sachar: Isn't the question academic in one sense, because in your study compatible partners who copulate throughout the cycle also have the highest frequency during the fertile period?

Goy: It is not significantly higher for compatible male partners in the data presented. This may be related to the fact that the hormones may influence the sexual arousability of the female herself. Perhaps there isn't a big difference between the more and the less compatible male partners, at the fertile period, because the females are highly aroused then. Alternatively, the failure to find different levels of performance by the two types of males at that time may be merely because the tests were of such short duration.

Beach: This sex difference in selectivity is not exclusively a primate characteristic. We find that female beagles exhibit selective choice and also show individual differences in finickiness. Some are quite indiscriminate; others are extremely selective. Some males are also selective, but to a lesser degree than females.

Dr Goy, have you ever considered a possible relationship of such observations to Darwin's concept of sexual selection as a force in evolution? Could sexual preferences function genetically in some way, some males getting a better chance to reproduce and perpetuate their genotypes and other genotypes being gradually selected against?

Goy: I don't know. Two sets of genes are involved. What would happen if the genes that make the female highly attractive are the same genes that make the male unattractive? If she mates with a very attractive male, that doesn't mean that her male offspring are going to be as attractive as their parents. The genetic picture is not understood.

Sachar: Would Dr Beach's question be clarified if we drew on another dimension of Dr Goy's data? Now that he has data on monkeys who are successful at copulating to ejaculation with a large number of females, and females who are successful in attracting males, if he had parallel data on their positions in the group and on how the group sorted itself out, we could see whether male sexual performance is correlated with dominance in the social structure; and likewise we could look at the place in the dominance hierarchy of those female monkeys who are particularly attractive to male monkeys.

Goy: In the social setting there may well be social attributes of the male and of the female that are part of the characteristics that indicate their sexual attractiveness, but I don't know of any evidence on this. The concept that the dominant males are the only ones that copulate or that they sire most of the young in macaques has been challenged. Eaton (1976) has shown that this is not a characteristic that influences the rate of production of offspring in Japanese macaques. The pairing process is highly individual. Although a female may have general characteristics that many males find attractive, the sorting-out process, especially in a natural situation, is still based on individual preferences, which I think would be reflected in latency to ejaculation and frequency of ejaculation for the pair.

Returning to Dr Short's comment that in a natural situation you might not see copulation throughout the cycle, we may in our studies be capitalizing on the fact that our animals are kept apart all the time and have no social companions. Heterosexual copulation may be being used by them, when they are allowed to be together briefly, as a bonding mechanism. This is all the more reason to say that this kind of behaviour *is* an index of compatibility and not of male sexual assertiveness, because the female is really involved. She can refuse if she wishes. Male rhesus monkeys do not beat up their females; they get along quite well!

Bancroft: Have you any measure of female proceptivity in the two groups?

Goy: It doesn't correlate with frequency of ejaculation. How proceptive the female is doesn't mean anything, because many of the ejaculatory latencies are one minute after the pair is put together. The female in a highly compatible pair doesn't have to display proceptive behaviour. She only has to show high levels of proceptive behaviour when she is strongly attracted to a male who is not so strongly attracted to her.

Bancroft: What about after castration? How much of that sexual behaviour depends on female proceptivity?

Goy: I haven't analysed these data for the effects of castration, and I should do so. I can only say that if one looked at how females behave toward the most popular males before and after castration, their proceptive behaviour might increase with those males, providing that castration did not reduce the sexual attractiveness of the males.

Green: I am confused. I thought you said a female *did* do different things with the shorter-latency males, in terms of making herself more attractive?

Goy: That is correct. According to the data obtained when a single female was tested with more than one male, neither her proceptivity nor her receptivity predicted male ejaculatory performance. But it could be that she shows more vaginal lubrication with the male she prefers; that hasn't been measured. But I don't believe that when there is short latency repeatedly in a pair it is because the female is urging the male on. It is something that happens immediately and spontaneously. The male gives no elaborate courtship signals to her and she doesn't give any to him.

Herbert: The discussion so far has centred very much on the question of measurement. I want to raise a point which applies both to the kind of work that we and Dr Goy do and to that of people working in the clinic. This is the question of *what* you measure. Dr Goy's data provide a good example of what happens when you measure end-points, such as ejaculation. This measure is very similar to that used in studies of sexual activity in people as 'copulation rates'. You then get changes which only occur at the extreme ends of the spectrum. But I would predict that if Dr Goy looks at some intervening behaviour, such as mounting rates or thrusting rates, he will find a different pattern, because different males ejaculate differently—they take longer times, or their mounting rates might be lower. And in certain males the mounting rate, say, would fall by a critical amount which is necessary for ejaculation. If you limit your measurement to 'ejaculation' you artificially get two classes, though there is in fact a continuum.

This also applies to people. Most clinical work is based on copulation frequencies, and the problem is the same. The data are artificially divided into classes, and similarly the effects are very marked; but you miss the intervening effects which don't change the end-point. You also miss the interactions. So my question is whether you think that in principle one should analyse intervening behaviour both in monkeys and in people and, if so, what should we be looking at, in order to get away from this end-point analysis?

Goy: It depends on what counts for the species. If heterosexual copulation to ejaculation is important, in terms of reproductive output, in terms of bonding and in terms of physical and emotional well-being, it is a useful index, even if not the only one. There is no reason one should *not* look at the behaviours of the female and the male that function to increase heterosexual copulation to ejaculation, but to look at them only for their own sake—to say that one is only interested in how often and how long a female sits close to the male—without relating it to other variables, is to my mind less defensible than looking only at the frequency of ejaculation.

Sachar: I am glad that Dr Herbert has brought in human couples and the intervening variables in the sexual process. In studies of subjective states during the menstrual cycle several reports agree that women's subjective feeling of well-being and affectional feelings peak at the time of ovulation (Bardwick 1976). This presumably could lead to the result that would be the best for the species, because they would be more receptive, and would feel like copulating more, and so on.

Goy: You make it sound as though they might become sexually indiscriminate at that time!

Sachar: A better way to put it is that the receptivity to the partner of their choice might be increased then.

Keverne: On the point of what is good for the species, I am not sure that copulation in the luteal phase of the cycle is necessarily of selective advantage to the species. It doesn't serve any reproductive function; and in terms of social bonding it is also not necessarily good for the species. For a start, social cohesion continues throughout the year and yet sexual behaviour is restricted to discrete breeding periods. In fact, during the breeding periods, it could be argued that sexual activity disrupts the social organization. This is the time of year when you see more group breakdown and high levels of aggressive interaction. So when one talks about sexual behaviour as a 'bonding process' in the adult rhesus monkey, I am not sure that it is always a prerequisite for social cohesion.

Goy: In seasonally breeding macaques, mounting behaviour – both homosexual and heterosexual mounting – does not cease outside the breeding season. Heterosexual mounting with copulation to ejaculation doesn't cease either but it decreases greatly. I would not say that macaque societies, anyhow, exist without sexual bonding devices. It is just a question of how far the sex behaviour goes.

Beach: It depends on the mechanism too. There is certainly sexual bonding in the hamadryas baboon, which forms one-male groups (Kummer 1971). There is almost no sexual behaviour except when one of the male's own females is in heat, but sexual bonding is continuous because she is bitten if she steps out of line; the sexual bond is maintained, through different mechanisms.

Green: Let me try to build a bridge and see if I can turn Dr Goy into a clinician! Many people who treat so-called sexual dysfunctions see human couples in which there is either a low sex drive or an incompatibility of sex drive. If you were a clinician and were consulted by one of these incompatible pairs, is there anything you might do with respect to endocrine status or behaviour that might make that couple less incompatible?

Goy: The problem is probably one of deficient mutual arousal, and I am not sure what one can do to each partner independently of the other to increase that, since to increase mutual arousal means that one necessarily must increase the inter-individual bond. I don't think we know how to increase the bond between two humans or between two monkeys. There may, however, be a way for monkeys to decrease the strength of inter-individual bonding.

We (Slimp *et al.* 1978) did some work on brain lesions in adult male rhesus monkeys. A lesion in the preoptic-anterior hypothalamic region of the brain greatly reduced heterosexual copulation to ejaculation. But lesioned males did not stop masturbating, and they masturbated as regularly as before the brain lesion. This could mean that this particular lesion produces a deficiency in heterophilic bonding behaviour. To test that hypothesis we made similar brain lesions in juvenile males (1 1/2–2 years old), because they mount their partners very frequently as part of both homophilic and heterophilic bonding behaviour, although they do not achieve intromissions or ejaculate. After these lesions the mounting behaviour of the 1 1/2-year-old males to partners of both sexes decreased greatly. Thus this brain area seems to be important to bonding, and homophilic and heterophilic processes in juveniles, and it may interfere with adult heterosexual copulation through this same mechanism.

Herbert: You would have to test that. I am not sure that you can extrapolate from non-mounting to bonding. You would have to look at a group of animals to see whether grooming relationships or other social interactions change as well. We are in some danger of using 'bonding' in rather restrictive ways.

Beach: What happens to play behaviour?

Goy: It goes on without any change. These young monkeys aren't good groomers, so we can't look at that. I have never regarded play as a bonding mechanism, in any case.

References

BARDWICK, J. (1976) Psychological correlates of the menstrual cycle and oral contraceptive medication, in *Hormones, Behavior and Psychopathology* (Sachar, E.J., ed.), pp. 95–104, Raven Press, New York

EATON, G.G. (1973) Social and endocrine determinants of sexual behaviour in simian and prosimian females, in *Primate Reproductive Behavior* (Phoenix, C.H., ed.) *(Symposia of the IVth International Congress of Primatology*, vol. 2), pp. 20–35, Karger, Basle

EATON, G.G. (1976) The social order of Japanese macaques. *Sci. Am. 235(4)*, 96–106

KEVERNE, E.B. (1976) Sexual receptivity and attractiveness in female rhesus monkeys. *Adv. Study Behav. 7*, 155–200

KUMMER, H. (1971) *Primate Societies: Group Techniques of Ecological Adaptation*, Aldine, New York

SLIMP, J.C., HART, B.L. & GOY, R.W. (1978) Heterosexual, autosexual and social behaviour of adult male rhesus monkeys with medial preoptic-anterior hypothalamic lesions. *Brain Res. 142*, 105–122

General discussion

SEXUAL DIFFERENTIATION OF THE BRAIN OF THE SHEEP: EFFECTS OF PRENATAL IMPLANTATION OF ANDROGEN

(Film by R.V. Short)

Short: The film shows the effects of implanting pregnant ewes with testosterone at different stages of gestation on the anatomical development of the external genitalia of their female offspring, and on the behavioural development of these female intersexes in later life. Androgenization of the female fetus in early gestation (Days 30–80) resulted in complete masculinization of the external genitalia, although the scrotum remained empty and the ovaries retained their normal intra-abdominal position. Androgenization in later gestation (Days 50–100 or 70–120) produced clitoral hypertrophy, but essentially normal female external genitalia.

Several aspects of behaviour were masculinized. The intersex ewes became incapable of displaying oestrous behaviour, even in response to exogenous oestrogen injections, but they showed male courtship and mounting with pelvic thrusting, and were markedly aggressive towards normal rams when put in a situation where they were in competition with a ram over a normal ewe in oestrus. This male-type sexual behaviour was most pronounced in the females masculinized in later gestation, who had *female* type external genitalia. The intensity of the male behaviour was markedly diminished if the female intersexes were ovariectomized, but it could be restored if they were given either oestradiol-17β or testosterone. Fetal androgenization also masculinized the urination behaviour of the intersexes, turning it into the male type. This behaviour could be induced by androgenization relatively late in gestation, after it was no longer possible to masculinize sexual behaviour. Finally, the positive feedback effect of oestrogen on luteinizing hormone (LH) discharge is a sexually dimorphic character in the sheep, being expressed by intact or castrate ewes, but never by intact or castrate rams. In some of the female intersexes this positive feedback mechanism was abolished, but the presence or absence of positive feedback gave no clue whatsoever to the type of sexual behaviour to expect from the animal (Short 1974; Clarke *et al.* 1976*a,b*; Clarke & Scaramuzzi 1978; Clarke 1977).

Bancroft: Do oestrogens restore sexual aggression in the male?

Short: Yes, completely. We have castrated stags and then given them an oestradiol implant; this has caused them to fight with other stags over the oestrous hinds, so it induces sexual aggression. But when we have given stags oestradiol implants at other times of the year, outside the rut, it did *not* affect their position in the social rank order, so oestrogen appears to be without effect on social aggression, unlike testosterone (Fletcher & Short 1974).

Ehrhardt: Are there any other kinds of sex-dimorphic behaviour one can study in sheep, such as sexual mounting behaviour?

Short: When we scored mounting, male soliciting, flehmen (curling of upper lip), aggression, female soliciting, and oestrous behaviour in control females and in different types of androgenized animals, depending on when they had the androgen, we found a spectrum of effects (Clarke 1977).

Ehrhardt: How about play behaviour in sheep?

Short: We haven't really looked at that. We did seem to notice a lot of copulatory behaviour among the androgenized lambs a few days after birth, but we subsequently found that it was just as common in the untreated controls.

Beach: In the rhesus monkey and in the dog there seem to be two different classes or kinds of behaviour which can be influenced by prenatal manipulation of androgen levels. One class is expressed in adulthood without concurrent stimulation of gonadal hormones; it appears in the untreated castrated animal. The other class can only be elicited while the animal is currently receiving exogenous androgen or oestrogen. In dogs we have observed masculinization of urination behaviour in prenatally androgenized females that have a penis. Postnatal treatment with testosterone has no effect on this behaviour. The adult pattern appears in the normal male at 5–7 months of age, and it also appears at the same time in males castrated at birth. Finally, the same behaviour appears in the masculinized female at about the same age, although she was ovariectomized months earlier. Now, the same female will exhibit vigorous male copulatory behaviour towards other females, but to elicit this effect of early androgen treatment on mounting behaviour we must give testosterone at the time of testing. This is true for some kinds of sex-related behaviour in the rhesus monkey as well. Is there anything like that in the sheep?

Short: This is an important point. If we ovariectomize our androgenized sheep in adulthood and leave them for several months, the amount of male sexual behaviour declines, although it is never completely abolished, whereas the male pattern of urination behaviour is totally unaffected. We have also made some intriguing observations on red deer stags (R.V. Short, G. A. Lincoln & F. Guinness, unpublished). In 1970 I castrated two wild red deer stag calves within a week of birth and we have followed their behaviour in the wild for seven years, comparing it to that of normal male and female calves. The two castrates never left their mothers, so that the mother-infant bond never broke, whereas in normal male and female calves it is broken after 2–3 years. Even more intriguing was the fact that at the rut, the castrated males, which looked like females, remained with their mothers. The stag who kept the mother in his harem failed to recognize her castrated offspring as a male, and so failed to drive it out. But there was enough residual androgenic imprinting of the castrated stag for him to serve his mother when she came into oestrus. Thus we had the incredible situation of a dominant stag allowing a castrated stag to serve its own mother, but not showing any aggression towards it, presumably because he failed to recognize it as a male. Thus male behaviour had persisted in the castrate for over six years.

Goy: Your demonstration in the sheep is so interesting because it indicates that for one kind of behaviour, namely sexual behaviour, there isn't any particular hormonal specificity, but another kind of behaviour that is important to mating, namely ram aggression, is highly specific in terms of the kind of hormone required for activation. In the rhesus monkey the mating behaviour of the male tends to be specific to the androgens. There is less specificity for female mating behaviour; both androgens and oestrogens can activate it, not necessarily to the same degree. For other behaviour there may or may not be hormonal specificities. It is an important theoretical question, and an empirically solvable one, as to which kinds of behaviour in which species are hormonally specific, and what that hormonal specificity means to the adaptive value of sex differences within the species. Those questions are the kinds that comparative behavioural endocrinologists could consider.

Short: One other point which is relevant to our understanding of hormones and sexual behaviour relates, as do most things in sexual behaviour, to experiments that Frank Beach did years ago in rats (Beach 1942). If we ovariectomize normal hinds or ewes and give them an implant of either testosterone or oestradiol, the initial behavioural response to either hormone is oestrus. But if the implant is left in place for several months, regardless of which hormone it is, the female behaviour is gradually replaced by more and more components of male behaviour (Clarke & Scaramuzzi 1978; Fletcher 1978). I find it fascinating that the same hormone can produce oestrous behaviour when given as a short pulse, but male behaviour if given for a long time. Thus it may be vital for the female to have cyclical ovarian activity, if she is to show female behaviour; if she had a constant high level of oestrogen secretion, she would do what the cow with cystic ovaries does, namely show male behaviour.

Goy: In your study, Dr Short, the occasions for the masculinized ewe fighting with the intact male were all occasions set by the circumstance that an oestrous female was also present. Is that the only time when the intersex fights with the male, and is it your impression that it is in competition for possession of the sexual incentive?

Short: Yes.

Ehrhardt: And that was without any postnatal treatment?

Short: There was no postnatal treatment at all.

Goy: It could happen in an intersex ewe that retained its vagina?

Short: Yes. We saw the most masculine behaviour in a group of sheep androgenized in mid-gestation who had minimal masculinization of their external genitalia, so it seems that the genitalia differentiate first and differentiation of the brain follows, as in the rat.

Goy: That is a model that I have been looking for in rhesus monkeys; I haven't yet found it. It is most interesting that you can successfully masculinize large segments of the social and sexual behaviour of the individual without morphological masculinity.

Beach: Is it possible to masculinize some kinds of behaviour and not masculinize other kinds?

Short: We have looked at the correlation between sexual behaviour and the presence or absence of positive feedback, because the ram and ewe show a marked dimorphism in this regard: the ewe always gives an LH discharge in response to oestradiol, providing a corpus luteum is not present, whereas the ram, whether intact or castrated, never gives it. We have therefore tested the intersex animals for positive feedback. In some females we have eliminated it by androgenization; in others we haven't. But there is no correlation between the presence or absence of positive feedback and the type of sexual behaviour we see, so it seems that hypothalamic sexual differentiation is completely different from the differentiation of sexual behaviour (Clark *et al.* 1976*b*).

Goy: Not necessarily different, but requiring a different period of androgenization?

Short: Yes. I don't know which areas of the brain regulate the sexual behaviour of sheep.

Beach: In the dog we can masculinize mounting behaviour without masculinizing urination behaviour. This is important, because we tend to talk about masculinization as though it always affected all systems, but that is not necessarily true.

Goy: It is just as important that we *can* affect all systems in some types of treatments that differ in systematic ways from those that only affect one or two characteristics.

Beach: Of course, but the assumption is sometimes made that one automatically always alters all systems, and that is incorrect.

Short: This is also true of urination in sheep. One can masculinize it very late in gestation when one can no longer masculinize any other behavioural character. Thus you can produce a ewe with female genitalia that urinates like a male but still shows oestrus.

Beach: The terms used here imply an important distinction. There is a significant conceptual difference between masculinization and defeminization. It is possible to reduce a female behavioural characteristic without any masculinization. A male can be demasculinized without being feminized.

Dörner: There are different regions in the brain that correspond to controllers of different behavioural patterns, such as male or female sexual behaviour. We also see that the organization (morphogenesis) of these regions begins and ends at different times. In other words, there are partially or even completely time-dependent dissociations in the organization of specific structures and functions of the brain.

Goy: Some traits such as pituitary function and lordosis are separable not only in terms of the period during which the individual is exposed to androgen but in terms of dosage. The first demonstration was by Barraclough & Gorski (1975), who showed that a very low dose of androgen (given postnatally) could block the cyclic function of the hypothalamus but didn't block the development of lordosis.

Dörner: I am not quite sure that it was proved to be only a question of dosage. When we give a specific dose of androgen or oestrogen to female rats in late prenatal or early postnatal life we can irreversibly influence gonadotropin secretion without markedly affecting sexual behaviour throughout life. The same dose given on the tenth day of life can irreversibly influence sexual behaviour without markedly affecting gonadotropin secretion in later life.

Goy: Duration is another critical factor; a higher dose given in a single injection lasts for a longer time.

Jost: Can we summarize how many species can be masculinized by prenatal or postnatal androgenization?

Goy: It has been achieved in every mammalian species in which it has been attempted, namely in hamster, rat, mouse, guinea-pig, dog, sheep, rhesus monkey and ferret – possibly in humans, but nobody has experimentally modified the human being in this way and this may partly explain discrepancies between the human and animal literature. The humans studied have all been instances of adrenal virilization. No control was exercised over the onset of the adrenal disorder, and no one knows the period of development or duration of androgenization, or the concentrations achieved.

Ehrhardt: Our study on girls with progestin-induced hermaphroditism gave the period of fetal development, the timing, and the dosage (Ehrhardt & Money 1967).

Dörner: But you don't know the exact sex hormone level in the fetus?

Ehrhardt: True, but we had the information concerning dosage and time of administration.

Goy: Norethisterone (Norlutin) has not been used in animals, which also makes comparison difficult.

Bancroft: In how many of the species listed can you androgenize with oestrogen?

Goy: I would say in most of the short-gestation rodents—mouse, rat and hamster.

Short: I don't know about the sheep.

Everitt: Dr Beach emphasized the distinction between masculinization and defeminization, but following from what Dr Goy has said there seems to be a real difference between primates and other species. It seems easy to masculinize a female monkey but not to defeminize her. Dr Goy's monkeys ovulate as adults and some have become pregnant so, presumably, their sexual behaviour is appropriate when they are paired with a male. This appears true, from Anke Ehrhardt's paper, for girls as well. However, masculinized rats are also defeminized; they don't ovulate (and display the persistent oestrus syndrome) and also they display masculine rather than feminine patterns of sexual behaviour.

Beach: We really should not skip quite so easily from gonadotropic function of the pituitary to behaviour. This tends to confuse two sorts of function that may be quite different.

Herbert: They are often congruent, are they not?

Beach: Of course, but we should examine them one at a time to discover whether they go together rather than assume that they do. I haven't considered the possibility of applying the concepts of demasculinization and defeminization to results on the rhesus monkey.

Goy: I don't think normal rhesus males show 'defeminization'; they show the female presentation posture when mounted by a partner. In male hamsters which complete their normal sexual differentiation and yet retain the potential for lordosis, would you call them 'not defeminized', or what?

Beach: If the behaviour is part of the normal male genetic pattern one cannot say that any defeminization *or* feminization is involved.

Goy: When testosterone is injected into a genetic female rhesus monkey prenatally, she still shows presenting, so testosterone given prenatally doesn't 'defeminize'. And that is comparable to what Baum (1976) has shown in ferrets. Some of these species differences may have to be understood in evolutionary terms; that is, female presentation behaviour in some species is essential for social bonding and for maintaining the social organization and the social group, and therefore that component is spared or protected, or there is an accumulation of genes that prevent androgens from acting on that particular substrate.

Beach: I can deal with these concepts most comfortably by considering one category of behaviour at a time, such as sexual or copulatory behaviour. Another category might be fighting or aggressive behaviour; another might be urination behaviour. When I separate these categories I can give examples in which one type of behaviour has been masculinized or demasculinized, feminized or defeminized. These concepts are of value only when the adult patterns are clearly sexually dimorphic.

Ehrhardt: In human research it is more difficult to use these concepts, since most aspects of sex-dimorphic behaviour differ only in frequency and intensity rather than being totally different in the two sexes.

Beach: Defeminization would mean reduction in feminine characteristics and demasculinization, reduction in masculine characteristics. The converse, feminization or masculinization, would mean an increase in feminine or masculine qualities. The very simple point is that defeminization need not involve obligatory masculinization, and loss of masculine traits does not automatically imply acquisition of feminine characteristics. Furthermore, masculinity and femininity do not represent polar opposites on a unidimensional continuum.

Bancroft: This view is reflected in the current vogue for the Bem androgeny scale (Bem 1974), because in all previous measures masculinity and femininity have been polarized. This new scale separates masculinity and femininity as orthogonal variables.

Goy: One can be high on both scales and low on both?

Ehrhardt: Human behaviour is much more complex. It is much easier talking about a dog that either lifts his leg or not!

Goy: Even that isn't clear-cut; there are female dogs who lift their legs a little bit! There certainly are male guinea-pigs that show lordosis; they all do so on the day of birth. I can't think of any absolute dichotomy in animals.

Ehrhardt: In what way, then, is it useful to talk about masculinization and feminization?

Goy: It is useful to think of them as polar conditions. Admittedly that is a

Jungian technique: you invent archetypes and then say that everything in the empirical world is imperfect, and why shouldn't it be? No two animals have the same developmental history. Why shouldn't they all be more conforming models of the archetype, or less conforming models? And why shouldn't they vary between polar opposites that we develop as part of a schema or way of looking at the world?

Short: Another distinction between primates and other mammals relates to the timing of ovulation in relation to puberty. The rhesus monkey, the chimpanzee and the human female all become sexually active at puberty, 1–4 years before they begin to ovulate, whereas in sheep, and I imagine in rats and mice, the first oestrus coincides with ovulation and the first copulation and hence the first chance of conception. There is surely some evolutionary significance in this; it must have been advantageous for pair-bonding primates to be able to practise their sexuality for a few years before they conceived, whereas in the sheep where there are no pair bonds the best strategy is to get pregnant as soon as she comes into oestrus.

Bancroft: Isn't that because the behaviour is less innately determined in the primate and must be practised before one can do it effectively, at least in the male? Harlow's data would suggest this (Harlow 1965).

Beach: The primate may have to learn something else about sex than just how to copulate.

Goy: Harlow's claim (1971) is that monkeys learn to love, and learn a specific motive behind sex. I would agree with that. It is not a question of learning a motor skill or a motor pattern. Juvenile sexual behaviour functions for social bonding and not for anything else.

Ehrhardt: You don't think it has any kind of rehearsal function?

Goy: No; and similarly I don't think rough-and-tumble play is a rehearsal for male aggression or male dominance behaviours in adults. The function of rough-and-tumble play is to sort out winners from losers in that particular group, and *at the time* it is displayed. The males are deciding and showing the female members of the group, while they are making their decisions, which of them will be the dominant male and which will be subordinate or peripheral. That is the function of juvenile play in rhesus monkeys.

Green: Didn't some of Dr Harlow's male monkeys reared without mothers approach females but initially misdirect the phallus, approaching them from the side?

Goy: Yes. They are erotically aroused but they can't get it together.

Green: Isn't that an argument against learning to love, as against learning to copulate?

Goy: No. Eroticism and love are not identical. The reasons for their side approach and so on may be their timidity and general lack of relationship with the individual animal and the lack of ability to establish appropriate affectional ties.

Bancroft: That is unconvincing. It could equally be that they haven't practised approaching from the right direction sufficiently.

Jost: From Dr Short's film it appears that sexual behaviour is much more stereotyped in sheep than in monkeys. Is that right?

Short: Yes, it is.

Sachar: It isn't a full courtship pattern, perhaps, but there has to be a certain amount of behavioural interchange before mounting. Perhaps Dr Harlow's monkeys lacked that behavioural repertoire so they could not give the right signals to the other partner and were awkward in that respect.

Keverne: One cannot rule out the fact that there must be some motor programming in the cerebellum, just as there is in learning to play bat and ball. It is not easy for a male rhesus monkey to grasp a female by the ankles with his hands on her back and to intromit. It requires motor programming. This doesn't detract from the fact that there might be an element of love too!

Goy: There has to be some competence in both members of the pair. I raised monkeys by giving them limited peer experience, only $^1/_2$–1 hour a day with their friends, beginning at three months of age. Although they played vigorously and did all the other social things characteristic of a group, those monkeys were deficient in the development of mounting. C.H. Phoenix (personal communication 1978) has shown that only a very small percentage of them ever copulate under any condition he has studied them in, in adulthood.

In contrast to that, I am now rearing monkeys in social groups where their peers are continuously present and also their mothers during the first years of life. Everyone can interact freely. Young males show this difficult task of the double foot clasp mounting, balancing delicately on their partner, as early as three weeks of age. So it is not the difficulty of the motor task that Harlow's adult animals are deficient in, and certainly males reared with limited social contact have well-practised cerebella, if one is to judge by their high levels of vigorous play.

Marteau: I am interested that the discussion is coming round from the hormones to learned behaviour relationships and is now using more my sort of language. I accept that there are differences that can be related to certain hormones, but this seems to be a chicken-and-egg problem. Which comes first? Even the fact that I can change people's behaviour by punishments or various forms of deprivation does not mean that whenever I see such behaviour it is necessarily the result of such punishment or deprivation. I gather that in the animal world too there can be an even greater change in behaviour produced by the rearing situation, by the learned situation, than by a change in the hormone level. I am thinking of studies like those of the Virgin Wives (Friedman 1971). Eleven men presenting as impotent were not seen for treatment, but their wives were taken into therapy. After the wives had had therapy the men's potency recovered. This had nothing to do with levels of hormones, or with the men at all; it was the 'castrating' influence of the wives on the men. On the other hand, one of my colleagues has been successful in treating vaginismus by taking the husbands into therapy rather than the wives. It is a pity that such studies in human behaviour have not been presented here, even though the clinician is somewhat inhibited by confidentiality. Perhaps we should have heard from behaviour therapists, who move more easily today between the world of animal experimentation and that of the psychoanalyst and see themselves as being concerned with maladaptive behaviour resulting from faulty rearing.

Goy: The behaviour therapist works with contrived learning systems and contrived rewards in his attempts to alter behaviour, and although I hate to enter the nature/nurture argument (and I am not trying to raise it but to bridge it), it is possible to adopt the view that everything is learned. Animals learn to walk, but nobody throws gum drops at them to get them to walk. The reinforcement or reward mechanisms for learning to walk or to mount or do any of these things are totally obscure to us. That doesn't mean they don't exist. James Olds (1976) should have proved to us that the brain *contains* drive and reward systems, and that such systems don't have to be activated by gum drops. More than that, the reward systems or reinforcing systems necessary for learning male behaviour by an individual may be programmed by the prenatal hormonal history.

Marteau: Indeed I think such results do exist and we certainly see them vividly in psychotherapy. However, on our side we have also failed you. We have not done those experiments which might have helped bridge the gap. For example, we might examine what hormone changes occur in people during psychotherapy. I have had patients in Gestalt therapy, who in a very short time have altered very much in appearance, in skin tone, in voice tone, and in their ability to relate as male or female. It would have been fascinating to have examined their hormonal levels before and after their therapy.

Sachar: There is no question that the psychosocial context has an influence on hormones, as well as vice versa. The classical animal experiment is that with the ring dove where each bit of courtship behaviour acts as a stimulus which turns on a hormone in the other bird, which then changes colour, which then stimulates further behaviour in the other (Lehrman 1964; Erickson & Zenone 1976).

The effects of the psychosocial environment on hormones have also been studied in monkeys. For example, Rose *et al.* (1975) transferred dominant males from one colony to another colony where they were no longer dominant but fell to the bottom of the hierarchy. Their testosterone levels also collapsed; when they were returned to an environment where they became dominant again, their testosterone levels rose. The role of stress in these changes, as opposed to pure dominance, is not clear, however.

One can do this the other way as well, by giving hormones and analysing the social effects. One can wonder how manipulating hormonal variables would alter the compatibility pairing in the situation that Dr Goy described in his paper. There were some unreceptive female monkeys who were not popular and males did not have a great success rate with them. We saw the influence of the cycle on that pattern, and perhaps Dr Goy might give hormones to these females, to see how that alters their receptivity to the male and the male's interest. Experimentally we have to hold one factor constant and manipulate the other, then try to hold the other factor constant. It isn't that we want to ignore one dimension but we are trying to tease one variable apart at a time.

Marteau: I thought our purpose was to bridge this gap.

Bancroft: Can I try to bridge it again and to emphasize the importance of peer group play in the human for the development of sexual behaviour, and the possible relevance of work of Harlow's kind and studies such as Dr Goy's in which he controls peer group structure in sub-human primates? I agree with Dr Ehrhardt (p. 79) that peer group play potentially has an enormous role in human sexual development and that hormones may be relevant to this process. It may be that at the time hormone levels are changing around puberty, things become either more or less difficult for different individuals in the peer group. We might learn from primates how crucial the timing of peer group interaction is and how this interacts with hormone changes. Are there ways in which we could do that?

Goy: Unquestionably. The study I described about raising peers with only a limited opportunity for social interaction—only half an hour a day—provides a condition where you give the wrong kind of peer experience. Qualitatively it is different from optimal peer experience because these males never have adequate time to sort out their status problems and to establish strong positive affectional ties with peers, as shown by the fact that they don't develop mounting—because mounting *is* the indicator of how strong the homophilic and heterophilic bonds are in the group.

Green: The feminine boys we studied (see p. 60) have a heterosocial (female) peer group and they, more often than masculine boys, become homosexual; whereas typical males who are pre-heterosexual have a homosocial (male) peer group during grade school years.

Goy: I have never observed a comparable phenomenon in developing rhesus monkeys. In heterosexual groups where the members have lived together all of their lives, competition for female partners can become intense when the males attain adolescence. Usually only one male in these small groups (containing only 2–4 males and 2–3 females) copulates with the females to ejaculation during adolescence. We have not studied them beyond this age.

Sachar: The previous bonds, one assumes, keep the social colony from falling apart?

Goy: Yes. They do more than that, I suspect. Long association with heterophilic and homophilic bonding behaviour allows those males who do not copulate with females in their peer groups to establish a relationship with a novel female and to show good copulatory behaviour.

Green: Were the males who spent half an hour each day with their peers raised with their mothers, or were they isolated?

Goy: They were with their mothers for the first three months of life. After that their only contacts were with peers for half an hour each day.

Ehrhardt: Did peer group experience compensate for absence of the mothers in Harlow's monkeys?

Goy: 'Compensation' depends on the extent of peer group interaction. If free and continuous access to peers is allowed for a long period (like a year) without the disruptiveness of daily separation and being put back together for a limited time, the monkeys develop reasonably well. But this observation does not deny a maternal role. The role of the mother may just be very difficult to show. It is extremely interesting that while the infants are with mothers the infants almost never have disputes. The mothers have disputes, but little or no antagonism is shown between infants in the presence of their mothers. The development of relations with peers in the presence of the mother is free of antagonism, and that may be a very important factor facilitating successful heterophilic and homophilic bonds.

References

BARRACLOUGH, C.A. & GORSKI, R.A. (1975) Studies on mating behaviour in the androgen-sterilized female rat in relation to the hypothalamic regulation of sexual behaviour. *J. Endocrinol. 25,* 175–182

BAUM, M.J. (1976) Effects of testosterone propionate administered perinatally on sexual behaviour of female ferrets. *J. Comp. Physiol. Psychol. 90,* 399–410

BEM, S.L. (1974) The measurement of psychological androgeny. *J. Consult. Clin. Psychol. 42,* 155–162

BEACH, F.A. (1942) Male and female mounting behaviour in prepubertally castrated female rats treated with androgen. *Endocrinology 31,* 673–678

CLARKE, J.J. (1977) The sexual behaviour of prenatally androgenised ewes observed in the field. *J. Reprod. Fertil. 49,* 311–315

CLARKE, I.J. & SCARAMUZZI, R.J. (1978) Sexual behaviour and LH secretion in spayed androgenised ewes after a single injection of testosterone or oestradiol-17β. *J. Reprod. Fertil. 52,* 313–320

CLARKE, I.J., SCARAMUZZI, R.J. & SHORT, R.V. (1976*a*) Effect of testosterone implants in pregnant ewes on their female offspring. *J. Embryol. Exp. Morphol. 36,* 87–99

CLARKE, I.J., SCARAMUZZI, R.J. & SHORT, R.V. (1976*b*) Sexual differentiation of the brain: endocrine and behavioural responses of androgenised ewes to oestrogen. *J. Endocrinol. 71,* 175–176

EHRHARDT, A.A. & MONEY, J. (1967) Progestin-induced hermaphroditism: IQ and psychosexual identity in a study of ten girls. *J. Sex Res. 3,* 83–100

ERICKSON, C.J. & ZENONE, P.G. (1976) Courtship differences in male ring doves: avoidance of cuckoldry? *Science (Wash.D.C.) 192,* 1353–1354

FLETCHER, T.J. (1978) The induction of male sexual behavior in red deer *(Cervus elaphus)* by the administration of testosterone to hinds and estradiol-17β to stags. *Horm. Behav.,* in press

FLETCHER, T.J. & SHORT, R.V. (1974) Restoration of libido in castrated red deer stag *(Cervus elaphus)* with oestradiol-17β. *Nature (Lond.) 248,* 616–618

FRIEDMAN, L. (1971) *Virgin Wives,* Tavistock, London

HARLOW, H.F. (1965) Sexual behavior in the rhesus monkey, in *Sex and Behavior* (F.A. Beach, ed.), Wiley, New York

HARLOW, H.F.(1971) *Learning to Love,* Albion Publishing Company, San Francisco

LEHRMAN, D.S. (1964) The reproductive behavior of ring doves, *Sci. Am. 211(5),* 48–54

OLDS, J. (1976) Brain stimulation and the motivation of behavior. *Prog. Brain Res. 45,* 401–426

ROSE, R.M., BERNSTEIN, I.S. & GORDON, T.P. (1975) Consequences of social conflict on plasma testosterone levels in rhesus monkeys. *Psychosom. Med. 37,* 50–61

SHORT, R.V. (1974) Sexual differentiation of the brain of the sheep. *INSERM (Inst. Natl. Santé Rech. Méd) Colloq. 32,* 121–142

Sexual and aggressive behaviour in social groups of talapoin monkeys

E.B. KEVERNE

Department of Anatomy, University of Cambridge

Abstract In social groups not all monkeys are equal, in terms of either their behaviour or their endocrine status. When a dominant monkey is compared with one that is subordinate the level of sexual behaviour is high in the dominant and low in the subordinate monkey, while levels of aggression received follow an inverse pattern. Attention in terms of visual monitoring is primarily focused on the dominant animal even when overt aggression is extremely low. Cortisol and prolactin concentrations tend to be higher in subordinate monkeys while only the dominant male shows elevated testosterone levels during group interactions with attractive females. A question of some importance is whether these differences in endocrine status are a determinant of the differences in behaviour or whether they reflect the behaviour and, if the latter, to what purpose. Recent attempts to answer this problem have focused on the hypothalamo-pituitary axis in order to examine whether differences in behaviour between dominant and subordinate monkeys are reflected in differences in its responsiveness to endocrine changes.

A highly organized social structure is characteristic of most primate species including man, and this social structure has a profound effect on each individual's behaviour. Hormonal changes are also important determinants of behaviour, particularly sexual behaviour, and in laboratory primate dyads the effects of sex hormones on different components of sexual behaviour are well understood (Keverne 1976; Baum *et al.* 1977). Such laboratory studies where variables can be controlled or reduced to a minimum have proved immensely important for understanding the mechanisms and sites of action of hormones. Nevertheless, because the social context plays such an important part in behaviour, it is not possible to gain a complete understanding of sexual behaviour in isolation from the total social fabric of which it is part (Beach 1976).

It is important to determine not only the extent to which an animal's sexual behaviour is influenced by its social position, but to what extent this is itself reflected in endocrine changes. Let us not forget that social structure is determined by behavioural interactions, many of which influence those endocrine systems responsible for sex-hormone secretions (Bernstein *et al.* 1974; Rose *et al.* 1972). It is this primary interaction between behaviour and neuroendocrine secretions, taken within the context of a primate social group, that is to be considered here. In particular, I shall be comparing the sexual and aggressive behaviours of the most dominant and subordinate individuals, and the endocrine correlates of such behaviour. It is hoped to shed some light on the mechanisms responsible for any neuroendocrine changes, and also the significance, in terms of reproductive success, of these changes.

MATERIALS AND METHODS

The gap between the primate sociobiologist and neuroendocrinologist has been technical rather than philosophical. The sociobiologist cannot be expected to sample plasma from feral monkeys living in inhospitable surroundings, and the neuroendocrinologist, like most laboratory workers, is restricted by space. It requires an enclosure of several acres to house a social group of rhesus monkeys. We have attempted to overcome these problems by moving to a less familiar laboratory primate, the talapoin monkey. This species has the advantage of being the smallest Old World monkey (weight 0.8–1.6 kg), with a true menstrual cycle and with most of the behavioural history already established (Dixson *et al.* 1975; Wolfheim & Rowell 1972; Gautier-Hion 1971). The restraints on repeated plasma sampling in such a small primate are becoming less severe with the development of progressively more sensitive radioimmunoassays requiring less plasma for analysis.

Two social groups of talapoin monkeys each consisting of four adult males and five (Group 1) or four (Group 2) adult females were observed in these studies. Each group was housed in a large cage (8 feet × 11 feet × 5 feet) and has been observed for 3½ years (Group 1) or 2½ years (Group 2). In Group 1 males and females lived permanently together while in Group 2 males and females lived in the same cage but were partitioned and only given access to each other for the duration of testing. Both groups were observed for 50 minutes twice daily (09.00 and 16.00 hours B.S.T.), and plasma samples were collected at two-day intervals (at 17.00 hours), after which at least one day was permitted for recovery before further behaviour was scored. Sexual, aggressive and social interactions were recorded together with the identity of the animals concerned, observations being made behind a one-way mirror (Keverne *et al.* 1978*a*).

For ease of presentation and in order to draw attention to the marked contrasts, only the most dominant and subordinate individuals will be considered in this paper. Dominance is defined according to the direction of aggressive behaviour, such that if A attacks B and is never attacked by B, then A is said to be dominant to B. Among talapoin monkeys females may, and frequently do, dominate males (Dixson & Herbert 1977).

Females in both groups were ovariectomized and at intervals received oestradiol-17β in silastic implants designed to release 2–3 μg/24 hours, sufficient to develop fully the sexual skin swelling. This rate of release of hormone from a single implant produced plasma levels of oestradiol similar to those found in the follicular phase of the menstrual cycle, while a further two silastic implants produced an oestradiol surge similar to that found before ovulation. This is the standard technique adopted for inducing an LH surge in neuroendocrine studies on the rhesus monkey (Knobil 1974).

MALE DOMINANCE, SEXUAL AND AGGRESSIVE BEHAVIOUR, AND CHANGES IN PLASMA TESTOSTERONE

In both social groups there was little sexual interaction before the females were given oestrogen implants. None of the males, dominant or subordinate, showed many mounts or ejaculations and inspections of the female's perineum were rare. Administration of oestrogen to the females increased sexual interactions, but this was the prerogative of the dominant male, with the subordinate still showing few mounts or ejaculations (Fig. 1). All males showed some interest in the females and inspected their perineal regions, the dominant male showing the greatest number of inspections and the most subordinate male very few. Masturbation increased in the lower-ranking males when the females received oestradiol but decreased in the dominant male whose sexual behaviour was now high with females.

Levels of aggressive behaviour were initially low in the presence of ovariectomized females with the most dominant males rarely attacking or threatening other males, and displacing them only occasionally (Fig. 2). The dominant males showed little withdrawal behaviour, indicating very low levels of aggression received. The subordinate males displayed no aggressive behaviour, but exhibited high levels of withdrawals. When the females received oestrogen the male aggressive hierarchy did not change but dominant males were significantly more aggressive. When females were given oestrogen, the dominant male demonstrated significantly more attacks, threats and displacements of other males (Fig. 2). The most dominant males received little

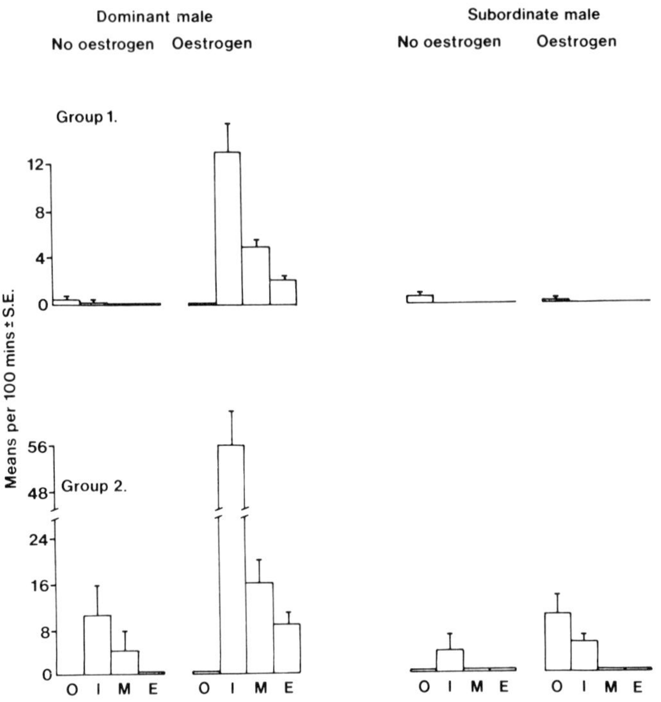

FIG. 1. The distribution of sexual behaviour between dominant and subordinate males in two social groups of talapoin monkeys. Observations on each group for each treatment lasted 1000 minutes during a three-week period. The females were initially ovariectomized with no oestrogen replacement and received oestradiol in a silastic implant. O, masturbation; I, inspection of female perineum; M, mounts; E, ejaculations. (From Keverne *et al.* 1978*a* by kind permission of Academic Press.)

aggression, while withdrawals in subordinates remained high or increased, indicating receipt of high levels of aggressive behaviour.

Out of the social group, during an 11-week period of isolation when no males had access to females, both the putative dominant and subordinate males had low levels of plasma testosterone which were not significantly different from each other (Fig. 3). In social groups with oestrogenized females there was a significant increase in plasma testosterone in the dominant males (Group 1, $t = 4.6, P < 0.001$; Group 2, $t = 3.83, P < 0.001$) but not in the subordinates, where if anything there was a tendency for plasma testosterone levels to fall. In the social group the dominant males now had plasma testosterone levels significantly higher than those of the subordinates (Fig. 3). Thus, the behavioural correlates of dominance (high levels of sexual

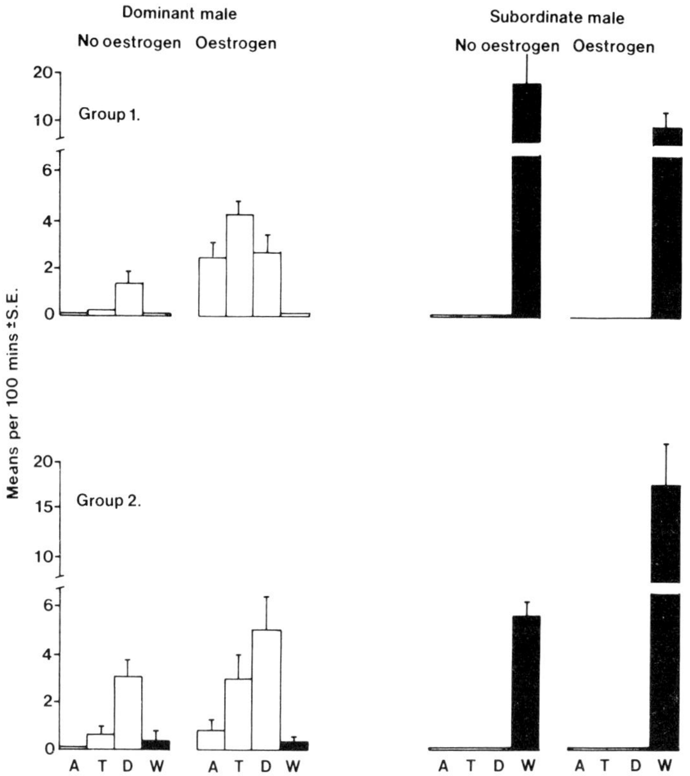

FIG. 2. Effects of treating ovariectomized females with oestradiol on the aggressive behaviour of dominant and subordinate males. A, attack; T, threat; D, displace; W, withdraw. Observations on each group for each treatment condition lasted 1000 minutes during a three-week period. (From Keverne *et al.* 1978*a* by kind permission of Academic Press.)

behaviour and the giving of high but the receipt of low levels of aggressive behaviour) are reflected in increased plasma testosterone, whereas no increase in plasma testosterone is observed in the subordinate males which receive high levels of aggression, and show neither aggressive nor sexual behaviour. A question of some importance is why the increase in plasma testosterone is observed in only the dominant male and not the subordinate, and whether or not this is primarily associated with aggressive or sexual behaviour. This question can be answered by looking at behaviour and plasma hormone changes in an all-male social group where sexual behaviour is absent but aggressive behaviour present.

In this all-male situation the dominant male is attacking and threatening

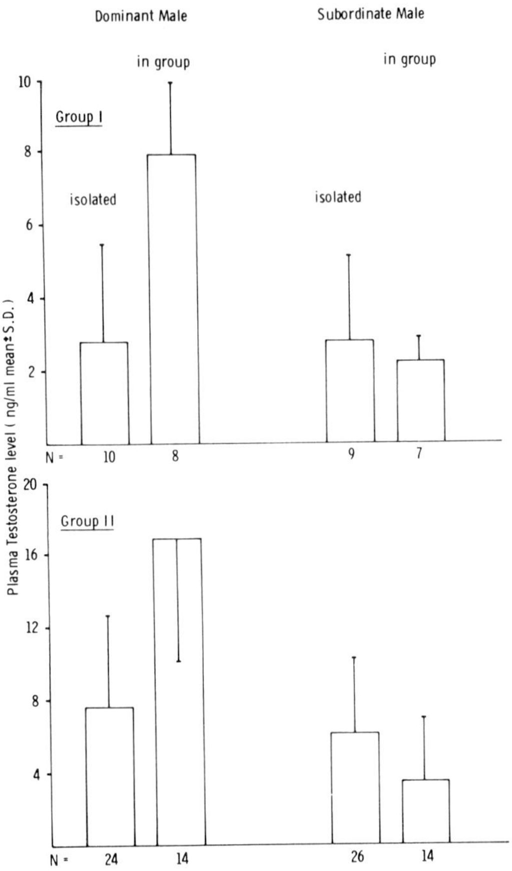

FIG. 3. Differences in plasma testosterone levels between dominant and subordinate males in response to oestrogenized females. Samples collected weekly during a 10–12-week period in isolation and a 7–8-week period in the social group with oestrogenized females.

others in the group (Fig. 4) but it is only when females are introduced that sexual behaviour occurs and plasma testosterone levels increase ($t = 3.38$, $P < 0.001$). At this time, the aggressive behaviour of the dominant male does increase, and one cannot rule out that aggression given in the context of sexual activity may contribute in some way to the increase in male plasma testosterone. Likewise, the increased aggressive behaviour received by the subordinate male in the presence of females may also have been instrumental in preventing both sexual behaviour and increased plasma testosterone.

To test this possibility, both the dominant and subordinate males were taken first into isolation and then from isolation returned to the social group of

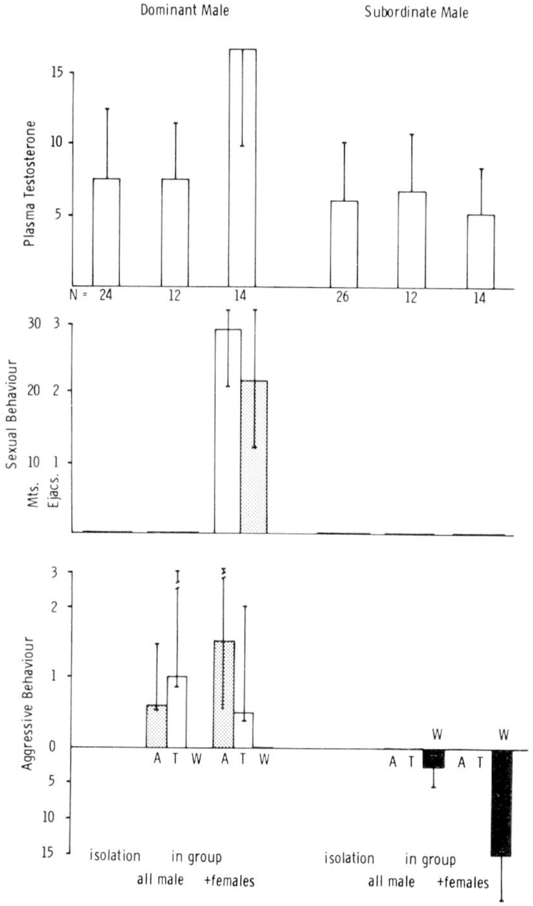

FIG. 4. Changes in sexual and aggressive behaviour (medians and interquartile ranges) and plasma testosterone levels (mean ± standard deviations) in the dominant and subordinate males during a 12-week period in isolation, a six-week period in an all-male group without females and a seven-week period in the social group with oestrogenized females. A, attack; T, threats; W, withdrawals.

females, but in the absence of any other males. In this situation both males showed high levels of sexual behaviour, and both showed a significant increase in plasma testosterone (Fig. 5). Neither male was receiving or giving high levels of aggression because no other males were present, and aggressive interactions with females remained unchanged, although this has not always been the case (see Keverne *et al.* 1978*a*).

If the suggestion is that specific behaviours given or received in the social

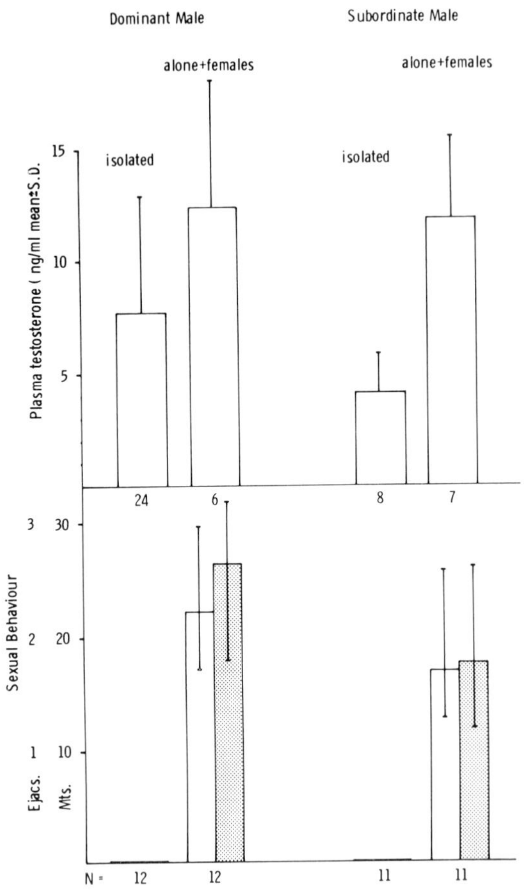

FIG. 5. Increases in plasma testosterone (mean ± standard deviation) and sexual behaviour (medians + interquartile ranges) in dominant and subordinate males on moving from isolation into the oestrogen-treated female group for three weeks, in the absence of other males.

group are primarily determining the different neuroendocrine responsiveness, then it is pertinent to examine the hypothalamo-pituitary axis, to look for differences at this level and to establish that increases in plasma testosterone are not simply a result of increased testicular blood flow. The two pituitary hormones on which we have focused attention are luteinizing hormone (LH) and prolactin. In the dominant male, levels of plasma LH ($t = 2.32, P < 0.05$) and plasma testosterone ($t = 3.27, P < 0.001$) increase in the social group situation (that is, in a group containing females and other males), when this male is showing sexual behaviour (Fig. 6). In the subordinate male, plasma

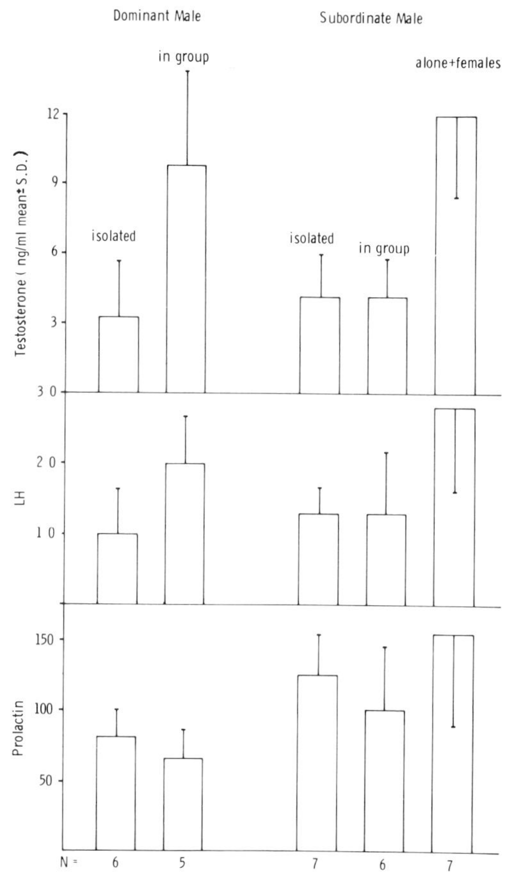

FIG. 6. The increase in LH concentration when plasma testosterone increases in dominant and subordinate males. The plasma prolactin concentration is significantly higher in the subordinate than in the dominant male. LH expressed as μg/ml LER 1909/2 standard. Prolactin expressed as ng/ml of human prolactin standard.

LH (t = 2.54, P <0.05) and testosterone (t = 4.41, P <0.01) do not increase until this male is alone with females, is therefore not receiving aggressive behaviour from other males, but is showing sexual behaviour. These changes in LH suggest that the behaviour is exerting its influence on the gonads via the hypothalamo-pituitary axis. Prolactin concentrations are always higher in the subordinate male, and do not decrease when this male is alone with the females, although levels of LH are, on the whole, higher in the subordinate than the dominant male at this time, and it could be that prolactin is influencing LH receptors in the testes (Bohnet & Friesen 1976). Since high levels of prolactin are measured in the subordinate male even in isolation, the possibility also exists that such a male is more stress-sensitive and shows elevation of prolactin concentrations even in response to the bleeding procedure. If this is the case, prolactin may serve as a predictor of dominance hierarchies, in that it reflects differences between animals in the context of their being able or unable to cope with stressful situations.

A second question that can be posed concerning the differences in plasma testosterone in the social group is the significance of elevated testosterone in the dominant male with respect to behavioural interactions. It is difficult to argue that such increases in plasma testosterone are primarily influencing the sexual motivation of the dominant male, because even after castration male monkeys continue to show sexual interest in females for months and even years (Wilson & Vessey 1968; Phoenix *et al.* 1973). I would like to suggest that increases in plasma testosterone are increasing the dominant males' attractiveness to females. Although a definitive experiment has not yet been done, there is no question that the dominant males are markedly more attractive to oestrogen-treated females than the subordinates, as judged both by increased visual monitoring (Keverne *et al.* 1978*b*) and sexual invitations. What has not yet been established is the degree to which non-behavioural or behavioural aspects of male attractiveness are increasing.

FEMALE DOMINANCE, SEXUAL AND AGGRESSIVE BEHAVIOUR AND CHANGES IN PLASMA PROLACTIN

Female talapoin monkeys, like the males, also form social hierarchies and although aggressive behaviour among females is not as frequent as among males, the effect of social rank on the behavioural interactions of individuals is very marked. When the two extremes of dominance and subordination are contrasted (Fig. 7), the high-ranking female is found to receive more sexual attention from males, and less aggressive behaviour, than the subordinate female. The subordinate female additionally receives relatively high levels of aggression from other females. Since all these females are ovariectomized and receive oestradiol implants it is not possible to look at ovarian hormones, but two stress-related hormones, prolactin and cortisol, have been measured and show marked differences between dominant and subordinate females (Fig. 7). Thus in the course of a year prolactin ($P<0.0001$) and cortisol ($P<0.001$) are significantly higher in the subordinate female which is receiving little sexual attention but high levels of aggression.

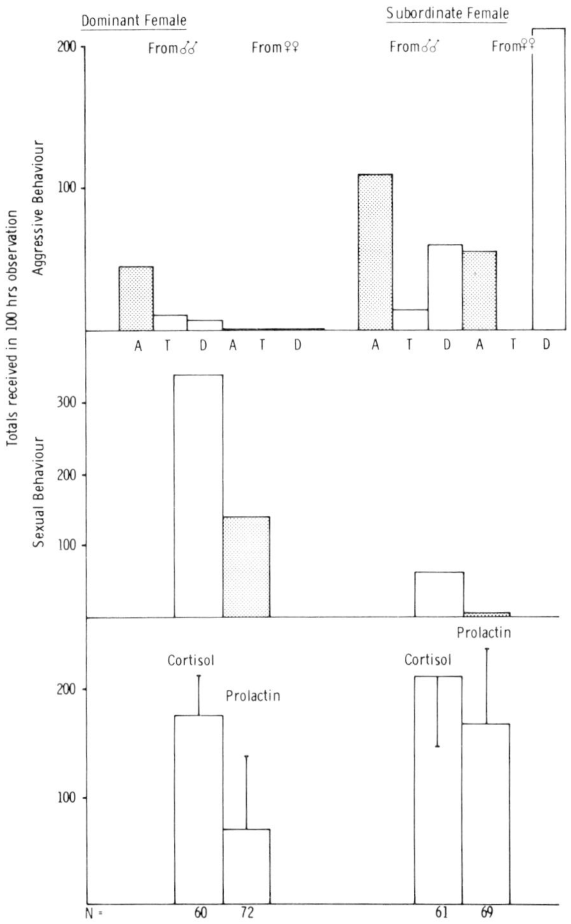

FIG. 7. Total sexual and aggressive behaviour received by dominant and subordinate females when receiving oestrogen for five three-week periods during the course of a 15-month period. Plasma cortisol (ng/ml) and plasma prolactin (ng/ml) were both significantly higher in the subordinate female at this time. Sexual behaviour: open columns, mounts; shaded columns, ejaculations. Aggressive behaviour: A, attack (shaded); T, threat; D, displace.

A point of some controversy concerns the significance of higher levels of sexual interaction with dominant females. It could be argued, and frequently is by field workers, that low-ranking females do in fact receive sexual attention (Loy 1971; Drickamer 1974) and, providing it is near mid-cycle, there is no reason why they should not become pregnant. In any case, since the females do not all synchronize their menstrual cycles, there may be times when subordinate females have an advantage over the dominant female in being attractive to males and behaviourally receptive. Hence, most females may at some time receive sexual attention from the males. Nevertheless, recent field studies have shown that among female gelada baboons, not all are equally fertile, the dominant females scoring higher in terms of reproductive success (Dunbar & Dunbar 1977). In these talapoin monkeys we cannot check for pregnancy or ovulation, since all have been ovariectomized, but what we can do is challenge the hypothalamo-pituitary axis with an oestrogen surge in order to look for an LH surge and potential fertility, since the LH surge seems to be the trigger for ovulation.

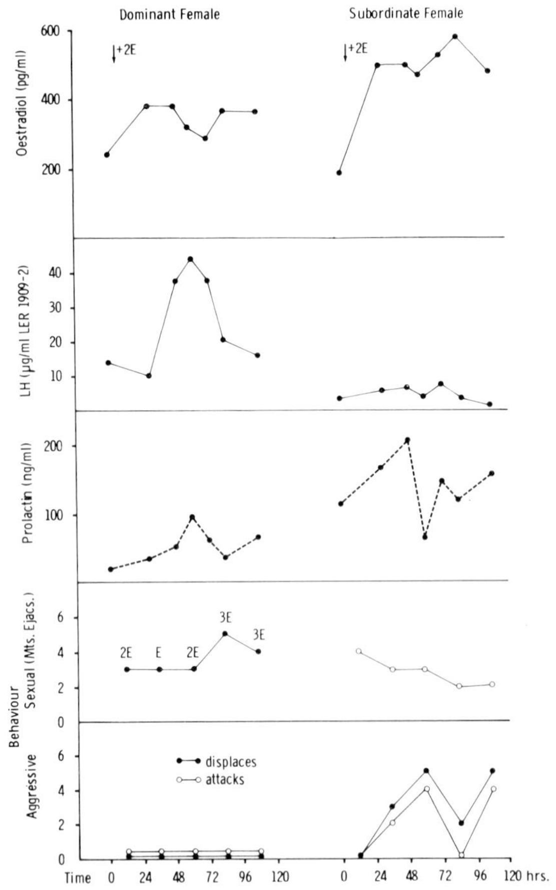

FIG. 8. Sexual and aggressive behaviour received together with plasma LH and prolactin in dominant and subordinate females when challenged with an oestradiol surge (+ 2E) over a five-day period. Sexual behaviour: •-•, mounts with ejaculations (2E denotes two ejaculations); o-o, mounts without ejaculations.

The outcome of challenging the hypothalamo-pituitary axis in the dominant and subordinate female, and the differences in the behavioural interactions of the two individuals, can be seen in Fig. 8. Although both females received equivalent oestradiol surges, only the dominant female responded with an LH surge. The prolactin concentration was significantly higher in the subordinate female (mean 135.7±46 ng/ml) than in the dominant female (mean 50.5±26 ng/ml; $P<0.001$). The behavioural interactions of the dominant and subordinate females were also markedly different. Thus, while the dominant female received high levels of sexual attention from the males in the group (18 mounts, 15 ejaculations) the subordinate female received little (14 mounts, 0 ejaculations). Aggressive interactions showed the opposite pattern, with the subordinate female receiving the highest number of attacks and 'displaces' and the dominant female receiving no aggression.

It is interesting to speculate that the subordinate female under the stress of constant attacks has elevated concentrations of prolactin (hyperprolactinaemia) producing high-prolactin amenorrhoea similar to that found in humans (Besser *et al.* 1972). If this is the case, then it should be possible to *(a)* induce ovulation in the subordinate female by lowering her prolactin concentration, and *(b)* block ovulation in the dominant female by elevating prolactin. Such procedures do, indeed, have the predicted effects on the induced LH surge in dominant and subordinate females (Fig. 9), although these effects are probably a result of changes in hypothalamic dopamine (Kordon & Ramirez 1975) rather than a direct action of prolactin itself. The dopamine agonist, bromocriptine, given daily (150 μg/kg) to the subordinate female, significantly lowered prolactin concentrations to levels similar to those found in the dominant female, and the subordinate female now showed an LH surge in response to an oestrogen challenge. Haloperidol, a dopamine antagonist, given daily (62.5 μg/kg) significantly elevated prolactin, although this was most marked in the few hours after injection (Fig. 9). Administration of haloperidol to the dominant female also blocked the LH surge in response to an oestrogen challenge.

Although there was a shift in male sexual interest away from the dominant female it is difficult at this stage to assert the causal factors. One of the problems of giving haloperidol is the extrapyramidal side-effects resulting from dopaminergic changes in the striatum. In the context of sexual behaviour, this resulted in presentation postures being maintained for prolonged periods, which may have contributed to the decline in the dominant female's attractiveness to males.

In conclusion, these experiments show that in the social group behaviours are not equally distributed among the individuals, and so far as sexual beha-

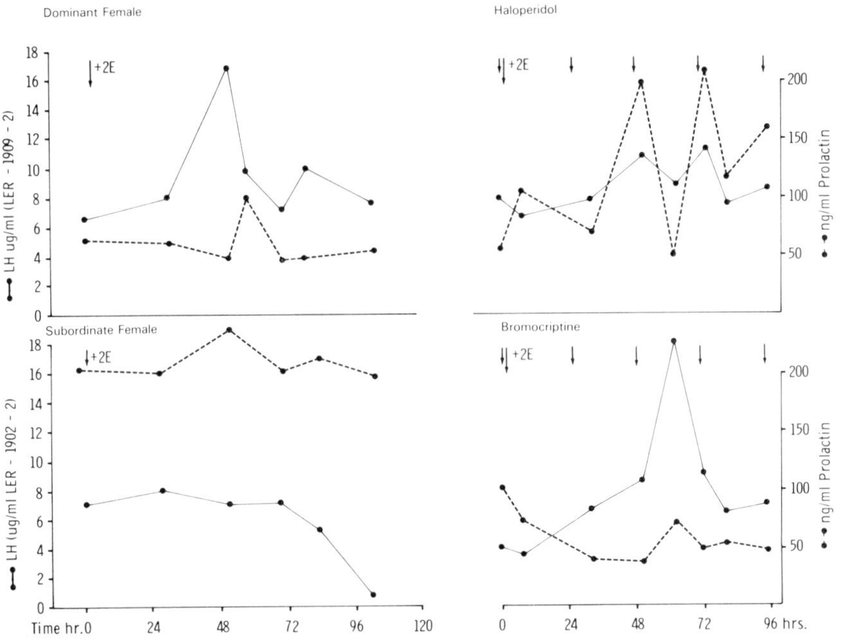

FIG. 9. Effects of suppressing or elevating prolactin on the oestrogen-induced LH surge. Bromocriptine and haloperidol were administered to subordinate and dominant females respectively by daily injection (indicated by ↓ on graph). +2E, each female receives an additional two silastic oestradiol implants. (From *Nature*, by kind permission of Macmillan Publications.)

viour is concerned it pays to be dominant. High-ranking individuals take part in more sexual interactions, receive little aggression, but show high levels of aggressive behaviour to others. In marked contrast, the lowest-ranking monkeys take little part in sexual activity, receive high levels of aggression, but are not themselves aggressive to others. Sexual and aggressive behaviour are therefore inclined to favour the reproductive success of high-ranking members of the group.

However, not only are the behaviours selectively advantageous to the reproductive success of dominant individuals, but so too are the neuroendocrine responses. Thus we see in the dominant male marked increases in plasma testosterone, with high levels of sexual performance possibly enhancing his attractiveness to females. Among the females, low rank is associated with high prolactin concentrations and a failure to show an LH surge in response to oestrogen challenge.

Thus although subordinate females are not entirely sexually excluded, a central neural mechanism appears to exist whereby the hypothalamo-pituitary axis is 'switched off' to the positive oestrogen feedback triggering the LH surge.

These experiments have demonstrated that the structure and composition of the social group have marked effects not only on an individual's behaviour, but also on the primary interaction between behaviour and neuroendocrine responsiveness. Clearly the data presented here have been selected for extremes, and those animals that are neither most dominant nor most subordinate fit less readily into these extreme behavioural or neuroendocrine patterns. However, it is only when extremes are compared that any picture emerges of which behaviours are a significant focus for future attention. While remaining relatively simplistic, this primate social model provides another dimension of complexity for the consideration of hormonal influences on sexual behaviour.

ACKNOWLEDGEMENTS

I wish to thank Susan Dilley and Lesley Bowman for doing the radioimmunoassays and Rachel Meller for help with testing and proof reading. Raith Overhill is thanked for drawing the figures and Liza Caldwell for typing the manuscript. Materials for radioimmunoassay were generously provided by Dr H.G. Friesen (prolactin antiserum), Dr G.D. Niswender (LH antiserum), Dr M.J. Wheeler (testosterone antiserum), NIAMDD (LH and prolaction standards) and the Medical Research Council (human prolactin for iodination). This work was supported by an MRC programme grant to Dr Joe Herbert, whose help and encouragement have been invaluable throughout.

References

BAUM, M.J., EVERITT, B.J., HERBERT, J. & KEVERNE, E.B. (1977) Hormonal basis of proceptivity and receptivity in female primates. *Arch. Sex. Behav. 6,* 173–192

BEACH, F.A. (1976) Cross species comparisons and the human heritage. *Arch. Sex. Behav. 5,* 469–485

BERNSTEIN, J.S., ROSE, R.M. & GORDON, T.P. (1974) Behavioural and environmental events influencing primate testosterone levels. *J. Hum. Evol. 3,* 517–525

BESSER, G.M., PARKE, L., EDWARDS, G.R.W., FORSYTH, I.A. & MCNEILLY, A.S. (1972) Galactorrhoea: successful treatment with reduction of plasma prolactin levels by bromergocryptine. *Br. Med. J. 3,* 669–672

BOHNET, H.G. & FRIESEN, H.G. (1976) Effects of prolactin and growth hormone on prolactin and LH receptors in the dwarf mouse. *J. Reprod. Fertil. 48,* 307–311

DIXSON, A.F. & HERBERT, J. (1977) Gonadal hormones and sexual behaviour in groups of adult Talapoin monkeys *(Miopithecus talapoin). Horm. Behav. 8,* 141–154

DIXSON, A.F., SCRUTON, D.M. & HERBERT, J. (1975) Behaviour of the Talapoin monkey *(Miopithecus talapoin)* studied in groups in the laboratory. *J. Zool. (Lond.) 176,* 177–210

DRICKAMER, L.C. (1974) Social rank, observability and sexual behaviour of rhesus monkeys *(Macaca mulatta). J. Reprod. Fertil. 37,* 117–120

DUNBAR, R.I.M. & DUNBAR, E.P. (1977) Dominance and reproductive success among female gelada baboons. *Nature (Lond.) 266,* 351–352

GAUTIER-HION, A. (1971) Répertoire comportemental du talapoin *(Miopithecus talapoin). Biol. Gabon. 2,* 311–329

KEVERNE, E.B. (1976) Sexual receptivity and attractiveness in the female rhesus monkey. *Adv. Study Behav. 7,* 155–200

KEVERNE, E.B., MELLER, R.E. & MARTINEZ-ARIAS, A. (1978*a*) Dominance, aggression and sexual behaviour in social groups of talapoin monkeys, in *Recent Advances in Primatology,* vol.1: *Behaviour* (Chivers, D.J. & Herbert, J., eds.), pp. 533–548, Academic Press, London & New York

KEVERNE, E.B., LEONARD, R.A., SCRUTON, D.M. & YOUNG, S.K. (1978*b*) Visual monitoring in social groups of Talapoin monkeys *(Miopithecus talapoin). Anim. Behav. 26,* 933–944

KNOBIL, E. (1974) On the control of gonadotropin secretion in the rhesus monkey. *Recent Prog. Horm. Res. 30,* 1–46

KORDON, C. & RAMIREZ, V.D. (1975) Recent development in neurotransmitter–hormone interactions, in *Anatomic Neuroendocrinology* (Stumpf, W.E. & Grant, L.D., eds.), pp. 409–419, Karger, Basel

LOY, J. (1971) Estrous behaviour of free-ranging rhesus monkeys *(Macaca mulatta). Primates 12,* 1–31

PHOENIX, C.H., SLOB, A.K. & GOY, R.W. (1973) Effects of castration and replacement therapy on sexual behaviour of adult male rhesuses. *J. Comp. Physiol. Psychol. 84,* 472–481

ROSE, R.M., GORDON, T.P. & BERNSTEIN, I.S. (1972) Plasma testosterone levels in male rhesus: influences of sexual and social stimuli. *Science (Wash. D.C.) 178,* 643–645

WILSON, A.P. & VESSEY, S.H. (1968) Behaviour of free ranging castrated rhesus monkeys. *Folia Primatol. 9,* 1–14

WOLFHEIM, J.H. & ROWELL, T.E. (1972) Communication among captive Talapoin monkeys *(Miopithecus talapoin). Folia Primatol. 18,* 224–255

Discussion

Abbott: I was very glad to hear your results on subordinate female monkeys, because when we set up groups of male and female marmosets we also find that only the dominant female breeds, as the subordinate females fail to ovulate (Abbott & Hearn 1978). We have shown that urinary oestradiol concentrations in these latter animals are typical of those in ovariectomized females (Lunn 1978), so the ovary in the subordinate female marmoset seems to be switched off. Is the behaviour of your groups changed in any way when the subordinate female starts to show a positive feedback of LH to oestradiol, in response to treatment with bromocriptine? Or, for example, does the treatment with haloperidol change the behaviour of the dominant female, or that of the dominant male towards her?

Keverne: This was difficult to assess because of the extrapyramidal side-effects of haloperidol. The behaviour in the group did change; the dominant male lost interest in the dominant female and switched his interest towards the lower-ranking females, but it is difficult to show whether this change in behaviour is primarily due to the lowering of their prolactin concentrations, or because of extrapyramidal side-effects producing changes in the dominant female's behaviour. The dominant females are not markedly different, but the fact that when in the presentation posture they don't show their normal running away, which is characteristic of talapoin monkeys (unlike the rhesus), but stay in a presentation posture, may explain why they may not be so attractive to the male.

Sachar: You gave both drugs at once, I gather? Why was that?

Keverne: We gave bromocriptine and haloperidol at the same time but to different monkeys, of course. There seemed to be no point making the high-ranking female less attractive, for whatever reason, if one left the low-ranking female in exactly the same state. By switching the two simultaneously we wanted to try to switch their behaviour.

Sachar: If the male transfers his attention to the subordinate female because of effects on the dominant female, you might see what effect that alone has if you left the subordinate's endocrine system the same.

Keverne: That is true, and we are now taking the subordinate female out of the stressful situation and putting her into a cage of her own. We find that her prolactin level has fallen, and we are challenging the hypothalamo-pituitary axis with another oestrogen surge. At the same time we are looking at the next lowest-ranking female who has now become subordinate, to see if we pick up the same kind of effects in her.

Besser: One would like to use a drug which doesn't have such large behavioural effects as haloperidol. Perhaps metoclopramide or sulpiride would be useful. There are also dopamine receptor blockers that raise prolactin levels at low doses. They have fewer central effects than haloperidol and are much less sedating, at least in the human.

I was fascinated by the similarities between what you have shown and our clinical experience. We are interested in stress infertility. There is a group of women who whenever they come to the outpatient department have high blood prolactin levels. These women are agitated and concerned about their infertility. But if we take them to the ward, insert an intravenous cannula, leave it for 45 minutes and then start sampling through the needle without venepuncture, every 15 minutes for two hours, the high prolactin levels fall progressively into the normal range. Yet each time the women come back to the hospital they have high prolactin levels again. We wonder if this is a form of stress infertility, because we know that hyperprolactinaemia stops ovulation. These women often have regular periods but they are not ovulating, or have an inadequate luteal phase. You are seeing a representation of this situation in your subordinate females. Those monkeys have high cortisol and prolactin concentrations, and these are two of the three stress hormones recognized in the human. Perhaps this explains why both the subordinate female and the subordinate male have high cortisol and high prolactin levels, as you suggest. It is a 'stressful' experience, if we interpret it in human terms, to be subordinate, and to be frustrated.

While we are talking of neurohormones, the endorphins and enkephalins are possibly stress-related neurohormones. We have recently shown in man that enkephalin (we used a long-acting analogue) releases prolactin and growth hormone (unpublished). If enkephalin is derived from ACTH one would expect ACTH, or the ACTH-lipotropin complex, to be secreted as well. It may be that within the enkephalin/endorphin system we shall see the way these various pituitary stress response hormones come together and how hyperprolactinaemia produces infertility. You have shown this very nicely in your study; and if we give bromocriptine to these stressed women they become fertile. Their anxiety state also improves, but that may be related to the resolution of infertility. Finally, the role of luteinizing hormone-releasing hormone (LH-RH) in sexual activity should be mentioned. Evidence in the rat suggests that LH-RH increases sexual activity in males and probably females as well (Moss & McCann 1973; Pfaff 1973). We have similar evidence in men (Mortimer *et al.* 1974, 1976).

When we take a gonadotropin-deficient male patient, irrespective of the cause (congenital LH-RH deficiency, Kallman's syndrome, or hypothalamic or pituitary tumour) and give him LH-RH, libido and erection rate increase consistently at 10–12 days, long before the testosterone concentration has risen to a level approaching normal. I wonder whether the neural-endocrine interfaces in terms of sexual activity in your male monkeys are in part mediated by LH-RH, rather than testosterone.

Nieschlag: Do you find this effect of LH-RH in castrates too?

Besser: We haven't done it in castrates.

Goy: Presumably castrated men release a lot of LH-RH all the time.

Besser: We assume so. They have no androgen or other gonadal steroid to provide the drive on which the LH-RH works, however.

Bancroft: But you say that the response occurs *before* the androgen levels increase?

Besser: There is some rise, but not into the normal range.

Sachar: We speculated earlier about a threshold. The testosterone concentration may not be within the normal range but it may still be up to the threshold for adequate sexual arousal.

Besser: These testosterone levels are in the range where we see impotence in patients being treated with testosterone.

Herbert: I wanted to agree with what Professor Besser says about the importance and interest of peptides. We are testing the effects of the morphine antagonist naloxone, and we shall see what happens with that.

We have data on LH-RH in the rhesus monkeys. The problem with LH-RH in this species is two-fold. There is a poor LH response to LH-RH given intravenously or intraventricularly. Even massive doses of LH-RH do not produce a real LH surge. We don't understand why, because it is effective in the human. So far as behaviour is concerned, our preliminary information doesn't encourage us to think that LH-RH is going to do anything dramatic to female sexual behaviour in the rhesus monkeys. It doesn't look as if native LH-RH has any effect; we are thinking about long-acting, more potent analogues.

Brawer: There are LH-RH terminals throughout the medial preoptic area and in the limbic system, including the amygdala, and the effect may be completely independent of testosterone and may be exerted by LH-RH acting as a neurotransmitter, since it is present in the regions of brain and hypothalamus which presumably account for this type of behaviour.

Bancroft: To return to prolactin, obviously it has some endocrine effect but in many of these situations it may be no more than an indicator of the state of the dopaminergic system. Until one can control prolactin without altering the dopaminergic system one cannot say what role it is playing.

Keverne: I agree. I don't know of any evidence that prolactin is having a behavioural effect on its own. Dr Everitt will be discussing this later (pp. 329–348).

Bancroft: LH-RH is surely very dose-sensitive? You see a strong inhibitory effect if you exceed a certain dose.

Herbert: Not in monkeys, because there is not much of a stimulatory effect on LH.

Besser: In patients we have to give big doses of the synthetic unmodified material. Therapy with LH-RH failed for a long time because of inadequate doses. We give 500 μg eight-hourly. We have kept patients on that regimen for 2½ years, both women and men. What you are referring to is very relevant, and relates to Dr Herbert's point about using analogues of LH-RH. When these are given total resistance develops rapidly (Tharandt *et al.* 1977), in terms of gonadotropin release; it is not due to antibody formation, although one such case has been described (Van Loon & Brown 1975). We have looked at this resistance *in vitro*. When we give a pulse of long-acting analogue, isolated rat pituitary cells initially respond and then become and remain resistant long after the analogue has disappeared from the perfusion system. Then responsiveness gradually returns. Clinically one has to be careful with the analogues that one is not giving them too frequently. We know that normally in human LH-RH secretion there are longer 'off' periods of secretion than 'on', and I believe this has a physiological meaning. One must be careful with the analogues not to overstimulate.

Sachar: On this question of trying to tease apart the hormonal and psychological variables using pharmacological methods, the dopamine system plays a role in LH release as well as prolactin release, so if you interfere with one pharmacologically, you affect the other also. Anxiety and stress stimulate cortisol and prolactin but using small doses of drugs like diazepam which don't have dopaminergic effects and don't directly affect prolactin or cortisol could allow you to reduce prolactin and cortisol by reducing anxiety.

Keverne: This is what we are thinking about doing now in our monkeys, using the anxiolytic drugs.

Nieschlag: I have two more technical questions concerning this monkey species. First, how do you measure their protein hormones? Do you have homologous assays?

Keverne: No. We use heterologous assays, an ovine–ovine system for LH and the Friesen antibody for prolactin. They tell us nothing about absolute levels but are helpful for looking at relative changes, within an individual and between individuals.

Nieschlag: Can you measure FSH?

Keverne: We haven't tried. This hasn't yet been done in talapoin monkeys so far as I know, because this is a relatively new species in neuroendocrinology.

Nieschlag: Do they show seasonality in their reproductive behaviour?

Keverne: These groups have been together for 1–3 years and we have been taking plasma samples twice weekly. We have no evidence of seasonal changes in behaviour or in plasma testosterone levels. In any case, this is a confused area. In the rhesus monkey, where this has been considered most thoroughly, and where we do see seasonal changes in testosterone and annual changes in sexual activity, at best we have only a correlation between the two. We don't know whether the testosterone changes are determining the behaviour or reflecting it. The confusion is illustrated in a recent study by Richard Michael in which he castrated rhesus monkey males and ovariectomized the females (Michael & Wilson 1975). The females were given constant daily doses of oestrogen and the males, constant daily doses of testosterone. He found the same kind of annual changes in behaviour as usual, so it looks as if some endogenous mechanism or possibly a central change in sensitivity to testosterone is producing these behavioural changes. We don't find any seasonal variations in endocrine state or behaviour in the captive talapoin, however.

Herbert: Talapoins have a definite breeding season in the wild.

Keverne: Yes. They are an equatorial species, however, so they experience no marked environment changes, unlike rhesus monkeys.

Crown: I have a methodological query. Those of us who work with people tend to accept the validity and reliability of the observations of animal experimenters somewhat uncritically, and I want to ask a general question. With observations of children, for example, it is difficult both to define the behaviour and to get reliable observations between observers. How do you approach this, in studying animals? For example, with the activity that you refer to as 'displace', do you decide in your laboratory what everyone means by it and observe how much you and your colleagues agree? And how do you communicate that to another laboratory, which might want to repeat the study, so they can be sure they are observing the same activity?

Keverne: Many behaviours such as mounting and ejaculation, inspection, attacks and threats, are all very clear. The one you mention, 'displace', is the one which is perhaps more uncertain. For example, even with the dominant male there are occasions when it looks as if he is showing withdrawal behaviour. We define the behaviour called 'displace' as one animal coming up to another and occupying its position, whether it pushes it out of the way or not. This may happen occasionally when the behaviour isn't 'intended' as an aggressive insult, but we still score it as such. To do otherwise would involve subjective interpretation. So there is some 'noise' in the system, but it is small when you get enormous changes like the ones I have described.

Crown: So these are not intrapsychic mechanisms? You are not saying that the animal wants to be aggressive but is forced to be permissive; it is not that kind of displacement activity?

Keverne: No; we only score what we observe. We try not to put a subjective interpretation on it.

Crown: Do different observers record these behaviours reliably and consistently?

Keverne: We have a training period where new observers sit and watch behaviour with someone experienced and they score it simultaneously, to get a correlation.

Goy: You remarked that the animals had lived together for some time. You then take the subordinate male out, put him in an individual cage and jazz him up so that he is now a cowboy, and his testosterone level goes up. What happens to him when you put him back in the group in that state?

Keverne: In fact, he stays in the group; we take the *other* males out. So he is alone in the group with the females, and his testosterone level goes up. Then we put the other males back and it falls.

Goy: Is he aggressive? Does he fight with those males?

Keverne: No; he knows his place! Learning plays a very important part here in determining dominance and subordination.

Goy: Have you any information on the intermediate-ranking males?

Keverne: I didn't present this information because it makes the picture more confusing, partly because intermediate monkeys are sometimes showing sexual behaviour and are also receiving aggressive behaviour. Their endocrine changes are not the same as those at the two extremes of dominance and subordination. It is less easy to dissect out the relevant behaviours and their influence on endocrine state for these intermediate males.

Goy: There is a lot of room in the middle in society, of course!

Keverne: But it is the extremes in society where most of the behavioural problems arise!

Sachar: One wonders what the subordinate monkeys get out of it all, however – no sex, and much aggression?

Keverne: In this laboratory situation the subordinate monkey certainly gets little in the way of sex and also experiences relatively high levels of aggressive behaviour, but I don't envisage precisely the same picture emerging in the natural environment of the forest canopy. Low-ranking individuals have the opportunity to seek consort relationships outside the sphere of the dominant male's influence and, furthermore, can avoid contact and frequent aggressive encounters. These laboratory conditions do not, therefore, attempt to emulate the feral situation but they do provide us with a primate model for investigating the interaction of certain behaviours with neuroendocrine status. In particular they allow us to examine the effects of social stress and anxiety on reproductive success and performance. While this may be a somewhat contrived situation from which subordinates have no escape, we should bear in mind that members of our own society also have to contend with social stresses from which they too have no escape. Such a primate model may well provide valuable insights into the behavioural and neuroendocrine consequences of social stress, anxiety and depression.

Pirke: What happens if you decrease the prolactin concentrations in male monkeys? Does the testosterone concentration increase, and how does this affect behaviour?

Keverne: We have some provisional observations on this. We have given bromocriptine to a male monkey with low plasma testosterone. His prolactin level went down markedly. Testosterone levels rose but we didn't see any change in behaviour. This was only done for a two-week period, however. I don't know whether behavioural changes would occur after a longer period. But certainly bromocriptine lowers prolactin levels and there is an increase in testosterone after that.

Green: I would like to ask about the temporal relationship between the rise in testosterone level and sexual behaviour. You draw your samples after copulation. Is there a way of introducing the animal to a receptive female, providing the opportunity for copulation, then withdrawing the male and taking the blood sample, to see whether it is anticipation or consummation that raises the level of testosterone?

Keverne: I think it requires a little more than just anticipation. When we have males alone in a cage and introduce females either with or without oestrogen but prevent male access to them, we don't see an increase in plasma testosterone. Only when males have access to the females does the testosterone level rise (Keverne *et al.* 1978). I conclude that the increases in testosterone are reflecting copulatory behaviour rather than determining it. But I think the significance or role of increases in testosterone level may be in terms of male attractiveness to females, because testosterone improves the sexual performance of the male, which makes him more attractive to the females.

Hutchison: Could you speculate on how androgens might make the male monkey more attractive? I am thinking particularly of a possible effect on attentional mechanisms, in view of the work by Andrew and his co-workers (see Andrew 1978). It could be that androgen makes the male attend more to the female's invitational gestures. Therefore, he is more attractive to her because he is looking at her more often or for longer periods.

Keverne: It is difficult experimentally to prove that it is specifically an increase in male attractiveness. Fig. 1 shows the 'attention structure' or visual monitoring of the dominant and subordinate male by females. We measure the looks given to the dominant male by females, which in turn give an indication of the female's interest in him. Females ovariectomized before being given oestrogen tend to look at the dominant male more than at the subordinate. When they are given oestrogen they increase their attention to the dominant male far more than to the subordinate, so the dominant male is now getting a higher proportion of the female's attention than before. Likewise, with ovariectomized females given oestrogen, their sexual invitations increase markedly to the dominant male and not at all to the subordinate male (Fig. 1, lower section).

As to *how* testosterone makes the male attractive, it seems to be primarily by influencing his behaviour – that is, his sexual performance. We took two dominant males, one intact and one castrated and receiving a testosterone implant. The intact dominant male can and does show an increase in testosterone levels whereas the castrate doesn't, being on constant testosterone replacement. If we compare mounts and ejaculations, 75% of mounts result in ejaculation in the intact male who experienced a testosterone increase. He receives high levels of sexual invitations. With the *same* females, the castrated dominant male (who didn't stay dominant for long) mounts the females but doesn't achieve ejaculation. He was a long-term castrate, which may have something to do with it, but the sexual invitations he received were not nearly so many as the same females gave to the intact male.

Some further evidence which may be more convincing is from a male in another group, when he was initially second-ranking and when he subsequently became first-ranking. When second-ranking, he was interested in the females, as witnessed by high levels of mounts, but achieved few ejaculations. This male received a reasonably high number of sexual invita-

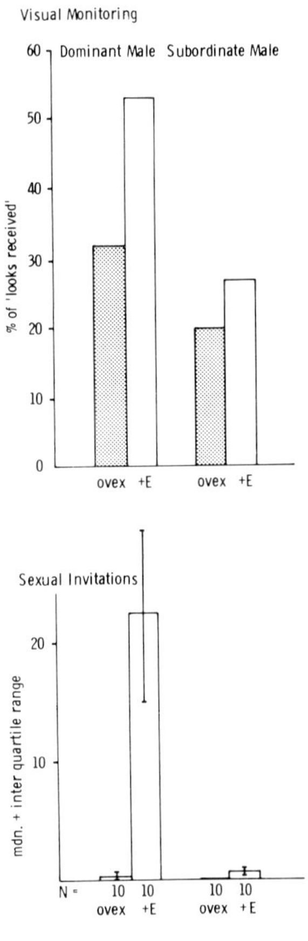

FIG. 1 (Keverne). Attention and sexual interest received by dominant and subordinate male talapoin monkeys in the group from all females, before (ovex) and after (+E) females were treated with oestrogen. Visual monitoring is expressed as % female 'looks' given to all males, and sexual interest as invitations to males.

tions. When he became first-ranking and experienced an increase in plasma testosterone, which he hadn't experienced before, the ratio of mounts to ejaculation went up to almost 100%. The same females now made many more sexual invitations to him.

Beach: Does physical interference by another male prevent the ejaculation?

Keverne: This was most certainly the case for this male when he was second-ranking. He would not mount a female in the presence of the dominant male; he tried to do it out of sight. So this represents a male showing fairly high levels of anxiety, if you like, because he is concerned about the high-ranking male.

Hutchison: Does the *male* pay more attention to the female under those conditions? It could be this attention which is making *him* more attractive to her?

Keverne: Yes, he does. But I am not sure whether visual monitoring is a two-way process. I am not convinced that the females are aware of it. I don't have evidence for that.

Beach: I don't understand why the castrate with the implant did not ejaculate. In most species, if you give enough testosterone this induces copulation, intromission and ejaculation.

Keverne: That may be exactly the reason – not 'enough' testosterone. He is initially receiving amounts of testosterone which mimic the levels a male shows *before* the increase, so he has the same testosterone levels as an intact male sitting alone in a cage. What the castrated male doesn't get is the surge or increase in testosterone which the intact male's testes produce. I suggest that the significance of the testosterone increase is that it improves sexual performance, which in turn makes him more attractive to females.

Sachar: You mean *after* the first copulation, because he doesn't get a rise in testosterone until he has copulated, according to your data? You are suggesting that he is more attractive the next time?

Keverne: Yes; the effect is over a period of time.

Sachar: Does this have anything to do with general secretions – pheromones?

Keverne: I don't think so.

Marteau: I am confused now, because from your paper I gathered that the most important part of the experiment was that you were able to show the way in which behaviour affected the hormonal balance in the animal; but now it is being suggested that it is the chemical which is affecting the behaviour.

Keverne: You are quite right that in my paper I showed that behaviour can influence the hormonal balance in the monkey. However, the question I have now posed, and attempted to answer, is whether such hormonal changes have any consequences for the behavioural interaction. I would like to suggest that they do, primarily in terms of making the dominant male more attractive to females. Taken simply, the behaviourally induced increase in testosterone could be viewed as a CNS-mediated event, with the increase in attractiveness being primarily a peripheral consequence of an increased testosterone concentration. In terms of sexual interactions, the latter will reinforce the former and hence be a less disruptive influence on the social organization than would be the case if females were to find the subordinate male more attractive and offered most of their sexual invitations to him.

Marteau: The second part of the experiment did in fact present you with a negative reinforcement of the first, that the hormone was unable to change the behaviour against the force of the social situation. Your experiment interested me greatly since it reflects vividly certain clinical situations in psychotherapy. I have had as patients women who seemed unable to conceive, even with hormonal help, and were in fact dynamically sub-dominant or subordinate characters within their own families. Their husbands were also. But once they had changed their attitudes, re-assessed themselves and become more dominant in the social situation, they became pregnant without any further problem. My question is that what you seem to be suggesting, or what seems to be accepted by endocrinologists, is that the answer to the problem is some form of chemical manipulation. But I would maintain that the chemical change is itself dependent on the social situation and on the feelings of the individual, and this is in fact what your experiment goes to validate.

Keverne: This may well be; but we haven't done that experiment. We were producing a neuroendocrine manipulation by altering prolactin levels. We were not affecting the behaviour as such. We should do that, as Dr Sachar suggested, by giving an anxiolytic drug.

Marteau: But manipulating behaviour is exactly what you have done.

Keverne: What we have done is taken out the subordinate female and put her on her own; her prolactin level has gone down and we are about to challenge her now with an oestrogen surge. By removing the female we have manipulated behavioural interactions. But it is very difficult to manipulate behaviour within the social situation, because of the learning factor. Although we can reduce prolactin in the subordinate female and artificially increase testosterone in the subordinate male, what we cannot easily do is make the animals forget all that they have learned about each other from their social interactions.

Marteau: It is a question of the chicken and the egg again.

Short: Can you tell us, Dr Keverne, about the rate of release of oestradiol from the implants in the ovariectomized females? How much oestradiol are they getting per day? And how long did you leave the implants in for? Did you notice any change in the behaviour of these females with time?

Keverne: The rate of release over a 24-hour period as assessed *in vitro* is about 5–6 μg. In the female the concentrations with one implant (about 1.5 cm of the standard silastic capsule) are equivalent to those in the follicular phase, about 200 pg/ml. We leave the implants in for a two- or three-week period. The data were collected at five periods during a year when they had implants.

Short: I was wondering whether your results could have been confounded by the effects we notice in red deer with long-duration treatment, where the behaviour gradually changes to a more male pattern; but if you remove the implants after 2–3 weeks there is no problem.

References

ABBOTT, D. H. & HEARN, J. P. (1978) Physical, hormonal and behavioural aspects of sexual development in the marmoset monkey, *Callithrix jacchus*. *J. Reprod. Fertil. 53,* 155–166

ANDREW, R. J. (1978) Increased persistence of attention produced by testosterone, and its implications for the study of sexual behaviour, in *Biological Determinants of Sexual Behaviour* (Hutchison, J. B., ed.), pp. 255–275, Wiley, Chichester

KEVERNE, E. B., MELLER, R. E. & MARTINEZ-ARIAS, A. (1978) Dominance, aggression and sexual behaviour in social groups of Talapoin monkeys, in *Recent Advances in Primatology,* vol.l: *Behaviour* (Chivers, D. J. & Herbert, J., eds.), pp. 533–548, Academic Press, London, New York and San Francisco

LUNN, S. F. (1978) Urinary oestrogen excretion in the common marmoset, *Callithrix jacchus,* in *The Biology of the Callitrichidae* (Rothe, H., Wolters, H. J. & Hearn, J. P., eds.), University of Göttingen Press, Göttingen, in press

MICHAEL, R. P. & WILSON, M. I. (1975) Mating seasonality in castrated male rhesus monkeys. *J. Reprod. Fertil. 43,* 325–328

MORTIMER, C. H., MCNEILLY, A. S., MURRAY, M. A. F., FISHER, R. A. F. & BESSER, G. M. (1974) Gonadotrophin releasing hormone therapy in hypogonadal males with hypothalamic pituitary dysfunction. *Br. Med. J. 4,* 617–621

MORTIMER, C. H., MCNEILLY, A. S. & BESSER, G. M. (1976) Gonadotrophin releasing hormone therapy. *Ann. Biol. Anim. Biochim. Biophys. 16,* 235–243

MOSS, R. L. & MCCANN, S. M. (1973) Induction of mating behavior in rats by luteinizing hormone-releasing factor. *Science (Wash. D.C.) 181,* 177–179

PFAFF, D. W. (1973) Luteinizing hormone-releasing factor potentiates lordosis behavior in hypophysectomized ovariectomized female rats. *Science (Wash. D.C.) 182,* 1148–1149

THARANDT, L., SCHULTE, H., BENKER, G., HACKENBERG, K. & REINWEIN, D. (1977) Treatment of isolated gonadotropin deficiency in men with synthetic LH-RH and a more potent analogue of LH-RH. *Neuroendocrinology 24,* 195–207

VAN LOON, G. R. & BROWN, G. N. (1975) Secondary drug failure occurring during chronic treatment with LH-RH: appearance of an antibody. *J. Clin. Endocrinol. Metab. 41,* 640

The effects of neonatal exposure to testosterone on the development of behaviour in female marmoset monkeys

DAVID H. ABBOTT and JOHN P. HEARN

MRC Unit of Reproductive Biology, Edinburgh

Abstract Experimental investigations of sexual differentiation in primates have been mainly confined to the rhesus monkey, a highly polygamous species with marked anatomical and behavioural sexual dimorphism. The marmoset is a monogamous monkey which shows little anatomical or behavioural sexual dimorphism, and both sexes exhibit positive feedback in response to the administration of oestradiol. This monkey has a relatively short gestation period of 144 days and usually gives birth to dizygotic twins. These share a common placental circulation and hence develop as haematopoietic chimaeras. However, a female with a male co-twin is not adversely affected as a result of this and the freemartin condition does not occur. Since the newborn male experiences raised testosterone levels soon after birth it is possible that the 'critical period' for sexual differentiation of the brain occurs after birth in the marmoset. Five female marmosets were implanted with 25 mg of testosterone for 50 days after birth. After removal of the implants their genitalia remained partly masculinized and they initiated more masculine rough-and-tumble play than their controls. After puberty they exhibited a mixture of male and female sexual behaviour when presented with unfamiliar normal males and females during 15-minute behavioural trials. Four of the implanted females have also ovulated. Neonatal administration of testosterone therefore has had an organizing effect on female behaviour. Whether the marmoset is exceptional in this respect, or whether other primates which exhibit a male neonatal testosterone surge, such as man and the rhesus monkey, also undergo some postnatal behavioural differentiation, remains to be seen.

INTRODUCTION

Administration of androgen to pregnant females during a critical stage of gestation has resulted in masculinization of the external genitalia and the Wolffian ducts of their female fetuses in many species, including rats (Greene *et al.* 1939), mice (Turner *et al.* 1939), hamsters (Bruner & Witschi 1946), guinea-pigs (Phoenix *et al.* 1959), dogs (Beach & Kuehn 1970), sheep (Short 1974), rhesus monkeys (Goy 1968) and humans (Wilkins *et al.* 1959). Behavioural masculinization, however, appears to occur later in gestation, as it was produced in response to prenatal androgenization only in animals with relatively long gestation periods, such as guinea-pigs (Phoenix *et al.* 1959), dogs (Beach & Kuehn 1970), sheep (Clarke 1976), rhesus monkeys (Goy & Resko 1972), and man (Money & Ehrhardt 1972). In species with relatively short gestation periods behavioural differentiation is affected by postnatal androgen treatment, as in rats (Harris 1964; Harris & Levine 1965), mice (Barraclough & Leathem 1954; Manning & McGill 1974) and hamsters (Swanson & Brayshaw 1973; DeBold & Whalen 1975). Furthermore, androgenized females in these latter species were rendered anovulatory in later life. In female rats this was attributed to an alteration in the hypothalamic control of gonadotropin release from the 'cyclic' pattern of the female to the 'tonic' pattern of the male (Barraclough & Gorski 1961). Hence, androgenization prevented these females from releasing an ovulatory discharge of gonadotropin in response to oestrogen feedback (Brown-Grant 1974). Normal female rats exhibit this positive feedback response, whereas normal males do not.

Paradoxically, neonatally administered oestrogen was found to be more effective than androgen in inducing sterility in genetically female rats (Gorski 1963; Harris & Levine 1965; Brown-Grant 1974). It was subsequently suggested that 'androgenization' of the hypothalamic centres controlling gonadotropin release was caused by aromatization of androgens to oestrogens within the brain cells (Reddy *et al.* 1974). This claim was supported by the greater aromatization capacity of hypothalamic tissue in neonatal male rats than in females (Reddy *et al.* 1974) and the failure of a non-aromatizable androgen, dihydrotestosterone, to induce the anovulatory condition in female rats (Whalen & Luttge 1971; Korenbrot *et al.* 1975). Further evidence for the lack of direct effects of androgen on the hypothalamus stems from the human. Genetic males suffering from the testicular feminization syndrome possess testes but develop phenotypically as females (Morris 1953). Their intra-abdominal testes secrete normal amounts of testosterone (Jeffcoate *et al.* 1968), but all their tissues are insensitive to it. Yet, when two such patients were examined, neither exhibited the positive feedback response to oestradiol administration characteristic of normal women (Van Look *et al.* 1977), suggesting that the hypothalamus had been masculinized in spite of the androgen insensitivity. However, it is interesting that the sexual behaviour of testicular feminization patients does not appear to differ from that of normal women (Masica *et al.* 1971).

The administration of oestrogen to neonatal female rats was also successful in inducing masculinized behaviour (Harris & Levine 1965; Whalen & Edwards 1967), whereas treatment with the non-aromatizable dihydrotestosterone was unable to masculinize the behaviour of female hamsters (Payne 1976). However, genetically female rhesus monkey fetuses were as effectively masculinized behaviourally by dihydrotestosterone as by testosterone (Goy *et al.* 1977). So apparently in the rhesus monkey, and maybe in the human, androgens can have a direct effect on the behavioural centres of the brain without first being converted into oestrogen. A further difference arises between rodents on the one hand, and primates like the rhesus monkey (Goy & Resko 1972) and man (Wilkins *et al.* 1955) on the other, because androgenization of female primate fetuses does not induce the anovulatory syndrome in adulthood. Nevertheless, the behaviour of these androgenized primates was as effectively masculinized as that of the rodents. Hence behavioural masculinization would appear to occur independently of hypothalamic sexual differentiation in some mammals.

In primates, experimental investigations of sexual differentiation have been mainly confined to the rhesus monkey (Goy & Resko 1972; Goy *et al.* 1977). This monkey is a highly polygamous species with marked anatomical and behavioural sexual dimorphism. The common marmoset, on the other hand, is an example of a monogamous monkey which exhibits little anatomical or behavioural dimorphism. Female marmosets neither menstruate (Hearn & Renfree 1975) nor show any physical signs of oestrus, but are spontaneous ovulators with a cycle length of 16.4 ± 1.7 days (Hearn & Lunn 1975). Both intact adult males and females exhibit a positive feedback response of luteinizing hormone (LH) to oestradiol administration (Hodges & Hearn 1978). These monkeys also have a relatively short gestation period of 144 days and usually give birth to dizygotic twins (Hearn *et al.* 1978). The twin embryos establish vascular anastomoses between their placental circulations within a few days of implantation (Wislocki 1939), and hence they develop as haematopoietic chimaeras (Benirschke & Brownhill 1962; Benirschke *et al.* 1962; Gengozian *et al.* 1964). Nevertheless females born chimaeric to their male co-twins are not adversely affected as a result of this: the freemartin condition does not occur (Wislocki 1939; Benirschke & Layton 1969), their ovaries and genital tract are normal, and there is no evidence of hypertrophy of any Wolffian duct derivatives (Wislocki 1939). These females also copulate and breed normally (Abbott & Hearn, unpublished observations). In other primates, such as the rhesus monkey (Resko 1974) and the human (Abramovich & Rowe 1973), normal male fetuses experience increased concentrations of plasma testosterone during early to mid-gestation, when sexual differentiation might be occurring. Rhesus monkey (Robinson & Bridson 1978) and human males (Forest *et al.* 1973, 1974) also show a brief elevation of testosterone levels neonatally. As yet we have no information on blood testosterone in early male marmoset fetuses, but the newborn male experiences raised levels of plasma testosterone soon after birth (Abbott & Hearn 1978), and the female does not. It is therefore possible that this monkey has delayed the sexual differentiation of its brain until after birth. In order to discover whether neonatal androgen treatment could influence sexual differentiation we implanted newborn female marmosets with testosterone and observed the effects on their external genitalia and their playful and sexual behaviour.

MATERIALS AND METHODS

Animals

Details of the management of the common marmoset *(Callithrix jacchus jacchus)* have been fully described elsewhere (Hearn *et al.* 1975). Animals were kept in natural light supplemented with artificial illumination between 07.00 and 19.00 hours.

Testosterone treatment

Five female marmosets were each subcutaneously implanted one to four days after birth with 25 mg of crystalline testosterone. The implants were inserted through a ventrolateral incision in the abdominal region and were removed fifty days later. The animals were given a local anaesthetic on both occasions (0.2 ml 'Lidothesin', 1% (10 mg/ml) plain. Lignocaine hydrochloride B.P.; Pharmaceutical Manufacturing Co. Ltd) and their co-twins or triplets were sham-operated in a similar manner (Table 1), but no implant was inserted. Pairs of animals in male–female (n = 8), male–male (n = 3) and female–female (n = 3) twin sets were also used as non-experimental controls.

When the implants were removed they were dried in an oven at 70 °C for 24 hours. Their weights were then compared with those obtained before implantation. The total dosage of testosterone received by each animal was calculated (Table 1) and, assuming a constant release of testosterone, the daily dosage was expressed in terms of mg/kg body weight.

TABLE 1

Age, body weight and total dosage of testosterone received in implanted female marmosets with their respective co-twin or triplet controls

Family	*Implanted females*			*Sham-operated controls*	
	Age (days)	*Body weight (g)*	*Total dosage of testosterone (mg)*	*Animals*	*Body weight (g)*
1	4-53[a]	30-90	-[a]	female[c]	29-68
2	1-51	30-60[d]	14.8	female[c], female[e,f]	28-69, 30-68
3	4-55[b]	30-97	14.9	female[e]	31-[c]
4	2-52	30-96	14.3	female[f]	32-100
5	4-54	32-91	16.5	female[e],male[f,c]	29-[e], 27-80

[a] Implanted for 49 days; implant lost *in situ*.
[b] Implanted for 51 days.
[c] Sham-operated only at implant removal.
[d] Only triplets to survive, hence reduced body weight.
[e] Died before puberty.
[f] Died after puberty.

Blood sampling

Blood samples of 0.3 ml were taken from the femoral vein using a heparinized syringe and a 0.41 mm diameter needle (27 gauge). All samples were taken between 09.30 and 12.30 hours and immediately placed on ice. The blood was centrifuged at 500 ***g*** for 20 min at 4°C and the plasma stored at −20 °C until assayed. Animals under 100 days of age were bled at 10–20 day intervals and at 50–100 day intervals thereafter. Androgenized females between 400–600 days of age were bled at 2–3 day intervals for two months on at least two occasions to see if they showed any ovulatory activity (progesterone concentration of $\geq$ 20 ng/ml). This frequency of sampling was sufficient to detect the luteal phase of the ovarian cycle, which normally lasts for 10–12 days (Hearn & Lunn 1975).

Hormone assays

All samples were assayed in duplicate. Plasma testosterone concentrations were measured by the specific radioimmunoassay of Corker & Davidson (1978). This assay cross-reacts 23.9% with 5α-dihydrotestosterone and by < 0.4% with all other androgens and oestrogens tested. The inter- and intra-assay variation was 12.0 and 4.5% respectively, with a detection limit of 1 ng/ml. Plasma progesterone concentrations were determined using the radioimmunoassay described by Neal *et al.* (1975). The inter- and intra-assay variation was 11.3 and 4.2% respectively, with a detection limit of 2 ng/ml.

Behavioural observations

The animals were all left with their families, which usually consisted of the parents and an older or younger set of twins, until puberty (at 400–500 days of age). Every experimental or control twin (or triplet) was observed in its family group for a total of 90 minutes at five different ages: 40–50 days (when the implants were in place), and 80–100, 150–180, 250–280 and 350–400 days (when the implants had been removed). Usually three observations were made at every age, with one in each of the three periods of the day ('morning', 09.30–12.00 hours; 'mid-day', 12.00–14.30 hours; 'afternoon', 14.30–18.00 hours). Each observation was made on a different day and the observation times were chosen to avoid disturbing the colony maintenance routine and to minimize diurnal variations in behaviour. Normally the animals were active from 05.30–07.00 hours until 18.00–19.00 hours, but they usually showed a period of inactivity of 0.5–2.0 hours between 11.30 and 15.00 hours.

During puberty (400–500 days of age) the twins were removed from their families and separated into peer groups (usually consisting of three males and three females). Each group was observed during the first two days after the animals were placed together and again 2–3 months later (Abbott & Hearn 1978). The dominance order in every group was assessed by scoring the dominant–subordinate interactions between pairs of animals (Abbott & Hearn 1978). A set of androgenized females (n = 5), normal females (n = 5) and normal males (n = 5) were then all observed in randomized combinations of unfamiliar pairs of animals. Each pair was observed for 15 minutes between 09.30 and 16.30 hours and neither animal was observed in any further trials for at least two hours.

The animals in family groups and unfamiliar pairs were observed through a one-way mirror in an observation room of 2.1 × 2.4 × 2.2 m fitted with branches. Their behaviour was coded onto magnetic tape by a computerized keyboard modified from Dawkins (1971). The peer groups were observed, directly, in an exercise cage of 2.0 × 1.0 × 2.0 m, connected by flexible ducting to their home cage of 1.0 × 0.5 × 0.75 m (Hearn *et al.* 1975). Cage sizes were identical in each of the four rooms used. Behaviour was recorded in abbreviated notes.

Behavioural categories

For the purposes of this study, the following behavioural categories were used:

Social play

Rough-and-tumble: contact play involving the most aggressive elements of marmoset play behaviour, including wrestling, grasping and inhibited biting, and hitting of the upper parts of the playmate's body with the arms or hands.

Aggression and submission

Threaten and pursue: one animal closely followed another while issuing vocal treats ('erh-erh'; Stevenson & Poole 1976).

Submission: animals displayed submissive vocalization, flattened their ear tufts, or fled from the proximity of another animal (Abbott & Hearn 1978).

Sexual behaviour

Pursuit courtship: one animal closely followed another, displaying rhythmical tonguing and lipsmacking.

Passive courtship: the animal remained almost stationary and displayed tonguing and lipsmacking movements accompanying nuzzling, licking and rubbing of the partner's head, face and body.

Head turning: the female turned her head backwards over her shoulder while being courted or mated.

Lordosis: the female remained motionless apart from head-turning, tonguing, lipsmacking and nuzzling movements.

Accept mount: the female displayed no active physical or vocal objection within 2–3 seconds of being mounted.

Attack, attempt mount, mount and *pelvic thrusting* are self-explanatory.

Play analysis

The rough-and-tumble play between the twins under observation was quantitatively assessed after each observation (the surviving triplet control was not included). The total rough-and-tumble initiated by one twin was subtracted from the total rough-and-tumble initiated by the other. The resulting positive or negative differences ($\pm\Delta$ R) from every observation were then analysed using the Sign test (one-tailed; Siegel 1956) and zero values were ignored. A positive value ($+\Delta$ R) was given to the twin which accumulated the largest number of differences by initiating more rough-and-tumble play than its co-twin in a larger number of observations. The negative value ($-\Delta$ R) was assigned to the other twin.

Behavioural trial analysis

The numbers of normal males, androgenized females and normal females displaying each behaviour were compared by using Fisher's Exact Test (Siegel 1956).

RESULTS

Testosterone dosage

The implanted females were exposed to testosterone doses of between 3 and 10 mg/kg body weight per day. The large variation in dose was due to the rapid growth of these animals, but they did not exceed the weight of their controls (Table 1). Circulating concentrations of testosterone were maintained at about 100 ng/ml in implanted females and these concentrations fell below the sensitivity limit of the assay when the implants were removed. Plasma testosterone concentrations in control females remained immeasurable throughout.

Effects of neonatal testosterone on female genitalia

By 40–50 days after implantation the clitoris of the androgenized females had become significantly hypertrophied and masculine scrotal and pudendal pad swelling was very marked (Fig. 1). The vaginal opening was obscured by the folds of the glandular pudendal pad but was not obstructed. In comparison, in a normal male of this age the penis was still concealed inside the prepuce. The scrotum was well defined but poorly developed and the testes were usually undescended. In a normal female the external genitalia were not grossly different from those of the normal male, and the clitoris and vaginal opening were tiny and obscured by the labia.

At 350 days of age, 300 days after the implants were removed, the androgenized females still possessed genitalia that were intermediate between those of a normal male and a normal female (Fig. 2). The androgenized females

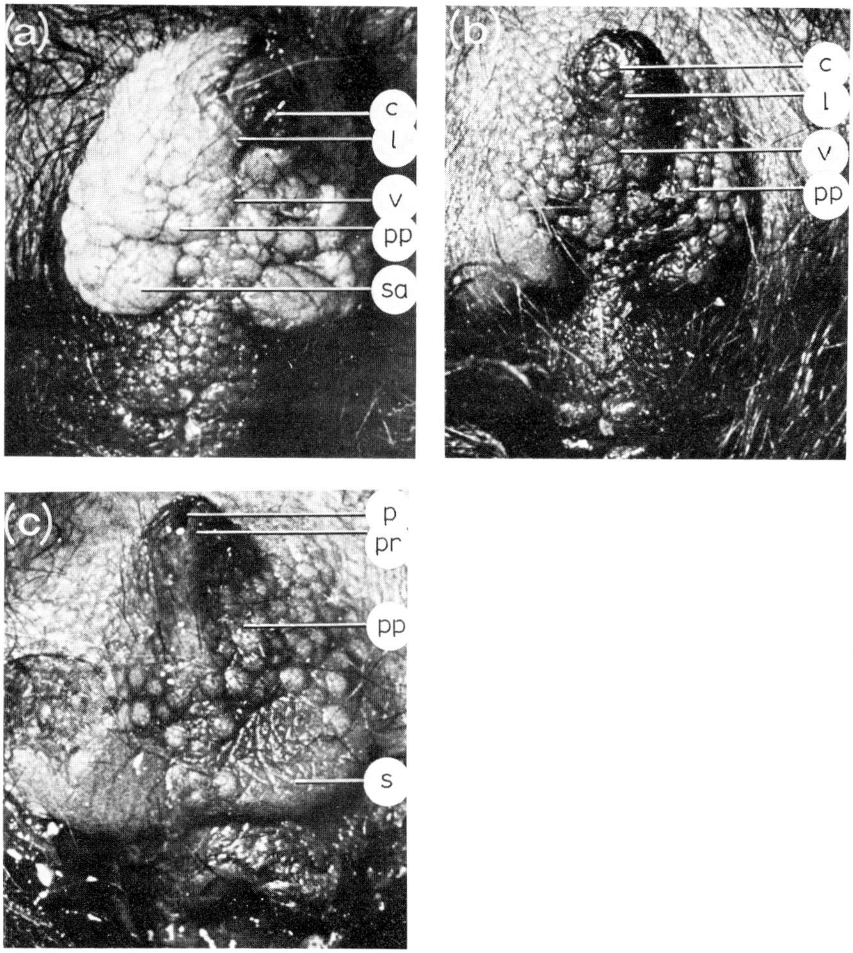

FIG. 1. The external genitalia of an androgenized female marmoset compared to those of the normal female and male at 50 days of age (× 6.4).

(*a*) The perineal area of an androgenized female showing the hypertrophied clitoris (c) protruding between the labia (1), the vaginal opening (v), the pudendal pad (pp) and the swollen but empty scrotal area (sa).

(*b*) The perineal area of a normal female showing the clitoris (c) obscured by the labia (1), the vaginal opening (v), and the pudendal pad (pp).

(*c*) The perineal area of a normal male showing the penis (p) obscured by the prepuce (pr), the pudendal pad (pp) and the empty scrotum (s).

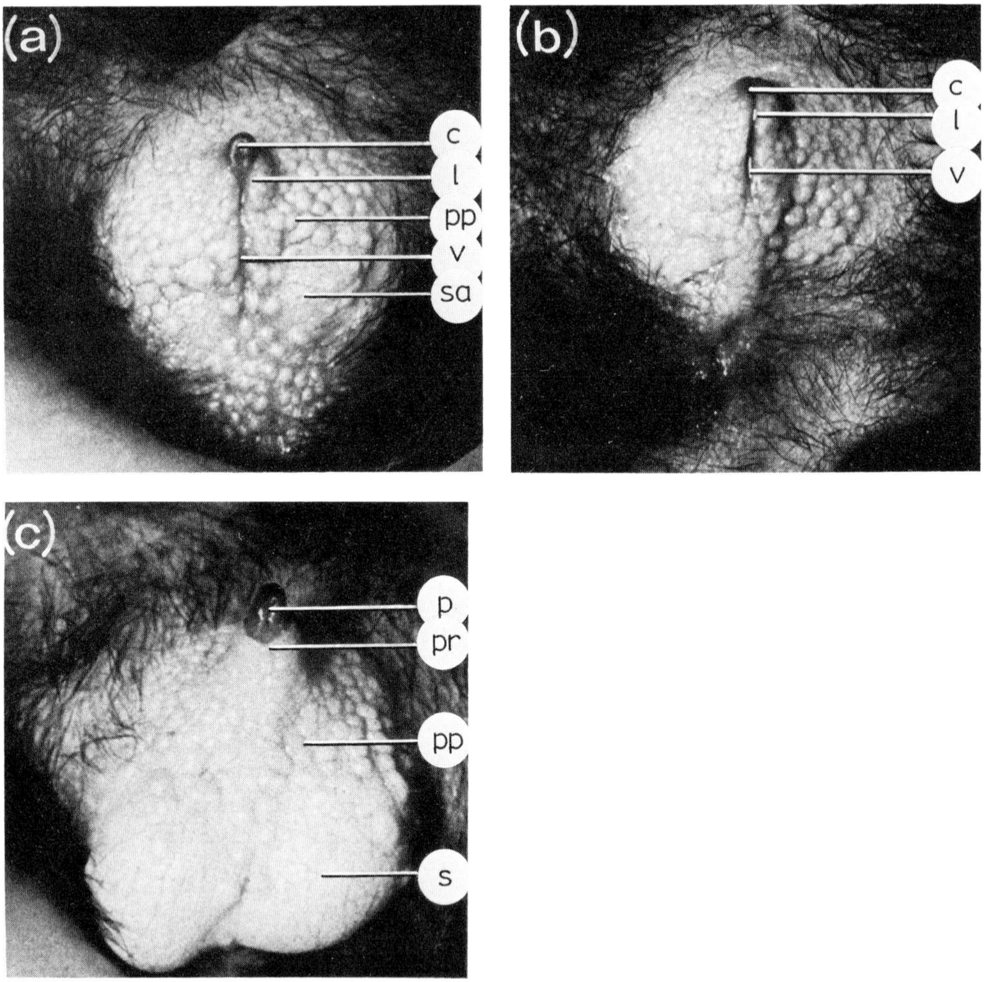

FIG. 2. The external genitalia of an androgenized female, 300 days after removal of the implant, compared to those of the normal female and male at 350 days of age (× 1.8).

(*a*) The perineal area of an androgenized female showing the hypertrophied clitoris (c), still protruding between the labia (l), the vaginal opening (v), the pudendal pad (pp) and the slight swelling of the empty scrotal area (sa).

(*b*) The perineal area of a normal female showing the clitoris (c) obscured by the labia (l) and the vaginal opening (v).

(*c*) The perineal area of a normal male showing the penis (p) protruding through the prepuce (pr), the pudendal pad (pp) and the well-developed scrotum (s) containing testes.

displayed a hypertrophied clitoris and some swelling of the empty scrotal area below the pudendal pad. The control females showed none of these features and the maturing male now possessed a well-developed penis and scrotum into which the testes had descended. The genitalia of the androgenized females did not subsequently change their appearance.

The effects of neonatal testosterone administration on female prepubertal behaviour

Sexual behaviour among young marmosets in family groups is rare (Rothe 1975; Abbott 1978*a*). However, social play is a frequent activity. In normal male–female twin pairs, males initiated more rough-and-tumble play than females when the twins played with each other (Table 2). In male–male and female–female twin pairs there was no difference in the amount of rough-and-tumble play initiated between each twin. Nevertheless, androgenized females with female co-twin controls initiated much more of the rough-and-tumble play, similar to the situation in normal male–female twin sets. Yet, on the one occasion when the control twin was male, the androgenized female did not initiate significantly more rough-and-tumble play.

TABLE 2

Analysis of rough-and-tumble play between marmoset co-twins in their family groups (A, androgenized; C, control; N, non-experimental)

Treatment	*Animal*	*Δ R sign*	*No. of twin sets*	*Δ R* +	*Δ R* −	*Total Δ R*
Testosterone implant	Female A Female C	+ −	4	27***	1	28[a]
Testosterone implant	Female A Male C	+ −	1	4	2	6
No implant	Male N Female N	+ −	8	21*	8	29
No implant	Male N Female N	+ −	3	5	3	8
No implant	Female N Female N	+ −	3	6	5	11

*$P < 0.02$, ***$P < 0.001$.
[a] Triplet not included.

The effects of neonatal testosterone on female sexual behaviour

During puberty, four out of five of the androgenized females ovulated, as indicated by their high concentrations of plasma progesterone ($\geq$ 20 ng/ml). However, when housed in peer groups, three out of the five initially displayed components of male sexual behaviour. All three displayed pursuit courtship towards normal males and females, one violently attacked and pursued any male attempting to mount her, and one also attempted to mount normal males and females. Subsequently, two of these three animals became the dominant females in their groups and formed a 'pair bond' with the dominant male in their group. The dominant male and female in a group normally form a pair bond, and this is usually expressed (in qualitative terms) by the two animals frequently remaining within arm's length of each other ($\leq$ 10 cm), following each other, huddling together and exhibiting intimate social grooming, courtship and copulatory behaviour. The remaining three androgenized females ranked as subordinate to the dominant female in their group and displayed no further sexual behaviour.

In the behavioural tests using pairs of animals, normal males displayed masculine copulatory and courtship behaviour and did not display any female courtship or copulatory behaviour (Fig. 3). Normal females showed feminine copulatory and courtship behaviour and only one displayed the pursuit courtship usually observed in males. Androgenized females, on the other hand, displayed components from both male and female sexual behavioural repertoires. Yet, when compared with normal males, significantly fewer exhibited pelvic thrusting behaviour and, unlike normal females, none of the androgenized females accepted any mounts (Fig. 3). Aggressive behaviour was not a sexually dimorphic characteristic in this monkey (Fig. 3), and passive courtship was also displayed by both sexes.

DISCUSSION

This is the first report of an effect of neonatal androgenization on behaviour in a primate. Female rhesus monkeys treated with 2 mg testosterone propionate, three times per week between 6.5 and 14.5 months of age, failed to show any signs of behavioural masculinization (Joslyn 1973), and only female rhesus monkeys treated with androgen before birth developed masculinized behaviour (Goy *et al.* 1977). However, the newborn male rhesus and pig-tailed macaque (Robinson & Bridson 1978), human (Forest *et al.* 1973, 1974) and marmoset (Abbott & Hearn 1978) all experience elevated concen-

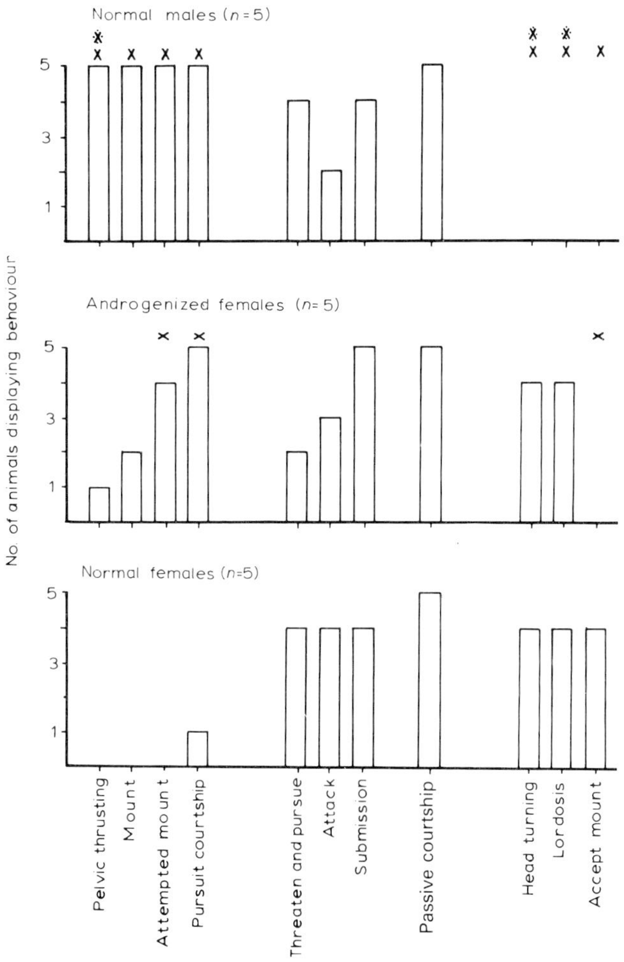

FIG. 3. Masculine and feminine behaviour displayed by normal male, androgenized female and normal female marmosets during 102 15-min trials. Significant differences ($P<0.05$) were found between (**X**) normal males and normal females, (**X̣**) normal males and androgenized females, and (**×**) normal females and androgenized females.

trations of plasma testosterone. Perhaps all these primates undergo some sexual differentiation in the immediate postnatal period, although this remains to be demonstrated.

The prepubertal rough-and-tumble play of androgenized female marmosets in female–female twin pairs was enhanced to an extent normally found in males in male–female twin pairs (Table 2), suggesting that neonatal exposure to testosterone had had some organizing effect on female behaviour. The fact that the normal male shows more of the aggressive elements in play than the female has been previously found in pubertal male marmosets (Abbott 1978*b*) and in many other male primates, such as rhesus monkeys (Mason 1960; Harlow & Harlow 1965; Goy & Resko 1972; Brandt & Mitchell 1973), baboons (De Vore 1963; Ransom & Rowell 1972), talapoin monkeys (Wolfheim 1977), vervet monkeys (Lancaster 1971), squirrel monkeys (Baldwin 1969), crab-eating macaques and patas monkeys (Seay *et al.* 1972), chimpanzees and orang utans (Nadler & Braggio 1974), and the human (Davenport 1965; Brindley *et al.* 1973; Blurton-Jones & Konner 1973).

Subsequently, in the behavioural trials, the androgenized female marmosets exhibited masculinized sexual behaviour, though not to the degree observed in normal males (Fig. 3). In addition, the androgenized females also showed normal female sexual responses, indicating that masculinization of their sexual behaviour could occur without defeminization. In rats (Clemens *et al.* 1969), hamsters (Payne 1976), dogs (Beach & Kuehn 1970) and sheep (Clarke 1976) androgenized females can also show enhanced masculine behaviour without the loss of their feminine sexual responses. Hence, as Beach *et al.* (1972) proposed, masculinization and defeminization of behaviour by androgen treatment are two distinctly separate processes and are not mutually inclusive. Yet the differences in sexual responses between normal male and female marmosets and androgenized females may not be exclusively due to the behavioural organizing effect of neonatal testosterone. The neonatal testosterone may have simply altered the hormonal state of the androgenized females by affecting ovarian, hypothalamic, pituitary or adrenal function, which in turn could be partly or wholly responsible for their altered behaviour. In agreement with the results from androgenized fetal or neonatal female rhesus monkeys (Goy & Resko 1972; Treloar *et al.* 1972) and humans (Wilkins *et al.* 1955; Polishuk & Anteby 1971), androgenized female marmosets did not develop the anovulatory syndrome in later life. In the marmoset this was understandable, since intact adult males and females retain the positive feedback response of luteinizing hormone to oestradiol administration (Hodges & Hearn 1978).

Aggression is also not a sexually dimorphic trait in the marmoset (Fig. 3), which is perhaps related to monogamy. In the polygamous rhesus monkey, males and androgenized females displayed more aggression than normal females (Goy & Resko 1972), and androgenized females began to develop some of the males' larger size by increasing their body weight (Wilen *et al.* 1977); they also showed delayed menarche (Goy & Resko 1972). Since there is no sex dimorphism in body size in marmosets, another consequence of monogamy (Short 1977), it was not surprising to find no effect of androgenization on the body weight of female marmosets (Table 1). It was not possible to ascertain whether androgenization delayed puberty, as this would have required serial determinations of progesterone throughout the pubertal period.

In conclusion, the marmoset monkey has much to offer as an experimental primate model for the investigation of behaviour. Its monogamous social structure may resemble the human norm of serial monogamy (Short 1976) more closely than does the extreme polygamy of the rhesus monkey.

ACKNOWLEDGEMENTS

We thank Professor R. V. Short for his criticism of the manuscript and Mr F. J. Burden and Miss C. Malcolm for care and maintenance of the animals.

References

ABBOTT, D. H. (1978*a*) The physical, hormonal and behavioural development of the common marmoset, *Callithrix jacchus jacchus,* in *The Biology of the Callitrichidae* (Rothe, H., Wolter, H.J. & Hearn, J.P., eds.), University of Göttingen Press, Göttingen, in press

ABBOTT, D. H. (1978*b*) Hormones and behaviour during puberty in the marmoset, in *Recent Advances in Primatology,* vol. 1: *Behaviour* (Chivers, D. J. & Herbert, J., eds.), pp. 497–499, Academic Press, London

ABBOTT, D. H. & HEARN J. P. (1978) Physical, hormonal and behavioural aspects of sexual development in the marmoset monkey, *Callithrix jacchus. J. Reprod. Fertil. 53,* 155–166

ABRAMOVICH, D. R. & ROWE, P. (1973) Foetal plasma testosterone levels at mid-pregnancy and at term: relationship to foetal sex. *J. Endocrinol. 56,* 621–622

BALDWIN, J. D. (1969) The ontogeny of social behaviour of squirrel monkeys *(Saimiri sciureus)* in a seminatural environment. *Folia Primatol. 11,* 35–79

BARRACLOUGH, C. A. & GORSKI, R. A. (1961) Evidence that the hypothalamus is responsible for androgen induced sterility in the female rat. *Endocrinology 68,* 68–79

BARRACLOUGH, C. A. & LEATHEM, J. H. (1954) Infertility induced in mice by a single injection of testosterone propionate. *Proc. Soc. Exp. Biol. Med. 85,* 673–674

BEACH, F. A. & KUEHN, R. E. (1970) Coital behaviour in dogs. X. Effects of androgenic stimulation during development on feminine mating response in females and males. *Horm. Behav. 1,* 347–367

BEACH, F. A., KUEHN, R. E., SPRAGUE, R. H. & ANISKO, J. J. (1972) Coital behaviour in dogs. XI. Effects of androgenic stimulation during development on masculine mating response in females. *Horm. Behav. 3,* 143–168

BENIRSCHKE, K. & BROWNHILL, L. E. (1962) Further observations on marrow chimerism in marmosets. *Cytogenetics 1,* 245–257

BENIRSCHKE, K. & LAYTON, W. (1969) An early twin blastocyst of the golden lion marmoset, *Leontocebus rosalia L. Folia Primatol. 10,* 131–138

BENIRSCHKE, K., ANDERSON, J. M. & BROWNHILL, L. E. (1962) Marrow chimerism in marmosets. *Science (Wash.D.C.) 138,* 513–515

BLURTON-JONES, N. G. & KONNER, M. J. (1973) Sex differences in behaviour of London and Bushmen children, in *Comparative Ecology and Behaviour of Primates* (Michael, R.P. & Crook, J.H., eds.), pp. 689–750, Academic Press, London

BRANDT, E. M. & MITCHELL, G. (1973) Pairing pre-adolescents with infants. *Dev. Psychol. 8,* 222–228

BRINDLEY, C. P., CLARKE, P., HUTT, C., ROBINSON, I. & WETHLI, E. (1973) Sex differences in the activities and social interactions of nursery school children, in *Comparative Ecology and Behaviour of Primates* (Michael, R.P. & Crook, J.H., eds.), pp. 799–828, Academic Press, London

BROWN-GRANT, K. (1974) Steroid hormone administration and gonadotrophin secretion in the gonadectomized rat. *J. Endocrinol.62,* 319–332

BRUNER, J. A. & WITSCHI, E. (1946) Testosterone induced modifications of sex development in female hamsters. *Am. J. Anat. 79,* 293–219

CLARKE, I. J. (1976) *The Effects of Prenatal Testosterone on Reproductive Patterns in Ewes.* Ph. D. Thesis, University of Edinburgh

CLEMENS, L. G., HIROI, M. & GORSKI, R. A. (1969) Induction and facilitation of female mating behaviour in rats treated neonatally with low doses of testosterone propionate. *Endocrinology 84,* 1420–1438

CORKER, C. S. & DAVIDSON, D. W. (1978) Radioimmunoassay of testosterone in various biological fluids. *J. Steroid Biochem., 9,* 373–374

DAVENPORT, W. (1965) Sexual patterns and their regulation in a society of the Southwest Pacific, in *Sex and Behavior* (Beach, F. A., ed.), pp. 164–207, Wiley, New York

DAWKINS, R. (1971) A cheap method of recording behavioural events for direct computer access. *Behaviour 40,* 162–173

DEBOLD, J. F. & WHALEN, R. E. (1975) Differential sensitivity of mounting and lordosis control systems to early androgen treatment in male and female hamsters. *Horm. Behav. 6,* 197–209

DEVORE, I. (1963) Mother-infant behaviour in baboons, in *Maternal Behaviour in Mammals* (Rheingold, H. C., ed.), pp. 305–335, Wiley, New York

FOREST, M. G., CATHIARD, A. M. & BERTRAND, J. A. (1973) Evidence of testicular activity in early infancy. *J. Clin. Endocrinol. Metab. 37,* 148–151

FOREST, M. G., SIZONENKO, P. C., CATHIARD, A. M. & BERTRAND, J. (1974) Hypophyso-gonadal function in humans during the first year of life. I. Evidence for testicular activity in early infancy. *J. Clin. Invest. 53,* 819–828

GENGOZIAN, N., BATSON, J. S. & EIDE, P. (1964) Hematologic and cytogenetic evidence for chimerism in the marmoset, *Tamarinus nigricollis. Cytogenetics 3,* 384–393

GREENE, R. R., BURRELL, M. W. & IVY, A. C. (1939) Experimental intersexuality. The effect of antenatal androgens on sexual development in female rats. *Am. J. Anat. 65,* 415–469

GORSKI, R. A. (1963) Modification of ovulatory mechanisms by postnatal administration of oestrogen to the rat. *Am. J. Physiol. 205,* 842–844

GOY, R. W. (1968) Organizing effects of androgen on the behaviour of rhesus monkeys, in *Endocrinology and Human Behaviour* (Michael R.P., ed.), pp. 12–31, Oxford University Press, London

GOY, R. W. & RESKO, J. A. (1972) Gonadal hormones and behaviour of normal and pseudohermaphroditic non-human female primates. *Recent Prog. Horm. Res. 28,* 707–733

GOY, R. W., WOLF, J. E. & EISELE, S. G. (1977) Experimental female hermaphroditism in rhesus monkeys: anatomical and psychological characteristics, in *Handbook of Sexology* (Money, J. & Musaph, H., eds.), pp. 139–156, Elsevier/North-Holland, Amsterdam

HARLOW, H. F. & HARLOW, M. K. (1965) The affectional systems, in *Behaviour of Non-human Primates* (Schrier, A. M., Harlow, H. F. & Stollintz, F., eds.), pp. 287–334, Academic Press, New York

HARRIS, G. W. (1964) Sex hormones, brain development and brain function. *Endocrinology 75,* 627–648

HARRIS, G. W. & LEVINE, S. (1965) Sexual differentiation of the brain and its experimental control. *J. Physiol. (Lond.) 181,* 379–400

HEARN, J. P. & LUNN, S. F. (1975) The reproductive biology of the marmoset monkey, *Callithrix jacchus,* in *Breeding Simians for Developmental Biology (Laboratory Animals Handbook* vol. 6) (Perkins, F. T. & O'Donoghue, P. N., eds.), pp. 191–202, Laboratory Animals, London

HEARN, J. P. & RENFREE, M. B. (1975) Prealbumins in the vaginal flushings of the marmoset, *Callithrix jacchus. J. Reprod. Fertil. 43,* 159–161

HEARN, J. P., LUNN, S. F., BURDEN, F. J. & PILCHER, M. M. (1975) Management of marmosets for biomedical research. *Lab. Anim. 9,* 125–134

HEARN, J. P., ABBOTT, D. H., CHAMBERS, P. C., HODGES, J. K. & LUNN, S. F. (1978) The use of the common marmoset, *Callithrix jacchus,* in reproductive research, in *Marmosets in Experimental Medicine* (Gengozian, N. & Deinhardt, F., eds.) *(Primates in Medicine 10,* Goldsmith, E.I. & Moor-Jankowski, J., eds.), pp. 40–49, Karger, Basle

HODGES, J. K. & HEARN, J.P. (1978) A positive feedback effect of oestradiol on luteinizing hormone release in the male marmoset monkey, *Callithrix jacchus. J. Reprod. Fertil. 52,* 83–86

JEFFCOATE, S. L., BROOKS, R.V. & PRUNTY, F.T.G. (1968) Secretion of androgens and oestrogens in testicular feminisation: studies *in vivo* and *in vitro* in two cases. *Br. Med. J. 1,* 208–210

JOSLYN, W. D. (1973) Androgen-induced social dominance in infant female rhesus monkeys. *J. Child Psychol. Psychiatr. 14,* 137–145

KORENBROT, C. C., PAUP, D. C. & GORSKI, R. A. (1975) Effects of testosterone propionate or dihydrotestosterone propionate on plasma FSH and LH levels in neonatal rats and on sexual differentiation. *Endocrinology 97,* 709–717

LANCASTER, J. B. (1971) Play mothering: the relations between juvenile female and young infants among free-ranging vervet monkeys *(Cercopithecus aethiops). Folia Primatol. 15,* 161–182

MANNING, A. & MCGILL, T. E. (1974) Neonatal androgen and sexual behaviour in female house mice. *Horm. Behav. 5,* 19–31

MASICA, D. N., MONEY, J. & EHRHARDT, A. A. (1971) Fetal feminization and female gender identity in the testicular feminizing syndrome of androgen insensitivity. *Arch. Sex. Behav. 3,* 143–149

MASON, W. A. (1960) The effects of social restriction on the behaviour of rhesus monkeys. I. Free social behaviour. *J. Comp. Physiol. Psychol. 53,* 582–589

MONEY, J. & EHRHARDT, A. A. (1972) *Man and Woman, Boy and Girl: The Differentiation and Dimorphism of Gender Identity from Conception to Maturity,* The Johns Hopkins University Press, Baltimore

MORRIS, J. M. (1953) The syndrome of testicular feminisation in male pseudohermaphrodites. *Am. J. Obstet. Gynecol. 65,* 1192–1211

NADLER, R. D. & BRAGGIO, J. T. (1974) Sex and species differences in captive-reared juvenile chimpanzees and orang-utans. *J. Hum. Evol. 3,* 541–550

NEAL, P., BAKER, T. G., MCNATTY, K. P. & SCARAMUZZI, R. J. (1975) Influence of prostaglandins and human chorionic gonadotrophin on progesterone concentration and oocyte maturation in mouse ovarian follicles maintained in organ culture. *J. Endocrinol. 65,* 19–25

PAYNE, A. P. (1976) A comparison of the effects of neonatally administered testosterone, testosterone propionate and dihydrotestosterone propionate on aggressive and sexual behaviour in the female golden hamster. *J. Endocrinol. 69,* 23–31

PHOENIX, C. H., GOY, R. W., GERALL, A. A. & YOUNG, W. C. (1959) Organising action of prenatally administered testosterone propionate on the tissues mediating mating behaviour in the female guinea pig. *Endocrinology 65,* 369–382

POLISHUK, W. Z. & ANTEBY, S. (1971) Testosterone in premature babies and its effect on sexual development. *Lancet 1,* 344

RANSOM, T. W. & ROWELL, T. E. (1972) Early social development of feral baboons, in *Primate Socialization* (Poirier, F. E., ed.), pp. 105–144, Random House, New York

REDDY, V. V. R., NAFTOLIN, F. & RYAN, K. J. (1974) Conversion of androstenedione to estrone by neural tissues from fetal and neonatal rats. *Endocrinology 94,* 117–121

RESKO, J. A. (1974) The relationship between fetal hormones and the differentiation of the central nervous system in primates, in *Reproductive Behaviour* (Montagna, W. & Sadler, W. A., eds.), pp. 211–222, Plenum Press, New York

ROBINSON, J. A. & BRIDSON, W. E. (1978) Neonatal hormone patterns in the macaque. I. Steroids, *Biol. Reprod.*, in press

ROTHE, H. (1975) Some aspects of sexuality and reproduction in groups of captive marmosets *(Callithrix jacchus). Z. Tierpsychol. 37,* 255–273

SEAY, B., SCHLOTTMANN, R. S. & GANDOLFO, R. (1972) Early social interaction in two monkey species. *J. Gen. Psychol. 87,* 37–43

SHORT, R. V. (1977) Sexual differentiation of the brain of the sheep. *INSERM (Inst. Natl. Santé Rech. Med.) Colloq. 32,* 121–142

SHORT, R. V. (1976) Definition of the problem: the evolution of human reproduction. *Proc. R. Soc. Lond. Ser. B Biol. Sci. 195,* 3–24

SHORT, R. V. (1977) Sexual selection and the descent of man, in *Reproduction and Evolution* (Calaby, J.H. & Tyndale-Biscoe, C.H., eds.), pp. 3–19, Australian Academy of Science, Canberra

SIEGEL, S. (1956) *Nonparametric Statistics for the Behavioral Sciences,* McGraw-Hill, New York

STEVENSON, M. F. & POOLE, T. B. (1976) An ethogram of the common marmoset *(Callithrix jacchus jacchus):* general behavioural repertoire. *Anim. Behav. 24,* 428–451

SWANSON, H. H. & BRAYSHAW, J. S. (1973) Effects of brain implants of testosterone propionate in newborn hamsters on sexual differentiation, in *Hormones and Embryonic Development (Advances in Biosciences 13)* (Raspe, G., ed.), pp. 119–136, Pergamon Press, Oxford, New York, Toronto & Sydney

TRELOAR, O. L., WOLF, R. C. & MEYER, R. K. (1972) Failure of a single neonatal dose of testosterone to alter ovarian function in the rhesus monkey. *Endocrinology 90,* 281–284

TURNER, D. C., HAFFEN, R. & STRUETT, H. (1939) Some effects of testosterone on sexual differentiation of female albino mice. *Proc. Soc. Exp. Biol. Med. 42,* 107–111

VAN LOOK, P. F. A., HUNTER, W. M., CORKER, C. S. & BAIRD, D. T. (1977) Failure of positive feedback in normal men and subjects with testicular feminization. *Clin. Endocrinol. 7,* 353–366

WHALEN, R. E. & EDWARDS, D. A. (1967) Hormonal determinants of the development of masculine and feminine behaviour in male and female rats. *Anat. Rec. 157,* 173–180

WHALEN, R. E. & LUTTGE, W. G. (1971) Perinatal administration of dihydrotestosterone to female rats and the development of reproductive function. *Endocrinology 89,* 1320–1322

WILEN, R., GOY, R. W., RESKO, J. A. & NAFTOLIN, F. (1977) Pubertal body weight and growth in the female rhesus pseudohermaphrodite. *Biol. Reprod. 16,* 470–473

WILKINS, L., BONGIOVANNI, A. M., CLAYTON, G. W., GRUMBACH, M. M. & VAN WYK, J. (1955) Virilizing adrenal hyperplasia: its treatment with cortisone and the nature of the steroid abnormalities. *Ciba Found. Coll. Endocrinol. 8,* pp. 460–481, Churchill, London

WILKINS, L., JONES, H. W., HOLMAN, G. H. & STEMPFEL, J. (1959) Masculinisation of the female foetus associated with administration of oral and intramuscular progestogens during gestation: non-adrenal female pseudohermaphroditism. *J. Clin. Endocrinol. Metab. 18,* 559–585

WISLOCKI, G. B., (1939) Observations on twinning in marmosets. *Am. J. Anat. 64,* 445–483

WOLFHEIM, J. H. (1977) Sex differences in behaviour in a group of captive juvenile talapoin monkeys *(Miopithecus talapoin). Behaviour 63,* 110–127

Discussion

Sachar: The marmoset seems to be an ideal primate for studying sexual behaviour. It is monogamous, it generates its own control animal, and it is small so it does not need large cages and ranging space.

Beach: I would like to know more about the sexual behaviour of the adults. Is it cyclic, for instance?

Abbott: We don't really know. This is a controversial point about the marmoset. It is difficult to get good data because the females show no physical signs of oestrus and they don't menstruate. In cycling non-pregnant females sexual behaviour is not well correlated with ovulation (Hearn & Lunn 1975), but there is some correlation of increased sexual behaviour with the postpartum ovulation period (Stevenson & Poole 1976). However, female offspring, left in their family groups until after puberty, will cycle, but do not show any overt sexual behaviour and do not become pregnant (D. H. Abbott & S. F. Lunn, unpublished work 1978).

Sachar: You mean that sexual activity is relatively continuous throughout the cycle?

Abbott: Yes, and they copulate throughout pregnancy (Rothe 1975; D. H. Abbott, unpublished work 1977), and even during parturition (Rothe 1974). The frequency of copulation depends on the pair; some copulate more frequently than others (Rothe 1975; Abbott & Hearn 1978).

Jost: In this monogamous species how does each partner select the other? How is this done in your colony or in the wild, to establish a family?

Abbott: In the wild, observers have found that social groups of marmoset and tamarin monkeys consist of a breeding pair and their offspring (Dawson 1976; Warner 1978; Stevenson 1978). Apparently the older offspring move about between groups (Dawson 1976; Warner 1978), but nobody has yet reported how new groups form or how breeding pairs become established. However, in captivity, when common marmosets are maintained in large family groups and one of the breeding pair dies (either the father or the mother), a son and a daughter will take over their role in the family and start breeding (Rothe 1978). This new pair become the dominant animals in the family after a brief period of squabbling and fighting between the siblings, but none of the new pair bonds formed have been between co-twins. In Edinburgh, when we put our peer groups together, only the dominant male and female pair up and breed (Abbott & Hearn 1978). Their rank order *within* their sex seems to determine whether they will pair and breed, and the dominant animals also tend to select each other because they are the only ones that don't run away from each other.

Green: You say that sexual interactions continue throughout pregnancy. Is there a decrease in late pregnancy or is it at a steady rate throughout gestation?

Abbott: Copulation rates can vary throughout pregnancy, and many instances of increased frequency have been reported throughout pregnancy, even to within a few days of birth (Rothe 1975).

Green: This is contrary to humans. Are there other primates in which copulation continues throughout pregnancy?

Goy: Bielert *et al.* (1976) studied this in rhesus monkeys in a few pairs. Copulation to ejaculation continued in those pairs through the first 90–100 days of the pregnancy and then ceased in the second half of pregnancy.

Herbert: A study in Thailand showed a similar result in human beings (Morris 1975). Copulation is very much determined by culture and by prevailing male opinion. Until recently this was against copulation during pregnancy in the Western world but this is changing and it is more common than it used to be.

Green: It is more common, but most women report lower rates of responsiveness and lower rates of orgasm, particularly in the third trimester.

Bancroft: In the second trimester there is often an increase in sexual responsiveness.

Green: Masters & Johnson (1966) reported an increase in the second trimester but another study (Kenny 1973) did not confirm that. The most consistent finding is the decrease in the third trimester of both desire and responsiveness in women.

Dörner: Dr Abbott, there is a clear-cut testosterone peak in the human lasting for 2–3 months after birth, but only for total testosterone levels and not for free testosterone, which even shows a decrease after birth. The explanation is that although total testosterone levels clearly increase between Days 5 and 50 after birth, the binding capacity increases even more, as shown by Forest *et al.* (1974). Therefore the level of free testosterone, which is considered to be the active component, actually decreases. It is most important to know what happens in newborn marmosets with respect to the biologically active free testosterone levels. I think it is also important to differentiate between an organization or differentiation period and a maturation period of the brain. Male rats castrated two weeks after birth – that is, at the beginning of the prepubertal maturation phase – show permanently decreased male sexual behaviour after androgen replacement in adulthood as compared to those castrated just before puberty (Götz & Dörner 1976). We also find permanently reduced male sexual activity in adult animals treated with the antiandrogen, cyproterone acetate, during the prepubertal maturation period. However, androgen deficiency during this maturation period of the brain results only in decreased sexual responsiveness of the males to females —that is, in male hyposexuality. On the other hand, androgen deficiency during the critical organization period (perinatally in rats) results not only in decreased sexual responsiveness of the males to females but also in increased sexual responsiveness of the males to other males—that is, in bi- or homosexual behaviour.

Beach: I am interested in the development of the Wolffian and Müllerian systems in marmosets. Is it complete at birth?

Abbott: Yes. Wolffian and Müllerian systems are fully developed at birth in males and females respectively (Wislocki 1939) and the external genitalia are completely formed. In males, the testes have still to descend, but they are palpable. The newborn infants also have a full covering of hair. Some infants have their eyes closed, but this is the only external sign that they are not completely developed at birth.

Dörner: Do you know more exactly when the differentiation of the external genitalia is complete in this species? There is usually a sequence of differentiation of internal genitalia, external genitalia, and then the brain. This may give an indication about the critical differentiation period of the brain.

Abbott: From hysterotomies we know that the gonads do not differentiate until about mid-pregnancy (70 days), and the external genitalia follow slightly later (W-S. O, P. L. Chambers & J. P. Hearn, personal communication). In the rhesus monkey (Van Wagenen & Simpson 1965) and the human (Moore 1973), these events occur relatively earlier in gestation.

Jost: You say that this sequence is the rule, Professor Dörner, but it is not so in all mammals. In ruminants, for example the calf fetus, the male external genitalia are the first sex character to appear after the testes are formed.

Goy: In some strains of rat the female develops a good part of the male prostate and retains it throughout life although it is not functional unless androgens are given in adulthood. Is there any evidence in female marmosets that are co-twinned with males that they have structures like the prostate or rudimentary Wolffian duct derivatives?

Abbott: In our colony, post-mortems of young and adult female marmosets known to be haematopoietic chimaeras revealed no Wolffian duct derivatives, but such structures may have been present earlier in development. Wislocki (1939) found no Wolffian derivatives in his examination of female marmoset fetuses.

Goy: One would have to look microscopically. The sexes in the marmoset may look quite different to you, Dr Abbott, but the newborn animals look very similar to me! But there might be some influence of the presence of the male fetus on internal structures which causes those structures to develop differently from female–female twins.

Short: Professor Jost, can you suggest how the female marmoset fetus protects itself from the potential masculinizing influence of its male co-twin? Your work on the bovine freemartin suggests, for example, that the Müllerian-inhibitory factor does cross from the male fetus into the female and interferes with her Müllerian duct development. As David Abbott said, there is no evidence that female marmosets co-twinned with males have any abnormality of the uterus, and they breed normally. Must we postulate that in the marmoset the organizing effects of the testis, both in Wolffian stimulation and Müllerian inhibition, are entirely local and the hormones don't spill out into the systemic circulation at all?

Jost: This would be my surmise; it is the easiest way to understand it. In rabbit fetuses the local effect is prominent in the early stages. Later in development hormones are distributed through the bloodstream. If one grafts the testis on one side of the genital tract of a female rabbit fetus the effect is localized to that side (Jost 1947). I would expect the fetal gonads of marmosets, cats and man to show very local effects.

Hutchison: I have a rather general question which relates to Dr Dörner's point. It concerns the critical period for the effects of hormones on sexual differentiation, and what determines the critical period in terms of brain function. In one avian species (the Japanese quail), where sexual differentiation appears to be an oestrogenic effect in the female during embryonic development (Adkins 1975), removal of the ovary immediately after hatching causes the earlier differentiating effects to disappear. Such females are essentially bisexual in adulthood (Hutchison 1979). In this species there would seem to be an early differentiating effect of oestrogen and also a later consolidating effect, which apparently involves ovarian hormones. So the critical period isn't limited in this species; it is an extended phenomenon. Does anyone really know what determines the limits of the critical period in terms of changes in brain structure? What is it about brain sensitivity to the hormone during early development that determines the subsequent behavioural effect of hormones in adulthood?

Goy: We have very few leads about this. Is it a synaptic effect of the hormone? There is no reason why in some species such a synaptic effect could not be reversible whereas in others it might be very resistant to change, once established. This example in a bird might indicate that synapses form in the presence of a hormone and when that hormone is withdrawn the synapses degenerate; they need some maintenance. There obviously have to be different synapses for different behaviours, and many of us make an error in communication here. We should think of behaviour not in terms of a motor response alone but in terms of an orderly and predictable relationship between a stimulus configuration and the response. If guinea-pigs and rats are fed from a food hopper, both sexes mount the hopper and the motor pattern is not so different from the mounting they show sexually, but it has nothing to do with the endocrine condition and cannot be influenced hormonally. The mounting behaviour *of a sexual object* is the behaviour we are considering, although we often talk only about the motor pattern.

Bancroft: I want to revert to the relevance of the postnatal androgen surge to human development. I am a bit concerned at what Dr Dörner was saying, because I had hoped that a primate such as the marmoset which shows such a surge might be relevant to the human and help us to study the relationship between the postnatal androgen surge and later development. But what is the function of this surge if the androgen is all mopped up by sex-hormone-binding globulin? Why does it occur, and do these conclusions mean that this species is not a useful model for the human?

Goy: The male rhesus monkey also shows this postnatal period of androgenization which lasts 2–3 months, just as in the human, according to Robinson & Bridson (1978). We haven't measured the percentage of bound and free testosterone, but even if testosterone is 100% bound, it is still an effective hormone, because if we castrate the males the pituitary secretion of gonadotropins increases greatly. There is an interesting effect; at a certain time in maturation, even though the animals have no testes, the pituitary turns itself off and gonadotropin concentrations fall to typical prepubertal levels until puberty. So the negative feedback is there. What this neonatal period of androgen secretion is accomplishing in terms of differentiation or maturational effects, I don't know. I have studied the behavioural development of male rhesus monkeys castrated on the day of birth; they perform their gender role in the infant and juvenile periods indistinguishably from intact male monkeys. Deficits might appear in their libido in adulthood, but during the juvenile period, which lasts four years, we haven't found any significant effect of neonatal castration.

Herbert: We are assuming that the neonatal testosterone surge has a physiological function, of course. We know that the fetus is subjected to hormonal control from itself and from the mother. How far is the neonatal testosterone surge a release, when the animal is removed from the uterus and now lacks the hormonal environment of the uterus? Its testes are functional because it is showing a surge; but in a few days it goes back to what it ought to be as a prepubertal animal.

Abbott: I don't think this is so, because we observed elevated testosterone levels in male marmosets between 15 and 100 days after birth (Abbott & Hearn 1978).

Bancroft: In the human the surge doesn't start until 3–4 weeks after birth, so it seems unlikely that this would be true.

Short: It is correlated with the rise in LH in the human male but the rise in LH in the female is not as pronounced (Faiman *et al.* 1974). It is a uniquely male effect in the human.

Dörner: In the human this increase in LH may be caused by the decreased biologically active free testosterone level in the male, due to the increased sex-hormone-binding capacity.

Jost: Roffi and his colleagues (Roffi *et al.* 1977; Corbier *et al.* 1977) showed that at birth in the rat there is a sudden burst of LH and testosterone which lasts for two hours or so.

Sachar: The neonatal period in both humans and monkeys clearly deserves more thorough endocrine evaluation. It could turn out to be an important period.

Bancroft: In the UK we have an ethical restriction in that one can't take blood from human infants for research purposes.

Sachar: Not even a heel stick?

Goy: That wouldn't be adequate; samples of blood in the rhesus monkey, even taken at the same time every day, vary greatly from day to day, and although there probably are significant differences between males, one could not show it from a single sample.

Sachar: What about measuring urinary testosterone in the newborn?

Goy: That seems possible.

Bancroft: Most of the data on postnatal androgen concentrations come from children coming up for adoption, who have to have blood tests. Blood taken immediately after birth isn't relevant anyway; it is later on that the testosterone surge occurs.

Sachar: There may be techniques that can be worked out. The other diurnal rhythms, like that of cortisol, are not established in the first month, so testosterone levels may not be so variable according to the time of day in the newborn human as in the monkey.

Ehrhardt: Dr Abbott, what do you make of your suggestion that the androgenized female marmoset shows more rough-and-tumble play than her normal male twin?

Abbott: In the one case where the androgenized female initiated more rough-and-tumble play than her male co-twin control the difference was not significant. However, as this was the only androgenized female with a male co-twin control it is difficult to conclude anything.

Ehrhardt: Do you have any plans for experiments like those Dr Goy did on rhesus monkeys treated with dihydrotestosterone, where he found little masculinization of the genitalia but still the effect on behaviour (Goy *et al.* 1977)?

Abbott: This would be a fascinating experiment to do.

Short: Dr Ehrhardt, what clinical evidence is there of abnormal behaviour in the 'Infant Hercules' syndrome where the male is precociously virilized at birth as a result of congenital adrenal hyperplasia?

Ehrhardt: We found no clinical abnormality when we compared them with other male children (Ehrhardt & Baker 1974). The only difference was that the androgenized boys showed somewhat more athletic and active play behaviour.

Herbert: One thing we lack is information on the role of androgens in the development of *masculine* behaviour in primates. There is hardly any evidence on that, and Dr Abbott has supplied some of the first information in the adult that androgen may be important. How sure are you that a female from a male–female twin pair doesn't behave differently from a female from an all-female twin pair? How carefully have you looked at behavioural differences?

Abbott: In the behavioural trials there were two females in the group of normal females which were born co-twins to males and they showed no masculine sexual behaviour at all. However, to answer your question fully we need to test such females rigorously over a long period of time. This has not yet been done.

Herbert: You showed that the androgenized females could show both masculine and feminine sexual behaviour, but the males didn't. This seems to imply that something has happened in the development of the normal male that doesn't happen in the androgenized females, to prevent them showing female type behaviour. It would suggest that male fetuses receive androgen prenatally as well as postnatally and therefore this may be responsible for this effect.

Abbott: This is possible. I have concentrated on investigating neonatal development in the marmoset and the results I obtained do not preclude the possibility that males experience elevated androgen levels before as well as after birth. We have tried to investigate sexual differentiation in fetal marmosets, and Dr John Hearn has implanted five pregnant female marmosets with testosterone. Unfortunately, the female marmoset 'dislikes' testosterone even more than the pregnant rhesus monkey does (Goy *et al.* 1977), because all five aborted. However, our studies of fetal development are continuing.

Herbert: You are working with intact females; even though you haven't been able to draw exact conclusions on the relation between hormones and adult behaviour it seems important to look at the endocrine function of these androgenized females in adulthood to see if they really are the same as normal females. Is ovarian function distinguishable from that of normal females, for instance?

Abbott: Unfortunately, I cannot answer your question completely. I know that the androgenized females cycle similarly to normal females but I don't know if their ovarian function is totally normal.

Short: Dr Herbert is saying that the androgenized females seemed to be halfway between normal males and normal females, so one cannot assume that neonatal androgenization has completely turned female behaviour into male, and presumably the additional male hormone needed is prenatal. That may not be a correct deduction, because David Abbott tested those androgenized females for behaviour in adult life when they were without the testicular testosterone levels of the normal male controls. Is not the evidence still compatible with the hypothesis that there is no sexual differentiation in the brain in fetal life in the marmoset and that it is entirely postnatal, with an initial organizing effect, produced by an early postnatal surge of testosterone, and then a later reinforcing effect with rising testosterone levels at puberty?

Abbott: My evidence is quite compatible with that hypothesis, but the data do not exclude the possibility of some fetal sexual differentiation.

Goy: This degree of bisexuality observed in the masculinized females is interesting. They are more bisexual than the normal female controls *and* more than the normal male controls. The bisexuality that develops in any given species differs with the species, however, and until you have tested normal males with their testes taken out and ovaries implanted, you don't know whether the bisexuality seen in your masculinized female marmoset is the same as males would show then or, conversely, whether it is the female marmoset that retains a high degree of bisexual potential, and if you took out her ovaries and implanted testes or testosterone, she might look like your modified females.

Abbott: We have exchanged gonads between male and female co-twins at birth and at 180 days of age. The males with ovaries behaved as though they were castrates when placed in the behavioural trial situation; they ran away from the others and didn't interact. Unfortunately, we don't know if the ovaries were functional. As yet we don't have any behavioural trial data on females with transplanted testes, but in peer groups they behaved like normal females. However, we have recovered a testis from one of these females, two years after implantation. This testis had grown the least of all those transplanted, but seminiferous tubules were easily identified in transverse sections of the tissue. No evidence of spermatogenesis was found.

Goy: These experiments need to be done if we are to learn more about this species and its potential for bisexual expression in adulthood, because species differ very much in that regard.

Short: One needs to do an extremely detailed behavioural study of females born as twins to females and females born as twins to males, because they are the interesting ones, as Dr Herbert said.

Herbert: One doesn't know to what degree the difference between the treated and control females is due to this unique experience or to ovarian function later in life. Obviously one must castrate such females and give them testosterone.

Bancroft: Or one could give cyproterone acetate during the neonatal period and leave them intact.

Goy: On the possible significance of the neonatal androgenization, Patricia Goldman has found a dimorphic effect of brain lesions in rhesus monkeys (Goldman *et al.* 1974). In certain cognitive tests, learning tests, in males operated on soon after birth, the deficits associated with the lesion appear as early as 2½ months of age. In females, comparable deficits do not appear until 15–18 months of age. The lesion is made in the orbitofrontal area, bilaterally. If androgen is given to the female postnatally she suffers cognitive deficits from this lesion at as early an age as the male does (P. S. Goldman, personal communication).

Sachar: The human male is notoriously more susceptible to all kinds of brain dysfunction than the female. There may be a hormonal basis for this difference in susceptibility.

Goy: Goldman's work is important precisely because it takes our thinking about hormonal influences into cognitive areas.

Bancroft: There is a difference in maturation of the CNS in humans, as shown in the EEG pattern. Females are ahead in development.

Green: Females are ahead on everything except field dependency tests. There is one type of cognitive test, best exemplified by the Embedded Figures Test (where the subject must distinguish an embedded figure from the background), in which males are generally superior. In our studies of the effects of prenatal sex hormones we looked for an effect in this test. In the first study (Yalom *et al.* 1973) we found that males exposed to oestrogen before birth took longer on this test, which is a trend in the female direction. However, this was not confirmed in the second study (Green *et al.* 1978). Zussman *et al.* (1975) were also unable to replicate this. Field independence is one capacity which appears to be superior in the male.

Dörner: Ladosky & Gaziri (1970) have shown a clear-cut sex-specific difference in serotonin concentration of the brain (forebrain plus midbrain) in rats as early as the 12th day of life. It was higher in females than in males. After a single androgen injection to females on the first day of life the serotonin level on the 12th day was decreased to the level found in males. More recently, the serotonin precursor tryptophan was also found to be significantly more abundant in the brain (cerebral cortex) of female rats at 12 and 60 days of age than in males (Vaccari *et al.* 1977). Hence, deficiency of this serotonin precursor during brain development may be more deleterious in females than in males. As I mentioned in my paper, we observed long-lasting harmful effects on brain development, particularly in girls, after bottle-feeding with tyrosine- and phenylalanine-rich but tryptophan-poor formulas for the first three months of life as compared to breast-feeding (Dörner & Grychtolik 1978).

References

ABBOTT, D. H. & HEARN, J. P. (1978) Physical, hormonal and behavioural aspects of sexual development in the marmoset monkey, *Callithrix jacchus*. *J. Reprod. Fertil. 53,* 155–166

ADKINS, E. K. (1975) Hormonal basis of sexual differentiation in the Japanese quail. *J. Comp. Physiol. Psychol. 89,* 61–71

BIELERT, C., CZAJA, J. A., EISELE, S., SCHEFFLER, G., ROBINSON, J. A. & GOY, R. W. (1976) Mating in the rhesus monkey *(Macaca mulatta)* after conception and its relationship to oestradiol and progesterone levels throughout pregnancy. *J. Reprod. Fertil. 46,* 179–187

CORBIER, P., PICON, R. & ROFFI, J. (1977) Elévation de la testostéronémie chez le rat nouveau-né. *C.R. Hebd. Séances Acad. Sci. Sér. D Sci. Nat. 285,* 1247–1249

DAWSON, G. A. (1976) Behavioural ecology of the Panamanian Tamarin, *Saguinus oedipus* (Callitrichidae, Primates). *Diss. Abstr. Int. B Sci. Eng. 37,* 645–646

DÖRNER, G. & GRYCHTOLIK, H. (1978) Long-lasting ill-effects of neonatal qualitative and/or quantitative dysnutrition in the human. *Endokrinologie 71,* 81–88

EHRHARDT, A. A. & BAKER, S. W. (1974) Fetal androgen, human CNS differentiation and behavior sex differences, in *Sex Differences in Behavior* (Friedman, R. C., Richart, R. M. & Vandewiele, R. L., eds.), pp. 53–76, Wiley, New York

FAIMAN, C., REYES, F. I. & WINTER, J. S. D. (1974) Serum gonadotrophin patterns during the perinatal period in man and the chimpanzee. *INSERM (Inst. Natl. Santé Rech. Méd.) Colloq. 32,* 281–298

FOREST, M. G., CATHIARD, A. M., BOURGEOIS, J. & GENOUD, J. (1974) Androgènes plasmatiques chez le nourrisson normal et prématuré, relation avec la maturation de d'axe hypothalamo-hypophyso-gonadique. *INSERM (Inst. Natl. Santé Rech. Méd.) Colloq. 32,* 315–335

GOLDMAN, P. S., CRAWFORD, H. T., STOKES, L. P., GALKIN, T. W. & ROSVOLD, H. E. (1974) Sex dependent behavioural effects of cerebral cortical lesions in the developing rhesus monkey. *Science (Wash. D.C.) 186,* 540–542

GÖTZ, F. & DÖRNER, G. (1976) Sex hormone-dependent brain maturation and sexual behaviour in rats. *Endokrinologie 68,* 275–282

GOY, R. W., WOLF, J. E. & EISELE, S. G. (1977) Experimental female hermaphroditism in rhesus monkeys: anatomical and psychological characteristics, in *Handbook of Sexology* (Money, J. & Musaph, H., eds.), pp. 139–156, Elsevier/North-Holland, Amsterdam

GREEN, R., KESTER, P., FINCH, S. & WILLIAMS, K. (1978) Prenatal female hormone administration and later psychosexual development in human males, in preparation

HEARN, J. P. & LUNN, S. F. (1975) The reproductive biology of the marmoset monkey, *Callithrix jacchus*, in *Breeding Simians for Developmental Biology (Laboratory Animals Handbook*, vol.6) (Perkins, F. T. & O'Donoghue, P. N., eds.), pp. 191–202, Laboratory Animals, London

HUTCHISON, R. E. (1979) Hormonal differentiation of sexual behaviour in Japanese quail. *Horm. Behav.*, in press

JOST, A. (1947) Recherches sur la différenciation sexuelle de l'embryon de lapin. III. Rôle des gonades foetales dans la différenciation sexuelle somatique. *Arch. Anat. Microsc. Morphol. Exp. 36*, 271–315

KENNY, J. (1973) Sexuality of pregnant and breastfeeding women. *Arch. Sex. Behav. 2*, 215–229

LADOSKY, W. & GAZIRI, L. C. J. (1970) Brain serotonin and sexual differentiation of the nervous system. *Neuroendocrinology 6*, 168–174

MASTERS, W. H. & JOHNSON, V. E. (1966) *Human Sexual Response*, Churchill, London, and Little, Brown, Boston

MOORE, K. L. (1973) *The Developing Human*, Saunders, Philadelphia

MORRIS, N. M. (1975) The frequency of sexual intercourse during pregnancy. *Arch. Sex. Behav. 4*, 501–507

ROBINSON, J. A. & BRIDSON, W. E. (1978) Neonatal hormone patterns in the macaque. I. Steroids. *Biol. Reprod.*, in press

ROFFI, J., CORBIER, P. & KERDELHUE, B. (1977) Stimulation de la sécrétion de LH et de FSH et augmentation du poids testiculaire à la naissance chez le Rat. *C.R. Hebd. Séances Acad. Sci. Sér. D Sci. Nat. 284*, 1313–1316

ROTHE, H. (1974) Further observations on the delivery behaviour of the common marmoset *(Callithrix jacchus). Z. Säugetierkd. 39*, 135–142

ROTHE, H. (1975) Some aspects of sexuality and reproduction in groups of captive marmosets *(Callithrix jacchus). Z. Tierpsychol. 37*, 255–273

ROTHE, H. (1978) Structure and dynamics of captive *Callithrix jacchus* groups, in *The Biology of the Callitrichidae* (Rothe, H., Wolters, H. J. & Hearn J. P., eds.), University of Göttingen Press, Göttingen, in press

STEVENSON, M. F. (1978) The behaviour and ecology of the common marmoset *(Callithrix jacchus jacchus)* in its natural environment, in *The Biology of the Callitrichidae* (Rothe, H., Wolters, H. J. & Hearn, J. P., eds.), University of Göttingen Press, Göttingen, in press

STEVENSON, M. F. & POOLE, T. B. (1976) An ethogram of the common marmoset *(Callithrix jacchus jacchus):* general behavioural repertoire. *Anim. Behav. 24*, 428–451

VACCARI, A., BROTMAN, S., CIMINO, J. & TIMIRAS, P. S. (1977) Sex differentiation of neurotransmitter enzymes in central and peripheral nervous systems. *Brain Res. 132*, 176–185

VAN WAGENEN, G. & SIMPSON, M. (1965) *Embryology of the Ovary and Testis. Homo sapiens and Macaca mulatta.* Yale University Press, New Haven

WARNER, P. F. N. (1978) The ecology and social behaviour of the cotton-topped tamarin in Columbia, in *Biology and Conservation of Marmosets* (Kleiman, D. G., ed.), Smithsonian Institution, Washington, D.C., pp. 39–71

WISLOCKI, G. B. (1939) Observations on twinning in marmosets. *Am. J. Anat. 64*, 445–483

YALOM, I., GREEN, R. & FISK, N. (1973) Prenatal exposure to female hormones: effect on psychosexual development in boys. *Arch. Gen. Psychiatr. 28*, 554–561

ZUSSMAN, J., ZUSSMAN, P. & DALTON, K. (1975) Post-pubertal effects of prenatal administration of progesterone. (Unpublished paper, Society for Research in Child Development, Denver, April 1975)

Monoamines and sexual behaviour in non-human primates

BARRY J. EVERITT

Department of Anatomy, University of Cambridge

Abstract The experiments described were concerned with elucidating the involvement of monoamines in the sexual behaviour of rhesus monkeys. The measurement of perturbations in the levels and turnover of the acid metabolites of serotonin and dopamine in cisternal cerebrospinal fluid, occurring in response to hormonal manipulations which alter proceptivity and receptivity, has not clarified the ways in which hormones and amines interact. However, the use of psychoactive drugs which alter the activity of monoamine neurons in the brain has demonstrated that sexual activity can be profoundly influenced by such procedures. Thus, depletion of serotonin (5-hydroxytryptamine) in the brain using *p*-chlorophenylalanine reversed the decrease in proceptivity that followed adrenalectomy. Conversely, inhibition of serotonin uptake using chlorimipramine reduced proceptivity and receptivity to very low levels. Both findings point to the apparently important role of serotoninergic neurons in the control of sexual behaviour. Low doses of the dopamine agonist α-bromocriptine enhanced the proceptivity of female rhesus monkeys but high doses had no such effect. This behavioural change was not related to the concomitant suppression of serum prolactin and may have been related to presynaptic actions of the drug in a manner postulated to explain similar behavioural effects in rats. The β-blocker oxprenolol had the interesting property of improving the sexual performance of male rhesus monkeys, a behavioural effect consistent with an anxiolytic action, although endocrine (prolactin, cortisol) measures did not provide support for such a view. Defining the nature of the interaction between hormones and monoamine-containing neurons in the brain in behavioural contexts is shown to depend largely on the application of precise neuroanatomical and neuropharmacological techniques. However, the use of systemic treatment with psychoactive drugs used widely in clinical practice, in carefully controlled, behavioural and endocrine experiments, is likely to provide invaluable information on where and how to investigate the neural mechanisms involved.

In recent years there has been considerable interest in defining the neural sites and mechanisms of action of hormones involved in the regulation of sexual behaviour and in anterior pituitary function. While there has been some degree of success with the former—the hypothalamus forming a focal point—it has proved more difficult to solve problems concerned with the ways in which hormones alter neural activity, and the neurochemical identity of the neurons with which they interact. However, a considerable body of evidence, derived largely from experiments on non-primate species, suggests that monoamine-containing neurons are closely related to the behavioural and feedback actions of hormones in the brain (Everitt 1977*a*; Fuxe *et al.* 1976*a*; Stumpf & Grant 1975). The experiments described in this paper are mainly concerned, therefore, with attempts to define the relationships between hormones and monoamines in the regulation of sexual behaviour in female primates.

ENDOCRINE MANIPULATIONS WHICH AFFECT PROCEPTIVITY AND RECEPTIVITY

It should be emphasized at the outset that the hormones which regulate proceptivity (Beach 1976) in female monkeys are androgens (e.g. testosterone, androstenedione from the adrenal and ovary—particularly at mid-cycle) and not oestrogen and progesterone, which are more important determinants of this behaviour in non-primate species. Receptivity is also influenced by androgens, and perhaps by oestradiol as well, but the precise mechanisms involved have proved extremely difficult to define. A full discussion of data on the hormonal determinants of sexual behaviour in female primates is given by Baum *et al.* (1977). Full details of the behavioural methods used in the experiments to be described may be found in Trimble & Herbert (1968) and Baum *et al.* (1977).

Do hormonal manipulations which alter sexual behaviour in female monkeys produce characteristic changes in the levels or turnover of monoamines in the brain? In Fig. 1 the effects on proceptivity and receptivity of suppressing the adrenal cortex with dexamethasone in oestrogen-treated, ovariectomized monkeys are summarized from a series of early experiments (Everitt & Herbert 1971). It can be seen that adrenal suppression resulted in decreased proceptivity and receptivity despite the continuous presence of oestradiol and that this was reversed by treatment with testosterone propionate. The effects of dexamethasone have been recently confirmed, although no attempt was made to reverse them with androgens (Johnson & Phoenix 1976). More recently, in experiments initiated with Michael Baum, the effects of these treatments on plasma testosterone and cerebral monoamines have been measured. Fig. 1 shows that changes in plasma testosterone (which decreases during dexamethasone treatment and increases during treatment with testosterone propionate) clearly mirror the changes in proceptivity and receptivity.

The most accessible compartment for measuring alterations in cerebral monoamines in primates used for long-term behavioural experiments is the cerebrospinal fluid (CSF). Levels of the principal metabolites of serotonin (5-hydroxytryptamine) and dopamine (5-hydroxyindoleacetic acid, 5-HIAA, and homovanillic acid, HVA, respectively) in CSF withdrawn from the cisterna magna did not change during any treatment (Fig. 1). HVA (i.e dopamine) turnover similarly did not change significantly but 5-HIAA (i.e. serotonin) turnover increased markedly during dexamethasone treatment, an effect which was partially reversed during treatment with testosterone.

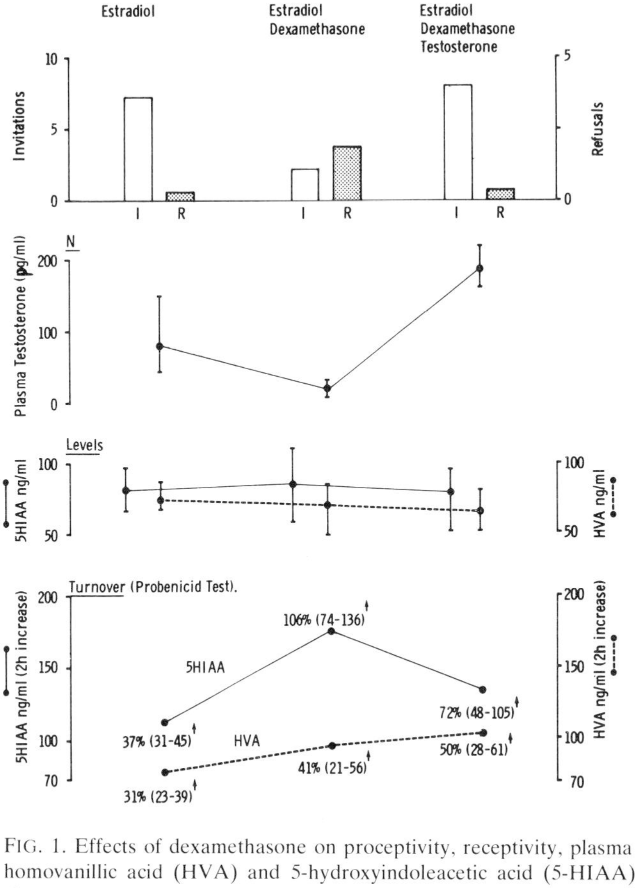

FIG. 1. Effects of dexamethasone on proceptivity, receptivity, plasma testosterone levels, and homovanillic acid (HVA) and 5-hydroxyindoleacetic acid (5-HIAA) levels and turnover in cisternal cerebrospinal fluid in ovariectomized, oestrogen-treated rhesus monkeys. Plasma testosterone was estimated using a radioimmunoassay. HVA and 5-HIAA were estimated by a spectrofluorimetric assay. Turnover of the acids was assessed by measuring the rate of increase in their levels 2 h after intravenous injections of the efflux blocker probenecid (see Gradwell *et al.* 1975). I, invitations, R, refusals. (Original behavioural data in Everitt & Herbert 1971.)

(Turnover was estimated using the probenecid test; see legend to Fig. 1 and Gradwell *et al.* (1975) for further details.)

Clearly, these findings fit—at least superficially—with existing dogma which suggests that serotonin exerts an inhibitory influence on the display of sexual behaviour and that hormones (e.g. testosterone) act by suppressing this influence (disinhibition; see Meyerson *et al.* 1978). But such a conclusion is unwarranted, not only because causal relationships have not been established in these experiments, but because the neurochemical effects of dexamethasone were only *partially* reversed by testosterone while plasma testosterone and sexual activity had completely returned to pre-treatment control levels. Thus, the effects of dexamethasone and testosterone on serotonin systems in the brain were dissociated and probably reflect the wider-ranging central effects of dexamethasone than those resulting simply from the loss of testosterone. Interference in the regulation of ACTH secretion, which is known to be dependent, at least in part, on serotonin mechanisms, probably represents one such effect.

If this is true, it should become increasingly difficult to measure changes in amines the more specific the hormonal manipulation used to alter sexual behaviour. Thus, adrenalectomized, oestrogen-treated, ovariectomized female rhesus monkeys receiving adequate mineralocorticoid and glucocorticoid replacement therapy are, essentially, lacking only adrenal sex steroids (notably androgens). Such animals show extremely low levels of proceptivity and receptivity (Everitt *et al.* 1972) but no alterations in 5-HIAA levels or turnover of 5-HIAA (P. B. Gradwell & B. J. Everitt, unpublished). Implanting small amounts of testosterone in the anterior hypothalamus completely reversed the behavioural effects of adrenalectomy (Everitt & Herbert 1975), but similarly caused no detectable alteration in 5-HIAA concentrations in cisternal CSF (unpublished).

Perhaps the most specific endocrine manipulation possible in behavioural experiments of this kind is the one which selectively eliminates the hormone being investigated. Fig. 2 shows some preliminary results of experiments involving passive immunization of ovariectomized, oestrogen-treated female rhesus monkeys against testosterone (N. Martensz & B. J. Everitt, unpublished). This treatment caused a temporal decline in proceptivity (invitations decreased) and receptivity (refusals increased and the females' acceptance ratios decreased) which correlated well with increased testosterone binding in Rivernol-treated plasma. These behavioural changes were reversed by treatment with methyltestosterone, which cross-reacts little with the antiserum (6%). Oestradiol, on the other hand, does not cross-react with the antiserum and was present throughout the experiment—so emphasizing the major role played by androgens in the control of sexual activity in female rhesus monkeys. Not surprisingly, levels of 5-HIAA in cisternal CSF did not change during the experiment. Turnover of serotonin has not yet been estimated.

Thus, little evidence has been derived from these experiments to suggest that monoamines (particularly serotonin) are intimately involved in the effects of hormones on proceptivity and receptivity. This is not to say that hormones are without effect on cerebral amines, since dexamethasone, testosterone and, indeed, oestrogen and progesterone given systemically in fairly large doses profoundly alter the turnover of serotonin (See also Gradwell *et al.*

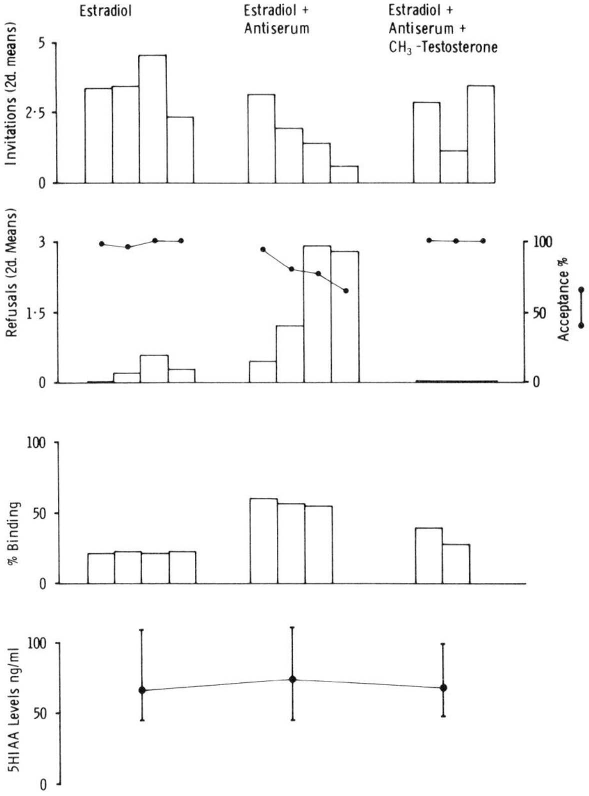

FIG. 2. The effects of passive immunization against testosterone on proceptivity, receptivity, plasma testosterone binding and 5-HIAA levels in cisternal CSF in ovariectomized, oestrogen-treated female rhesus monkeys. Behavioural data represented as consecutive two-day means from six pairs. Females received oestradiol-17β in the form of a subcutaneously implanted silastic capsule. Testosterone binding (%) was measured using Rivernol-treated plasma. (N. Martensz & B. J. Everitt, unpublished work).

1975). But such alterations represent widespread effects of hormones in the brain and they cannot be assigned specifically to the behavioural context under discussion. This is in large part due to the fact that CSF tapped from the cisterna magna is derived from the entire brain and hence changes in serotonin turnover may reflect, for example, the feedback action of these hormones in the regulation of anterior pituitary secretion, in addition to any effects they might have on regions of the brain more directly concerned with sexual behaviour. It is unlikely, therefore, that measuring perturbations in 5-HIAA, HVA or other amine metabolites in cisternal CSF will be of significant value in monitoring or explaining any central effects of hormonal manipulations which alter proceptivity and receptivity. Samples of CSF derived from a more relevant pool, such as the third ventricle, may yield more reliable and interpretable information, but there are serious technical problems associated with this approach.

PSYCHOPHARMACOLOGY: THE USE OF AMINERGIC DRUGS TO ALTER HORMONE-DEPENDENT BEHAVIOURS

Psychopharmacological techniques provide another means of studying the role of monoamines in behavioural systems, and experiments of this kind have been widely used in non-primate species. Data collected in this way have provided the major foundation of hypotheses implicating serotonin- (particularly), dopamine- and noradrenaline-containing neurons in the central (behavioural) actions of hormones (Meyerson *et al.* 1978; Everitt 1977*a*), although the interpretation of much of this work is open to major criticism (see below).

(1) It is particularly important in such experiments to have an appropriate behavioural model in which to explore, using drugs, the possible relationship between hormones and amines. It seemed that adrenalectomized, oestrogen-treated, ovariectomized female rhesus monkeys provided just such a model, since a particular component of their sexual behaviour, proceptivity, was consistently impaired and could be restored by injecting testosterone or implanting it in the anterior hypothalamus (see above). The problem addressed in these experiments was whether, as experiments on non-primate species predicted, lowering the levels of serotonin in the brain could reverse the behavioural effects of adrenalectomy—that is, could essentially replace testosterone in this context (Gradwell *et al.* 1975). Fig. 3 shows the effects of the tryptophan hydroxylase inhibitor, *p*-chlorophenylalanine (PCPA), on the proceptivity of adrenalectomized monkeys. It can be seen that decreasing serotonin levels in the brain, as shown by the low levels of 5-HIAA in cisternal CSF (bottom, Fig.3), reversed the behavioural effects of adrenalecto-

my. Furthermore, treatment with 5-hydroxytryptophan, the precursor of serotonin whose formation is blocked by PCPA, prevented the effects of the latter—and this was also mirrored by 5-HIAA levels in CSF (Fig. 3). Giving 5-hydroxytryptophan alone to intact female rhesus monkeys, on the other hand, significantly decreased their proceptivity (Gradwell *et al.* 1975). The real value of cisternal CSF measurements is shown in these experiments where 5-HIAA levels were used to monitor the drug's neurochemical actions.

The tempting conclusion to be drawn from these experiments (and comparable ones on non-primates) is that serotonin exerts an inhibitory influence on the expression of proceptivity and, since depletion of serotonin has similar behavioural effects to testosterone, that this hormone may exert its action via a serotonin-dependent mechanism (see p. 330 above and Gradwell *et al.*

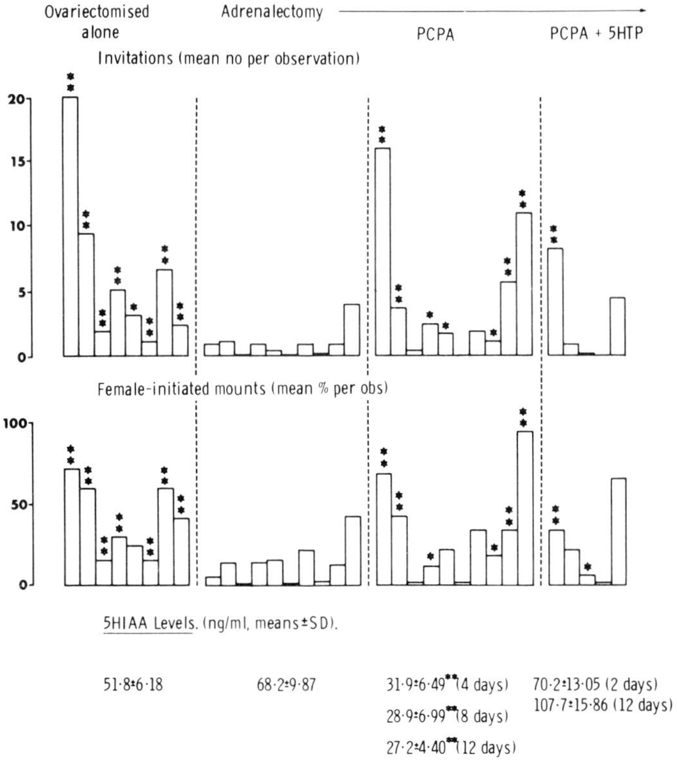

FIG. 3. The effects of *p*-chlorophenylalanine (PCPA) with and without 5-hydroxytryptophan (5HTP) on proceptivity and 5-HIAA levels in cisternal CSF of ovariectomized-adrenalectomized, oestrogen-treated female rhesus monkeys. Each column represents the mean score of an individual animal over 10 observations. (For full details see Gradwell *et al.* 1975.)

1975). But there are serious problems in accepting such a simplistic interpretation: first, PCPA does not specifically alter serotonin concentrations; it affects noradrenaline and dopamine in the brain as well, although reversal of its effects by 5-hydroxytryptophan strongly suggests that changes in serotonin levels were of major importance in mediating the behavioural changes. Second, and more important, is that there is no evidence suggesting a *direct* relationship between testosterone and serotonin: the mere fact that they both alter proceptivity is not sufficient to establish this, since each may affect the behaviour through different, even unrelated mechanisms. There is almost overwhelming circumstantial evidence that the two *are* related but direct, causal relationships have proved difficult to define (Meyerson *et al.* 1978).

(2) There are obvious limits to the amount of information on patterns of interaction between hormones and monoamines that experiments such as the one described above with PCPA will give—a problem discussed further below. But a more valuable side to this work involves the use of psychoactive drugs prescribed clinically, particularly in the treatment of affective behaviour disorders. Many of these compounds have well-defined neurochemical effects and are, therefore, powerful investigative tools. But although they are widely prescribed their behavioural and endocrine actions in man, outside the therapeutic context in which they are used, are little known (with few notable exceptions). This is particularly the case for effects on sexual behaviour, disturbances of which are quite often described by patients as side-effects. Thus, tricyclic antidepressants have been reported to impair the ability to achieve orgasm and to decrease libido in both men and women (Beaumont 1973; Micev & Marshall 1973). There are a number of similar reports in the literature (Couper-Smartt & Rodham 1973) but few if any have a behavioural analysis adequate enough to allow definitive statements to be made on the effect of any particular compound—except, perhaps, chlorimipramine (see Beaumont 1973).

Chlorimipramine is generally regarded as an inhibitor of the reuptake of serotonin, although it has considerable effects on noradrenaline reuptake as well. Inhibition of the reuptake of serotonin (or noradrenaline) causes the released transmitter to remain in the synaptic cleft for a long period and is, therefore, associated with prolonged stimulation of postsynaptic receptors. Thus, blockade of uptake represents an indirect means of activating postsynaptic receptors and is associated with enhanced transmission in the particular aminergic pathway. Fig. 4 shows that *in vitro* chlorimipramine is almost equipotent in inhibiting the reuptake of noradrenaline and serotonin in monkey hypothalamus. However, acute dosage *in vivo* results in much more marked inhibition of serotonin uptake (Fig. 4). If chlorimipramine is given

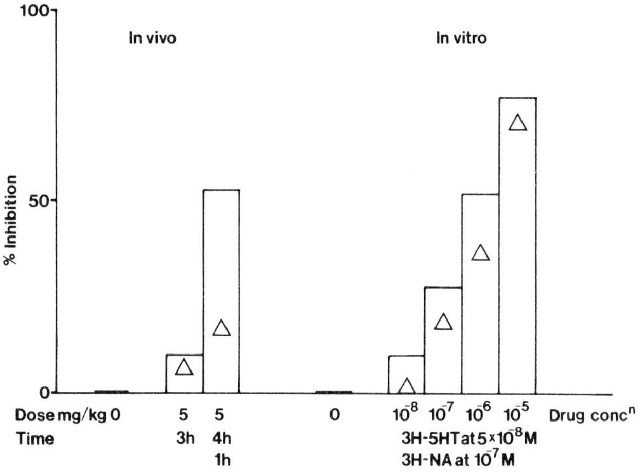

FIG. 4. The effects of chlorimipramine on the uptake of serotonin (columns) and noradrenaline (Δ), measured in two ways. *In vivo:* monkeys were injected with 5 mg/kg chlorimipramine, 3 h and 1 h before slices of the hypothalamus were incubated with [^{3}H]serotonin (5×10^{-8}M) and [^{3}H]noradrenaline (10^{-7}M) for 10 min. *In vitro:* hypothalamic slices from untreated monkeys were incubated with [^{3}H]serotonin and [^{3}H]noradrenaline, in the same concentrations as above, in the presence of chlorimipramine in the molar concentrations shown. Brains were obtained from post-mortem material through the kind cooperation of Huntingdon Research Centre. (For further details, see Everitt 1977*b* and Everitt *et al.* 1975*b*).

for longer periods the effect on noradrenaline is increased, because of accumulation of the principal metabolite desmethyl-chlorimipramine, a potent inhibitor of noradrenaline reuptake (Carlsson *et al.* 1969).

The effects on proceptivity and receptivity of acute treatment of female rhesus monkeys with chlorimipramine are shown in Fig. 5 (see also Everitt 1977*b*). There were two treatment periods, each of three days, when the animals received chlorimipramine (5 mg/kg twice daily), preceded and followed by three-day periods when they received only vehicle. All females were ovariectomized and implanted with a silastic capsule of oestradiol which remained in place throughout the experiment. Treatment with chlorimipramine caused a significant decrease in both proceptivity and receptivity: the number of sexual invitations made by females decreased and their refusal of mounting attempts by the male increased such that their acceptance ratios declined (Fig. 5). The copulatory performance of the males with whom they were paired also decreased during the females' treatment periods, and this was probably a direct consequence of their decreased proceptivity and receptivity at this time (Everitt 1977*b*).

Concentrations of 5-HIAA in cisternal CSF decreased significantly during

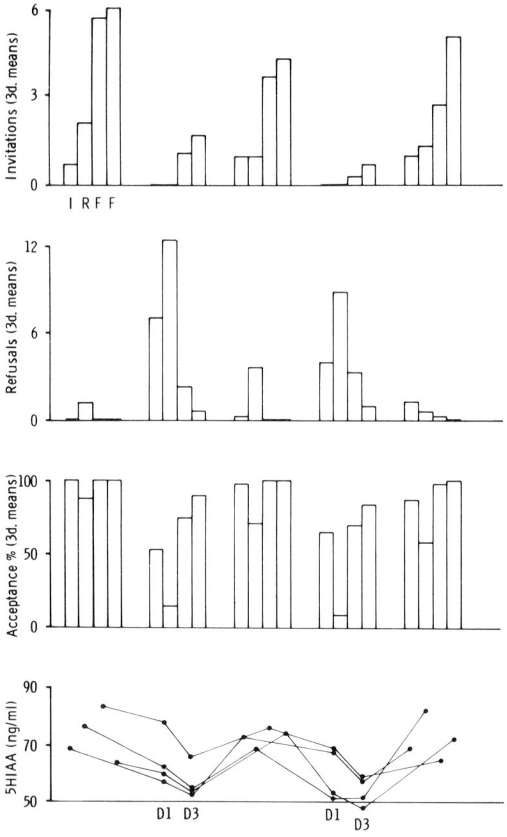

FIG. 5. The effects of chlorimipramine (5 mg/kg twice daily) on proceptivity, receptivity and 5-HIAA levels in CSF of ovariectomized, oestrogen-treated rhesus monkeys. Behavioural data represented as three-day means from four females (I,R,F,R) during two repetitions of each treatment. 5-HIAA levels were measured in the same females during a subsequent experiment not involving behavioural observations. D1 and D3, 1st and 3rd days of treatment. All females received a subcutaneous silastic capsule containing oestradiol-17β, in place for the duration of the experiment. (For further details see Everitt 1977*b*.)

chlorimipramine treatment, with a trend to lower levels from Day 1 to Day 3 (Fig 5). This decrease in 5-HIAA levels has also been seen clinically (Åsberg *et al.* 1977; Bertilson *et al.* 1974; Walinder *et al.* 1976) and presumably reflects the fact that serotonin is inaccessible to intraneuronal monoamine oxidase during inhibition of uptake. A significant correlation existed between 5-HIAA levels and the numbers of refusals before and during chlorimipramine treatment (r=0.72; P< 0.01).

The effects of chlorimipramine on the sexual behaviour of female monkeys emphasize again the profound consequences of modulating serotoninergic transmission. The postsynaptic serotonin receptor stimulation induced by the uptake inhibitor presumably underlies the behavioural change and provides complementary data to the results obtained with PCPA, described above. These results may also provide some explanation for the effects on sexual activity in patients receiving the drug, which may be severe enough to provoke discontinuation of their therapy (G. Beaumont, personal communication). The fact that chlorimipramine and other tricyclic and tetracyclic drugs are widely used in the treatment of affective behaviour disorders (particularly depression) raises the intriguing question of defining the relationship between mood and sexual behaviour. Clearly, mood is an important determinant of sexual arousal in man, but an extremely difficult variable to study experimentally (see also the chapter by Keverne in this volume).

(3) A compound which has been widely prescribed in clinical endocrinology in recent years is bromocriptine (2-brom-α-ergocriptine; CB154). It is a dopamine receptor agonist used especially in the treatment of hyperprolactinaemia, since one of its major actions is to reduce plasma prolactin levels—presumably by directly stimulating dopamine receptors in the anterior pituitary (Besser *et al.* 1972; Horrobin 1973; Fuxe *et al.* 1976*a*). This drug has also been used, with somewhat disputed success, in the treatment of impotence (see for, example, Ambrosi *et al.* 1977).

In female rats, bromocriptine and other dopamine receptor agonists have biphasic effects on sexual receptivity, enhancing it at low doses (which are, however, much larger than those used clinically) and inhibiting it at high doses (Everitt & Fuxe 1977). This biphasic dose-response relationship is explained by selective pre- and postsynaptic actions of the drugs at low and high doses respectively, hypotheses discussed more fully elsewhere (Aghajanian & Bunney 1974; Everitt & Fuxe 1977). But no reports on the effects of bromocriptine on sexual and associated behaviour in primates, including man, have appeared as yet.

Thus, bromocriptine (25, 50 and 100 mg/kg) was given to ovariectomized female monkeys (implanted with a silastic capsule containing oestradiol) and its effects on sexual proceptivity, serum prolactin and luteinizing hormone (LH) were measured. Fig. 6 shows that, while all three doses were equipotent in lowering serum prolactin levels (LH levels did not change throughout the experiment), only the smallest dose (25 μg/kg) had any consistent, significant, effect on proceptivity. The number of sexual invitations made by females and the proportion of sexual interaction (mounts) they initiated increased significantly during treatment with 25 μg/kg bromocriptine; the 50 and 100 μg/kg doses were without effect (Fig. 6).

It is quite clear that the actions of bromocriptine on sexual behaviour did not depend on the lowering of prolactin levels, since there was a clear dissociation between the two effects. The data also emphasize the peculiar sensitivity of pituitary dopamine receptors to bromocriptine, as reflected in its ability to maximally lower prolactin levels at very low doses. This could be explained by the fact that systemically administered drugs have privileged access to

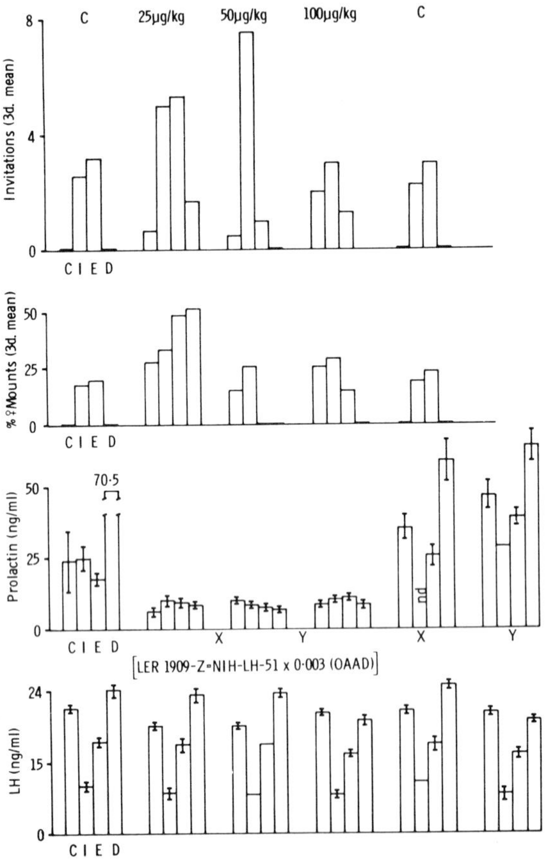

FIG. 6. The effects of 2-Br-α-ergocriptine (bromocriptine, CB154) on proceptivity and serum prolactin and LH levels in ovariectomized, oestrogen-treated rhesus monkeys. Behavioural data represented as three-day means from four females (C,I,E,D). Prolactin and LH levels measured using a radioimmunoassay. Details of the LH standard are shown, the concentrations (ng/ml) having been corrected to the standard. All females received a silastic oestradiol implant. Bromocriptine was injected 30 min before testing.

dopamine receptors in the pituitary (which are outside the blood-brain barrier), or that bromocriptine preferentially occupies the particular configuration of these receptors (if indeed they are different from those in, say, the striatum or nucleus accumbens). The fact that this drug changes dopamine turnover in hypothalamic and limbic areas at lower doses than in the striatum provides some support for this view (Everitt & Fuxe 1977).

There are insufficient data in the lower dose range (less than 25 μg/kg) for us to state at present whether the effects of bromocriptine on proceptivity in female monkeys are truly biphasic, as in rats. If they are, it provides a special challenge to assess whether they are explainable in terms of selective presynaptic and postsynaptic dopamine receptor activation at low and high doses and, more important, where in the brain the relevant dopamine neurons are situated (see below).

(4) The above experiments have all been done on female monkeys; indeed, there have been very few psychopharmacological experiments on the sexual behaviour of male monkeys. But there have also been comparatively few studies of the endocrine and neural determinants of sexual behaviour in male primates, and good data on this subject have appeared only recently (Slimp *et al.* 1978). The last experiment I shall describe, then, involves male rhesus monkeys. It is related to the experiments in which chlorimipramine and bromocriptine were used, described above, in that it involves the use of one of a family of clinically prescribed drugs which are gaining wide acceptance in the control and treatment of hypertension, namely the β-blockers. More recently, however, these drugs have been reported to possess anxiolytic properties (James *et al.* 1977) and it is partly in this context that they have been used here. But, in addition, β-blocking drugs have been seen to enhance sexual behaviour in female rats when given both systemically (Everitt 1977*c*; Fuxe *et al.* 1976*b*) and intrahypothalamically (Ward *et al.* 1975), while α-blocking drugs have the opposite effect (Everitt 1977*c*).

Four male rhesus monkeys, new to the colony in Cambridge, who were rather inconsistent and unusual performers during observations of sexual behaviour when they were paired with females, were selected for this experiment. They formed a somewhat heterogeneous group, two of the males (M15 and M17) mounting the female only once per test and ejaculating immediately, while the remaining two (M13 and M14) ejaculated after some 10-15 mounts, of which a very low proportion were associated with intromissions and thrusts (Fig. 7). Their mounting rates and ejaculation times were very variable (Fig. 7). Besides these quantitative measures, a necessarily subjective assessment of these animals suggested that they were 'stressed' or 'anxious' during the observation periods. They spent much of the time pacing round the cage, ignoring the female and not engaging in grooming activity with her. There are obvious difficulties in using terms such as 'anxious', which are essentially human in concept, to describe the behaviour of non-human primates, but the hypothesis tested in these experiments was that the drug oxprenolol, a β-blocker with reported anxiolytic properties, could exert its 'anxiety-reducing' actions in these males such that they could engage in more consistent sexual interaction when paired with females in the laboratory.

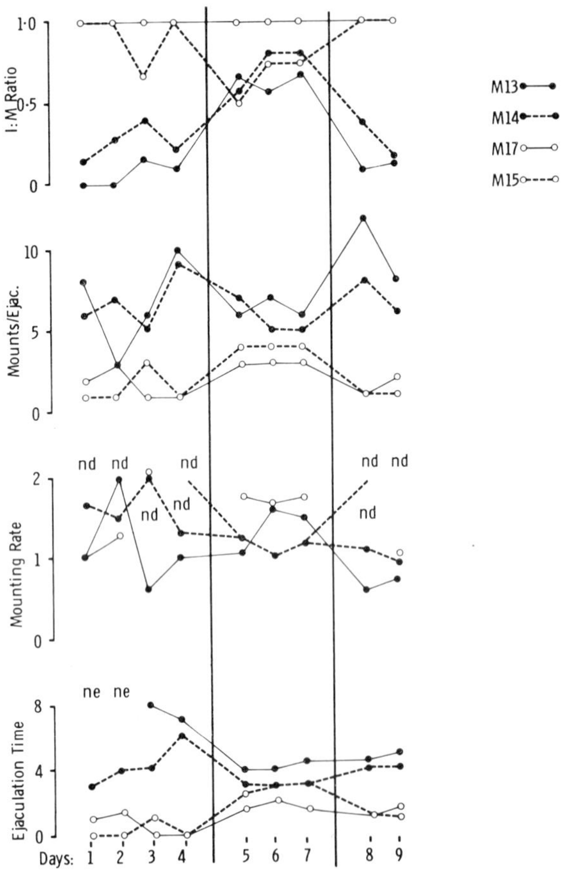

FIG. 7. The effects of oxprenolol (1mg/kg) on components of sexual behaviour of intact male rhesus monkeys. I : M ratio, intromission/mount ratio. Mounts/Ejac., no. of mounts to ejaculation. n.d., no data; n.e., no ejaculation. Oxprenolol was injected subcutaneously 1 h before testing. The points represent data from individual observations.

Fig. 7 shows that oxprenolol (1 mg/kg per day) had marked effects on the sexual activity of each male which were as heterogeneous as the baseline levels of behaviour. Thus, those males who ejaculated during the only mount of the test period (M15 and M17), began making more mounts, with intromissions, before ejaculating (Fig. 7). Conversely, M13 and M14 began making fewer mounts with higher proportions of intromissions before ejaculating (Fig. 7). Mounting rates and ejaculation times became much more consistent during treatment and, indeed, the behavioural parameters shown became similar for all four males at this time. When the drug was withdrawn the males' behaviour tended towards pretreatment levels, producing the 'butterfly-shaped' patterns in Fig. 7.

These experiments are preliminary in nature, but the behavioural effects of oxprenolol may be interpreted to be consistent with the original hypothesis and to be those predicted of an anxiolytic drug. However, measurements of serum prolactin and cortisol levels before, during and after treatment did not reveal any endocrine picture which might be expected to reflect 'stress' or 'anxiety'. Thus, there were no significant differences in prolactin levels, measured immediately after testing, before or during oxprenolol treatment. Cortisol levels were also similar at these times and were not significantly different from levels in other monkeys in the colony. It may be that the concentration of prolactin (a characteristic 'surge' hormone) became elevated at the start rather than the end of an observation period, and this will be investigated. But it should be stated here that there is no support for the suggestion of an anxiolytic effect of oxprenolol in these monkeys other than that derived from the behavioural results. These may, of course, reflect the effects of the drug on β-receptor mediated mechanisms underlying sexual behaviour (Everitt *et al.* 1975*b*; Everitt 1977*c*; Fuxe *et al.* 1976*b*), but this awaits further investigation.

SUMMARY AND GENERAL DISCUSSION

Although, from experiments described in the first section (p. 330), little evidence was obtained of aminergic involvement in the effect of hormones on proceptivity and receptivity, the experiments described in the second section (p. 334) make it clear that manipulating cerebral monoamines with drugs results in major alterations in sexual behaviour. The simple conclusions arising from this work are that serotonin (from the use of PCPA, 5-hydroxytryptophan and chlorimipramine) and dopamine (bromocriptine) are two important transmitter substances in the context of sexual behaviour. But the likelihood that these types of experiments will give precise information about the nature of the link between hormones and monoamines in specific areas of the brain, known from other research to be important for the expression of sexual behaviour, is strictly limited. This is not to say the information is not useful: first, I feel it has particular value in a clinical setting, a subject to which I shall return below. Secondly, it provides a clear guide as to where to look more closely, using refined techniques, at this neuroendocrine system. Such techniques, which form the basis of a closely related approach to these problems, involve precise intervention with monoamine neurons in the brain and represent, therefore, a marked improvement over the systemic administration of psychoactive drugs. In these experiments neurochemically specific neurotoxic drugs (e.g. 6-hydroxydopamine; 5,7-dihydroxytryptamine) are injected intracerebrally into small components of the aminergic projections in order to produce regional denervations of areas in the brain which selectively involve one transmitter system. Measuring the endocrine and behavioural effects of these lesions, both directly and after a challenge with hormones or receptor-acting drugs, yields information of a much more precise kind than that obtained by other techniques. In another context, the tremendous breakthrough in understanding the pathology and pharmacology of Parkinson's disease which followed exploration of the nigro-striatal dopamine neurons with 6-hydroxydopamine (Ungerstedt 1971) represents a good example of the power of this approach.

To do these experiments efficiently it is necessary to know precisely which sites in the brain actively accumulate sex steroids (Pfaff 1971; Pfaff *et al.* 1976); where, in the brain, lesions and hormone implants affect sexual behaviour (Davidson 1972; Everitt 1978); and the stereotaxic co-ordinates of the origins, projections and terminations of monoamine neurons. These are all well known for the rat, and the first two for primates (at least in part), but the absence of a stereotaxic map of monoamine neurons in the monkey brain has been an important limitation in experiments on neurochemical mechanisms of sexual behaviour in primates. A major project, undertaken by Sue Schofield in this laboratory and now almost complete, has been to map monoamine neurons in the rhesus monkey (and in talapoin monkeys, to some extent) using Falck-Hillarp fluorescence histochemical techniques in association with stereotaxically placed lesions. The terminations of serotoninergic neurons, which are virtually impossible to visualize, are being defined using a highly sensitive radioenzymic assay for serotonin in combination with micro-dissection of small areas of the brain. It is already apparent that important differences between rodents and the rhesus monkey exist in the locations of cell groups in the brain stem and, more critical for subsequent lesion placements, in the courses taken by ascending projections (S. Schofield &

B. J. Everitt, unpublished). Thus we feel poised to initiate behavioural and neuroendocrine experiments utilizing the approaches outlined above.

A number of experiments have been done using these techniques in rats with very interesting results (Everitt *et al.* 1975*a*; Wright & Everitt 1977; Larsson *et al.* 1978).

Thus, 5,7-dihydroxytryptamine lesions of serotoninergic projections to the diencephalon (particularly hypothalamus) and septal nuclei enhance sexual behaviour in female and male rats (Everitt *et al.* 1975*a*; Larsson *et al.* 1978). In females, the effect takes the form of increasing the animal's sensitivity to oestradiol such that progesterone is unnecessary for the display of proceptive and receptive behaviour. These lesions have subsequently been made more specific in attempts to define which divisions of this subcortically projecting serotoninergic system are particularly important in mediating the behavioural changes (see Everitt 1978).

Thus these techniques are powerful, but it remains vitally important to understand which kinds of events, in the context of sexual behaviour, the aminergic systems mediate and how they interact with hormone-dependent functions of the brain (see Herbert 1977). In particular, the relationships between recently described systems of peptidergic neurons (luteinizing hormone-releasing factor, LRF (LH-RH); thyrotropin-releasing factor, TRF, etc.) (see Fuxe *et al.* 1976*c*), aminergic neurons and hormone-sensitive areas of the brain are likely to prove most interesting in this respect—as they are known to be, for example, in the control of anterior pituitary function (Herbert 1978*a*; Everitt 1978).

But, to return briefly to the subject of psychopharmacology, I believe it to be of great, albeit different, value to assess in primates the behavioural and endocrine effects of drugs used widely in psychiatry. This is not simply because all too little is known of the effects of such drugs, or that they have well-defined properties which make them useful investigative tools. It is more because many of these compounds are used in man to alter mood (to alleviate depression or anxiety, for example) and, as referred to above, mood is an important determinant of sexual arousal (in man at least) as well as an important consequence of social interaction. The chapter by Keverne in this volume emphasizes very clearly the major effects that the social interactions underlying dominance hierarchies have on endocrine and behavioural functions in talapoin monkeys. Whether or not this provides an opportunity to study affective behaviours experimentally is discussed elsewhere (Everitt & Keverne 1978), but much must be done to devise an efficient system of behavioural analysis before we can be sure (see also Herbert 1978*b*).

In attempts to study behaviour in monkeys, in either social or experimental (psychopharmacological) situations, endocrine measures such as prolactin, cortisol and LH levels in blood are likely to be of considerable importance in establishing correspondences between these behaviours and those described in man. This is particularly the case when words such as 'depressed' and 'anxious' are used in experimental studies, since the essentially human, verbal component used to define these terms is lacking and they must be described, therefore, in different ways, based on behavioural observations of the kind discussed above and by Keverne earlier in this symposium.

ACKNOWLEDGEMENTS

I express sincere thanks to my collaborators in these experiments, namely Joe Herbert, Kjell Fuxe, Mike Baum, Nick Martensz and Sue Schofield. Excellent technical help has been provided by Maureen Newton, Sue Dilley and Lesley Bowman. Financial support was provided by the Medical Research Council, The Royal Society and Geigy Pharmaceuticals, UK and is gratefully acknowledged. Sandoz generously provided the bromocriptine.

References

ÅSBERG, M., RINBERGER, V. A., SJÖQVIST, F., THOREN, P., TRÄSKMAN, L. & TUCK, J. R. (1977) Monoamine metabolites in cerebrospinal fluid and serotonin uptake inhibition during treatment with chlorimipramine. *Clin. Pharmacol. Ther. 21*, 201–207

AGHAJANIAN, G. K. & BUNNEY, B. S. (1974) Pre- and post-synaptic feedback mechanisms in central dopaminergic neurons, in *Frontiers of Neurology and Neuroscience Research*, (Seeman, P. & Brown, B. G., eds.), pp. 4–11, University of Toronto Press, Toronto

AMBROSI, B., BARA, R. & FAGLIA, G. (1977) Bromocryptine in impotence. *Lancet 2*, 987

BAUM, M. J.,EVERITT, B. J., HERBERT, J. & KEVERNE, E. B. (1977) Hormonal basis of proceptivity and receptivity in female primates. *Arch. Sex. Behav. 6*, 173–192

BEACH, F. A. (1976) Attractivity, proceptivity and receptivity in female mammals. *Horm. Behav. 7*, 105–138

BEAUMONT, G. (1973) Sexual side effects of chlorimipramine (Anafranil). *J. Int. Med. Res. 1*, 469–472

BERTILSON, L., ÅSBERG, M. & THOREN, P. (1974) Differential effect of chlorimipramine and nortriptyline on cerebrospinal fluid metabolites of serotonin and noradrenaline in depression. *Eur. J. Clin. Pharmacol. 7*, 365–368

BESSER, G. M., PARKE, L., EDWARDS, C. R. W., FORSYTH, I. A. & MCNEILLY, A. S. (1972) Galactorrhea: successful treatment with reduction of plasma prolactin levels by bromoergocryptine. *Br. Med. J. 3*, 669–672

CARLSSON, A., CORRODI, H., FUXE, K. & HÖKFELT, T. (1969) Effects of antidepressant drugs on the depletion of intraneuronal brain 5-hydroxytryptamine stores caused by 4-methyl-α-ethyl metatyramine. *Eur. J. Pharmacol. 5*, 357–369

COUPER-SMARTT, J. D. & RODHAM, R. (1973) A technique for surveying side-effects of tricyclic drugs with reference to reported sexual effects. *J. Int. Med. Res. 1*, 473–476

DAVIDSON, J. M. (1972) Hormones and reproductive behaviour, in *Reproductive Biology* (Balin, H. & Glasser, S., eds.), Elsevier/Excerpta Medica/North-Holland, Amsterdam

EVERITT, B. J. (1977*a*) Cerebral monoamines and sexual behaviour, in *Handbook of Sexology* (Money, J. & Musaph, H., eds.), Elsevier/North-Holland, Amsterdam

EVERITT, B. J. (1977*b*) The effects of chlorimipramine and other inhibitors of monoamine uptake on the sexual behaviour of female rats and monkeys. *Postgrad. Med. J. 53,* Suppl. 4, 202–210

EVERITT, B. J. (1977*c*) Adrenergic mechanisms in the control of sexual behaviour: the relationship to depression and its treatment, in *Depression – the Biochemical and Physiological Role of Ludiomil* (Jukes, A., ed.), pp. 59–67, CIBA-GEIGY, Basle

EVERITT, B. J. (1978) A neuroanatomical approach to the study of monoamines and sexual behaviour, in *Biological Determinants of Sexual Behaviour* (Hutchison, J. B., ed.), pp. 555–574, Wiley, Chichester & New York

EVERITT, B. J. & FUXE, K. (1977) Dopamine and the sexual behaviour of female rats. Effects of dopamine receptor agonists and sulpiride. *Neurosci. Lett. 4,* 209–213

EVERITT, B. J. & HERBERT, J. (1971) The effects of dexamethasone and androgens on the sexual receptivity of female rhesus monkeys. *J. Endocrinol. 51,* 575–588

EVERITT, B. J. & HERBERT, J. (1975) The effects of implanting testosterone propionate into the central nervous system and sexual receptivity of female rhesus monkeys. *Brain Res. 86,* 109–120

EVERITT, B. J. & KEVERNE, E. B. (1978) Models of depression based on behavioural studies of experimental animals. *British Association of Psychopharmacology Monograph No. 1,* Clarendon Press, Oxford, in press

EVERITT, B. J., HERBERT, J. & HAMER, J. (1972) Sexual receptivity of bilaterally adrenalectomized female rhesus monkeys. *Physiol. Behav. 8,* 409–415

EVERITT, B. J., FUXE, K. & JONSSON, G. (1975*a*) The effects of 5,7-dihydroxytryptamine lesions of ascending 5-hydroxytryptamine pathways on the sexual and aggressive behaviour of female rats. *J. Pharmacol. (Paris) 6,* 25–32

EVERITT, B. J., FUXE, K., HÖKFELT, T. & JONSSON, G. (1975*b*) Role of monoamines in the control by hormones of sexual receptivity in the female rat. *J. Comp. Physiol. Psychol. 89,* 556–572

FUXE, K., HÖKFELT, T., LÖFSTROM, A., JOHANSSON, O., AGNATI, L., EVERITT, B. J., GOLDSTEIN, M., JEFFCOATE, N., WHITE, N., ENEROTH, P., GUSTAFSSON, J.A. & SETT, P. (1976*a*) On the role of neurotransmitters and hypothalamic hormones and their interactions in hypothalamic and extrahypothalamic control of pituitary function and sexual behaviour, in *Subcellular Mechanisms in Reproductive Neuroendocrinology* (Naftolin, F., Ryan, K. J. & Davies, J., eds.), pp. 193–290, Elsevier, Amsterdam & New York

FUXE, K., BOLME, P., & EVERITT, B. J. (1976*b*) The effects of beta- adrenergic blocking agents on arterial blood pressure and central monoamine turnover: possibility of agonist activity at central adrenaline receptors, in *Beta Adrenergic Blockers and Hypertension* (Ganten, D., Dietz, R., Luth, B. & Gross, F., eds.), pp. 131–142, Georg Thieme-Verlag, Stuttgart

FUXE, K., HÖKFELT, T., JOHANSSON, O., GANTEN, D., GOLDSTEIN, M., PEREZ DE LA MORA, M., POSSANI, L., TAPIA, R., TERAN, L., PALACIOS, R., SAID, S. & MUTT, V. (1976*c*) Monoamine neuron systems in the hypothalamus and their relation to GABA and peptide-containing neurons, in *INSERM Colloque de Synthésis 1976. Actions thématiques 22 et 35 Neuroendocrinologie,* pp. 17–40, INSERM, Paris

GRADWELL, P. B., EVERITT, B. J. & HERBERT, J. (1975) 5-hydroxytryptamine in the central nervous system and sexual receptivity of female rhesus monkeys. *Brain Res. 88,* 281–293

HERBERT, J. (1977) Hormones and behaviour. *Proc. R. Soc. Lond. Ser. B Biol. Sci. 199,* 425–443

HERBERT, J. (1978*a*) Neuro-hormonal integration of sexual behaviour in female primates, in *Biological Determinants of Sexual Behaviour* (Hutchison, J. B., ed.), pp. 467–491, Wiley, Chichester & New York

HERBERT, J. (1978*b*) Neurobiological concepts and methods in the study of sexual behaviour. *Arch. Sex. Behav.* in press

HORROBIN, D. F. (1973) *Prolactin: Physiology and Clinical Significance,* M.T.P., Lancaster

JAMES, I. M., PEARSON, R. M., GRIFFITH, D. N. W. & NEWBURY, P. (1977) Effect of oxprenolol on stage-fright in musicians. *Lancet 2,* 952–954

JOHNSON, D. F. & PHOENIX, C. H. (1976) Hormonal control of female sexual attractiveness,

proceptivity and receptivity in rhesus monkeys. *J. Comp. Physiol. Psychol. 90,* 473–483
LARSSON, K., FUXE, K., EVERITT, B. J., HOLMGREN, H. & SÖDERSTEN, P. (1978) Sexual behaviour of male rats after intracerebral injection of 5,7-dihydroxytryptamine. *Brain Res. 141,* 293–303
MEYERSON, B. J., MALMNÄS, C. O. & EVERITT, B. J. (1978) Neuropharmacology, neurotransmitters and sexual behaviour in mammals, in *Handbook of Behavioral Neurobiology* (Goy, R. W. & Pfaff, D. W., eds.), Plenum Press, New York, in press
MICEV, V. & MARSHALL, W. K. (1973) Undesired effects in slow intravenous infusion of chlorimipramine (Anafranil). *J. Int. Med. Res. 1,* 452–455
PFAFF, D. W. (1971) Steroid sex hormones in the rat brain: specificity of uptake and physiological effects, in *Steroid Hormones and Brain Function* (Sawyer, C.H. & Gorski, R. A., eds.), pp. 103–112, University of California Press, Berkeley
PFAFF, D. W., GERLACH, J. C., MCEWEN, B. S., FERIN, M., CARMEL, P. & ZIMMERMAN, E. Z. (1976) Autoradiographic localization of hormone-concentrating cells in the brain of the female rhesus monkey. *J. Comp. Neurol. 170,* 279–294
SLIMP, J. C., HART, B. L. & GOY, R. W. (1978) Heterosexual, autosexual and social behaviour of adult male rhesus monkeys with medial preoptic-anterior hypothalamic lesions. *Brain Res. 142,* 105–122
STUMPF, W. E. & GRANT, L. D. (eds.) (1975) *Anatomical Neuroendocrinology,* Karger, Basel
TRIMBLE, M. R. & HERBERT, J. (1968) The effect of testosterone or oestradiol upon the sexual and associated behaviour of the adult feral rhesus monkey. *J. Endocrinol. 42,* 171–185
UNGERSTEDT, U. (1971) *Acta Physiol. Scand.* Suppl. 367, 1–122
WARD, I. L., CROWLEY, W. R., ZEMLAN, F. P. & MARGULES, D. C. (1975) Monoaminergic mediation of female sexual behaviour. *J. Comp. Physiol. Psychol. 88,* 53–61
WRIGHT, CH. & EVERITT, B. J. (1977) The effects of dorsal noradrenaline bundle lesions on the sexual behaviour of female rats. *Exp. Brain Res.,* EBBS Suppl. R48–R49 (abstr.)
WALINDER, J., SKOTT, A., CARLSSON, A., NAGY, A. & ROOS, B. E. (1976) Potentiation of the antidepressant action of chlorimipramine by tryptophan. *Arch. Gen. Psychiatr. 33,* 1384–1389

Discussion

Sachar: I gather that if you reduce testosterone levels in the female monkey, sexual behaviour is reduced; at the same time you show that serotoninergic activity increases. Is that correct?

Everitt: This was only the case in the experiment in which dexamethasone was used to reduce testosterone levels. I suggested that the changes in levels of 5-hydroxyindoleacetic acid (5-HIAA) in cisternal cerebrospinal fluid (CSF) reflected much wider effects of dexamethasone in the brain than those simply related to suppressing adrenal androgens. The fact that no changes in 5-HIAA concentration were measured when the hormonal intervention was more precise (e.g. by implanting testosterone in the hypothalamus) supports this view. Many of these problems are associated with the large size of the CSF pool tapped, so that any *regional* change in 5-HIAA concentration is diluted by the time we measure it in the cisterna magna.

Sachar: You gave *p*-chlorophenylalanine (PCPA), which generally reduces serotonin levels in the brain, and then sexual activity increased. Then you selectively destroyed serotoninergic neurons to the hypothalamus by injecting 5,7-dihydroxytryptamine into serotonin axons in the midbrain and sexual activity again increased. So it looks as if testosterone may exert its effects on sexual behaviour by effects on the serotonin system, by reducing serotonin activity?

Everitt: That is how the data have been interpreted by many workers. I am more cautious, because it is apparent that the neurons which bind sex steroids are not serotonin neurons. It is also clear that giving testosterone or decreasing central serotonin activity could affect sexual behaviour in different ways. An important question is the nature of the interaction between neurons which accumulate steroids in the hypothalamus and, for example, serotonin neurons which project to them from the mesencephalic raphe nuclei. In other words, what kinds of influences (environmental or endogenous) do the aminergic neurons mediate and how is this related to the functions, behavioural or endocrine, of the steroid-concentrating neurons they project to? This is easier to answer in the framework of anterior pituitary function, at present.

Sachar: In your bromocriptine experiments you saw a biphasic effect on behaviour and a uniphasic effect on prolactin secretion. Carlsson, looking at effects of dopamine receptor stimulants on behaviour in rats, finds a similar biphasic effect (Carlsson 1976). Low doses of apomorphine have a sedating effect on activity; with increased doses the rats become very active. He believes that the dopamine neuron has an auto-receptor, a presynaptic receptor, and that at low doses the auto-receptor is activated, which turns off the presynaptic neuron and reduces net dopaminergic activity. At higher doses, the postsynaptic receptor is activated, giving behavioural activation. We have looked at the differences between this system and the pituitary system regulating prolactin secretion in man. There are dopamine receptors on prolactin-secreting cells in the pituitary. We studied the effects of the dopamine agonist piribedil (ET-495) (B. Angrist, M. Ain, J. Rotrosen, S. Gershon, F. S. Halpern & E. J. Sachar, to be published). At low doses our subjects were very sedated, which fits with Carlsson's data. But if the pituitary system were behaving precisely like the behavioural system studied by Carlsson we should have seen a paradoxical rise in prolactin and also dopamine inhibition, but we didn't. We found that while behaviourally the subjects were sedated, prolactin secretion was suppressed. So it looks as if the dopamine agonists have a uniphasic effect on the pituitary, suppressing prolactin, but the dopamine receptor system in the brain which regulates behaviour works differently and dopamine agonists may affect it biphasically. That is what you found in rhesus monkeys. You are therefore right to be cautious about interpreting the effects of bromocriptine on behaviour as purely due to a suppression of prolactin secretion. They may be recruiting a different population of auto-receptors in the brain from the pituitary receptors.

Brawer: The serotoninergic pathway, at least as studied in adult rat neocortex, is not really a classical synaptic pathway, in that the serotoninergic terminals don't form synaptic contacts on recipient cells (Descarries *et al.* 1975). The terminals are very large. They may form a few spine terminals, but are presumed to work by releasing serotonin and bathing vast areas of tissue in serotonin in a non-specific way rather than by point-to-point synaptic contact. It is a unique system, because catecholaminergic systems seem electrophysiologically and anatomically to be of the classical form. The serotoninergic system has to be looked at in this light rather than as a system of discrete neuronal connections.

Herbert: In electron micrographs of any part of the central nervous system the majority of terminals seen are *not* forming synapses. The question is whether they form synapses in a different plane of the section, or whether our conventional view is true. There is also the point that Descarries *et al.* (1975) didn't find all serotonin terminals looking the way you describe; 5% of them formed conventional synapses.

Brawer: Five per cent is after all only five per cent. Furthermore, there is evidence in other monoaminergic systems that classical synapses are formed.

Herbert: Is that true for noradrenaline? Has it been shown that noradrenaline neurons form true synaptic contacts?

Brawer: According to the group at Karolinska Institute, probable noradrenergic terminals in the hypothalamus are associated with Gray-type I synaptic specializations (see Fuxe *et al.* 1970). More recently it was shown that a significant proportion of noradrenergic terminal profiles in the hippocampus show typical synaptic specializations (Koda *et al.* 1978).

Everitt: Hökfelt (1968) has always maintained in his electron microscopical study of aminergic neurons that, for example in the caudate, the dopamine terminals are not associated with true synaptic contacts.

Beach: Going back to the studies of PCPA and recalling the claims that it produces 'hypersexual' behaviour (Ferguson *et al.* 1970), can you relate those claims to your own work? I am interested in this because research in my laboratory on male cats failed to confirm the original reports (Zitrin *et al.* 1970).

Everitt: Where that has been looked at carefully, for example in your study, hypersexual behaviour did not follow serotonin depletion induced by PCPA. But I am not sure of the value of taking animals already performing optimally in the behavioural situation in which they are placed and treating them with often very large doses of a non-specific drug like PCPA and trying to make statements about the mechanisms underlying any behaviour change.

Sachar: But you did find an effect on sexual behaviour?

Everitt: Yes, but our monkeys were not 'hypersexual'. In the work Dr Beach refers to, which claims hypersexuality after PCPA treatment, the behaviours measured involved rabbits mounting anaesthetized cats, and 10 rats all mounting one another. It was difficult to sort out the effects of the drug on the mounting animal and on those being mounted, and whether or not the mounts were sexual or represented a general increase in activity. In the experiments I described the monkeys had one component of their behaviour (proceptivity) impaired by removal of androgens. Treatment with PCPA restored their behaviour, perhaps by mimicking the actions of androgens. The latter is the real problem—how are serotonin depletion and androgen action related?

Green: Loss of sexual interest is one of the ways we define depression in man. Are there any studies in which depressed people with low sex drive have been given antidepressants and a dissociation has been found between the effects of the drug on affect and on sexuality? Or do both always improve together?

Sachar: Usually when you treat a patient with an antidepressant all the symptoms improve together. When there has not been a total return to full sex drive this has usually been associated with a modified general clinical response. There is no obvious dissociation. But the fine analysis of this point hasn't been done.

Bancroft: My impression is that there isn't the necessary precise information on sexual behaviour to enable one to answer Dr Green's question.

Green: Has anyone taken people with low sex drive who are *not* depressed and attempted to treat them with antidepressants?

Bancroft: Ivor Mills (personal communication) thinks that the treatment of many cases of sexual dysfunction of various kinds is to give antidepressants, mainly tricyclic drugs.

Everitt: These are a very varied group of drugs in their neurochemical effects. Thus, to take two which Mills uses (Mills 1977), amitriptyline and nortriptyline, the former combines serotonin receptor blockade with inhibition of noradrenaline reuptake; the latter is a relatively clean inhibitor of noradrenaline uptake alone. There seems to be no clear rationale behind the use of either drug in Mills' work—or, indeed, for their differential prescription in the treatment of depression. Interestingly in this respect, chlorimipramine has been used with apparent success to treat premature ejaculation, although the trial was not controlled (Eaton 1973).

Hutchison: Dr Everitt, how do you know that serotoninergic neurons don't bind oestrogen?

Everitt: The identity and sites of neurons which specifically take up and bind oestrogen are well known from the work of Donald Pfaff (1971). They lie in three major areas: the medio-basal hypothalamus and preoptic area; the septal nuclei; and the amygdala and entorhinal cortex. The sites of serotonin neurons are also well known; the ones which project rostrally (B5, B6, B7, B8 and B9) lie in the pontine and mesencephalic raphe and, clearly, do not take up and bind oestradiol. They may, however, project to neurons in the anterior hypothalamus, for example, which do concentrate the hormone, and it is here that efforts to discern the patterns of interaction between hormones and amines should be focused. The only aminergic neurons which have been seen to bind oestradiol are the dopamine neurons of the arcuate nucleus and noradrenaline neurons in cell groups A1, A2, A5, A6 and A7. This was demonstrated in a combined autoradiographic/fluorescence histochemical study (Grant & Stumpf 1975; Heritage *et al.* 1977).

Hutchison: However, the autoradiographic label may not be oestrogen. But the question I wanted to ask is how close you think we are to finding a relationship between effects of steroids at the level of the hypothalamus and the effects obtained with neurotransmitters. What intermediates do you see between binding of the steroid to intracellular receptors and genomic effects of the steroid at the level of the cell nucleus, and the eventual transmitter effects?

Everitt: This is a particularly interesting question which, I think, brings us to the additional question of peptide-containing neurons in the brain and the way they may interact with, and provide the key to, hormone-amine interactions. Since he has a vested interest in this subject, I would like to ask Dr Herbert to reply to this question.

Herbert: Could I add another question: what do we know of the exact anatomical relationship between amine terminals and steroid-binding neurons? For example, do they end directly on such neurons or is there an intermediate cell? Demonstrating such relationships is a formidable problem, bearing in mind the different techniques involved (but see Grant & Stumpf (1975) for an attempted synthesis). We also need to know exactly how altering monoaminergic activity modulates the functions of steroid-sensitive systems. It has always seemed to me that many of the data resulting from modifying monoamines in this way can be interpreted in terms of changing an animal's sensitivity to its own steroids; thus the animal may respond to doses of hormone which, before treatment, were ineffective. This kind of result can be obtained if one looks at either neuroendocrine function or a behavioural response to steroids in animals given drugs which alter monoamines. One basic question is whether monoamines have a direct effect on steroid-sensitive systems or whether these transmitters have a pervasive effect on a variety of stimuli, of which a given behaviour is but one.

Finally, there is a problem of how neuropeptides relate to monoamines and steroids, since peptides may turn out to have great importance in the behavioural mechanisms we are discussing. We know that the action of peptides on the pituitary is modulated by steroids (see Discussion in Gainer 1977) and the same process may occur in the brain. We also know that the action of certain amines (eg.dopamine) can be modulated by peptides. So we have a potential three-component system, and we have to specify the role of each component in a given behavioural context, such as sexual behaviour. I can't give you any answers; I can only pose some further questions.

Bancroft: When we stopped giving androgen to hypogonadal men the effect of the androgen went on for 2–3 weeks. What is the process that continues after the steroid is removed?

Herbert: That question was put by Stone in 1927, and nobody has answered it yet!

Hutchison: There is some indication that the maintenance of copulatory behaviour in the rat after castration may be influenced by vasopressin (Bohus 1977). The suggestion is made that vasopressin, which is known to influence memory of learned behaviour (de Wied *et al.* 1976), may also act to maintain memory processes associated with sexual behaviour.

Besser: Another variable related to the three being considered is the effect of catecholamines on peptide hormone responses. We have some indication that this takes place in the pituitary; the TSH response to TRH can be varied by means of a dopamine agonist, for example (Besser *et al.* 1975; Scanlon *et al.* 1977). You can impair this response by adding the agonist and enhance it with a dopamine receptor blocker.

I would like to comment on the point that responses to a compound, a dopamine agonist or whatever, have hormonal and behavioural components but the two are not necessarily dependent. I am surprised we should think that they should be. There is much clinical evidence from the use of bromocriptine that these effects can be totally dissociated. Bromocriptine suppresses prolactin at very low doses; prolactin secretion is exquisitely sensitive to dopamine agonists. Again, a normal person shows growth hormone release whereas an acromegalic patient shows growth hormone suppression in response to bromocriptine. There are opposite actions in different circumstances. Yet the dose of a dopamine agonist required to reduce growth hormone concentrations in the acromegalic patient is many times greater than that required to lower prolactin levels in patients with simple prolactinaemia. Only in patients receiving large doses of bromocriptine do we begin to see certain central effects such as insomnia. This is common in acromegalic patients treated with large doses of bromocriptine, whereas I have seen it only once in 250 patients on the low doses used for hyperprolactinaemia.

In Parkinsonism, where we also use bromocriptine, the dose required is another order of magnitude higher than for acromegaly. We suspect now that dopamine receptors fall into different categories, like the adrenoreceptors. The striatal and pituitary receptors are different, for instance. Drugs such as bromocriptine are 'dirty' drugs, in that they react with different types of receptor differently. I am not surprised to see different sensitivities and we should not try to explain all the actions of dopamine agonists according to the responses seen at the pituitary.

Green: Are there any controlled studies which relate sexual interest and sexual activity to Parkinsonism, before and after treatment with monoamines?

Everitt: Two careful studies on the effects of L-dopa in Parkinsonian men have been by Benkert (1973) and Hyyppä *et al.* (1970). Increases in sexual activity were reported in both studies but the effects were very slight. In addition, Benkert showed that the effect was not enhanced by also giving androgen. It remains unclear whether the effects of L-dopa really reflect an increase in libido or whether they are explained in large part by the reversal of akinesia and improvement in overall motor performance.

Green: Is there a reduction in sex interest as Parkinsonism develops, independent of the other bad effects?

Everitt: So far as I am aware, this question has not been specifically asked in studies of Parkinsonism. But it must be very difficult to dissociate changes in libido *per se* from the developing akinesia and motor symptoms such as tremor. The patients are also generally older people, and changes in libido may be those associated with ageing as well as with the disease itself.

Herbert: I agree entirely with Professor Besser that of the triad we have been discussing—peptide, steroid and monoamine—each interacts both ways with each of the other two. It is not a simple, straight-line situation. But we are also tending to think of monoamines as a group, like peptides or steroids. We should consider the different monoamines a little more carefully. In view of the different topography of dopaminergic and serotoninergic systems in the brain, should we expect to find a dissociation between behavioural and endocrine effects for serotonin comparable to the dissociation described by Dr Everitt for dopamine?

Everitt: As Dr Herbert knows, that is an extremely difficult if not impossible question to answer. It is true that the organization of nigro-striatal and mesolimbic dopamine systems appears, at least at first sight, not to have a parallel in the serotonin systems. Efforts to dissect out different functional roles of components of the widespread serotonin projections have not been as successful as those made on dopamine systems. I think this is in large part due to the scarcity of specific receptor agonists and antagonists with which to manipulate serotoninergic systems and hence make use of phenomena such as postsynaptic receptor supersensitivity, which have been so useful in functional studies of, particularly, striatal function. In inadequate answer to your question, I suppose I would not expect to find the behavioural and endocrine separation resulting from the effects of drugs on striatal, limbic and hypothalamic dopamine systems when manipulating serotoninergic transmission. Of course, the involvement of serotoninergic systems in endocrine mechanisms is rather obscure in any case.

Herbert: And you haven't got pituitary receptors for serotonin like those for dopamine.

Beach: Do you find serotonin-sensitive neurons in the cerebral cortex of the rat?

Everitt: Yes.

Beach: It appears, then, that by destroying serotonin neurons by intracerebral injection of 5,7-dihydroxytryptamine you might be removing a source of inhibition from other neurons which are oestrogen-sensitive. We know we can increase lordosis in female rats by removing or temporarily suppressing the cerebral cortex. Can you make anything of this connection?

Everitt: My impression is that the attempts to relate the mesencephalic reticular formation projections to the cerebral cortex to the actions of progesterone on lordosis, while interesting, are extremely difficult to understand and to fit into a meaningful picture.

The experiments of Yanase & Gorski (1976) are particularly important in this respect since they show that progesterone implanted in the midbrain tegmentum does induce sexual receptivity in oestrogen-primed female rats. It is true that many workers, including myself, believed that manipulations of serotoninergic transmission which enhanced sexual activity in female rats were closely related to the actions of progesterone, but I feel now that this belief is untenable. Such manipulations are more profitably to be regarded as changing the animal's sensitivity to oestrogen such that progesterone is no longer necessary for the complete expression of sexual receptivity. It is well known that increasing the dose of oestrogen given to spayed female rats effectively eliminates the necessity of injecting progesterone in order to induce sexual receptivity, so we may be dealing with a dose-response relationship in any case.

Lesions of the dorsal noradrenergic bundle, which arises from neurons in the locus coeruleus and is the most important noradrenergic projection to the cortex, almost completely prevent oestrogen and progesterone from activating receptivity in female rats (Wright & Everitt 1977). But careful examination of dose-response relationships showed that it was the effects of oestrogen that were impaired, not progesterone.

In answer to your question, then, I know of no good data which tie together the effects on lordosis of cerebral cortical ablation, the ascending projections of the reticular formation, monoamine neurons, and hormones (particularly progesterone).

Goy: Gorski and his co-workers induced receptive behaviour in rats to an otherwise subthreshold dose of oestrogen by means of a lesion in the septal region. The question is whether, if you injected a neurotoxic drug locally in very small quantity into the septal region of the brain, you would get this effect.

Everitt: The effects of septal lesions have been particularly well studied by Gorski's group (Nance *et al.* 1974, 1975*a,b*) and their results showed that electrolytic lesions of the lateral septal nuclei caused female and male rats to become extremely sensitive to oestradiol such that they displayed lordosis very readily in response to low doses of the hormone. We repeated and confirmed their experiments and showed in addition that these lesions in male rats caused the animals to respond to progesterone, which they do not normally do (J. C. Sterling, J. Chambers & B. J. Everitt, to be published). We went on to ask the question to what extent are the effects of septal lesions due to disruption of its serotonin, noradrenaline or dopamine inputs, knowing that fornix transections or lesions of the stria terminalis are without effect. Briefly, in female rats, lesions of serotoninergic neurons in the medial forebrain bundle produced by injection of 5,7-dihydroxytryptamine only increased their behavioural response to oestrogen if made caudal to the hypothalamus (Everitt *et al.* 1975). Lesions in the medial forebrain bundle rostral to the hypothalamus in the preoptic area, which depleted septal serotonin, were without effect. As I said, lesions of the dorsal noradrenergic bundle actually prevented the behavioural response to oestradiol so, clearly, this did not explain the effects of septal lesions either. Recently, we have shown that lesions of the lateral and to a lesser extent the medial part of the A10 dopamine cell group in the midbrain, produced by injecting 6-hydroxydopamine intracerebrally, cause an increase in the behavioural response of female rats to oestradiol, but these are best correlated with dopaminergic denervation of the nucleus accumbens and not the septum (E. Alton & B. J. Everitt, to be published). Clearly, these experiments have yet to be completed.

However, in male rats, 5,7-dihydroxytryptamine lesions of serotoninergic neurons in the diagonal band region of the preoptic area (tractus septohypothalamicus) beautifully mimicked the behavioural changes which follow electrolytic lesions of the septum. Thus, these animals displayed lordosis in response to low doses of oestradiol, and progesterone could enhance this response (J. Chambers & B. J. Everitt, to be published). These data need amplifying but they demonstrate clearly the power of selective neurotoxic lesions and also that, at least in part, the sex-hormone-dependent effects of septal lesions on behaviour are due to disruption of amine inputs to the septum or of axons running to nearby structures such as the nucleus accumbens.

References

BENKERT, O. (1973) Pharmacological experiments to stimulate human sexual behaviour, in *Psychopharmacology, Sexual Disorders and Drug Abuse* (Ban, T. A. *et al.*, eds.), pp. 489–495, North-Holland, Amsterdam

BESSER, G. S., BURROW, G. N., SPAULDING, S. W. & DONABEDIAN, R. K. (1975) Dopamine infusion actively inhibits the TSH and PRL response to TRH. *J. Clin. Endocrinol. Metab. 41,* 985–988

BOHUS, B. (1977) *Exp. Brain Res.,* E.B.B.S. Suppl. R8 (abstr.)

CARLSSON, A. (1976) Some aspects of dopamine in the basal ganglia, in *The Basal Ganglia (ARNMD 55)* (Yahr, M.D., ed.), pp. 181–189, Raven Press, New York

DESCARRIES, L., BEAUDET, A. & WATKINS, K. C. (1975) Serotonin nerve terminals in adult rat neocortex. *Brain Res. 100,* 563–588

DEWIED, D., VAN WIMERSMA GREIDANUS, T. B., BOHUS, B., URBAN, I. & GISPEN, W. H. (1976) *Prog. Brain Res. 45,* 181–191

EATON, H. (1973) Clomipramine in the treatment of premature ejaculation. *J. Int. Med. Res. 1,* 432–438

EVERITT, B. J., FUXE, K. & JONSSON, G. (1975) The effects of 5,7-dihydroxytryptamine lesions of ascending 5-hydroxytryptamine pathways on the sexual and aggressive behaviour of female rats. *J. Pharmacol. (Paris) 6,* 25–32

FERGUSON, J., HENRIKSEN, S., COHEN, H., MITCHELL, G., BARCHAS, J. & DEMENT, W. (1970) 'Hypersexuality' and behavioural changes in cats caused by administration of *p*-chlorophenylalanine. *Science (Wash. D.C.) 168,* 499–501

FUXE, K., HÖKFELT, T. & UNGERSTEDT, U. (1970) Morphological and functional aspects of central monoamine neurons. *Int. Rev. Neurobiol. 13,* 98–126

GAINER, H. (ed.) (1977) *Peptides in Neurobiology,* Plenum Press, New York

GRANT, L. D. & STUMPF, W. E. (1975) Hormone uptake sites in relation to CNS biogenic amine systems, in *Anatomical Neuroendocrinology* (Stumpf, W. E. & Grant, L. D., eds.), pp. 445–463, Karger, Basle

HERITAGE, A. S., GRANT, L. D. & STUMPF, W. E. (1977) ^{3}H-estradiol in catecholamine neurons of rat brain stem: combined localizations by autoradiography and formaldehyde-induced fluorescence. *J. Comp. Neurol. 176,* 607–630

HÖKFELT, T. (1968) *Electron Microscopic Studies on Peripheral and Central Monoamine Neurons.* M. D. Thesis, Stockholm, pp. 7–30

HYYPPÄ, M., RINNE, U. K. & SONNINEN, V. (1970) The activating effect of L-dopa treatment on sexual functions and its experimental background. *Acta Neurol. Scand. 46,* Suppl. 43, 223

KODA, L., SCHULMAN, J. & BLOOM, F. (1978) Ultrastructural identification of noradrenergic terminals in the rat hippocampus: unilateral destruction of the locus coeruleus with 6-hydroxydopamine. *Brain Res. 145,* 190–195

MILLS, I. H. (1977) The role of noradrenaline reuptake blockers in the treatment of disturbed sexual functioning in men and women, in *Depression – the Biochemical and Physiological Role of Ludiomil* (Jukes, A., ed.), pp. 69–76, CIBA-GEIGY, Basle

NANCE, D. W., SHRYNE, J. & GORSKI, R. A. (1974) Septal lesions: effects on lordosis behaviour and pattern of gonadotropin release. *Horm. Behav. 5,* 73–81

NANCE, D. W., SHRYNE, J. & GORSKI, R. A. (1975*a*) Effects of septal lesions on behavioural sensitivity of female rats to gonadal hormones. *Horm. Behav. 6,* 59–64

NANCE, D. W., SHRYNE, J. & GORSKI, R. A. (1975*b*) Facilitation of female sexual behaviour in male rats by septal lesions: an interaction with estrogen. *Horm. Behav. 6,* 289–299

PFAFF, D. W. (1971) Steroid sex hormones in the rat brain: specificity of uptake and physiological effects, in *Steroid Hormones and Brain Function* (Sawyer, C. H. & Gorski, R. A., eds.), pp. 103–112, University of California Press, Berkeley

SCANLON, M. F., MORA, B., SHALE, D. J., WEIGHTMAN, D. R., HEATH, M., SNOW, M. H. & HALL, R. (1977) Evidence for a dopaminergic control of thyrotrophin secretion in man. *Lancet 2,* 421–423

STONE, C. P. (1927) The retention of copulatory ability in rats following castration. *J. Comp. Psychol. 7,* 369–387

WRIGHT, CH. & EVERITT, B. J. (1977) The effects of dorsal noradrenaline bundle lesions on the sexual behaviour of female rats. *Exp. Brain Res.,* E.B.B.S. Suppl. R48–R49 (abstr.)

YANASE, M. & GORSKI, R. A. (1976) Sites of estrogen and progesterone facilitation of lordosis behaviour in the spayed rat. *Biol. Reprod. 15,* 536–543

ZITRIN, A., BEACH, F. A., BARCHAS, J. D. & DEMENT, W. C. (1970) Sexual behaviour of male cats after administration of parachlorophenylalanine. *Science (Wash. D.C.) 170,* 868–870

Final general discussion

Sachar: Inevitably, a number of topics have not been touched on. We have not considered the evidence in animals and humans on the behavioural effects of antiandrogens and antioestrogens. There has been interesting research on the XY and XYY human subjects, in terms of their hormonal status and their psychological profiles, which we have not considered. There have been questions about improving our measures of sexual arousability in animals, as opposed to relying purely on the end-point of sexual activity. Dr Bancroft had some interesting data in the human, on the measurement of reflections of sexual arousal in women.

The subject of pheromones came up briefly (p. 295) and disappeared with a very short half-life! What is the current status of this topic? Some comments on our understanding of the relation of sex hormones to psychopathological states such as premenstrual tension and postpartum depression would also be in place.

Beach: Conventional measures of sexual 'motivation' may reflect what we are calling 'arousability'. These would include procedures such as the interpolation of an electrified grid between the test animal and the incentive animal. One interesting alternative is to vary the adequacy of the evoking stimulus. For example, Calvin Stone (1924) measured the responsiveness of naive male rats by determining the 'minimally adequate' stimulus capable of inducing mounting behaviour. Some males would mount only an extremely receptive female whereas others readily mounted dioestrous females or even immature masculine stimulus partners. In a somewhat similar fashion individual differences in the responsiveness of female rats could be quantified in terms of the intensity or frequency of physical stimulation necessary to evoke lordosis.

I have attempted to measure arousability by presenting naive male rats with a variety of stimulus partners, ranging from a newborn guinea-pig to a receptive female rat, an unreceptive female rat, a castrated male, and so on. Normal males raised in isolation show different degrees of arousal in response to different types of partners. For example, an oestrous rat is most exciting and a neonatal guinea-pig elicits the least interest (Beach 1942*a*).

Males injected with supraphysiological amounts of testosterone before any contact with stimulus animals display the same *relative* responsiveness to the different types of partners but *absolute* arousability is increased, so that the degree or intensity of sexual reaction is increased overall. The threshold for copulation occurs lower on the scale of hierarchically ordered potential partners (Beach 1942*b*).

Sachar: That is dose-dependent, which is interesting. You found the same as you did with latency to copulation, as you go higher; so it isn't simply a threshold.

Goy: It seems difficult to do something in animals parallel to what investigators are doing in humans. You have been measuring essentially a consummatory response, involving skeletal muscle and so on, to an array of stimuli, which correlates highly with mating outcomes. Investigators of human responses have been using conscious influences on autonomic responses such as erection and vaginal sweating, which are quite different end-points. If animal workers could do something comparable to measurements made by investigators of human beings it would build a bridge between the two areas.

Beach: It is possible to condition penile erection in the dog. It might be feasible to establish erection to a conditioned stimulus and then investigate the effects of castration and hormone replacement on that reflex.

Green: Can you use a controlled stimulus? The research on human subjects uses a standardized stimulus and measures genital response.

Beach: I think you could, and that would certainly be worth trying.

Bancroft: We are making recordings from the vagina, using photoplethysmography. Working with humans we have more difficulties than you have in monkeys in distinguishing between proceptivity and receptivity, because of the subtle interaction between partners. I was interested in what Dr Goy said in his paper about changes through the menstrual cycle. In the human, part of the problem is to distinguish to what extent we are looking at the effects of the male and the female respectively. One advantage of being able to take an individual into the laboratory, away from the influence of his or her partner, is that we can measure individual changes.

The photoplethysmograph is inserted into the vagina in the form of a probe. We get two signals from the photo cell, a slow d.c. change and an a.c. signal. Fig. 1 shows what happens at the onset of an erotic film. Fairly quickly we see a shift in the d.c. signal which probably reflects the total amount of blood in the vaginal wall. (Blood has special optical properties in diffusing light, and the more blood there is in the tissue, the less light is reflected back to the photo cell. So it gives an indication of an increased amount of blood in the vaginal tissues.) By looking at the rapid a.c. changes we get a measure of the amplitude, or pulse pressure, in that tissue. One can use either or both signals. In the normal woman there is a rapid response, in 15 seconds or so, when the stimulus changes.

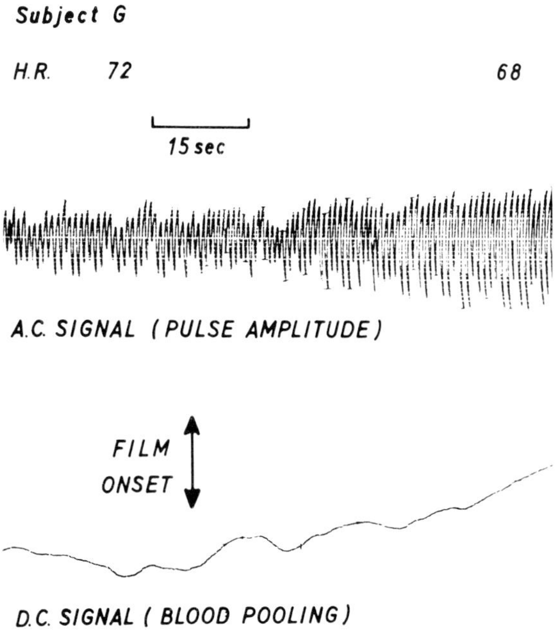

Fig. 1 (Bancroft). Vaginal photoplethysmography in the human, showing rapid changes in both pulse amplitude and blood pooling in response to an erotic stimulus (film).

Fig. 2 shows a case where the change is maximal in the pulse amplitude with little in the way of blood pooling. There are problems in calibrating this device, in the relevance of its position in the vagina, and in some other aspects of interpreting the data, but basically it is an easy physiological response to measure and perhaps could be used in a female monkey.

Goy: We have mentioned the influence of hormones on ease of arousability. What do you think about the possibility that hormones may make it difficult or impossible to *inhibit* arousability?

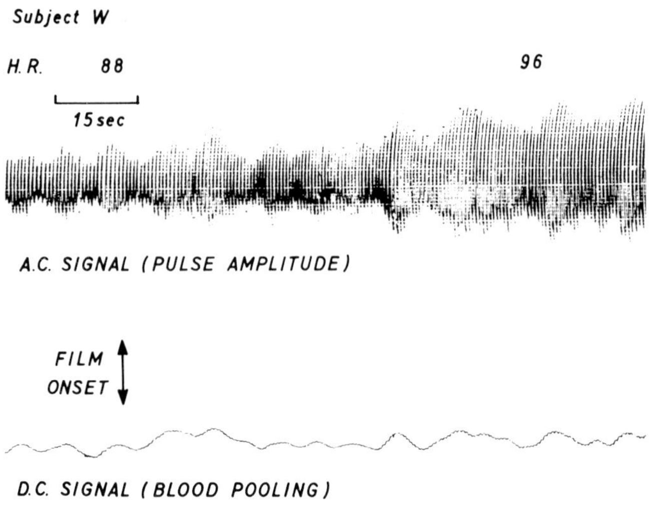

Fig. 2 (Bancroft). A second example of vaginal photoplethysmography showing the response in pulse amplitude but not blood pooling to an erotic film.

Bancroft: So that one would have less control of one's arousability? I don't know how to answer that question.

Herbert: I am particularly interested in the question of cognitive input and its transmission to limbic areas of the brain. If you showed a castrated man a series of sexually arousing stimuli of graded intensity, without telling him that they were sexually arousing, would he still classify them as sexual stimuli even though he may not show arousal to them? In other words, does the cognitive definition of what is sexually arousing correspond with the behavioural response to that stimulus?

Bancroft: Men have a tendency to equate sexual arousal with having an erection. Therefore there is a higher correlation between subjective ratings of arousal and erection in a man than in a woman, presumably because she more easily dissociates, or has greater difficulty in relating, vaginal change (which is much less distinct perceptually) and subjective arousal. So men would tend to answer you on the basis of how much erection they are getting.

Green: What about impotence? Patients describe situations which they label as sexual, in which they don't get erections, but they find them to be exciting.

Bancroft: The two aspects of response can be separated. There is a lot of individual difference. A hypogonadal male whom we are testing produced a full erection to an erotic film and rated his subjective arousal as low; he didn't actually *like* the film. Whereas a fantasy of having intercourse with his wife, to which he got only a slight erection, was rated very highly by him. He was probably using the concept of sexual arousal differently to another person.

Herbert: I wasn't thinking so much of erection as of cognitive recognition of sexual stimuli. I asked the question because of results obtained by R. W. Sperry in experiments on humans with split brains. It was found that a sexually arousing stimulus that was allowed access to either hemisphere of a split-brain person, either a so-called verbal or non-verbal stimulus (although these separations are not complete), produced sexual arousal (see Gazzaniga 1967), whereas only if it ended up in the left hemisphere could it be verbalized. I am trying to get at the nature of sexual arousal. It doesn't seem to depend on either verbal or indeed visuo-spatial analysis to the degree that some other kinds of experience do.

Bancroft: This question of whether there is any cognitive mediation between a visual sexual stimulus and a sexual response is extremely interesting but difficult to answer. If you simply ask people, they say that when looking at an erotic film they seem to be looking at the film and get an erotic response; whereas if they are looking at an erotic slide, it is as though they are turning that slide, by some active cognitive process, into a film. On the other hand, when we ask people to avoid cognitive processes, it does seem to inhibit their response to erotic stimuli. There are ways to approach this, by using the 'expectancy wave', or 'contingent negative variation', as an indicator of interest which does not necessarily reflect cognitive processes. This slow surface-negative shift in the baseline of a scalp potential has been shown to occur in anticipation of an interesting stimulus and has been used to distinguish between erotic stimuli (Costell *et al.* 1972).

Ehrhardt: There is a fundamental problem with vaginal measures of sexual arousal in women. Whenever they do not correlate, investigators tend to assume that women don't know when they are aroused and have a dissociation of vaginal changes and cognitive arousal. The alternative explanation is not often considered, namely that some vaginal changes are not specifically linked to sexual arousal.

Bancroft: I think you are right; the genital response is the response most specifically related to the sexual stimulus, but it is a mistake to equate a genital response with arousal. The only thing one can say is that the vagina is aroused!

Ehrhardt: Even that may not be a correct way of putting it.

Bancroft: It is changed, at least! Levi (1969) did some interesting work measuring catecholamines in response to erotic stimuli. He found that women had a much higher correlation between their subjective rating of arousal and their catecholamine excretion in urine than men.

Sachar: There, unfortunately you really have a very non-specific measure. The hormonal response could be from anxiety or excitement or sexual arousal. Presumably with your vaginal measure, however, if you show terrifying films and then, say, erotic films, you will be able to make the discrimination much better than with simply urinary or plasma catecholamine or cortisol measures.

Bancroft: Yes, it is a more specific measure, but Dr Ehrhardt is right that we should not assume that if someone has a genital response she or he is aroused in a way that would be reflected in catecholamines. The men in Levi's (1969) study showed much lower correlations between subjective rating of arousal and catecholamine excretion. This could be because they were basing their ratings on a genital response, whereas the women were basing theirs on how they were feeling, which would be more closely linked to catecholamines.

Green: I would like to make a plea for a study of another kind of sexuality, namely asexuality! In the human and in other species a small percentage of individuals do not seem to show any sexual behaviour, and we don't understand this. There may be something to be learned by contrasting extremes, setting up models of either hypersexual or normosexual animals against asexual animals, be it from the point of view of chemical mechanisms, neural connections, or early social learning conditions. There has not been enough study of asexuality, clinically or otherwise, and it could enhance our understanding of sexual behaviour.

Sachar: We have heard about monkeys who become asexual in the social context, essentially subdominant males who are really sexually emasculated.

Green: But given the right circumstances they will become sexual. Some animals will not show sexual behaviour in any circumstances.

Short: There is an animal model of this which derives from our work on wild red deer. They are seasonal breeders and the males only show sexual activity in the autumn. They will show this even though kept in complete isolation and don't seem to need the presence of females to show it. But sexual behaviour does require testosterone. However, if you give a castrated animal testosterone in the spring, it will produce immediate social changes and induce social aggression but it will not switch on sexual behaviour until the appropriate time of year, in the autumn (Lincoln *et al.* 1972).

There are similar data in birds. It does seem that there is a higher circannual control mechanism in some species which overrides the presence or absence of a hormone and decides whether or not sexual behaviour will be displayed. I don't know whether there is information on this in primates.

Sachar: Is sexual activity dependent on cues from female deer?

Short: No, because sexual behaviour occurs in male deer kept in isolation who have never seen a female. The one point where the experiments were at fault is that we cannot say whether it is only as a result of previous experience that the stag knows that the autumn is the time of year to rut, since we have not been able to do the appropriate control experiments in naive animals. In birds the experiments are better controlled.

Herbert: To go back to what Barry Keverne said in his paper (pp. 271-286), behavioural stimuli affect monoamines, and it could be simply that the animals turn off their own hormones.

Beach: Dr Green may be referring to a different kind of unresponsiveness. In purchasing rats from commercial breeders I have always found that a certain percentage of apparently healthy males won't copulate. This clearly is not due to testosterone deficiency in adulthood.

Bancroft: The assumption tends to be made in humans that such people are inhibited, but that is a rather dubious (if not tautological) assumption.

Herbert: Another problem with examining asexuality was raised by Dr Beach, namely the refractory period in the male. This is a time of temporary asexuality, and if we understood what happens after ejaculation in the male we might know much more about what causes 'sexuality'.

Green: Do any species *not* show the post-ejaculatory refractory period?

Beach: None that I know of. However, androgen-insensitive rats of the Stanley-Gumbreck strain may, very rarely, show ejaculatory reflexes, and when this occurs there is no clear-cut post-ejaculatory refractory period (Beach & Buehler 1977).

Bancroft: Have your experiments on electroejaculation in the rat, showing the absence of a refractory period (Beach *et al.* 1966), been repeated on other species?

Beach: There is no really satisfactory evidence on this score save for our work on the rat which showed that ejaculation induced by brain stimulation does not influence subsequent copulatory behaviour to the same extent as ejaculation induced by mating with a female (Beach *et al.* 1966).

Bancroft: Electroejaculation is being used in men now, especially for paraplegics, and it may enable us to see if they have the same refractory period as is found after normal ejaculation.

Sachar: In man the refractory period increases with age, which has been assumed to have something to do with declining testosterone levels. Has the refractory period been manipulated hormonally?

Beach: In rats, yes. The refractory period actually consists of an absolute and a relative phase, and you can reduce the relative phase with large amounts of testosterone but you cannot eliminate the absolute phase.

Sachar: That is an interesting question for future research. The latency period and refractory period haven't been studied in terms of hormonal effects in humans.

Can we turn now to the question of pheromones in primates? What is the current status of this field?

Keverne: I have a certain axe to grind on this. When we introduced the term pheromone to studies of primate behaviour our data seemed to fit at least with the definition of the term, in that we were able to change behavioural interactions in oppositely sexed pairs of monkeys by altering an olfactory cue (see Michael & Keverne 1968). It was unfortunate that we chose the term because many people tend to associate pheromones with insect behaviour, where there is a stereotyped release of behaviour. This isn't true of the monkey. Our mistake was in failing to put the behavioural changes we observed into context, and although we said we could produce changes in behaviour by altering olfactory cues, we were not excluding the fact that visual cues, auditory cues, certainly behavioural cues, would also influence the behavioural interaction. Thus, although we produced remarkable responses, they were in a contrived situation with highly selected males which responded to odour extremely well. Nevertheless, I still feel (and Bob Goy probably disagrees with me here) that odour cues are important in primate sexual behaviour. The olfactory sense is of special interest in that it is the only sensory system having a direct input into the limbic brain. It is therefore a sensory input which might influence mood changes and arousal without the individual being consciously aware of it. From that point of view it may well be of significance in man, but I wouldn't think that pheromones are active in humans in the sense that they attract us to one person or another. The context where they may have a function would be within a sexual relationship and their effect might be on, say, the time taken for consummation of sexual activity.

Sachar: You are making a distinction between a true pheromone and an olfactory cue. Surely cats and dogs run for miles when certain scents are detected?

Keverne: In mammals other than primates, pheromonal effects are well established.

Beach: Wilson & Bossert (1963) make a useful distinction between two different pheromonal effects. *Releaser* pheromones evoke an immediate behavioural response by the receiving individual. *Primer* pheromones have a delayed effect because they modify the receiver's physiological state and thus indirectly influence behaviour. When one male mouse attacks another in response to the odour of the second individual's urine a releaser pheromone is indicated (Mugford & Nowell 1970). When a female mouse reaches puberty prematurely as a consequence of exposure to adult male urine, a primer pheromone is involved (Vandenberg 1973).

Sachar: This hasn't been demonstrated to be more than an olfactory cue in primates? A pheromone is an olfactory cue, but an olfactory cue isn't necessarily a pheromone?

Beach: Studies of primates have concentrated on releaser effects of putative pheromones.

Goy: The work of Barry Keverne and Dr Richard Michael was a demonstration of the effectiveness of a certain group of odours on a behavioural end-point, done in an abstract and fairly specific situation with a fairly specific methodology (Michael & Keverne 1968). Although statistically significant effects were obtained, they could hardly be called world-shaking. The effects clearly did not control everything about the sexual interaction. Whenever one finds a small and statistically significant effect of a stimulus in even one situation it is often worth looking to see whether the same stimulus functions effectively in another situation. For example, it would be interesting to see what effect these odours have in social groups of monkeys, but that has never been done. Goldfoot *et al.* (1976) asked questions about different kinds of situations and whether the cue would have any measurable effect. No effects of the vaginal aliphatic acids on male ejaculation were found.

I specifically do *not* think that the vaginal odours can be a relevant source of information about female attractiveness and on that basis explain cyclical changes in behaviour of the pair, because we have shown here (see pp. 227-249) that one male rhesus monkey may show cyclical variations in sexual performance and another male, with the same partner during that same cycle for that partner, won't show any cyclical variation. So the odour of the female is not explanatory.

I don't know what the vaginal aliphatic acids do during pregnancy, but it might be interesting to examine this, because copulation goes on through much of pregnancy in pairs of rhesus monkeys, as we discussed earlier (p. 318).

Beach: I would expect olfactory stimuli to be less important in microsomatic primates than in macrosomatic rodents and carnivores, where they may play a primary role.

Goy: Certainly, but my comments are not a denial of the effect that Michael & Keverne (1968) obtained; it has been well demonstrated in one situation. But one has to ask what the significance of the vaginal odour might be in the life of the species. We don't know that, for monkeys or for most mammalian species. There are suggestions that it might work in the wild, where the monkeys have to locate each other, or the male might have to find and single out a cycling female from many who are not cycling.

Short: We looked for the existence of sex-specific odours in human urine (R. V. Short, unpublished observations) by taking samples from 15 men and 15 women, making a male and a female pool, labelled A and B, and having 30 students sniff each individual urine sample and label it A or B without telling them which was male or female. When we broke the code there was no evidence that those 30 individuals could discriminate between male and female urine.

Sachar: Before ending the symposium we should say at least a little about the relationship between sex hormones and psychopathological states, and the current status of that field. On premenstrual tension, it seems clear that this is not simply a cultural phenomenon or one relating to feminine attitudes about the menses, but that there is a change with the cycle. Dr Ehrhardt's case of a $1^1/_2$-year-old girl with precocious puberty and severe premenstrual tension should indicate that.

Ehrhardt: It seems clear that for a subgroup of women premenstrual tension is a real phenomenon and is related to hormonal changes. Where the controversy comes in is when these findings are generalized and said to be true of all women, which is not the case, and also enlarged to include a much broader range of behaviour. But for the subgroup of women in whom irritability and mood changes such as depression appear, the syndrome seems real.

Sachar: Even in a large group of non-symptomatic women is there a trend in the data towards a small but significant increase in depression and irritability in the few days before menstruation?

Ehrhardt: Only for a subgroup. There is a large group of women in whom this does not hold at all.

Beach: Are there any observations on premenarcheal girls? Do any of them begin to experience times of depression at monthly intervals before they start to menstruate?

Ehrhardt: Clinically it has often been reported that a mother says that her daughter is probably going to menstruate soon because she is moody, but it has not been well established.

Sachar: The question of whether there is anything different hormonally about the women who get premenstrual tension is quite open still.

Bancroft: Bäckstrom in Sweden claims that the psychological symptoms of the premenstrual syndrome are related to an abnormal oestrogen: progesterone ratio in the late luteal phase, with a high oestrogen level relatively unopposed by progesterone (Bäckstrom & Carstensen 1974).

Sachar: Once again, we need replication. One idea was that increased prolactin had something to do with the syndrome but I gather that the evidence on the effect of bromocriptine is not firm.

Besser: Several double-blind trials on the effect of bromocriptine in premenstrual tension have been done. Some appeared to show that the symptoms are improved by this therapy; some failed to show anything. The first problem is to define the syndrome, but even accepting that some well-designed studies have shown a preference for bromocriptine, it has usually been given for 10 days premenstrually and it is constantly forgotten that all dopamine agonists are natriuretic agents, producing sodium and water loss by an action on the kidney. So is it a non-specific effect? No one has done a double-blind trial comparing bromocriptine with a small dose of a thiazide diuretic.

Sachar: The diuretics have been shown to help the part of the syndrome associated with discomfort from fluid retention, but do not affect the mood changes.

Besser: The problem is that a group of workers must select patients in such a way that they show an effect in a double-blind trial of bromocriptine, and then the same group must select patients on the same basis to compare bromocriptine with a thiazide. Until this is done it remains a totally open question. That is also a different question from whether prolactin concentrations are abnormal in women with premenstrual tension or merely permissive to that effect.

Short: An interesting clinical observation was that of Beumont *et al.* (1975) who did hysterectomies on women complaining of premenstrual tension. They conserved the ovaries and showed that taking the uterus out abolished all the symptoms of premenstrual tension, including the effects on mood, although hormone estimations showed that the ovaries continued their normal cyclical function with ovulation. This suggests that premenstrual tension may be a result of steroids acting not directly on the brain but on the uterus, to influence for example prostaglandin secretion, which itself has the central effects we know as premenstrual tension.

Herbert: There used to be a story about a relationship between women undergoing hysterectomy and a history of mental disease.

Sachar: This is a whole complicated area. There is a certain category of women who have a lot of operations; it is part of Briquet's syndrome, for example (formerly termed hysteria and in the future to be termed Somatization Disorder in the US), and often they persuade someone to take out their uterus as well as other organs.

However, while we are considering depression, we should just comment that we are completely ignorant in another respect, too. There is a considerable incidence of at least mild depression after parturition, not necessarily on the fourth day, when it was originally thought to be, the so-called 'milk blues', but in the first few days after delivery (Hamburg *et al.* 1968). It is very common to find a depressed mood, crying spells and so on. Tremendous hormonal changes occur then and there is the immense psychological significance of having had a baby, with a temporary 'let down' effect, but any attempts to explain the depression by the hormone changes remain at the level of speculation. I don't know any systematic research on hormonal manipulations during that period, done to attempt to prevent these post-partum blues.

References

BÄCKSTROM, T. & CARSTENSEN, H. (1974) Estrogen and progesterone in plasma in relation to premenstrual tension. *J. Steroid Biochem. 5,* 257–260

BEACH, F. A. (1942*a*) Analysis of stimuli adequate to elicit mating behaviour in the sexually inexperienced male rat. *J. Comp. Psychol. 33,* 163–207

BEACH, F. A. (1942*b*) Effects of testosterone propionate upon the copulatory behaviour of sexually inexperienced male rats. *J. Comp. Psychol. 33,* 227–247

BEACH, F. A. & BUEHLER, M. G. (1977) Male rats with inherited insensitivity to androgen show reduced sexual behaviour. *Endocrinology 100,* 197–200

BEACH, F. A., WESTBROOK,W. H. & CLEMENS, L. G. (1966) Comparisons of the ejaculatory response in men and animals. *Psychosomat. Med. 28,* 749–763

BEUMONT, P. J. V., RICHARDS, O. H. & GELDER, M. G. (1975) A study of minor psychiatric and physical symptoms during the menstrual cycle. *Br. J. Psychiatr. 126,* 431–434

COSTELL, R., LUNDE, D., KOPELL, B. & WITTNER, W. (1972) The contingent negative variation as an indicator of sexual object preference. *Science (Wash. D.C.) 177,* 718–720

GAZZANIGA, M. S. (1967) The split brain in man. *Sci. Am. 217 (2),* 24–29

GOLDFOOT, D. A., KRAVETZ, M. A., GOY, R. W. & FREEMAN, S. K. (1976) Lack of effect of vaginal lavages and aliphatic acids on ejaculatory responses in rhesus monkeys: behavioural and chemical analyses. *Horm. Behav. 7,* 1–27

HAMBURG, D., MOOS, R. H. & YALOM, I. D. (1968) Studies of distress in the menstrual cycle and the postpartum period, in *Endocrinology and Human Behaviour* (Michael, R. P., ed.), pp. 94–118, Oxford University Press, London

LEVI, L. (1969) Sympatho-adrenomedullary activity, diuresis, and emotional reactions during visual sexual stimulation in human females and males. *Psychosom. Med. 31,* 251–268

LINCOLN, G. A., GUINNESS, F. & SHORT, R. V. (1972) The way in which testosterone controls the social and sexual behaviour of the red deer stag *(Cervus elaphus). Horm. Behav. 3,* 375–396

MICHAEL, R. P. & KEVERNE, E. B. (1968) Pheromones in the communication of sexual status in primates. *Nature (Lond.) 218,* 746–749

MUGFORD, R. A. & NOWELL, N. W. (1970) Pheromones and their effect on aggression in mice. *Nature (Lond.) 226,* 967–968

STONE, C. P. (1924) The awakening of copulatory ability in the male albino rat. *Am. J. Physiol. 68,* 407–424

VANDENBERG, J. G. (1973) Acceleration and inhibition of puberty in female mice by pheromones. *J. Reprod. Fertil.,* Suppl. 19, 411–419

WILSON, E. O. & BOSSERT, W. H. (1963) Chemical communication among animals. *Recent Prog. Horm. Res. 19,* 673–716

Concluding remarks

E.J. SACHAR

Department of Psychiatry, College of Physicians and Surgeons of Columbia University, New York

I would like to congratulate all the participants on several counts.

First, both the animal and human data presented were of high quality, and provided most valuable information about the numerous aspects of this rapidly developing field – anatomical, neuropharmacological, psychopharmacological, behavioural, experiential, and social.

Secondly, in each area the designs and methods of study illustrated ingenious approaches which should be of considerable use to investigators in many disciplines.

Thirdly, the group in its discussion was willing to accept the challenge of this symposium, to consider seriously the implications that the animal and human studies might have for each other. It is always difficult for data-oriented scientists to risk speculating for the record, but in this instance we were all rewarded by the effort. At the same time, we saw that such speculation could be conducted responsibly, with a full awareness of the limitations of animal observations for explaining the complexities of human experience and behaviour.

An especially useful aspect of this interchange was the mutual clarification of our various languages for describing these phenomena.

Finally, the conference, while emphasizing how much we don't know, has shown us a great many exciting avenues for future study. These fascinating questions now appear truly researchable, not only because the appropriate methods are becoming available, but also because the intellectual climate for responsible investigation is now favourable. The talons which hampered serious study of the psychobiology of sexual behaviour for so many years have at last been relaxed, and we are grateful to the pioneers who worked through those difficult times for pursuing their efforts, and for participating in this conference.

The next Ciba Foundation Symposium on sex hormones and behaviour will surely document a quantum leap in our knowledge, but will just as surely show that this understanding grew from the lines of inquiry described in this conference.

Index of contributors

Entries in **bold** *type indicate papers; other entries refer to discussion contributions*

Indexes compiled by William Hill

Subject index